SHIPWRECK

Diving the Graveyard
of the Atlantic

Second Edition

SHIPWRECKS

Diving the Graveyard of the Atlantic

Second Edition

Menasha Ridge Press

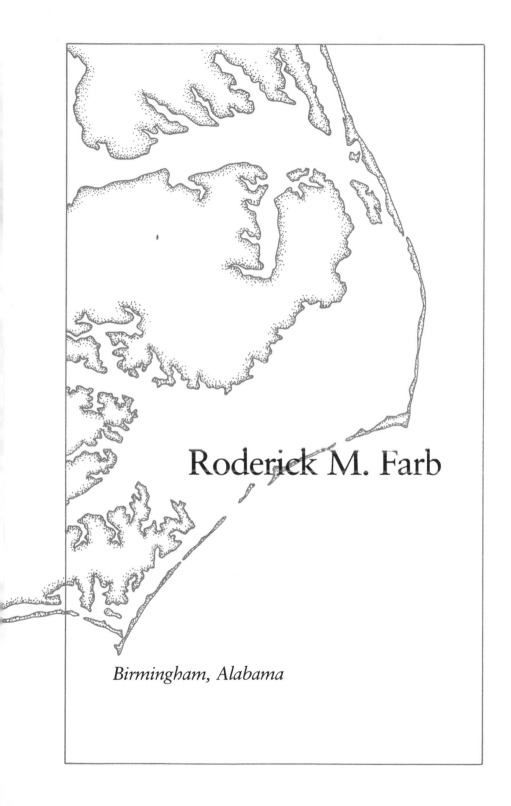

Roderick M. Farb

Birmingham, Alabama

Diagrams by Eva Holdenried
Maps by Karen Wysocki

Library of Congress Cataloging-in-Publication Data:
Farb, Roderick M., 1946—
Shipwrecks: diving the graveyard of the Atlantic
revised edition
Roderick M. Farb   p.   cm.
Includes bibliographical references (p. 11) and index.
ISBN 0-89732-034-4
1. Scuba diving—North Carolina. 2. Shipwrecks—North Carolina—
History. I. Title.
GV840.S78F36 1990
622'.19'0247972—dc20
90—44234
CIP

to
Laurie

CONTENTS

Preface   xii

Foreword   xv

Introduction

Diving the Graveyard of the Atlantic   3

Overview of the Wrecks   7

Wreck Diving from a Boat   11

Beach (Walk-in) Diving   17

Adventures in Locating Shipwrecks   18

Sharks and Shipwrecks   25

PART ONE: OFFSHORE WRECKS

1. Nags Head

Buarque   32   Zane Grey   46

Byron D. Benson   34   Dionysus   48

Norvana   37   Marore   49

U-85   39

2. Ocracoke-Hatteras

Ciltvaira   52   Keshena   92

U-701   54   F. W. Abrams   94

City of Atlanta   64   Dixie Arrow   96

Australia   66   Proteus   103

USS Monitor   68   USS Tarpon   113

Empire Gem   82   British Splendour   124

City of New York   84   Manuela   128

Malchace   87

E. M. Clark   90

3. Ocracoke to Cape Lookout

Aphrodite   132   Amagansett   142

Tamaulipas   136   Caribsea   143

Atlas   139   Ario   147

Ashkhabad   149   Thistleroy   155
Portland   152   Central America   157

4. Cape Lookout
   HMS *Bedfordshire*   162   *Ella Pierce Thurlow*   204
   Ea   168   *Papoose*   208
   Fenwick Island   169   *Naeco*   212
   Senateur Duhamel   170   *Theodore Parker*   217
   Aeolus   174   *Suloide*   221
   U-352   177   *W. E. Hutton*   225
   USS *Schurz*   197

5. New River Inlet
   Cassimir   230   *Esso Nashville*   241
   The "Lobster Wreck"   236   *Normannia*   244

6. Cape Fear
   Alexander Ramsey   250   *George Weems*   270
   USS *Peterhoff*   251   *Mount Dirfys*   273
   John D. Gill   255   *Raritan*   274
   City of Houston   261

PART TWO: NEAR SHORE WRECKS

7. Late 19th and Early 20th-Century Wrecks
   Metropolis   280   *Kyzickes*   285
   Carl Gerhard   283   USS *Huron*   288

8. Cape Fear Civil War Shipwreck District   295
   Oriental   305   *General Beauregard*   313
   Phantom   307   *Modern Greece*   314
   Nutfield   308   *Condor*   315
   Fanny and Jenny   309   *Douro*   316
   Sophia   310   *Ella*   317
   USS *Columbia*   310   *Bendigo*   318
   Venus/Lynx   311   USS *Iron Age*   319
   Hebe   312   *Ranger*   320

Vesta   321   USS *Aster*   324

CSS *Raleigh*   322   *Stormy Petrel*   324

Unknown Vessel   322   *Elizabeth*   325

USS *Louisiana*   323   *Wild Dayrell*   326

Arabian   323

9. New Artificial Reefs   327

Appendixes

  A. Underwater Photography   329

  B. Federal Laws: Abandoned Shipwreck Act of 1987   335

  C. NC Statute on Underwater Salvage   338

  D. Divers Alert Network   340

  E. North Carolina Dive Stores and Charterboats   342

  F. Charter Dive Services   345

  G. Type, Tonnage, and Depth of Offshore Wrecks   361

  H. Fate of U-Boats Involved in Sinking Ships Off the NC Coast   364

Selected Bibliography   366

Glossary   369

Index   371

LIST OF SHIPWRECK DIAGRAMS

U.S.S. *Monitor*   70

Malchace   88

Dixie Arrow   101

Proteus   110

U.S.S. *Tarpon*   121

British Splendour   125

Manuela   129

Tamaulipas   137

Caribsea   145

Portland   153

H.M.S. *Bedfordshire*   165

Senateur Duhamel   172

U-352   195

U.S.S. *Schurz*   201

Ella Pierce Thurlow   205

Naeco   215

Theodore Parker   219

Suloide 222

W. E. Hutton   227

Cassimir   233–34

The "Lobster Wreck"   238

Normannia   247

John D. Gill   259

George Weems   271

U.S.S. *Huron*   290

PREFACE

I HAVE WRITTEN this book to provide the shipwreck enthusiast with the only comprehensive guide to North Carolina shipwrecks, their history, photographs of their remains, and how to dive them. Over the past eleven years I have visited the offshore wrecks and many of the near shore beach wrecks, often several times each year during the eight-month-long diving season. The information presented here about the wreck sites and the photographs of them are the result of many hours of underwater exploration. To do such exploration required the services of a number of dive charter boats and experienced captains to take me out to the wrecks, and as a consequence I have used most of the dive charter services listed in this book.

Several boat captains supplied valuable information about wrecks in their area and provided exceptional service in getting me and my dive charters to the appointed wreck sites. I am especially grateful to the following boat captains for their help: Art LePage, Wanchese, NC; Bob Eastep, Beaufort, NC; Mike McKay, Buck Wilde, Scot Whitfield and George Purifoy, Morehead City, NC; Don Huneycutt and George Harper, Swansboro, NC; Ed Wolfe, Doug Grant and Doug Dudley, Wrightsville Beach, NC; and Wayne Strickland, Southport, NC.

There are several dive shops that provided diving and camera equipment and air fills for me. For this assistance I give my sincerest thanks to Debbie Wilkinson, Discovery Diving Company, Beaufort, NC; Ron Thrower, Undersea Specialists, Cary, NC; John Renfro, Blue Water Dive Shop, Raleigh, NC; David Katzenmeyer, Water World Marine Service, Durham, NC; Bob Horne, Piedmont Drivers Supply, Burlington, NC; and Mike McCarley, Undersea Sales, Wrightsville Beach, NC. I also wish to thank Foister's Camera Store, Chapel Hill, NC, for providing photographic assistance. Special thanks to Bennett Frankel of Los Angeles, California, for his support of this project.

The following dive club organizations and their members are due thanks for providing additional corroborative information regarding the physical condition of the wrecks: Triangle Dive Club, Durham, NC; North Carolina Wreck Divers, Raleigh, NC; Charlotte Scuba Club, Charlotte, NC; and the University of North Carolina Scuba Club, Chapel Hill, NC. Without the participation of the members of those clubs on my dive charter trips, this project would have been infinitely more difficult.

Although many divers have taken part in my dive charters to various wrecks, I would especially like to thank Jim, Bob, and Karin Pickard,

Joe and Jay Harris, Gail Covington, Myra Lemley, Klaus Ford, Wayne Frazier, Don Gladstone, Ed Bachmann, Judy Dolce, David Tyson, Beverly White, John Iredale, Ken Rankin, Paul Hudy, Chris Wachholz, Paul Sullivan, Steve Burris, Sam Ranzino, Wes Devaney, Ron Thrower, Mike Simmons, Bill Thomas, Art Peters, John R. Moore, Branch Bissette, Stan Davis, John Kernodle, Susan Haberland, Danny and Sheila Arnold, Jim Garrison, Louis Payne, Doris Rouse, Blake Wilson, Ted Womack, Danny Campbell, Wayne Grabowski, Chris Walker, Joe Poe, David Katzenmeyer, Maris and Marilyn Kazmers, Steven Cook, Helmut Horn, Bonnie Cardone, Howard Hall, Jack and John McKenney, Stan Waterman, and Bill Gleason for their pleasant company on my dive trips.

Other divers whom I would also like to thank for providing additional physical information about certain shipwrecks are Art LePage, George Purifoy, Mike Sheen, Wayne Strickland, Ron Thrower, Bob Eastep, Mike McKay, and Jim Bunch.

I would like to thank the following companies for their support of my work for this book: U.S. Divers, Viking, Poseidon, IBM, Xerox Imaging, Helix, Hypertech, Sony, Zodiac, Evinrude, Bio-Scan, Data Translation, Light and Motion, Ikelite, Orca Industries, Tekna, Underwater Kinetics, Equinox, Southern Nikonos, Probe Electronics, Amphibico, and Jack McKenney Film Productions.

Historical information and photographs about the ships were obtained from many different institutions. Although I could never offer sufficient thanks for all they provided me, I am, nevertheless, grateful to the following institutions for the use of their photographs and their invaluable help in my research and preparation of this book: National Archives, Washington, DC; Library of Congress, Washington, DC; Lloyd's of London; Department of the Navy, Washington, DC; The Mariners' Museum, Newport News, VA; Steamship Historical Society of America, Baltimore, MD; Peabody Museum of Salem, Salem, MA; WZ-Bilddienst, Wilhelmshaven, West Germany; The Essex Institute, Salem, MA; Naval Historical Center, Washington, DC; U.S. Naval Institute, Annapolis, MD; Submarine Force Library and Museum, Groton, CT; National Oceanic and Atmospheric Administration, Washington, DC; National Maritime Museum of San Francisco, CA; North Carolina Department of Cultural Resources and North Carolina Department of Natural Resources and Community Development, Raleigh, NC; and Southern Historical and North Carolina Collections, University of North Carolina, Chapel Hill, NC. I would especially like to thank the following individuals who, while serving with the aforementioned institutions, provided unstinting assistance in obtaining materials and guiding me to appropriate sources of information during my research into these shipwrecks: Laura Brown, Steamship

Historical Society of America; Charlotte Valentine, The Mariners' Museum; Kathy Flynn, Peabody Museum; Ilene Byron, Ed Miller, and Dr. Ervan Garrison, National Oceanic and Atmospheric Administration; D. C. Allard and Richard T. Speer, Naval Historical Center; Elaine C. Everly and Harry E. Riley, National Archives; James Delgado, National Park Service; Robin Chandler, National Maritime Museum of San Francisco; R. L. Sheina, Historian, U.S. Coast Guard; Lisa Halttunen, Mystic Seaport Museum; Jim Brown, NC Department of Natural Resources and Community Development; Steve Murphy, North Carolina Division of Marine Fisheries; Robert J. Zollars, Director, Submarine Force Library and Museum; and Dr. Tom Burke, Richard Lawrence, and Leslie Bright, Underwater Archaeology Unit, NC Department of Natural Resources.

Thanks are due the following individuals for providing additional historical material for several of the shipwrecks: Bill Lovin, Mike McKay, Joe Friday, Jr., Homer Hickam, L. Van Loan Naisawald, Dave Bluett, George Purifoy, Judy Dolce, Paul Payne, Wes Hall, Dave McGee, and Don Shomette. Special thanks to Captain Arthur R. Moore for allowing me to use historical material from his excellent reference book on American merchant ships sunk during World War II, *A Careless Word . . . A Needless Sinking*. Portions of historical information for accounts of the *Esso Nashville, Dixie Arrow, John D. Gill*, and the *Atlas* were kindly provided by Truman R. Strobridge from his "Tanker Losses of WWII."

I would like to thank Korvettenkapitän Hellmut Rathke, Ret., for historical photographs and information about his submarine, the *U-352*. I would also like to thank Dr. Gunde Reiger for the numerous German translations she did for me.

Photographs not credited to other sources are my own.

Special appreciation is given to Sheila Davis who typed the manuscript from my often illegible handwriting.

I would like to express my deep appreciation to my friend Jim Pickard for his constant support and encouragement without which I would have fallen far short of what I actually accomplished diving and researching these wrecks. And last, but not least, special thanks to my wife Laurie, who encouraged me and kept my spirits high, for putting up with it all.

FOREWORD

THE POPULARITY OF SPORT SCUBA DIVING has increased tremendously over the past ten years. Each year nearly a quarter of a million people in the United States alone learn to dive. Twenty-five years ago nothing more than the ability to read a set of instructions that came with the equipment was required to dive. Nowadays, however, a person has to have genuine training in the sport in order to be a certified scuba diver.

That training can only be acquired from qualified instructors through scuba courses taught year-round at YMCAs, city and county recreation centers, universities, and other places with access to swimming pools. The training programs are regulated by several national agencies which are self-governed organizations set up to establish uniform guidelines for teaching scuba diving and to promote safety in the sport. The courses may last a few days or a few weeks. Students are evaluated for their ability to handle themselves in water, and they are taught about dive gear, the physics and physiology of diving, dive safety, and emergency procedures. At the end of the course there is a written evaluation and the student participates in an open water dive that brings all of the accumulated knowledge into practical use. The test dive is a shallow one in a quarry, a lake, or the ocean in the presence of an instructor.

Upon successful completion of a course, the student is awarded a certification card, and it is this scuba diving certification card that permits a person to participate in the sport today. The self-regulating group of national certifying agencies makes it nearly impossible for a person to obtain equipment and air refills or to participate in diving activities without prior certification and a certification card.

The macho image of diving prevalent several years ago is by and large gone, and men and women of all ages and from many diverse backgrounds now learn to scuba dive and actively participate in the sport. Dive stores, YMCAs, and community centers in your area can provide information about scuba diving lessons. For more information about this exciting sport, you can also contact any of the following certifying agencies:

1. Professional Association of Diving Instructors (PADI), 1251 East Dyer Road, Suite 100, Santa Ana, CA 92705. Tel.: (714) 540-7234.
2. YMCA Scuba Program (YMCA), Oakbrook Square, 6083-A

3. National Association of Underwater Instructors (NAUI), P.O. Box 14650, Montclair, CA 91763. Tel.: (714) 621- 5801.
4. National Association of Scuba Diving Schools (NASDS), 5200 Warner Street, Suite 209, Huntington Beach, CA 92649. Tel.: (714) 846-0367.
5. Scuba Schools International (SSI), 2619 Canton Court, Fort Col-

SHIPWRECKS

*Diving the Graveyard
of the Atlantic*

Second Edition

INTRODUCTION

Diving the Graveyard of the Atlantic

OFFSHORE NORTH CAROLINA is well known as the "Graveyard of the Atlantic" for good reason. Scores of vessels throughout the past few centuries have come to rest in the waters off a coastline that has three large capes (Cape Hatteras, Cape Lookout, and Cape Fear), numerous shoals, treacherous currents, and unpredictable weather. Hurricanes, the passage of cold fronts across the coast, seasonal storms, fog, and war have taken a toll of ships estimated to be well over 2,000 since the 1500s when the earliest explorers became acquainted with the vagaries of coastal North Carolina.

The location of most of the shipwrecks is not known, and of those whose coordinates are known only a small percentage lie in waters of a divable depth (less than 240 feet). Of the offshore wrecks located in divable depths, fewer than 120 or so are wrecks that charter boat captains or others are willing to take divers to visit. These 120 odd wrecks, however, present some of the best and most varied diving to be found anywhere in the world. They lie from a few hundred feet to 60 miles offshore in water ranging from 30 to 240 feet deep.

The water off the coast of North Carolina is blessed by the presence of the tropical Gulf Stream which flows northeast past the North Carolina coast, swinging closer to shore in summer and moving further out in the winter. The Gulf Stream, the warm "river in the ocean" comes closest to the East Coast at North Carolina than anywhere else except the tip of Florida. North Carolina's coastline protrudes far out into the Atlantic Ocean bringing its offshore waters out to mingle with azure water of the Gulf Stream. Eddies of the Gulf Stream bathe the shipwrecks with warm, nutrient-filled water which brings a wide variety of tropical marine life up from the Caribbean to live in and among the remnants of these vessels. To view a North Carolina shipwreck at a distance is much like looking at an oasis in a desert of ocean bottom. The entire ocean food chain is present and utilizes these broken man-made structures for attachment, food acquisition, shelter, and growth. A diver may see beautiful corals, sponges, moray eels, blue angelfish, butterflyfish, lobsters, anemones, arrow crabs, groupers, amberjacks, sharks, manta rays, sea turtles, porpoises, starfish, sea urchins, sea cucumbers, triggerfish, and a wide variety of other tropical marine life usually associated with Caribbean diving.

Underwater visibility varies depending upon how far the wreck lies from shore. Inshore wrecks, within 10 or so miles from shore, are shallower and more affected by wave action and surging; on those wrecks, a diver can expect to find visibility in the range of 10–30 feet or less, but several times during the summer months visibility anywhere inshore may exceed 70–80 feet. The visibility on wrecks lying 20 or more miles offshore ranges from 80 to 150 feet, although occasionally visibility in the range of 30–40 feet occurs offshore because of local weather conditions and currents. The water temperature inshore is somewhat cooler than offshore, with April and May inshore temperatures running around 65 degrees while offshore the temperature will be in the upper 70s and low 80s. During June, July, August, and September, inshore and offshore temperatures are about the same—in the upper 70s and 80s.

Because the Labrador Current flows south and meets the Gulf Stream around Cape Hatteras, diving conditions north of Cape Hatteras are different than off the coast to the south. North of Hatteras, water temperatures are considerably colder, and the visibility is less on shipwrecks located in this area. In July, although the air temperature may be in the 80s and 90s, the surface temperature may be 60 degrees, while at depth the temperature may be 55 degrees or colder. Visibility ranges from 1 to 50 feet, and on an average day a diver might have 15–20 feet of visibility. Therefore, diving north of Cape Hatteras requires the use of a full wet suit with hood and gloves even during the hottest summer months and a bright dive light.

Diving on wrecks south of Hatteras may be done without the use of a wet suit. However, because of stinging nematocysts, corals, and other sharp objects, a diver would do well to protect legs and other body parts from stings and abrasions. From mid-May to October many divers wear just a pair of blue jeans or "Farmer John" pants while diving.

Given the large numbers and diversity of wrecks in divable depths, the warm Gulf Stream water bathing those south of Cape Hatteras, the good visibility, and the abundance of beautiful Caribbean marine life in and around the wrecks, shipwreck diving off the coast of North Carolina is unique and the best of its kind in the world. Whatever your preference, be it the visual delights of beautiful marine life or the adventure and excitement of investigating the remains of sunken ships, the Graveyard of the Atlantic provides something for all levels of divers. Indeed, maritime buffs from all over North America and the world come to visit the wreck diving mecca of underwater America that is offshore North Carolina.

The wrecks described in this book are divided into two groups: offshore wrecks and near shore wrecks. Within each group, the wrecks appear in order of their location off the coast, beginning with the most northerly of the wrecks located off Nags Head and proceeding southwest to wrecks off Southport.

Although many of the ships were renamed several times as their ownership changed over the years, I have used throughout the book the name by which a given vessel was known at the time it sank.

The wrecks are given approximate locations, and divers wishing to visit a particular site must depend on a dive boat captain to get them to the site. Because the wrecks are often located many miles from shore and deep beneath the ocean, boat captains use sophisticated electronic equipment to find wreck sites. One such piece of equipment is loran C, which uses radio waves to direct a boat to the spot on the ocean beneath which lies the wreck; and another is a recording fathometer, which draws a profile of the wreck on the bottom. All experienced dive charter captains use these devices to locate shipwrecks, and the surest bet in selecting a charter boat is to pick a boat captain who has already been to the site you have in mind. To some extent, one has to act on faith. However, when a reputable boat captain says he has the coordinates for a site and can find the wreck because he has been there before, he usually does.

The depths listed here for wrecks are as accurate as my depth gauge, and depth indications in this book should not be used in lieu of an accurate depth gauge worn by the diver.

While some of the offshore wrecks are relatively intact, many of them are broken up to a greater or lesser degree, with much of the superstructure scattered about the bottom in pieces having less than 10 feet of relief. There are two main reasons many of the offshore wrecks are broken up: wire-dragging and depth-charging. When a wreck's superstructure lies close to the surface it becomes a hindrance to navigation. During and after World War II, the Navy and the Coast Guard employed wire-dragging and depth-charging as the primary means of reducing the amount of wreck superstructure that came to within forty feet of the surface. Wire-dragging was accomplished by dragging a cable or cables between two ships across a wreck site, thereby tearing all obstructions away. Depth-charging a wreck was a very expedient alternative to wire-dragging and also served another purpose. During WWII, German submarines operating off the coast of North Carolina could escape detection by surface vessels by lying alongside a shipwreck site and appearing as part of the wreckage to the electronic sensors above. Realizing the implication of this camouflage technique, the Navy and the Coast Guard had its vessels depth-charge any metal contact for good measure. As a result, some of the sites are pretty disheveled. Nature, too, has taken its toll on the appearance of many shipwrecks. Over the years underwater, ships that sank more or less intact to the bottom and escaped depth-charging during

WWII gradually deteriorated, with the amidships portion slowly settling directly to the bottom and thereby pulling the bow and stern sections upwards. Several of the wrecks have their bows and sterns tilted up at 45 degrees to the bottom. Other vessels are remarkably intact sitting upright on the bottom, while some rest on their sides and some are upside down.

Shipwrecks that lie within approximately three miles of shore fall under the jurisdiction of the State of North Carolina. These include all of the Civil War blockade runners and blockaders discussed in this book. The North Carolina Department of Cultural Resources through its Underwater Archaeology Branch at Fort Fisher oversees these wreck sites. Although the state allows and even encourages diving on nearshore and beach wrecks, you must obtain a permit if you plan to remove artifacts from such sites. Detailed information about the wrecks and permits can be obtained from the Underwater Archaeology Branch, Division of Archives and History, P.O. Box 58, Kure Beach, NC 28449.

The USS *Peterhoff* is the only vessel covered in this book that is under Federal jurisdiction. The blockader actually falls under the jurisdiction of at least two Federal departments, Defense and Interior. Because the U.S. Navy never decommissioned the USS *Peterhoff* after it sank in 1864, it still owns the vessel. To remove artifacts from the *Peterhoff*, a diver must apply to the Navy for a permit. The *Peterhoff* is also listed in the National Register of Historic Places, which means that the site is regulated by the National Park Service of the U.S. Department of Interior.

One other wreck off the coast of North Carolina comes under Federal jurisdiction: the U.S.S. *Monitor*. It is an absolute requirement that permission be obtained before visiting the *Monitor*, and no sport diving is allowed at the site, which has been designated a National Marine Sanctuary. The National Oceanic and Atmospheric Administration (NOAA) of the U.S. Department of Commerce oversees the site. In any event, the *Monitor* lies in water too deep for sport diving.

Shipwrecks that lie further than three miles from shore can be freely visited, and any artifacts taken from sites that far out to sea belong to the diver who recovers them.

Divers who visit a wreck site must exercise good judgment about artifact collection. The wrecks described here are not only the remains of ships where a diver can explore; they also provide a habitat for hundreds of marine creatures. Over the years, these inhabitants develop into extensive communities comprising the entire ocean food chain. Of course, every diver wants a souvenir from a wreck, and over time many artifacts have been removed from North Carolina shipwrecks—though many still remain. As artifacts become ever more difficult to obtain, there is an ever-increasing temptation to destroy a wreck in order to uncover an otherwise inaccessible find. Such destruction for the sake of a few brass artifacts ruins living marine habitats and leaves little shipwreck legacy for future divers. If you must bring anything back from a wreck dive, take a camera and bring back pictures. Enjoy the beauty, mystery, and excitement of these exotic shipwrecks, and leave them intact for others to enjoy for years to come. Above all, preserve our marine environment.

Overview of the Wrecks

EDDIES OF THE LABRADOR CURRENT bring cold water from the north past the Nags Head area of the North Carolina coast. Here lie the remains of several WWII vintage wrecks, the most notable of which is the *U-85*. The German submarine was the first U-boat sunk off the East Coast by the Allies, and that sinking marked the beginning of the end of the U-boat stranglehold on Allied shipping to and from the U.S. during the war. The *U-85* sank in 100 feet of water and lies near the wrecks of the *Norvana* and the *Byron D. Benson*, both of which were tankers built in the early 1920s and torpedoed by German U-boats early in 1942. The *Norvana* lies in 100 feet of water northeast of the *U-85*, and to the northeast of the *Norvana* is the much larger wreck site of the *Byron D. Benson*, which rests in 90 feet of water. The Brazilian passenger-cargo vessel *Buarque* was torpedoed in 1942 and now lies in 140 feet of water, 40 miles northeast of Oregon Inlet. The *Buarque* is the wreck furthermost from land in divable waters off this section of the North Carolina coast.

Southeast of Oregon Inlet, off Avon, North Carolina, lie two more wrecks, the *Ciltvaira*, a freighter torpedoed early in 1942, and the *City of Atlanta*, another freighter which was also torpedoed in 1942. The sea offshore of this point along the Outer Banks marks a dividing line. Down to Avon the water is still kept cold by the eddies of the Labrador Current. South of Avon, however, the waters are warm and tropical due to the eddies of the Gulf Stream which flows nearby. Thus the *Ciltvaira* is a "tropical" wreck that is home for many corals, sponges, and other marine life usually found in the Caribbean. Inshore of the *Ciltvaira*, which lies in 105 feet of water, is the wreck of the *City of Atlanta* sunk in 80 feet of water.

In and around the Cape Hatteras area are some unique shipwrecks. On the northeast side of Diamond Shoals lies the *Empire Gem*, a British tanker torpedoed in January 1942. Southwest of Hatteras off Hatteras Inlet are the wrecks of the *City of New York*, the *Keshena*, the *F. W. Abrams*, the *Dixie Arrow*, the *Proteus*, the *British Splendour*, the *Manuela*, and the USS *Tarpon*. The *F. W. Abrams*, the *Dixie Arrow*, and the *British Splendour* were tankers torpedoed by German U-boats in 1942.

The *Dixie Arrow* lies in 90 feet of water, while the *British Splendour* lies in 110 feet. The *F. W. Abrams* is at a depth of 85 feet, and the *Manuela*, a freighter, is in 170 feet of water, which is out of the depth range of sport divers. The *F. W. Abrams* is located about 10 miles southeast of Hatteras Inlet, and the *Dixie Arrow* is about 10 miles further southeast. The *British Splendour* is located closer inshore and is upside down, with her keel at 90 feet and the bottom at 110 feet. The corals, sponges, and other marine life on these wrecks are quite beautiful.

In the same general area—south of Hatteras Inlet—divers can visit several other interesting wrecks. The *City of New York* was a small coastal trading ship which sank in a storm two miles offshore of Hatteras in January 1862 and settled in 70 feet of water. The *Keshena* was a small ocean tug which was accidentally sunk in 1942 when it ran over an American mine off Hatteras. The wreck is located about a mile from the *F. W. Abrams* and is in 70 feet of water. Something to avoid when diving this site is the large net caught on the port side forward of amidships of the wreck.

Offshore of the *British Splendour*, southwest of Hatteras Inlet, lie two of the most fascinating wrecks off the North Carolina coast. These are the *Proteus*, a passenger ship built in 1899, and the USS *Tarpon*, a WWII U.S. fleet submarine built in 1933. These two wrecks lie within one-quarter mile of each other in warm, clear water and contain very interesting artifacts. The wreck of the *Proteus*, sunk in a collision in 1918, lies in 125 feet of water, and the nearby *Tarpon*, sunk on its way to being scrapped, lies at a depth of 140 feet. Both wrecks provide a habitat for some of the most exquisite marine life to be seen on an offshore wreck site, and both attract sand tiger sharks, especially the *Tarpon*. The sharks have not presented any problem to divers and are quite a sight.

Several wrecks are located in the warm, clear water offshore between Ocracoke Island and Cape Lookout, and charter dive boats from the Morehead City and Beaufort areas frequently visit these sites. The wrecks are the tankers *Tamaulipas* and *Atlas*, and the freighters *Portland* and *Ashkhabad*, all of which were torpedoed by U-boats during WWII. The *Tamaulipas* lies in two sections about a mile apart from each other; the bow section is the larger of the two and lies upside down in 150 feet of water, while the keel lies at 130 feet. Closer to Cape Lookout is the *Atlas* tanker, one of the top five wrecks off the North Carolina coast; it rests in 130 feet of water. Inshore of the *Atlas* is a smaller freighter, the *Caribsea*, which lies in 85 feet of water, a relatively shallow depth that inexperienced wreck divers should be able to handle. The American freighter *Portland* and the Russian freighter *Ashkhabad* lie closer to Cape Lookout Shoals in shallow depths (around 55 feet); they are extensively broken up and spread over a large area of ocean bottom.

From Cape Lookout to Frying Pan Shoals off Cape Fear lie nearly a dozen shipwrecks that are accessible to divers. Inshore wrecks are quite numerous in this area. One such wreck, the *W. E. Hutton*, was torpedoed in 1942 and sank in 70 feet of water about 10 miles offshore of Beaufort Inlet. One year later, the freighter *Suloide* struck the wreck of the *Hutton* and sank about a mile away in 65 feet of water. Divers frequently visit these two sites, where many scuba classes also conduct checkout dives. Though the site of the *Hutton* is much larger than that of the *Suloide*, both wrecks are fun to dive. They are recommended for first-time North Carolina wreck divers because of their shallow depths and the short boat trip to the sites. Two other wrecks in this area, the *Senateur Duhamel* and the *Ea*, lie closer to the south side of Cape Lookout Shoals. The *Senateur Duhamel* is a WWII-vintage British armed trawler which was sent to aid the Americans in their battle with the U-boat menace. The trawler was accidentally rammed in the shipping lanes off Morehead City and sank in 70 feet of water. A buoy designated "8" marks the site. The *Ea* was a small coastal freighter sunk in a storm in 1902. Lying nearby is the wreck of the *Fenwick Island*, a 125-foot-long menhaden fishing vessel that went down in a storm near Cape Lookout Shoals on December 7, 1968. It is completely intact, lying on its side in 65 feet of water.

Off Cape Lookout and to the south of that area are some of the best offshore wrecks to be found in North Carolina waters. They lie twenty or more miles offshore in clear, warm tropical waters, and the marine life on these wrecks is the same as that found in the Caribbean or the Florida Keys. The wrecks in this area include the U.S.S. *Schurz*, a WWI U.S. Navy cruiser which sank as a result of an accident in 1918; the *U-352*, a U-boat sunk in 1942; the *Papoose*, the *Naeco*, the *Cassimir*, and the *John D. Gill*, four large tankers torpedoed in 1942 by U-boats; and the *Normannia*, a Danish freighter sunk in a storm in 1924. The USS *Schurz* was a confiscated German cruiser used by the U.S. Navy for antisubmarine duty off the Atlantic coast during WWI; she collided with a freighter offshore of Morehead City and sank in 110 feet of water. The *U-352* was sunk by the Coast Guard cutter *Icarus* and now lies intact in 115 feet of water about 10 miles from the *Schurz*. The German submarine is probably the most visited wreck off of the North Carolina coast; with the usual visibility on the wreck in the range of 70–100 feet, the remains of this submersible from the past make quite an impression when first glimpsed.

Further offshore lie two of the top five North Carolina shipwrecks: the *Papoose* and the *Naeco*, which were tankers torpedoed by U-boats in 1942. The *Papoose* lies upside down in 130 feet of water 35 miles offshore of Morehead City with her keel at a depth of 80 feet. The *Naeco* lies about ten miles further out past the *Papoose* in about 140 feet of water. The wreckage of the *Naeco* consists of two sections, the bow section being about two miles from the stern. The stern wreckage comprises about 80 percent of the ship, sits upright, and is the more interesting of the two sections.

Further west of the *Naeco* lies the *Cassimir*, another tanker sunk by a U-boat in 1942. Also one of the top five North Carolina wrecks, the *Cassimir* is a buoyed wreck with the designation "WR-2" and lies in 120 feet of water. The bow section lies about 50 yards away from the larger stern section, and the stern proper is at 45 degrees to the bottom. Nearby lies the *Normannia*, a Danish freighter which foundered in a storm off Cape Fear in 1924. She sank in 110 feet of water. The marine life on this wreck is beautiful, and the *Normannia* also ranks among the top five offshore wrecks.

Closer to shore, the *John D. Gill* was the largest ship sunk off the coast of North Carolina during WWII; the tanker was torpedoed early in 1942 on her second run in service. She sank in 90 feet of water and sits upright with her deck at 60 feet. Her above-deck superstructure has been cleared away. The stern section lies broken up about 50 yards from the much larger main section, which comprises about 70 percent of the ship. Soft corals, sponges, and other marine life abound on this wreck. The relatively shallow depth and the marine life on the wreck make the *Gill* an excellent dive for divers new to North Carolina wreck diving.

On the southeast side of Frying Pan Shoals lies the wreck of the *George Weems* in 40 feet of water. Sunk in 1908, the *Weems* is, in terms of marine life, one of the most beautiful wreck sites, lying in often unusually clear water on the edge of the shoals. On the southwest side of Frying Pan Shoals are three wrecks, the *Mount Dirfys*, *City of Houston*, and the *Raritan*. The *Mount Dirfys* was a freighter which sank in a storm in 1936 in 55 feet of water. The *City of Houston* was a passenger liner which sank in 1878 in a storm in 90 feet of water on Frying Pan Shoals. The ship was loaded with Christmas goods and supplies bound for Galveston, Texas, when she went down. The *Raritan* was a freighter which ran aground on Frying Pan Shoals in 1942 and sank in about 75 feet of water in two sections now lying about 100 yards apart. All three of these wrecks are excellent dives for inexperienced wreck divers.

There are a number of Civil War blockade runners and blockaders that lie very close to shore along the North Carolina coast, often at or inside the surf zone. Many are located offshore of Wilmington, which was an important Confederate harbor during the Civil War. The *Modern Greece*, the U.S.S. *Peterhoff*, the *Ranger*, the *General Beauregard*, the *Fanny and Jenny*, the *Condor*, and the *Iron Age* are but a few of the vessels that were sunk during the Civil War off the south coast of North Carolina.

A number of other vessels lie close to shore and are easy walk-in dives, but divers should be aware that low visibility and turbulence are the rule on close-to-shore dives. The two sections of the tanker *Kyzickes*, sunk in

1927, and the freighter *Carl Gerhard*, sunk in 1929, make up the "Triangle Wrecks" located 200 yards offshore near Nags Head.

Powered by sail and steam, the U.S.S *Huron* was a Federal gunship which ran aground off Nags Head in 1877 with the loss of 98 of her crew. The *Huron* lies in about 20 feet of water about 200 yards north of Nags Head Pier and about 100 yards offshore. The *Metropolis*, a small freighter, foundered and sank in a storm off Currituck Beach in 1878 with the loss of 85 lives. The wreck is located three miles south of Currituck Beach Light and about 100 yards offshore in the surf zone at a depth of 15 feet.

Four Liberty ships have been sunk as artificial reefs off the coast of North Carolina. The *Zane Grey* was sunk five miles southwest of Oregon Inlet and sits upright on the bottom at a depth of 80 feet, while her deck is at 40 feet. The *Dionysus*, a Liberty ship similar to the *Zane Grey*, was sunk 300 yards away from her look-alike in 80 feet of water. The *Alexander Ramsey* was sunk off Wrightsville Beach in 70 feet of water and is located three miles due east of Wrightsville Beach Inlet. The *Theodore Parker* was sunk off Morehead City and now lies one-and-a-half miles off Bogue Banks and three miles west of Fort Macon in 50 feet of water with her upper deck at 30 feet. The *Aeolus* was a troop transport ship converted to a transoceanic cable layer which was sunk in 110 feet of water off Morehead City in 1988 as an artificial reef. The hull of the cable ship may be reached at 60 feet.

By arranging charters through local coast dive shops, divers can visit dozens of other wrecks whose identities are unknown. In addition, dive charter boat captains will occasionally take divers out to "private" wreck sites, and many interesting types of dives can be had on such charters.

Wreck Diving from a Boat

MANY GOOD AND SAFE WRECK DIVING TECHNIQUES have been developed, refined, and perfected on North Carolina shipwrecks. This type of diving can be among the most demanding and strenuous, and anyone considering it should be in good physical shape. Wreck divers can encounter long boat rides, deep dives, strong currents, and other problems, but the difficulties are more than compensated for by the rewards of the dive. Warm, clear water teeming with beautiful, colorful tropical marine life amidst the remains of sunken wrecks is an experience to be found nowhere else but offshore North Carolina.

The most arduous part of wreck diving is often the boat trip. Not everyone gets seasick, but occasionally even the most seasoned divers will find themselves queasy from motion sickness during a long boat trip to a dive site. It is therefore important that, prior to a dive, one be adequately prepared not only for the dive itself but also for the lengthy trip out to the wreck.

A good night's sleep, no hangover, and a good breakfast are the keys to successfully avoiding seasickness. Breakfast is very important. Many divers have the mistaken conception that an empty stomach will keep them from experiencing motion sickness. Nothing could be further from the truth. Eat a moderate amount of non-greasy, non-acidic food in the morning prior to a dive, even if you don't feel like it. Most people find it difficult to face a meal at five o'clock in the morning, but those who eat will definitely benefit. Being in good physical shape also helps guard against motion sickness. Prior to the diving season, you should jog, swim, or engage in other regular exercise to improve not only your diving skills but also your boat-riding ability.

If all else fails in preventing seasickness, you can try one of the several antinausea medications that are readily available without a prescription. Everyone has his or her favorite, and it is basically a trial-and-error procedure to determine which is the best one for you. The relatively new Transderm-Scop patches, which contain scopolamine in a special time-release base, work well for many people—although they don't work for some. The patches are expensive and can only be obtained with a prescription. However, if you find that the patches work for you, you can save money by cutting them in half and applying only half the dosage. Dramamine, Marezine, scopolamine capsules, Bonine, and a wide variety of other remedies for motion sickness have been used with varying degrees of success by divers. The U.S. Navy has done studies on seasickness remedies and has found that Phenergan with ephedrine works well. I have seen people helped by the Phenergan-ephedrine elixir after they have tried all else to no avail. The elixir requires a doctor's prescription, and like many of the over-the-counter remedies may produce drowsiness. The Phenergan produces the sleepy effect, and the ephedrine is supposed to help keep you awake.

The best regimen for taking any seasickness remedy is to take a dose the night before a dive trip to acclimate your body to the drug's effects. Take another dose with breakfast, paying heed to the manufacturer's or pharmacist's directions. Once aboard the boat, choose a comfortable bunk or spot on deck and relax. Try to sleep on the way out if time permits, and have someone wake you at least 45 minutes before you reach the dive site. If you are the least bit susceptible to seasickness, do not stare at the water, read a book, or look at the sloshing water in the cockpit. If you must stare at something, stare at the horizon. That will make make your inner ear balancing mechanism believe things are more or less level, and you should then be fine. If you find yourself getting queasy, get some fresh air, lie down in a breezy area (and definitely not in a cramped, stuffy compartment), and try to relax. If you feel you are going to vomit, go to the side of the boat and don't be embarrassed to relieve yourself over the side. Often after vomiting a person will feel much better and—believe it or not—may feel like eating a little bland food. Don't rush to the head (bathroom) on the boat and lock yourself in to vomit in privacy. The small enclosed space will generally make you feel worse, and other divers entering the head after you will certainly not appreciate your efforts. If nothing works, lie down in a bunk or in a cozy place on deck and pray for the end of the trip or death, whichever comes first. However, you will always survive seasickness, though you may never set foot on a boat again. There are always shore dives.

Once breakfast is over, check to be certain that you have all of your gear and that it is loaded onto the boat. You will need two tanks of air, a weight belt, a gear bag, food, a cooler with drinks, dry clothes, a wet suit, and a towel or two. A sleeping bag, a camera, a radio, a tape player, and other amenities may also be carried on board, but a diver must be sure that all of the gear required for not only the dive but the whole trip will be at hand when needed. Store tanks safely and securely so they won't roll around on the deck, and don't throw weight belts, tanks, and other heavy objects onto the boat as though the deck were made of steel instead of fiberglass or wood. Check to be sure there is air in your tanks before you leave the dock, or else you may find your dive ruined before you ever get to the site.

During the trip out, someone familiar with the wreck should brief all of the divers by giving an informal "pre-dive" talk. Among the expected diving conditions that should be discussed are such matters as depth to the wreck, depth to the bottom, currents, visibility, how the wreck lies, and any other factors that would help orient divers who have never been on the wreck before. The pre-dive talk may also help to allay any anxieties that divers may be experiencing.

A good first-aid kit, medical O_2, and an O_2 regulator should be available on the dive boat, and their location and directions for their use should be pointed out to each diver. Be sure to attach the O_2 regulator to its bottle before the dive, and store the unit in a safe place accessible to all divers.

The captain should be told to notify the dive party when the boat is about 45 minutes away so that everyone can prepare his or her gear in advance. At that time, divers can start attaching regulators to scuba tanks, securing backpacks, and donning wet suits.

The wet-suit donning process requires a bit of thought to make it as comfortable as possible. If it is a hot day, don't suit up too far in advance because overheating will make worse any queasiness you may be feeling. If you are too hot in your wet suit, ask someone to put a bucket over the side for water to be poured over your head. Let the cool water get into the suit to cool the body skin.

Buckets for collecting water are always carried on board by a boat captain to rinse things off. A rope, with a loop on the free end, is usually tied to the bucket handle. Secure the loop to your wrist and throw the bucket over the side open end down and in the direction the boat is moving. When the bucket hits the water, pull it up quickly; it should then be more or less filled with water. Tossing the bucket toward the stern of the boat will result in a sudden and tremendous drag when it fills with water, and several consequences will follow: the bucket will be snatched off your wrist; you will have to reimburse the captain for his lost container; and there will not be a bucket to cool off divers or to wash out masks.

Once the captain nears the dive site he will usually throw a buoy to mark the location and begin to search the area for a while to locate the wreck on his depth finder. This search pattern is usually circular and results in a lot of turbulence as the boat hits its own swells. You must take care not to be thrown off balance while putting on your wet suit during this time, and tanks that were unsecured to attach the regulator must be secured to prevent them from being knocked about. When the wreck is finally located, the boat's engine will be slowed considerably and diver activity on the boat will pick up proportionately. The mate is usually on the bow waiting for the captain's signal to toss the anchor, and when the signal is given, the divers must wait to be certain the anchor is secured into the wreck before entering the water. Often several tries are necessary to accomplish this, and again the bucket is useful for cooling overheated divers during this period.

Once the anchor is securely hooked into the wreck, other lines and equipment should be prepared so that they can be put over the side.

The tag line, usually 50–100 feet in length, is tied to the stern on one end and attached to an inner tube or float on the other and allowed to drift away from the boat, thus effectively lengthening the craft by its own length. A diver can hold on to this line while waiting for his buddy to enter the water; or, more importantly, a diver drifting in a current on returning from the wreck can swim to the tag line and then pull himself to the stern. The tag line also serves as a place where divers can queue up to await their turn to board the boat.

A dive flag is usually attached to the inner tube at the end of the tag line. These days, it is probably best to fly two dive flags: the international blue and white flag as well as the one it has superseded, the old familiar red flag with a diagonal white stripe. The international flag is the only one that gives divers specific legal rights while it is flown over a dive site, but it is not as familiar to boatmen, who will more readily recognize the old red flag. Thus the use of both means that boatmen in the area will know that divers are below and that the diver's legal rights will be guaranteed in the event of a boating accident.

Another important line that should be put over the side is the current line which is clipped to the anchor line so that it falls freely into the water while attached there, and, running the length of the boat, is tied to the stern. After rolling into the water, divers can use this current or lead line to pull themselves to the anchor line in the event there is a current.

Someone should be stationed at the bow or bridge watching divers as they make their way forward to the anchor line to assist them if there are any problems. Once at the anchor line, buddies should descend to around 10–20 feet or so, check on each other, and with the O.K. signal continue their descent to the wreck by pulling themselves down the anchor line.

The first buddy team to reach the anchor should tie it securely to the wreck by means of a small line (3–4 feet) carried for that purpose. Once secured, the anchor cannot leave the wreck without being untied. The first or second buddy team to reach the wreck should also carry a spool of small line several hundred feet in length which can be tied to the anchor and played out over the wreck to provide a means of returning to the anchor line under conditions of limited visibility. The use of this so-called cross-wreck line is governed by common sense, in that if the visibility is 75–100 feet or more, there is no need to play it out.

A good compass, a dive light, and a signalling device, such as a whistle, are important items for each member of a buddy team to have. Wrecks tend to be disorienting, especially if there is limited visibility, and a compass bearing taken near the anchor will usually ensure an easy return to begin the ascent. A dive light is quite useful for illuminating nooks and crannies and for bringing out the natural colors of various kinds of marine life. Even the deepest wrecks off the coast of North Carolina have plenty of light at depth for a diver to see well enough to navigate, and the dive light is strictly for looking into dark recesses; it is not for illuminating the dive for the divers.

Until sufficient experience is gained, a good rule of thumb is that once divers have decided which direction to investigate, they should swim out from the anchor line until they have used 1,000 psi of air and then return to the anchor line, arriving with around 1,000 psi of air remaining for the balance of the dive (assuming an 80-cubic-foot scuba cylinder with 3,000 psi fill). An additional 500 psi may then be used while investigating the wreck within sight of the anchor, and when a diver is down to the last 500 psi of air the buddy team should begin its ascent up the anchor line.

If you should lose the anchor line, don't panic. Search for a few minutes, and if you still cannot locate it, begin your ascent watching your depth gauge and air bubbles. Look around as you are ascending to see if you can locate the anchor line. Also look up at the surface to see if you can locate the dive boat. Failing this, keep ascending slowly. If you have made a "no-decompression" dive and you are sure about your depth and bottom time, continue to the surface. Alternatively, if there is no current, stop your ascent at 10 feet, adjust your buoyancy compensator, and make a prophylactic decompression stop for three minutes. After the brief stop, surface, blow up your buoyancy compensator, and fin back to the boat. Signal the boat that you are O.K. as you make your way there.

If you have overstayed your bottom time and must decompress and there is a current running, you have a bit of a problem. Ascend to 10 feet, adjust buoyancy, and decompress the appropriate amount of time. Do not rush this decompression even though the current is taking you away from the boat while you decompress. After decompressing, surface and locate the boat, which may be some distance away. Generally, a diver cannot dive in a current greater than a knot (around one mph). At one mph, the current during a five-minute decompression stop will not carry a diver much farther than 400–500 feet away from the boat. Use your whistle or signalling device to signal your location to those on the dive boat, but realize that if there is any sea at all, a diver's head and shoulders are difficult to see among the waves. Don't try to swim against the current to reach the boat. Wait until the boat comes and picks you up. Don't expect fast service because the boat has to collect all the rest of the divers in the water first. It really is a hassle for everyone on a dive trip if divers come up away from the anchor line, especially if there is a current. Know the location of the anchor at all times.

Most divers find the anchor line and ascend with no problems. Surface and await your turn to board while holding on to the tag line. When it is your turn, keep your regulator and mask in place until you are up the ladder. Remove your fins before climbing the ladder and hand them to someone on the boat or put them over your wrist and carry them on board. Once on board, move yourself and all your gear away from the ladder area and begin to remove your equipment. Store all your gear together and out of the way, and then relax; the dive is over. The last buddy team to ascend must untie the anchor line from the wreck before surfacing.

Someone on the boat should keep track of each diver's bottom time and time out of the water so that an appropriate surface interval is allowed while travelling to a second shallower dive. At all times that divers are in the water someone should be on the bow or bridge of the boat watching for divers coming up away from the boat. A pair of binoculars is useful for this purpose. If divers are spotted away from the boat, they should be signalled that they have been seen and someone should watch them until they are back on the boat. Divers away from the boat should signal whether or not they are O.K. If they are not O.K., a buoy should be tied to the anchor line, the anchor line should be cut from the boat, and a diver equipped with a buoyancy compensator, mask, fins, and snorkle should be put over the side to assist divers in the water while the boat leaves to assist the divers in distress. Once the boat returns, all divers at the site of the anchor line should be put on board. Under any circumstances, before the boat gets underway a head count should be made to determine that all divers are on board.

Once all divers are on board, the gear has been stowed properly, and the dive ladder and all lines and cylinders have been put aboard as well, the anchor can be pulled and the boat gotten underway. Divers can then break out lunch and refreshments and swap stories about the dive they have just made. Divers should also report any problems they may be experiencing after surfacing.

Wreck diving, properly carried out, is safe, exciting, and fun for all divers. Novice and experienced alike will return for dive after dive to visit these vessels from the past.

Beach (Walk-in) Diving

WALK-IN BEACH DIVING can be as much fun as diving off of a boat offshore, and it is certainly much cheaper. However, there are certain factors to consider before attempting a walk-in dive. Most walk-in wreck sites are located in the very turbulent surf zone located just off the beach. A diver must negotiate his way through this turbulence to reach the wreck. If conditions are really tumultuous, it is always best to wait until a better day to dive. Currents and surge must also be taken into consideration. If there is a current running down the beach, it will be extremely difficult and tiring to try to swim across it to reach the wreck site. Under such conditions, it would again be wiser to wait until a better day.

If conditions are found to be acceptable, locate the wreck using a prominent landmark or two on shore for reference, put on all of your dive gear including your fins, and walk or shuffle backwards into the water until you reach deeper water where you can conveniently begin to swim. Be careful during your walk through the turbulence that you do not lose your balance and become a piece of flotsam tossed about by the waves. Keep your regulator in your mouth so it will not fill up with sand and keep track of your mask, holding it if necessary when waves hit. It is quite easy to have your mask torn off by vigorous wave action if you are not careful. Dive buddies should stay close enough to help each other out if necessary but far enough apart not to be knocked into each other in the surf. Once you have made it to waist-deep water, join up with your buddy, turn forward, and begin to swim toward the wreck, checking your landmarks frequently to keep on course. Once you are away from the shore it becomes somewhat easier to swim toward the wreck, and often some portion of the wreckage will be sticking out above the water, making navigation easier.

Once you have reached the wreck, do not expect the visibility to be much, as the water is kept stirred up by wave action. Also, care must be taken to avoid being pushed or pulled by the surge into sharp pieces of the wreckage, and gloves and protective clothing or a wet suit should be worn. A bright dive light, a compass, and a cross-wreck line are useful aids to navigation under conditions of limited visibility.

When you and your buddy are ready to make your way back to shore after the dive, make certain you are aware of any changes in the current and wave action because after the trip out and diving on the wreck, you are going to be very tired. Be prepared to inflate your buoyancy compensator and rest on the trip in if you get really tired. Make your way to shore keeping your regulator in your mouth as you did on the trip out. Once you can touch bottom, do not stand up but allow the waves to carry you in as close to the beach as possible. When you get to the beach, crawl away from the water and rest. Stand up only after you are sure you are out of the reach of waves.

Adventures in Locating Shipwrecks: A Personal Account

NOT ALL OF THE SHIPS that have gone down off of the North Carolina coast have been identified or even located. Once in a while word will begin to spread that a particular wreck has at last been found, but even then it's not always easy to track down a charter boat captain who can get divers to the presumed site of the wreck. Sometimes, it also happens that a wrecked ship has been misidentified or confused with another wreck in the vicinity where it sank. Twice now, I have had the good fortune of coming upon newly discovered wrecks. On such occasions one may have to endure considerable frustration before one can savor the thrill of discovery.

A couple of years ago, I was searching for a charter boat captain who would take me out to shipwrecks off Hatteras and Ocracoke when I met Art LePage, captain of the *November Gale* and owner of the Outer Banks

Dive Shop in Wanchese, which is located near Manteo 70 miles north of Hatteras Inlet. (The *November Gale* was his boat at that time; he now runs the *Beaudine* as a charter boat.) Art regularly takes divers out from Oregon Inlet to nearby wrecks, such as the *U-85*, the *York*, the *Benson*, and the *Ciltvaira*. I told him about my project of photographing shipwrecks off the North Carolina coast and about how I would be very interested in diving on some of the wrecks south of his normal stomping grounds. As it turned out, Art said he would be willing to move his boat down to Hatteras if I could charter both days of a weekend. He added that he could take me to the *Dixie Arrow*, the *F. W. Abrams*, the *Keshena*, the *City of New York* (also known as the "Urn Wreck"), the *Malchace*, the *Empire Gem*, the *Australia*, and several other wrecks.

I quickly booked the Memorial Day weekend, and several divers made the long trek with me from the Chapel Hill area to Hatteras. Fears of spending several hours on the road getting to Hatteras and then being blown out by bad weather permeated the atmosphere as we drove to the coast. It had happened that way the previous summer every single time we went to that part of the coast. However, our fears were never realized; the weather was cooperative and the dives we made that weekend to the *Dixie Arrow*, the *Abrams*, the *Keshena*, and the *City of New York* were excellent.

The dives were so good in fact that I booked another charter weekend with Art for a few weeks later. We discussed a trip to a wreck he had been fishing on for years, a wreck to which he had taken a small group of divers six or seven years previously when the only dive at the site had been made. This was apparently the wreck of the *Malchace*—a vessel sunk during WWII which is thought to be located about an hour further offshore than the *Dixie Arrow* at a depth of 130 feet. We set the date and a few weeks later I and several divers were headed to Hatteras once more. The usual fears were discussed during the long drive from Chapel Hill, but once again we were in luck.

As we headed out to the dive site on Art's boat, the seas were choppy, but the weather was beautiful. After a three-hour boat ride, we quickly hooked the wreck, and into the water I went, carrying all of my camera gear. The water was very warm and the visibility around 60 feet as I descended in currentless waters. When I reached the wreck I was absolutely stunned by what I saw. There were portholes scattered all over the bottom, some stuck into the sand and several just sitting on the bottom waiting to be picked up. Interspersed among the portholes were huge generators, an anchor windlass, pipes and valves, and a huge "old-fashioned" anchor complete with chain standing upright in the sand. We were most certainly on the bow of the wreck, and from all appearances no one had ever visited this wreck before. A virgin wreck. I photographed the entire bow area including some of the most beautiful corals and sponges I'd seen off the North Carolina coast.

We were all exhausted when we finally made it back to the dock through weather that had taken a decided turn for the worse. The next day of diving was blown out, but nothing could contain the euphoria all of us felt about having dived an untouched wreck. We made plans for another trip over the Labor Day weekend, and everyone left Hatteras in high spirits.

A few weeks later, word circulated back to me that George Purifoy, a boat captain and diver from Morehead City, had discovered another wreck off of Ocracoke and was planning a trip up there in the near future. It was the same wreck to which Albert Wadsworth had been carrying divers since mid-July 1983, from Atlantic Beach on his boat, the *Mary Catherine*. This wreck had yielded the most startling types of artifacts seen by area divers, the most notable of those artifacts being large, rectangular brass windows, complete with stained glass in the top portion. Regular portholes were a dime-a-dozen, and other artifacts were plentiful on this newly found wreck.

The vessel was apparently an old one sunk before WWII, and it seemed to be a diver's delight. I signed on for the trip, and at 3:00 A.M. on the appointed morning we cast off for a six-hour journey from Morehead City on very calm seas. By 9:30 we were in the water where we were treated to visibility of over 100 feet and the largest wreck I have ever seen scattered over the ocean bottom. Completely dominating the ship's remains were three of the largest boilers I had yet encountered (over 15 feet in diameter) and more portholes and brass windows than I had ever observed on a wreck site. In addition to the multitude of windows and portholes recovered by the divers on that day, George Purifoy managed to find and bring up a large capstan cover with the name of the ship that we had been diving on. It was the *Proteus*. The wreck had been positively identified. Happiness prevailed as we headed home.

I asked George the question I had been putting all summer long to other boat captains who travelled to these waters to dive. "Do you know the location of any other wrecks in these parts?" Always the standard answers. "Well, we've got the loran C numbers for a few but we haven't checked them out yet." "Do you have the numbers to the U.S. submarine *Tarpon*?" I would ask. The answer was always negative, and people would say, "Besides the *Tarpon* is in 160–80 feet of water. But we're working on it." For several months I had also been asking Art LePage to try to find the sub's location during his fishing trips to the Hatteras area.

He told me he was trying to do just that and had a few contacts among area fishermen that might pan out.

Meanwhile, I concentrated on other wrecks in the area. I was very happy about having been on the *Proteus* and about the nameplate having been found. I wanted to know more about the *Proteus*. Where was she located off the coast? I decided to call Albert Wadsworth and ask him a few questions since he had been carrying divers out to the *Proteus* most of the summer. I explained who I was and what I wanted, and he very graciously told me several interesting facts about the *Proteus*. One fact nearly knocked me out of my chair. Albert told me that in order to find the location of the *Proteus*, one merely had to know the loran C numbers for the *Malchace*. "The *Malchace*?" I asked. "Yes," he said, "All these years, the wreck reported to be the *Malchace* was really that of the *Proteus*." I asked him to wait a minute while I went to get a copy of a new wreck chart I had acquired from Buck Wilde (captain of the *Sea Wife IV*) three days earlier. On the chart were loran C numbers for several wrecks in the Hatteras-Ocracoke area including the *Malchace*. I read the numbers out to Albert who responded, "Yes, those would get you real close, but the map printers inverted the next-to-last digit of one of the coordinates and rather than a six it should be a nine. With that correction you would be able to locate the *Proteus*." I told him about Art LePage and his trips out to the *Malchace*. Was this the same wreck? Al suggested I call Art and see if he would give me the numbers to the wreck he had been taking me to for comparison.

I called Art and explained the whole story to him: Albert, George Purifoy, the *Proteus*, the new wreck chart, the *Malchace* numbers, the works. Would he please tell me the numbers of the wreck he had taken me to. After having me promise not to publish the numbers and saying that he had also seen a copy of the new wreck chart, Art gave me the numbers. They were identical to the corrected numbers Al Wadsworth had given me. The wreck we had visited several weeks earlier with Art LePage, thinking it was the *Malchace*, the wreck where we had seen the "old-fashioned" anchor and the bottom littered with portholes, our virgin wreck was in fact the wreck of the *Proteus*.

I called Albert and told him about the numbers, and he wasn't really surprised. A few weeks later word filtered back to me that Albert had taken a four-day charter trip from Atlantic Beach up to Hatteras to visit the *Proteus* several weeks earlier and had stopped on the way to check out some loran numbers a fisherman had given to him. Neither he nor the fisherman knew what was at the site except that it was metal and lots of fish hung about there. It wasn't too far from the *Proteus* so he swung by and put a couple of divers into the water to check it out. Lo and behold, what did they find but the wreck of the *Tarpon*. The sub I had been hoping to find and photograph had been found, and it was in divable waters, 130 feet deep.

I phoned Albert the night that I heard the report about his finding the *Tarpon*, and he confirmed it. We then arranged the first of three possible trips on which I would go to photograph the sub. Albert had taken divers out to the sub only once—a group from the Washington, D.C. area. The three upcoming trips he had planned involved groups from the same area, so he thought I could get on one of those charters or ride on the boat with him from Atlantic Beach up to Hatteras, stopping off to make a dive on the sub. As luck would have it, the weather and a boat malfunction cancelled the trips. I was so close to reaching the *Tarpon*, but it was not to be, at least not right away.

In the meanwhile, my Labor Day dives with Art LePage had come and gone. We had two spectacular days of diving on the *Proteus*, making three dives on her and wondering where the *Tarpon* was. We knew she was nearby. Art would keep checking.

I also participated in a several charters with Buck Wilde on the *Sea Wife IV*. Buck, it turned out, wanted to go to the site of the *Proteus* himself because he had the corrected numbers from the wreck chart but had never been there. A date was set, and 18 divers arrived at the dock on a cold, windy morning at the end of September 1983, took one look at the seas and wind, and promptly cancelled the trip. It was rescheduled for the following weekend as we hoped the weather would be more accommodating. It didn't look very good during the course of the week, however, because tropical storm Dean had developed, blowing gale force winds in the Hatteras area. Understandably, not as many divers wanted to make the long trip now, fearing bad weather, even though by the end of the week the skies were clearing and it appeared that the weekend was going to be beautiful.

On October 2 at 5:00 A.M., nine divers arrived at the dock where Buck's boat was tied up, and the *Sea Wife IV* headed out under cloudless skies, with no wind blowing. The seas were flat and calm with an occasional one-to-two-inch ripple during the five-hour trip. Although the day was projected to be especially nice by the weather forecasters, there were several signs that suggested the day was not going to be a good one for me. As though it were not enough that I had gotten a $45 speeding ticket driving to the boat, and that my twin 50's were empty (the valves had been inadvertently opened sometime during the trip), Buck's loran unit began to malfunction just as we approached the site of the wreck. Was this dive really going to be, and if it was, how were we going to find the

Proteus? Buck thought he knew what the problem with the loran was but could not be absolutely certain without a known point of reference. Sunny skies, flat, dead calm water, five hours from home, and no wreck. We searched and searched every combination and permutation of the numbers for two-and-a-half hours and never marked as much as a fish. We couldn't find the *Proteus*.

Buck reset the loran once more to the way it was when we left the dock originally, and we took up the search again. Nothing. We searched some more, and suddenly he marked something that appeared to be metal. Immediately we threw a buoy over and got into position to anchor. What a relief. It was almost noon. Anchors away. Nothing. The anchor was dragging sand. We pulled up the anchor and attempted another pass. Anchors away. Nothing again. What was going on? We were marking something but nothing could be hooked. Was it just a fish? No, it marked like metal.

We decided to pull up the anchor and send it and a diver down to hook into the wreck. We were all nervous and concerned. Was this to be a wasted day? The diver who was sent down the anchor line went to five or ten feet above the anchor and saw nothing but sand. He returned to the boat and reported seeing nothing; he also said that the visibility was only 40 or so feet. We were panic-stricken. There goes the dive.

We hauled up the anchor and moved to another location we had been searching earlier in the morning. Nothing. We had run out of options. I tried to think of something to do. My $45 speeding ticket was to be for nothing and a beautiful dive day wasted. I asked Buck to turn around and go back to the site where we had marked something and placed the buoy. There I wanted to go down and actually search the area for whatever we were marking. He agreed.

Back we went and again we marked the same thing. I geared up and gathered my camera equipment. As soon as the anchor was dropped I went into the water determined that if anything metal was down there I was going to take a photograph of it. The visibility was about 40 feet, and when I reached the anchor at 125 feet all I saw was sand. I looked around and saw what I thought was a darker area of the bottom some distance away. I really couldn't be sure because if I stared into the distance, everything looked the same. I quickly took a compass bearing and swam about 20 feet toward the apparent object and realized it was getting darker as I approached it. I still could not make anything out, but I returned to the anchor and carrying my camera gear in one hand and the anchor in my other I "walked" on my knees toward the object. There was no current, and the anchor rope floated limply in the water as I made my way to the dark object.

After travelling about 60 feet or so, I found myself at the bottom of a

Atlantic sand tiger shark in its aggregation area near the wreck
of the American submarine, U.S.S. *Tarpon*.

large metal wall which I immediately thought was the starboard wall of
the *Proteus* because it had about the same relief (around 15 feet). Still
something wasn't right. In order to set the anchor I had to get it to the top
of the wall, so I put a little more air into my BC, finned like crazy, and
using the anchor as a grappling hook pulled myself to the top. Gasping, I
threw the anchor into the nearest crevice and looked at the wreck. The
first thing I realized was that I could easily see across it to the sand on the
other side, maybe 20 feet away. I turned to my left and found myself looking at a large hatch at 45 degrees to the surface. I turned to my right and
saw a conning tower. My God! We had found the wreck of the *Tarpon*.

I raced from bow to stern photographing the sub. Almost 50 percent
larger and wider than the *U-352* or the *U-85*, the sub sits on top of the
sand listing to port. Her props and deck gun barrel are gone, and the
hatches are wide enough to accommodate twin scuba cylinders.

After about 20 minutes I returned to the surface with the good news,
and the rest of the divers poured into the water to view a submarine divers had been seeking for the past 25 years. Late in the 1950s, the *Tarpon*
sank while being towed to Baltimore to be scrapped. No one had seen the
sub again until the summer of 1983.

Sharks and Shipwrecks

I STUMBLED UPON THIS LOCATION by accident five years ago. Few had ever seen it and nobody knew its secret. Clues were seen that first October but there was little else to reveal what was really going on. Today, after scores of dives, I've sorted out much of the story but certainly not all of it.

What I had discovered in October of 1983 while searching for another shipwreck was the wreck of an American submarine, the U.S.S. *Tarpon*. More importantly, what I didn't realize at the time was that I had found an aggregation and mating ground of the Atlantic sand tiger shark, *Eugomphodus taurus* (formerly *Odontaspis taurus*).

The wreck of the *Tarpon* is about twenty miles south of Ocracoke Island, North Carolina and lies at the northwestern edge of the area now believed to be the shark's breeding ground. Near here the northerly-flowing, warm Gulf Stream water comes closest to the East Coast than anywhere else except the tip of Florida. To the north of the *Tarpon*, off of Cape Hatteras, the Gulf Stream meets the southerly-flowing, cold water of the Labrador Current. At their confluence, both currents turn east and flow further out into the Atlantic Ocean. The sand tiger sharks aggregate in a large area south of Cape Hatteras where the Caribbean-like temperature of the water is moderated by the influence of the Labrador Current. The warm-temperate sharks have been reported by scientists and fishermen to migrate up the entire eastern seaboard from as far south as Cape Canaveral, Florida.

The dive on the *Tarpon* is deep, slightly over 140 feet to the bottom. The water here is azure blue, clear, and warm. It is indescribably beautiful descending through schools of amberjack and Atlantic spadefish in water with 100 or more feet of visibility. As your eyes stare and strain toward the bottom, the submarine slowly comes into view. Upon reaching forty or fifty feet above its hull you can begin to see large fish swimming slowly or hovering motionless just off the bottom. Dozens of them. Turning to scan through 180 degrees brings you to the realization that they are everywhere as far as the visibility allows you to see. These are the Atlantic sand tiger sharks that aggregate and mate here. As you reach the hull and stop, several very large sharks swim towards you. Notwithstanding the magnification effect of the water, some look as big around as fifty-five gallon drums. Your pulse quickens and air consumption rises as the sharks approach within a few feet. Some of them turn away at the last minute while others glide effortlessly inches away overhead. They have a ferocious look because of the teeth that protrude from their mouth. None of them attack. It is quite exhilarating. Several of the largest sharks of both sexes may be seen surrounded by many tiny fish. These fish are thought to be seeking the protection of the sharks from other predators such as amberjack and barracuda which are prevalent on the site. In the five years that I have taken visitors to see the sharks, no one has ever been attacked or aggressively approached. These sharks eat small fish such as spade fish, not people.

Grant Gilmore, a scientist from the Harbor Branch Oceanographic Institution, who has spent the past twenty years studying sand tiger sharks, visited the aggregation area in the summer of 1989. My observations of the past five years recorded on film and videotape and his recent observations of the site provide evidence that this is a spawning area because of the presence of males and females together which is rare except at mating. In April and early May, many young sharks of about three feet in length may be seen alongside dozens of large females. Female sharks from six to eight feet in length are present in great numbers throughout the spring and summer while the number of small sharks decrease and the number of males increase as the summer proceeds. By the fall, all sharks in the area decrease dramatically in number. In the spring and early summer, there are usually four or five dozen sharks visible around the *Tarpon* at any time. In the fall, there may be only two or three sharks seen over three or four dives on the site.

One of the first things I noticed when I discovered the wreck of the *Tarpon* was the presence of large numbers of shark's teeth on the hull of the submarine. Divers could pick up a dozen or more teeth on a single dive. The sand bottom around the wreck was also littered with teeth. An area of sand the size of an average diver's length on a side may contain two to three teeth or more. It was the presence of these teeth that provided the first clue as to what was happening in the area. Males, prior to mating, bite the female behind her head and forward of the first dorsal fin. In the process the male shark loses some of his protruding teeth and these fall to the bottom. Ordinarily, teeth lost during mating would go unnoticed on the bottom unless they fell on a substrate that would prevent them from being covered by sand. The *Tarpon's* hull provides this substrate. I have surveyed other shipwrecks that are a few miles further offshore of the submarine. Not only are there many sand tiger sharks present on these other sites but the wreck hulls and adjacent sand bottom are also littered with their teeth. According to Gilmore, the presence of the teeth are a further indication that the area is a mating ground for the sharks. Exploring the many wreck sites in this area may be useful to scientists in determining the boundaries of the mating ground.

Why is the discovery of the Atlantic tiger sharks' mating ground important? In addition to being the first occasion to document mating of large sharks in the wild, it also provides the opportunity to study and film the sharks close-up and naturally without baiting them to the site. Unlike many other sharks, the female sand tiger bears only two offspring each season. Although she carries several embryos during early gestation, only one will survive in each of her two oviducts to reach birth; the survivors eat the other embryos before birth. Other shark species that are popular for food in fishmarkets around the world are diminishing in number because they have been over-harvested by fishermen. Now, there are fisheries that wish to harvest thousands of pounds of the sand tiger shark each year for the commercial marketplace. Fish species with such low reproductive output as the sand tiger shark could not survive such pressure upon their population.

To make the future of the Atlantic sand tiger shark even more precarious, the state of North Carolina has leased to oil companies sixty sites on the ocean bottom off its coast for oil and gas exploration. That several exploratory sites lie near the mating/aggregation area raises serious questions about the biological consequences of a spill on the shark nursery area. Much more information about the behavior and reproduction of this species is needed in order to determine how many, if any, may be removed from the sea before man will devastate another of the ocean's dwindling populations. It is hoped that this aggregation and mating area off of the North Carolina coast will be helpful in providing this information.

PART ONE

Offshore Wrecks

I. *Nags Head*

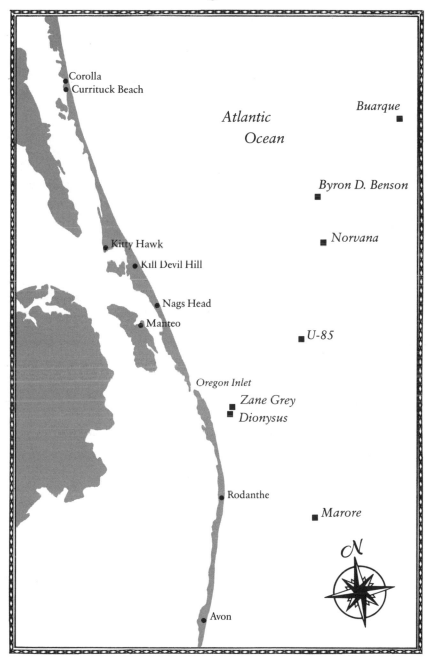

Corolla
Currituck Beach

Atlantic
Ocean

Buarque ■

Byron D. Benson
■

■ *Norvana*

Kitty Hawk
Kill Devil Hill

Nags Head
Manteo

■ *U-85*

Oregon Inlet
■ *Zane Grey*
■ *Dionysus*

Rodanthe

■ *Marore*

cN

Avon

Buarque

THE *Buarque* was the only passenger ship torpedoed off the coast of North Carolina during WWII that sank in a divable depth of water. Built in 1919 by the American International Shipbuilding Corporation at Hog Island, Pennsylvania and originally named *Scaupenn* and then *Bird City*, the vessel was 5,152 tons (3,155 net tons) and 390 feet long. It was later sold to Brazilian interests and renamed *Buarque*. On February 15, 1942, bound from Rio de Janeiro to New York, the *Buarque* was about 40 miles southeast of Cape Henry, Virginia, and 35 miles due east of Currituck Beach, sailing with all lights on and her Brazilian flags spotlighted. She was not zigzagging and was cruising at 15 knots on calm seas with good visibility when, shortly after midnight, a torpedo struck her starboard bow near the #1 hatch. The *Buarque* stopped and began listing heavily to starboard, starting down by the bow. Passengers, asleep in their cabins at the time of the attack, were abruptly awakened by the explosion. After the torpedo struck, an SOS was sent by radio, and that was the first time during the entire voyage that the radio had been used for transmission since leaving Rio. The crew had used the radio only for listening. The captain gave the order to abandon ship shortly after the SOS was transmitted, and he, the crew, and the passengers (including two Americans) left the stricken vessel within 20 minutes of the initial attack. Ten minutes later a second torpedo struck the engine room causing the boilers to explode and sinking the *Buarque* within 30 seconds. The captain, passengers, and crew were rescued after daylight and returned safely to shore.

Sitting upright on the bottom, the *Buarque* lies in 140 feet of water 37 miles northeast of Oregon Inlet, on a heading of 47 degrees, and approximately 35 miles due east of Currituck Beach. The uppermost deck of the vessel is located at 100 fsw. Divers seldom visit the wreck, but the U.S. Coast Guard conducts training dives on the wreck once a year. The *Sea Fox*, operated by the Nags Head Pro Dive Shop, will carry divers to the *Buarque* via Oregon Inlet and makes the trip in a fast two hours. The water temperature is cold even in the summer when bottom temperatures of 60–65 degrees will be encountered even though surface temperatures may be in the mid-70s. A full wet suit with hood and gloves is advisable. The visibility is usually 40–50 feet although occasionally visibility extends to the 80-foot range. The wreck is relatively intact with many artifacts to be found, and a good dive light is recommended for investigating murky portions of the wreck. The bow and midship portions of the wreck are the least intact and are areas where a dive light is useful for illuminating in and around the exterior debris. Because of its depth, the long boat ride to it, and the cold water, this wreck is recommended for divers with wreck-diving experience.

1.1　*Buarque*. U.S. Coast Guard.　　Courtesy of The Mariners' Museum, Newport News, Virginia.

Byron D. Benson

THE *Byron D. Benson*, a tanker of 7,953 tons (4,932 net tons) and 465 feet long, was built in Tampa, Florida, in 1921 by the Oscar Daniels Company for the Tide Water Associated Oil Company of New York, New York. The vessel was powered by a triple expansion engine built by Vulcan Iron Works of Jersey City, New Jersey, having four cylinders of 24, 35, 51, and 75 inches in diameter with a 41-inch piston stroke. Although her home port was Wilmington, Delaware, the *Benson* spent most of her time transporting petroleum products between Texas and New Jersey and other ports on the East Coast. In early April 1942, the ship left Port Arthur, Texas, loaded with 100,000 barrels of crude oil bound for the refineries at Bayonne, New Jersey. As Captain John McMillian and the 37 crewmen on board passed less than 10 miles off Currituck Beach and about 10 miles northeast of Oregon Inlet in the company of two Navy escorts and another tanker, the *Gulf of Mexico*, the commander of the German submarine *U-552* lined up the starboard side of the *Benson* in his periscope sight. Korvettenkapitän Erich Topp then ordered his submarine's torpedoes to be fired and several minutes later torpedoes from the *U-552* struck the *Benson* amidships, igniting the whole starboard side. Locked in a starboard turn by the blast, the ship could not be stopped and continued to circle spreading flaming fuel over the sea. Lifeboats #1 and #3 had been destroyed in the blast, and all that remained available for Captain McMillian and his crew were the #2 and #4 lifeboats and a raft. Two men in life-jackets jumped overboard and were later rescued by the USCG cutter *Dionne* and a British armed tanker, HMS *Norwich City*. Twenty-five crewmen abandoned ship aboard the #4 lifeboat and were rescued by the USS *Hamilton*. Captain McMillian, the radio operator, and eight other crew members abandoned ship in the #2 lifeboat but for some unexplained reason began drifting into the burning fuel and were never seen again.   [From Arthur R. Moore, 1983]

The *Benson* drifted for three days before sinking on April 7, 1942, off Kill Devil Hills, 28 miles northeast of Oregon Inlet on a heading of 44 degrees. She lies in 110 feet of water 25 miles from the Sea Buoy off Oregon Inlet. Brian Pledger (*Sea Fox*), of the Nags Head Pro Dive Center runs dive charters to the *Benson*. The ship lies in the cold waters north of Cape Hatteras and consequently there is not much in the way of tropical marine life on the wreck. There are a few coral heads here and there, but by and large the most prevalent creatures on the wreck are snails, starfish, and tautogs. The wreck is relatively intact and sitting upright. There are

1.2   *Byron D. Benson*. U.S. Coast Guard.   Courtesy of The Mariners'
Museum, Newport News, Virginia.

1.3   *Byron D. Benson* in flames.   Courtesy of The Mariners' Museum,
Newport News, Virginia.

1.4   *Byron D. Benson.* Valve wheel.

holds and cabin areas that may be penetrated, and the deck is covered
with fuel transport pipes. The water temperature during the summer is
55−60 degrees on the bottom and about 75−80 degrees on the surface.
Wear a full wet suit with hood and gloves because it gets chilly. Carry a
dive light to explore the holds and cabin areas. Occasionally, current will
be running on the wreck but usually it is not a problem. Average visibility
is around 10−15 feet although on occasion it will be 70−80 feet. Many
artifacts have already been taken off the wreck, but brass valves, valve
handles, pulleys, and other artifacts may still be found throughout the
wreck. The wreck site is quite large, probably 500 feet by 100 feet or so.
Various portions of this wreck have 20 feet or more of relief. The *Byron
D. Benson* is one of the more interesting wrecks off the North Carolina
coast and certainly the largest in the Nags Head area.

Norvana

THE *Norvana* was a rather small freighter of 2,677 gross tons built in the genre of many Great Lakes freighters. Launched in 1920 at Saginaw, Michigan, the 253-foot vessel was originally named *Lake Gatun*; then later her name was changed to *York* and finally to *Norvana* when the Merchants and Miners Transportation Company of Baltimore, Maryland, purchased her. Captain Ernest J. Thompson and his crew of 29 arrived in Cuba in January 1942 to take on a load of sugar which was bound for Philadelphia, Pennsylvania. Late in January, with the cargo aboard, the *Norvana* departed Nuevitas, Cuba, and headed for the East Coast of the United States. However, she failed to arrive at Philadelphia. Though an extensive search was undertaken, nothing was ever again heard from anyone aboard the *Norvana*. It was only after WWII and German submarine records were obtained that a very limited account of the demise of the jaunty little freighter came to light. Late in the evening of January 22, 1942, the German *U-66*, with Frigattenkapitän Richard Zapp in command, found the *Norvana* about 25 miles northeast of Cape Hatteras and torpedoed her. There were no survivors of the attack. The *Norvana* was one of nine vessels sunk by the *U-66* before the U-boat itself was sunk by Allied forces off the Cape Verde Islands on May 6, 1944. [From Arthur R. Moore, 1983]

The *Norvana* went down in 100 feet of water, approximately six miles northeast of the wreck of the *U-85*, five miles south of the wreck of the *Byron D. Benson*, and 12 miles northeast of the Sea Buoy off Oregon

1.5   *Norvana*. U.S. Coast Guard.   Courtesy of The Mariners' Museum,
Newport News, Virginia.

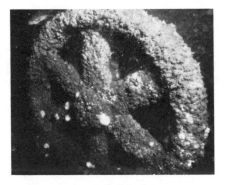

1.6   *Norvana*. Windlass.

Inlet. From Oregon Inlet, the wreck is 22 miles out to sea on a heading of 52 degrees. Though similar to the *Caribsea* wreck, the *Norvana* has much more relief. The most prominent features are two large boilers and a propane tank-like structure. Several large beams protrude above the wreck, and there is a small room that divers can penetrate. In addition, there are several large walls standing and several portholes visible on bulkheads. In spite of the fact that the *Norvana* lies in relatively cold water, sponges and corals are growing on all parts of the wreckage, and many curious tautogs (grouper-like fish) can be found in crevices and caverns throughout the wreck site. Artifacts other than portholes can also be found throughout the wreck, including large gears, valves, and valve handles. The water temperature in summer is a cold 55–60 degrees on the bottom with surface temperatures of 75–80 degrees. The visibility is usually about 10–20 feet, but it may be considerably more or less depending on weather and sea conditions. I have seen it very clear (90–100 feet) to a depth of about 60 feet and then found the visibility drop to 25 feet on the bottom. Wear a full wet suit and hood and bring a bright dive light for investigating numerous nooks and crannies. The wreck is spread out over an area about 300 feet by 75–100 feet. Currents may be a problem on occasion but usually if there is any current, it is less than a quarter knot.

Brian Pledger runs the *Sea Fox* out of Nags Head through Oregon Inlet for a two-and-a-half hour ride to the wreck. Captain Pledger runs the *Sea Fox* for the Nags Head Pro Dive Shop, which sends along a competent divemaster to assist on each dive trip.

Locally, the wreck is known by its previous name, *York*, because a diver once recovered a brass plate with the name "York" embossed upon it, a remnant of pre-*Norvana* days.

U-85

THE *U-85* was a 220-foot-long, 500-ton type VIIb U-boat built in Lübeck, Germany, early in 1941. Kapitänleutnant Eberhard Greger commanded the *U-85* on its first tour of duty off Norway to prey on British convoys plying off the coast. On September 10, Greger and the *U-85* encountered their first British convoy. Not a timid man, Greger, in spite of air cover, attacked the convoy, but his first five torpedoes went wide of the target. Greger was forced to follow the convoy through very heavy seas while American destroyers tried repeatedly to drive the submarine off with gunfire and depth charges. With each attack, the *U-85* was forced to submerge and hide from the pursuers on the surface. Finally she was able to evade the attackers and moved on, gradually drawing ahead of the convoy to position herself for a new attack. By the afternoon of September 11, Greger's perseverance paid off as he maneuvered the *U-85* into position. The first torpedoes made a direct hit on a 6,000-ton steamer. Within a half-hour the *U-85* had attacked two more merchant ships in the convoy, but by then the destroyer escorts gave chase and launched a depth-

1.7   U-85   Courtesy of William H. Hughes.

charge attack, severely damaging the submarine. Surviving this close brush with death, the *U-85* limped home for repairs.

After the damaged submarine was repaired, she left for another war mission to Newfoundland. This was probably her next-to-the-most disappointing tour and did not result in any ship sinkings. Her third tour was to the heart of Allied shipping lanes, the western Atlantic approaches to New York. She chased many convoys, always to no avail. Returning to Germany in February 1942, for a month's leave while their ship was being refitted, Commander Greger and his crew looked forward to their return to the war even though they had rough times surviving two airplane and four destroyer attacks during their previous tours. On March 21, 1942, with a brass band playing, the *U-85* set out once more for America, her fourth trip out to battle. By early April, the *U-85* was on station running up and down the East Coast of the U.S. On April 10, the *U-85* sank a large steamer with two torpedoes, but otherwise there were few targets to attack. Greger decided to head south towards easy pickings off Cape Hatteras. As they made their way southward the crew of the *U-85* were buoyed by their second Allied ship sinking and feeling somewhat confident after having survived several attacks during their last three tours of duty. Indeed, Greger and his crew should have felt confident. The German U-boats were exerting a strangle hold on Allied shipping in the Atlantic.

During 1941 and 1942, the undersea battle against Atlantic shipping by the U-boats was taking a tremendous toll on Allied ships. Operation Paukenschlag (Drumroll) against the U.S. began in January 1942 in response to what Admiral Karl Doenitz, commander of the U-boat fleet, perceived to be better hunting grounds for his submarines. However, the German submarine fleet was spread so thinly that by 1942 he could only send five out of 91 submarines which were operational at that time to the East Coast of the U.S. The East Coast was a virtual shooting gallery for the U-boats primarily because the U.S. was unprepared for these submersible warships. Lacking new destroyers, the U.S. Navy was forced to use WWI four-stack destroyers taken out of mothballs to fight the U-boat menace. The defenses of the East Coast in the spring of 1942 consisted of 10 WWI wooden sub-chasers, three converted yachts, four blimps, and six Army bombers. When the U-boats reached America, they struck on the surface at night, not even bothering to submerge. Eight submarines were on station off the East Coast during the early months of 1942 and ship after ship was sunk off Morehead City, Wilmington, Hatteras, and Virginia Beach. Coastal cities were favorite target areas for the submarines since at this stage of the war U-boats had no radar and could use the glow of these towns to silhouette targets. It took many months for Americans ashore to realize they were unwittingly aiding the enemy by

1.8   U.S.S. *Roper*. U.S. Navy.   Courtesy of the U.S. Naval Institute
Photo Library.

not blacking out coastal cities at night. By March of 1942, three ships
were being sunk every day along the East Coast. With the sinkings were
lost many lives as well as ammunition, tanks, guns, gasoline, diesel fuel,
iron ore, and other freight. Coastal shipping would have to halt if the
U-boat menace could not be stopped.

One of the means of stopping the submarines was the USS *Roper*, a
1,200-ton, four-stacked destroyer, an old ship in 1942 and not much
larger than the *U-85*. Built in 1918 to combat the first U-boat invasion,
the *Roper* was not completed until WWI was over. After a tour in waters
off Turkey in 1918 and then some Pacific duty, she was laid up in San
Diego in 1922. She was recommissioned in 1930 and transferred to the
Atlantic Fleet for patrol duty. Early in WWII, the *Roper* did convoy patrol
duty in the North Atlantic but never saw the enemy. By March of 1942
the convoy patrol duties of the *Roper* were decreased to the point that she
was reassigned to East Coast patrol duty.

By early April, both the *U-85* and the USS *Roper* were patrolling the
same waters off North Carolina. On the night of April 13 the *U-85* moved
south and close enough to shore such that beacons and searchlights were
easily visible to her crew. At midnight on the 13th the *Roper* was headed
south off Bodie Island. The night was clear, stars were bright, and the

Bodie Island light was visible to starboard. Shortly after midnight the *Roper*'s radar detected a small blip about a mile and a half dead ahead. The officer of the deck thought it was another small boat, probably a Coast Guard boat on patrol, one of the many they had detected that night. He also knew that Naval Intelligence reports acknowledged that German sympathizers on shore were rendezvousing with U-boats and re-supplying them offshore from small boats. He ordered a slight change in course to present as small a target as possible, just in case. Lieutenant Commander Hamilton Howe, captain of the *Roper*, was summoned to the bridge. Howe ordered an increase in speed and by now the crew on the *Roper* could see the wake of whatever was ahead. It still could be a Coast Guard patrol boat. General quarters alarm was sounded and gun and depth-charge batteries were manned while the *Roper* closed on the mysterious ship. Now only a few hundred yards astern, the captain and officers strained to see what was ahead in the darkness. Was it a submarine? No one aboard had seen a German sub before. It looked too small.

Still, knowing the U-boats carried stern torpedo tubes, Howe kept the *Roper* to the side of the wake. Howe realized that both ships were slowly turning and that if the other ship was a submarine, its stern tubes would soon be pointing directly at the *Roper*. He immediately ordered the searchlights turned on. Out of the darkness the searchlight beam caught the conning tower of the *U-85* with five men running along her half-submerged deck towards her gun. The *Roper*'s 50-caliber machine guns were brought to bear on the Germans and they were cut down instantly. At the same time, crewmen on the *Roper* shouted at a sparkling trail in the water. Howe was to recall later that he first thought it was a porpoise but then immediately realized it had to be a torpedo passing only a few yards from the ship. By this time, the *U-85* began to submerge to escape and Howe ordered the *Roper*'s three-inch guns to open fire. One of the three-inchers misfired, but was quickly reloaded and fired at the fleeing submarine. Their target was at point-blank range now and it seemed to be getting smaller and smaller. It was getting away and soon it would be completely submerged. Just as the last shots were fired the *Roper*'s crew saw a direct hit at the base of the conning tower where it joined the pressure hull.

The *U-85* was finished. Water poured into the submarine and her crew bailed out, many without life-jackets. Screaming and shouting, they plunged into the water to await rescue and capture. Greger ordered the submarine scuttled and she sank slowly and finally went down stern first. Forty men from the *U-85* were swimming in the water when the sub sank beneath the waves. The men on the bridge of the *Roper* saw the Germans

1.9   Digging graves for dead U-*85* crewmen at the National Cemetery, Hampton, Virginia.   Courtesy of the National Archives.

1.10   Burial of the dead U-*85* crew at the National Cemetery, Hampton, Virginia.   Courtesy of the National Archives.

in the water; but, fearing that another U-boat was in the same spot as the survivors, Howe ordered depth charges to be fired. A barrage of 11 depth charges was fired in the midst of the Germans and seconds later 3,300 pounds of TNT exploded, killing all 40 men in the water. The *Roper* took no prisoners, and at daylight all that remained was an oil slick and 29 dead bodies in life-jackets. Empty life-jackets bore mute testimony to the death of other crewmen from the *U-85*. The 29 dead Germans were hauled aboard the *Roper*. Two of the dead were officers, but the body of the skipper, Eberhard Greger, was never found.

Thus the first U-boat kill of WWII was recorded by the U.S., and the killing of the Germans in the water reflected the tremendous frustration the Navy felt about the casualties the U-boats had inflicted upon the U.S. However, no prisoners meant no information about these mysterious U-boats, and it was clear from then on that capturing downed submariners was preferable to killing them. The *U-85* was one of 781 submarines the Germans lost during WWII, and four out of every five German submariners lost their lives. For this price, the U-boats accounted for the sinking of over 3,000 ships during the war.

The bodies of the 29 crewmen of the *U-85* were buried in numbered plots in the Hampton National Cemetery. No official attempt to notify the families of the identified deceased German crewmen has ever been made.

The *U-85* now lies in 100 feet of water approximately 14 miles northeast of Oregon Inlet on a heading of 75 degrees. The site is regularly visited during the summer by dive charter boats from Wanchese and Nags

1.11   *U-85*. Conning tower.

Head. One of the most popular wrecks off this area of the coast, the submarine has been virtually stripped clean of artifacts by visiting divers. Her deck gun points upward at about 60 degrees and one of her propellors is still intact on the vessel, which lists about 45 degrees to starboard. All of her five hatches are open and the hatch covers have been removed. Her conning tower looms high above the hull and reaches nearly 80 fsw. Water temperature on the wreck is cold most of the time: usually 65 degrees in the summer when the surface temperature is 80 degrees. A full wet suit with hood is recommended for this dive. Visibility is usually 10–30 feet, although visibility in the range of 70 feet may be encountered. Currents are frequently found on the wreck, and when currents are running visibility drops to less than 10–15 feet. The wreck attracts a lot of bottom-dwelling fish and is covered with coral and sponge growth. However, much of the marine life has been removed from the *U-85* by the scores of divers who visit her each summer. Although the depth is moderate, this dive is for wreck-divers with previous offshore diving experience.

Zane Grey

THE *Zane Grey* was a Liberty ship of 7,176 tons (4,380 net tons) and 441 feet long which was built in January 1943 by the California Ship-building Corporation at Terminal Island, Los Angeles, California. The ship's engine was built by Joshua Henry Ironworks of Sunnyvale, Califor-nia, and powered a large four-blade propellor (18 feet 6 inches in diame-ter) which pushed her through the water at 11 knots. The *Zane Grey* served as a supply ship ferrying equipment and cargo across the Atlantic during WWII. After the war, the Liberty ship was consigned to the Mer-chant Marine Reserve Fleet Site 2 on the James River near Newport News, Virginia. Purchased in late 1974 by the State of North Carolina for use as an artificial reef, the *Zane Grey*'s superstructure was cut down to deck level, giving it a 40-foot-high profile, and towed out to its site off Oregon Inlet where it was sunk on December 12, 1974.

The ship is resting upright five miles southwest of Oregon Inlet in 80 feet of water with its deck at 40 feet. Several open holds allow sunlight and divers to penetrate below decks where one can find an abundance of pipes, the engine, machinery, valves, ladders, catwalks, and other compo-nents of large ocean-going vessels. Because of its close proximity to shore the visibility is usually less than 10 feet but occasionally may reach 40–50 feet. Currents and surge are often present and under these condi-tions the visibility becomes quite poor. Care must be taken while below deck in the presence of surge to avoid being pushed and pulled into the numerous sharp objects present. The water temperature is cold even in the summer and a full wet suit with hood is recommended. A bright dive

1.12 *Zane Grey.* Courtesy of The Mariners' Museum, Newport News, Virginia.

light is also useful for illuminating nooks and crannies below decks. There is some marine life growing on the deck, which resembles a large, flat field, and the vessel provides a good habitat for bottom-dwelling fish and attracts ocean-ranging fish as well. Because of the relatively shallow depth and short boat ride to the site, the *Zane Grey* is sometimes used by scuba classes for checkout dives. The Liberty ship is a good dive for those who have little or no experience with wreck diving and can often be dived when weather prevents diving on wrecks located further offshore. Dive charter boats from Wanchese and Nags Head frequently carry divers to the *Zane Grey*.

Dionysus

THE Liberty ship *Dionysus* was the second such vessel to be sunk off Oregon Inlet by the State of North Carolina as an artificial reef. Like her three counterparts also sunk off the coast, the vessel was 7,176 tons (4,380 net tons) and 441 feet long. Before she was sunk, her superstructure was cut down to the second deck level, giving her a 30-foot-high profile. Sunk November 30, 1978, five miles southeast of Oregon Inlet and 300 yards from the *Zane Grey*, the *Dionysus* sits upright in 80 feet of water with her deck at 45 fsw. She is very similar to the *Zane Grey*, and diving conditions on this wreck are identical to those found on her nearby counterpart. A full wet suit is advised because of summer water temperatures in the mid-60s. A bright dive light is recommended as well. Though the visibility is usually 5–10 feet, it occasionally reaches 20 feet or more. There are holds in the deck that allow penetration below and, as on the *Zane Grey*, there is much machinery and equipment to be seen. This wreck is a good dive for inexperienced wreck divers and is often used by scuba classes for checkout dives. Dive charter boats from Wanchese and Nags Head take divers to the *Dionysus* frequently during the summer.

Marore

THE *Marore* was the longest ship to be sunk off the North Carolina coast during WWII. The 550-foot-long bulk carrier was 27 feet longer than the *John D. Gill*, which—in terms of tonnage—was the largest ship to be sunk off North Carolina during the war. The *Marore* was only 8,215 tons (4,172 net tons), about three-quarters the tonnage of the *Gill*. The *Marore* was built in 1922 by the Bethlehem Shipbuilding Corporation of Sparrows Point, Maryland, for the Ore Steamship Company of New York. The twin-screw vessel was commanded by Captain Charles E. Nash and carried a crew of 39 men. At the end of February 1942, the *Marore* departed Cruz Grande, Chile, loaded with iron ore bound for Baltimore, Maryland. On February 26, passing northeast of Hatteras, 30 miles offshore of Wimble Shoals, the *Marore* was struck amidships by a torpedo fired from the German submarine *U-432*, which was under the command of Kapitänleutnant Heinz-Otto Schultze. Captain Nash immediately ordered his crew to abandon ship, whereupon three lifeboats were lowered. Safely launched, the captain and his crew began the long row to shore. By three o'clock that afternoon, Coast Guard cutter #3843 picked up Captain Nash and 13 crewmen from the #1 lifeboat and took them to just offshore the Kinnakeet Lifeboat Station. The cutter then stood by while a boat was sent from shore through the surf to carry the survivors, seven at a time, back to shore. The remaining 25 crewmen in the other two lifeboats were rescued by the tanker

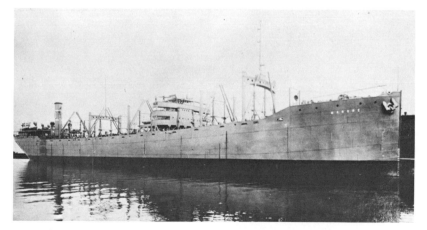

1.13   *Marore.*   Courtesy of the Peabody Museum of Salem, Salem, Massachusetts.

John D. Gill. Ironically, the *Gill* was on her way to Texas to pick up a load of crude oil to carry back up the East Coast to Philadelphia, Pennsylvania, on what would be her second and final trip in service. Two weeks after rescuing crewmen of the *Marore*, the *John D. Gill* was sunk 200 miles southwest of the *Marore*, off Cape Fear.

Captain Nash and his crew survived a close brush with death with the sinking of the *Marore*, but this wasn't to be the end of torpedo troubles for Captain Nash. Five months after the *Marore* sinking, Captain Nash was in command of a brand-new Liberty ship, the *Christopher Newport*, which was headed through the Barents Sea when a torpedo struck amidships and destroyed the vessel's engine room. This time, however, the attack did not come from a U-boat but rather a German Heinkel Torpedo Bomber. Once again, Captain Nash was forced to abandon ship and was rescued.   [From Arthur R. Moore, 1983]

The *Marore* sank only 12 miles offshore of Wimble Shoals in 125 feet of water. The wreck site is 30 miles northeast of Hatteras and 10 miles south of Oregon Inlet on a heading of approximately 159 degrees. Relatively intact, the wreck has around 25 – 30 feet of relief in many areas of the site, and the deck is at 90 feet. Because of the *Marore*'s close proximity to shore, visibility is in the range of around 25 – 30 feet, but it may sometimes reach 70 feet or more. Water temperatures are somewhat cooler than further south but not as cold as offshore of Oregon Inlet. Summer temperatures at depth are in the 70s. Current and disorientation caused by low visibility are the biggest problems for divers at this site. Captain Mike McKay (*Saltshaker*) will take divers out to the *Marore* via Hatteras Inlet.

2. Ocracoke-Hatteras

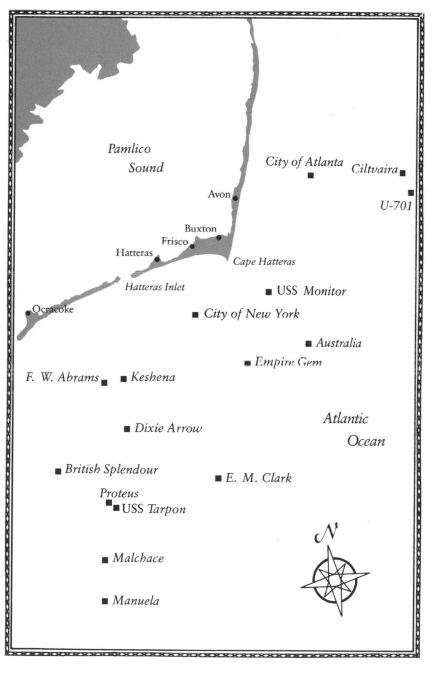

Pamlico
Sound

City of Atlanta   Ciltvaira ■

Avon ● ■ U-701

Buxton
Frisco ●
Hatteras ●

Cape Hatteras

Hatteras Inlet

Ocracoke ●

■ USS Monitor

■ City of New York

■ Australia

■ Empire Gem

F. W. Abrams ■   ■ Keshena

Atlantic
Ocean

■ Dixie Arrow

■ British Splendour   ■ E. M. Clark

Proteus
■ ■ USS Tarpon

■ Malchace

■ Manuela

Ciltvaira

THE FREIGHTER *Ciltvaira*, 3,779 tons (2,372 net tons) and 347 feet long, was built in 1905 by J. L. Thompson Sunderland for the Latvian Shipping Company and was originally named the *Twyford.* (During her career on the seas, the freighter bore several other names, including *Vironia, President Bunge,* and *Endsleigh.*) On January 19, 1942, under conditions of no wind and calm seas, the unarmed *Ciltvaira* was proceeding south along the North Carolina coast running at six knots under full lights and running lights. The vessel was about 30 miles north and east of Avon at 5:00 A.M. when an explosion tore a gaping hole in the port side amidships. The ship's radio operator was awakened by the explosion but was cut off from the radio room and did not attempt to try to go to it. The captain and first mate tried to determine their position on the charts but were unable to do so. The order to abandon ship was given and an SOS was sent out from an emergency set in the lifeboats. The ship continued to float for several hours and finally sank 10 miles north and east of Avon. There was no loss of life. In an interview afterwards the chief engineer said that, in his opinion, the vessel had been struck by a torpedo that hit the port side amidships. However, no one saw a submarine and the ship was not shelled after the explosion, which led investigators to conclude that probably the *Ciltvaira* had struck a magnetic mine. After the war it was determined that the *U-123*, commanded by Kapitänleutnant Reinhard Hardegan, had torpedoed the vessel the day after the *U-123* had torpedoed and sunk the *City of Atlanta.*

The ship lies 10 miles offshore near Avon in 120 feet of water with her uppermost deck at 75 feet. From Oregon Inlet, the wreck site is 31 miles out to sea on a heading of 150 degrees. Although it lies north of Cape Hatteras and Diamond Shoals, this is a "tropical" wreck on which corals, sponges, and other tropical marine life may be seen. There are numerous brass artifacts at the site. The *Ciltvaira*'s engine and boilers are prominent and the bow is more or less intact, but the wreck is very broken up from forward of amidships to the stern. For some mysterious reason, the bell on the bow section still remains. The wreck is less intact than the *Benson* but more intact than the *Norvana.*

Divers don't often visit the *Ciltvaira,* but the *Sea Fox* runs to it out of Nags Head and Art Kirchner's boat, the *Margie II,* runs to it out of Hatteras. This wreck will be the warmest dive undertaken out of the Nags Head—Wanchese area and is a good wreck for photography, artifact collecting, and spearfishing. Because of the *Ciltvaira*'s close proximity to shore the visibility is usually in the range of 40–50 feet; however, 70–100 feet of visibility may be had occasionally. Sometimes the visibility is such that the wreck may be seen from the surface. This wreck is one of the best dives in the area between Diamond Shoals and Nags Head.

U-701

THE *U-701* was a 220-foot-long type VII-C U-boat built in 1941 by
Strucken Sohn Shipyard at Hamburg, Germany. Launched in April of
1941, the *unterseeboot* was armed with a 88mm deck gun, a 20mm anti-
aircraft gun, and sixteen torpedoes. In July, command of the submarine
and its forty-three member crew was assigned to Kapitänleutnant Horst
Degen. Earlier in his career, Degen had honed his submarine command
skills while serving briefly on a war cruise under the tutelage of ace
U-552 commander, Kapitänleutnant Erich Topp. Ironically, it would be
one of the lessons learned from Topp during this time that would lead to
the later demise of Degen's submarine. Topp taught Degen that the disadvantages of running the U-boat on the surface, even during the day when
there was a chance of being spotted by patrol aircraft, was far out-
weighed by the several knot speed advantage surface running offered over
that while submerged. Greater distances could be traveled on the surface
and hence, increased possibility of encountering enemy shipping. This
was, after all, why U-boats were sent out to sea, to sink enemy ships. As
for running on the surface during daylight, Topp utilized sharp-eyed
lookouts to warn of approaching patrol craft. This tactic worked well
for Topp, for by the end of the war he and his crew had sunk 34 enemy vessels, third among all U-boat commanders during World War II.
Degen was very impressed by the boldness and attention to detail of Kapitänleutnant Topp.

One of Degen's first concerns about the newly constructed U-boat
was how well it was built. Because this was the first such vessel constructed by the shipyard, Degen rigorously scrutinized its performance
during sea trials at Kiel shortly after taking command. Attention to the
smallest detail meant the difference between success and failure. He and
his men would spend months aboard the boat in hostile waters and everyone wanted to feel confident that the craft would perform properly.
Degen had already heard many stories from other submariners about
production problems discovered aboard their boats at the most inoppor-
tune time. Degen was determined not to have that happen to the *U-701*.

The sea trials revealed a large number of construction defects that had
to be repaired before the vessel could enter the war. So many problems
had to be corrected that six weeks in Hamburg were required to bring the
U-boat up to standards. After the repairs were made, the submarine returned to Kiel for more trials and tests of her deck and anti-aircraft guns.
This time all of her systems checked out properly. The only thing that

2.1   *U-701*.   Courtesy of WZ-Bilddienst,
Wilhelmshaven, West Germany.

remained to be completed before the submarine and crew could be certified fit for duty was torpedo practice.

The *U-701* departed Kiel for Warnemunde in mid-September for torpedo firing exercises. While stationed there for two weeks, the town of
Warnemunde adopted the U-boat and crew as one of their own. So be-
loved became the *U-701* that the town emblazoned the submarine's conning tower with a red sea robin, the emblem on the pennant of the town's
successful rowing club. If success could be transferred by such means, the
imprimatuer of the rowing club and its supporters would surely carry the
U-701 all the way up the Thames to Whitehall. Those were heady days of
the war when U-boat commanders were filled with dreams of glory. During this time German submarines were exacting a tremendous toll from
British shipping. Merchant ships were unprotected and became easy pickings for the prowling submarines. A U-boat commander's career could be
made in a single war cruise.

At this time there were also persistent rumors that the United States
would soon enter the war against the Germans. U-boats would become
even more vital as instruments of the Reich's war strategy. Most certainly
they would be dispatched to the western Atlantic to cut off the flow of

supplies to the Allies in Europe at the source. Submarines were destined to become the vanguard of German forces to the west. They would bring the war in Europe directly to the shores of America. Degen thought about all of this as his submarine completed training exercises in November and prepared for their first war cruise.

On December 12, Degen and the *U-701* were in Kiel loading fuel, torpedoes, and other supplies when the United States declared war on Germany. Submarine commanders were anxious to get out to sea. They could not help the war effort moored at dockside. Thus, it was with great anticipation that Degen and the other U-boat commanders awaited their orders. When the *U-701*'s orders finally arrived, it wasn't duty off the American shores that called but rather more arduous North Sea duty. Degen was ordered to proceed to Newfoundland to guard the northwest approaches to England. Two days after Christmas, the U-boat left Kiel via the Kiel Canal and proceeded to the mouth of the Elbe and out into the North Sea to begin its first war patrol. Although the route to Newfoundland took the U-boat past northern England and Scotland and possible targets for action, the gale force weather encountered along the way prevented the submarine from doing much more than holding its course through the North Atlantic. Tragedy struck as the submarine rounded the tip of Scotland. In the midst of a blinding snowstorm at night, the first watch officer was swept off the deck after he left the conning tower to secure gear below. A search of the area was unsuccessful as snow and darkness severely hampered visibility and communication. The loss of their fellow crewman did little to relieve the crew's apprehension about events to come as their untested craft was buffeted by the freezing gale force winds.

On January 6, 1942, the *U-701* had made it halfway across the Atlantic when Degen spotted an unescorted freighter. Ordering his crew to battle stations, the submarine fired two torpedoes in its first attack of the war. As he watched through the periscope, the crew waited intensely to find out if their training had paid off. Up to now, the loss of the watch officer and the rough crossing had created a funereal atmosphere on board. Degen knew that this attack, if successful, would do much to improve the morale of his dispirited crew. As he watched through the periscope, both torpedoes slammed into the freighter and exploded. A cheer went up from his men as he announced the sinking. As the crewmen on board the freighter abandoned ship into lifeboats, the U-boat approached the survivors and asked the name of the ship. They received no answer, only hostile glares. Degen ordered the submarine away from the area and reported that the 3,391-ton British freighter *Baron Haig* was the victim. Only hours after the attack, gale force winds blew twenty-foot high seas through the area. Degen knew that none of the lifeboats could have survived the storm. Later it was determined that the vessel was actually the 3,657-ton British freighter *Baron Erskine* and that all of the crew were lost without a trace.

By mid-January, the U-boat reached its station off Newfoundland. There it remained until early February without engaging any enemy shipping. Returning in mid-February to the U-boat repair facilities at Saint-Nazaire, France, located at the mouth of the Loire River, the *U-701* remained here for three weeks while its storm damage and minor construction defects were repaired.

By this time, Admiral Karl Doenitz, commander of the U-boat fleet, had commenced Operation *Paukenschlag*, whereby German submarines were dispatched to the western Atlantic, all the way to the shores of America to destroy shipping bound for Europe. U-boat commanders had been reporting that it was a virtual shooting gallery along America's East Coast. There was no blackout of coastal cities, ships traveled alone and unprotected and ship's running lights burned brightly at night. It is no wonder that every U-boat commander's dream was to be assigned to American waters. Degen's dream was no different. Again he awaited his new orders. In late February, he received orders for his U-boat's second war cruise. If he was disappointed, he did not let it be known. This time he was being sent to the east coast of Iceland. More North Sea duty.

Leaving Saint-Nazaire in early March, the submarine skirted the south coast of England and the west coast of Ireland on its way to Iceland. En route on March 6, the submarine encountered the 272-ton Danish trawler *Nyggjaberg* and torpedoed it. The next day, a small steamer was fired upon south of Iceland but the torpedo missed and the vessel escaped unharmed. On March 8, the *U-701* came upon the 541-ton British armed trawler, *Notts Country* and quickly dispatched it with a single torpedo. Never had hunting been so good for Degen and his crew. These targets may not have been the large ships other U-boat commanders were sinking, nevertheless they provided suitable targets until larger prey became available. The area was quiet for the next couple of days and no enemy ships were seen. Then, on March 11, Degen spotted another British armed trawler, the 440-ton *Stella Capella*. As he lined up his target, Degen reflected that even though the target was small, it was another anti-submarine vessel and every one of those removed from the battlefield, the better off would be the U-boat fleet. He fired a single torpedo that dispatched another enemy vessel to the bottom of the ocean. Over the next few days, the weather off Iceland took a turn for the worse. There were plenty of enemy ships to be seen but sea conditions made it impossible to get into position to torpedo them. Gale force winds and heavy seas forced Degen to abort attack after attack. Running out of patience and fuel, Degen ordered his boat back to France early in April. He had already received word that Saint-Nazaire had been heavily damaged by a British attack in late March, so he set a course for Brest, France, near the entrance to the English Channel. Arriving there in mid-April, Degen and his crew looked forward to the time ashore away from the battlefront and the icy North Sea. Surely, the next cruise would be to a more temperate climate. The *U-701* remained in France until mid-May when, finally, Degen was ordered to America. However, what would begin as a dream war cruise for Degen and the *U-701*, would end up being their worst nightmare realized. The cruise to America was the beginning of the end for the *U-701*.

Degen's orders for the third war cruise were to mine the harbor at Norfolk, Virginia. A major U.S. Navy base was located there that also served as a large supply depot for materiel bound for Europe. In addition to military ships, there was a substantial amount of commercial shipping in and out of the harbor. The *U-701* was in Lorient, France, taking on fuel in preparation for the long journey when the mines were loaded on board. Although the submarine was carrying torpedoes, each of its torpedo tubes were loaded with three magnetic mines instead of the usual deadly metal fish. Mining the harbor was the main mission of the cruise but if any large ships were encountered along the way that could be sunk without jeopardizing the mission or if any ships were encountered after the mines were deployed, then torpedoes could certainly be fired at the ships. On May 20, with preparations completed and amid a flurry of goodbyes to loved ones, the U-boat cast off for its long trip across the Atlantic.

The crossing to America was rough at times and Degen ran at slow speed to conserve fuel. He encountered two large ships during the trip but did not attack either one because conditions were not favorable. The trip was taking long enough as it was and Degen did not wish to delay it any longer than necessary. When sea conditions permitted, Degen would have his crew practice crash diving until the shortest times to submerge were consistently achieved. The training alleviated boredom on the long trip and maintained Degen's philosophy of attention to detail. Reaching the American coast on June 12, Degen had hoped to keep his arrival a secret for as long as possible. But, the U-boat was spotted on the surface immediately by a patrol plane. Lookouts on the conning tower saw the plane and sounded the alarm. Crash diving practice was all that saved the submarine from disaster, as moments after reaching a depth of forty feet, depth charges exploded alongside the hull. Continuing the crash dive in darkness as the lighting system on board was knocked out of commission by the first series of explosions, the boat began to leave the detonations farther behind. Although the initial attack had punished the submarine severely, the actual damage inflicted was minor and would not interfere with the mission. Degen and his crew were exhilarated to have survived the attack and were thankful to be alive. The successes of the first two war cruises and their survival this day imparted a feeling of invulnerability among some of the crew. But the wiser men on board knew that luck would carry them only so far. Eternal vigilance and attention to detail were the ultimate keys to success. Nonetheless, no one had been hurt, the submarine was still intact, and their target was less than a day's run away. Degen turned his boat toward the Virginia coast.

Degen had studied maps of the Norfolk area and knew that the city was located just inside the mouth of Chesapeake Bay. Ships leaving the Norfolk area had to pass out the mouth of the bay to reach the open ocean. Two bright lighthouses at Cape Charles and Cape Henry conveniently marked, respectively, the northern and southern ends of the mouth of the Chesapeake. Since there was no blackout along the East Coast, Degen used the lighthouses to aid him in planting the fifteen mines at the entrance to the bay. The Americans are their own worst enemy, he thought, as the final mine left his U-boat. Mission accomplished, the *U-701* turned south and headed for the ship-rich area of the North Carolina coast. He ordered all torpedo tubes loaded in anticipation of enemy shipping. Once well clear of the Virginia Capes, Degen surfaced and radioed his U-boat command that the mission was a success. Degen would not know for several days how successful the mission really was. Over the next four days the mines would sink or damage four ships including sinking the British armed trawler, *Kingston Ceylonite* and the freighter, *Santora*. More importantly, the attack caused disruption and panic that resulted in closing the entrance to the Chesapeake for a couple of days. It tied up men and ships for several days while they searched for more mines. Shipping was brought to a virtual standstill while the navy and Coast Guard determined if U-boats were still in the area. Admiral Dönitz was very pleased with Degen and the *U-701*.

Well south of the Chesapeake, Degen cautiously guided the submarine toward North Carolina waters. He knew that only weeks before, the *U-352* had been sunk by the U.S. Coast Guard off Morehead City, North Carolina, and that a month before that, the *U-85* was sunk by the U.S. Navy off Nags Head, North Carolina. Thus far, the waters off the Carolina coast had claimed two of the U-boat fleet. He did not want to be the third. He wondered whether there was something about the Carolina coast that did not bode well for U-boats. He had orders to stay submerged during the day and to run on the surface during the night.

U-boats operating in American waters were being stretched thin with the loss of the two boats in Carolina waters.

Reaching Cape Hatteras on June 17, Degen surfaced at night only to be spotted by a Coast Guard cutter. Submerging immediately, the *U-701* escaped unharmed but Degen wondered again if there was something about the North Carolina coast that was the undoing of U-boats. For the next two nights the *U-701* was dogged by this cutter. It survived a depth charge attack and managed to escape unharmed. Finally, its luck turned for the better. The night of June 19 was foggy when the submarine surfaced. There, just inside the range of visibility, loomed a large hull. Degen silently slipped up to within 100 feet of what he could now see was his nemesis of the past few days, the Coast Guard cutter. Too small to sink with a torpedo, Degen chose to use the submarine's guns on the unsuspecting cutter. Opening fire with his deck gun and machine guns, the *U-701* quickly sank the *YP-389*.

For the next week, the submarine harassed shipping along the Carolina coast damaging the British tanker *Freedom* and sinking the 14,000-ton tanker *William Rockefeller*. It became impossible to sit on the bottom all day as the ventilation system was rendered inoperable during one of the depth charge attacks. So it became necessary to surface regularly to ventilate the submarine. Several times lookouts would spot patrol aircraft and the submarine would have to cut short its visit to the surface and crash dive. By this time, the routine was becoming boring. No shipping had been seen in over a week and constantly breathing the impure air was taking its toll on the men. Resting in the hypooxygenated atmosphere did not revive the crew from their weary labors. They became even more tired. Reflexes were slower and exhaustion was telling on the faces of his men. When they were on the surface, lookouts had to strain to maintain alertness. Degen and his executive officer often relieved the regular lookouts.

By July 7, the situation was critical. His executive officer that morning had failed to see a patrol plane until the last minute but the U-boat still managed to escape. Degen reprimanded the officer but knew his men were too tired to be effective. One man could cost him his submarine. Degen knew that it was time to return to France for rest and repairs. They sat on the bottom until the afternoon. After the near fatal encounter with the plane that morning Degen had decided to surface and radio his plans for the return trip to Doenitz. The errant lookout begged to be allowed to return to the conning tower. He would stay alert and be vigilant. Degen relented because he was his executive officer. He must set an example for the rest of the crew. It was Degen's choice. The U-boat surfaced and the lookouts raced to their positions. There was low cloud cover which made the lookouts especially nervous.

Unknown to the *U-701*, only a few hours before the submarine surfaced, Lt. Harry Kane and his crew, aboard a Lockheed-Hudson bomber, had taken off on a routine ocean patrol from the Marine Corps Air Station at Cherry Point, North Carolina. Kane did not know that July 7 would be a day he would remember for the rest of his life.

Rather than fly beneath the cloud cover during their mission, the bomber flew in or above the clouds out of sight of anything below. At various intervals, Kane would drop his plane out of the clouds to see what they could surprise. Thus, it was on one of these surprise maneuvers that the army bomber dropped down out of the clouds onto the unsuspecting *U-701*. Coming in toward the submarine's stern, the bomber was on top of them before the executive officer could shout the alarm. The airplane had come out of the sector for which he was responsible. Twice in a single day the executive officer had allowed an enemy plane to sneak up on the U-boat. He had seen the plane too late. This time his failure would probably kill them, Degen reflected as they raced into the submarine and began to dive. The submarine had barely submerged when three depth charges exploded around the hull. Two of the bombs tore open the hull and the dying U-boat filled with water. Within minutes the submarine had settled to the bottom. Degen and sixteen men were trapped in the control room with no knowledge of the fate of the other men on board. Certainly those in the stern were dead, but what of the others. There was no time to think about anything except survival as the control room had flooded nearly to the ceiling by the onrushing water. They grimly noted that the depth of the water was nearly 200 hundred feet according to instruments in the control room. Degen ordered the conning tower hatch opened and he and his men exited the drowned submarine propelling themselves to the surface. They had undergone emergency exit procedures at submarine school in Germany but nothing had prepared them for this. Everyone surfaced and those with life jackets supported those without. All were thankful to be alive. Lt. Kane and his bomber continued circling the area because they knew they had hit the U-boat. When Degen and his men surfaced, Kane ordered the bomber's life preservers and life raft thrown to the foundering submariners. The effort was futile, however, as only one life preserver reached the survivors. The raft and the rest of the preservers drifted off with the Gulf Stream. Kane noted his position and radioed for help from rescue vessels. Meanwhile, another group of eighteen men who were in the forward torpedo room managed to escape through the forward torpedo loading hatch. They surfaced some distance away from the first group and began to drift farther away from them. Because Kane had not given the position of the sinking accurately, rescue craft did not find any wreckage nor submariners at the spot where Kane said they should be.

Degen and his group of seventeen drifted away from the site. Almost immediately, four of the men, injured or non-swimmers, gave up the struggle to survive and drowned. Shortly afterward, the executive officer and another crewman decided to swim to shore and were never seen again. The survivors drifted for two days losing one of their numbers every few hours as each gave up hope. The warmth of the Gulf Stream sustained them but it also carried them farther away from rescue. Degen lost consciousness several times during this period. It took all of the effort of three of his crewman to keep his head out of the water to prevent him from drowning. Late in the afternoon of July 9, fifty hours after they had been sunk, the survivors, now only four in number, were sighted by a Navy K-8 blimp. They were picked up shortly thereafter by a seaplane and were surprised to see three others on board who had escaped from the forward torpedo room. These men had been picked up earlier in the day. Thus, of the forty-three crew on board only seven had survived the sinking. The seven were returned to Norfolk and hospitalized. Badly sunburned and dehydrated, the prisoners gave little information about their activities. They said nothing about the mining of the mouth of the Chesapeake Bay. Shortly afterward, Lt. Kane was brought to meet Degen while he was hospitalized. The two met briefly as Degen gave his congratulations to Kane for a "good attack." Kane received the Distinguished Flying Cross for the sinking. Degen and the six other survivors spent the remainder of the war in POW camps in Florida and Arizona. Their capture and internment was ultimately responsible for their survival during World War II. Of the 39,000 men in U-boat crews, 28,000 lost their lives and 5,000 were captured. Seven out of ten U-boats were sunk by the Allies. Had the *U-701* escaped the attack to return to the fray, likely as not they would not have survived the war. In a bizarre twist of irony, it could be argued that the errant executive officer, who missed seeing an attacking plane twice in the same day and whose oversight caused the deaths of thirty-six of his fellow crewmen, was responsible for assuring the lives of seven other crewmen for the rest of the war.

In 1982, Harry Kane traveled to Germany to meet Horst Degen for the first time in forty years. Kane had located Degen in 1979 and began corresponding with him. They had survived a period of history when the world was torn by a cataclysmic war the likes of which had never been experienced before or since. These two men, both survivors, once adversaries, had now become good friends.

As for the *U-701*, it still rests undisturbed on the bottom of the Atlantic off the coast of North Carolina. Over the years many groups have tried to find its location without success. It is believed to be in divable depths that can be reached with scuba equipment. The most frequently given location is in an area about twenty miles due east of Avon, North Carolina. Recently, in the fall of 1989, rumors were heard that the submarine had been found in shallow water by a diver who stumbled upon it by accident. He had been given loran numbers for a good fishing hole. When he visited the site in his own small boat, he became curious about what was on the bottom attracting so many fish. He put on his diving gear and dived down to find the *U-701*. To date no one can verify the story. The location of the *U-701* still remains a mystery.

City of Atlanta

THE FREIGHTER *City of Atlanta*, 5,433 tons (4,111 net tons) and 378 feet long, was built in 1904 at Chester, Pennsylvania, for Ocean Steamship Company of Savannah, Georgia. Captain Leman Chapman Urquhart and 45 crewmen were aboard the vessel as she steamed unarmed offshore of Wimble Shoals, northeast of Cape Hatteras, early in the morning of January 19, 1942, unknowingly under the watchful eyes of Kapitänleutnant Reinhard Hardegen of the German submarine *U-123*. Shortly after 2:00 A.M., Hardegan fired two torpedoes into the port side of the freighter which struck forward of the #3 hold causing the ship to instantly roll severely over to port before Captain Urquhart could order the ship slowed to decrease her headway. Urquhart ordered an immediate SOS sent out and gave the order to abandon ship. Lifeboat #1 on the starboard side was rendered useless as it was swung inboard, and although 18 men managed to get into the #2 lifeboat on the port side, the severity of the ship's list caused the small craft to capsize, throwing all of them into the sea. Fifteen of the 18 crewmen were lost and the remaining 28 men on board including Captain Urquhart went down with the ship. The three survivors in the water managed to remain afloat until they were picked up by the SS *Seatrain Texas* after daylight. [From Arthur R. Moore, 1983]

The *City of Atlanta* lies in 100 feet of water east of Avon on a heading of 82 degrees, 14 miles northeast of Cape Hatteras on a heading of 53 degrees, and 27 miles southeast of the Sea Buoy off Oregon Inlet on a heading of 170 degrees. The wreck is in two sections. The stern section lies about one mile east of the bow section. The name "City of Atlanta" may be seen on the stern. The letters are screwed-on and are located underneath the stern area. The stern is tilted up at an angle which makes seeing the letters difficult unless you are beneath the stern and looking up. The wreck site is visited very infrequently by dive charter boats; the *Saltshaker,* skippered by Mike McKay, will take divers to the wreck, heading out via Hatteras Inlet. The wreck is partially intact with the highest point on the wreck reaching 85 fsw. Listing to port, the remains of her masts are still visible, but much of the superstructure has been destroyed by wire-dragging and depth-charging to remove a hazard to navigation. Much of what does remain consists of broken bulkheads, twisted beams, steel plates, pipes, machinery, and other structures destroyed during clearing operations. There are many brass artifacts to be recovered from

64

2.2   *City of Atlanta.*   Steamship Historical Society Collection, University of Baltimore Library.

the site including portholes, gauges, valves, and fittings, and the wreck is covered with marine life including corals, sponges, tautogs, and other bait and game fishes. The water temperature is usually in the low to mid-70s, and the visibility is generally around 30 to 40 feet or so, although visibility exceeding 70 feet may be encountered occasionally. A full wet suit with hood is recommended, and a bright dive light will help illuminate the dark recesses created by the hodge-podge of twisted and broken structures. A compass and cross-wreck line are recommended for navigation on the site. Strong currents are sometimes encountered on the wreck. Because of those currents and the long boat ride to the site, diving on the *City of Atlanta* is recommended for the experienced wreck diver and other divers if accompanied by an experienced guide.

Australia

THE *Australia* was the second largest vessel sunk off the coast of North Carolina during WWII. The tanker, 510 feet long and 11,628 tons, was built in 1928 at Chester, Pennsylvania, by the Sun Shipbuilding and Dry Dock Company and originally named *Mary Ellen O'Neill*. Sold to Texaco, the *Australia* made the trip between Texas and New York carrying fuel oil. In March 1942, Captain M. Ader and his 40 crewmen watched over the loading of a full cargo of fuel oil at Port Arthur, Texas, and made ready for a trip to New Haven, Connecticut. After an uneventful trip across the Gulf of Mexico and up the East Coast, the *Australia* was 25 miles east of Cape Hatteras on the afternoon of March 16 when a torpedo fired by the German submarine *U-332*, commanded by Kapitän-leutnant Johannes Liebe, struck the starboard side amidships in the engine room. Four crewmen on watch in the engine room were killed, and one of the starboard lifeboats was destroyed, but the remaining 36 crewmen and Captain Ader were able to escape in the three remaining lifeboats. Luckily, no cargo tanks ruptured in the attack, and the last time the captain and crew saw their ship she was sinking, with her stern on the bottom but her bow still afloat. All of the survivors were rescued about an hour and a half after abandoning ship by the SS *William J. Salman* and taken to Southport, North Carolina, by the USS *Ruby*.   [From Arthur R. Moore, 1983]

Sometime later the *Australia* completely sank in 80 feet of water 19 miles southeast of Hatteras Inlet on a heading of 110 degrees and 11.5 miles southeast of Cape Hatteras on a heading of 143 degrees off the tip of Diamond Shoals. The wreck of the large twin-screw vessel lies on the tip of Diamond Shoals and is mostly broken up because it was wire-dragged and depth-charged by the Navy as a hazard to navigation. Some sections of the wreck have 15–20 feet of relief, and wreckage is scattered over a large area of sea bottom. The *Australia*'s large boilers provide the greatest relief on the site, and twisted beams, steel plates, bulkheads, machinery, and pipes are strewn about, much as in the case of the *Ashkhabad*. Corals, sponges, and other marine life inhabit the wreck, and flounders and large groupers may be found in abundance. A compass and a cross-wreck line are recommended for navigation, and a bright dive light facilitates exploring the many nooks and crannies of the wreckage. A full wet suit is also recommended as there are many sharp objects to scrape and cut bare skin. Water temperature on the site is generally in the

2.3   *Australia*. U.S. Coast Guard.   Courtesy of The Mariners' Museum, Newport News, Virginia.

70s during the summer. Because it lies so close to Diamond Shoals, the visibility is usually less than 15 feet and strong currents are often a problem. This dive is recommended for experienced wreck divers primarily because of the extremely poor visibility and the presence of strong currents. Mike McKay (*Saltshaker*) will take divers to visit this wreck from Hatteras or Ocracoke. It is a long boat trip and charter boats must cross or go around Diamond Shoals to reach this wreck.

USS *Monitor*

WHEN the beginning of the Civil War was signalled by the bombardment and capture of Fort Sumter, South Carolina, in April of 1861, President Lincoln ordered a U.S. naval blockade of the entire coastline of the south from Virginia to Texas. Even before the outbreak of hostilities, the largely non-industrialized South was heavily dependent upon ocean shipping to bring it the necessities of life. Lincoln reasoned that if southern ports were closed, then vital military supplies would be unavailable to the Confederacy thus severely hindering their war effort.

After the fall of Fort Sumter, the Confederates captured the Gosport Navy Yard at Norfolk, Virginia. The largest and most modern shipyard of its day, Gosport was taken after Union troops burned and abandoned the facility including the frigate USS *Merrimack*. The *Merrimack* was in drydock awaiting repair of its condemned boilers and engines. Following capture by the Confederates, the *Merrimack*'s superstructure was taken down to its main deck and the ship was converted into an ironclad. It was cheaper and less time-consuming to convert an already existing ship into an ironclad than to build one up from its keel especially since the South lacked the ironworks for the job. Once word of the *Merrimack*'s conversion became known in Washington, DC, Lincoln immediately asked for plans from designers for building a Union ironclad. Ironclads were not a new invention at the time of the Civil War. Britain and France had built a few ironclad vessels as early as 1853. In 1854, John Ericsson, a Swedish engineer and designer, had submitted plans for such a ship to Napoleon III for his battles in the Crimean War. The plan was never accepted and sat in limbo for many years until the American Civil War. After much urging, Ericsson also answered the call from Lincoln to design a Union ironclad. His design for the U.S. ironclad was quite similar to the one he did for the French. The deck was designed to be awash and there was a revolving gun turret. After much debate and with reluctance, Ericsson's design was finally accepted by the Navy and work was begun building the ship in New York. The designer called for several unique features that had never been seen before on a naval warship. These included a revolving gun turret which was twenty feet in diameter with eight-inch thick iron walls and armed with two eleven-inch Dahlgren guns, a unique anchor, underwater windlass room, protected anchor well, pressurized engine room, forced-air draft boiler, no exposed deck, and a pilot house forward with a sight-slit for viewing. The 173-foot-long, 981-ton warship was launched on

January 30, 1862. Some of those present at the launching did not believe the all-iron ship would float but when the ship slid into the water, she drew ten feet and floated within three inches of where Ericsson predicted it would. Commissioned on February 25, 1862, under the command of Lt. John Worden, the ironclad, named *Monitor* by its inventor, had been built in 147 days from contract to commissioning. But, the *Monitor* had to prove itself in battle before it could be accepted by the Navy according to the terms of the contract. With only nine days of trials between commissioning and sailing for Hampton Roads, there was little time to train her all-volunteer crew. They had many problems learning how to operate the newfangled machinery on board the strange craft. Nonetheless, the *Monitor* departed New York under tow on March 6, 1862, and headed for Hampton Roads where it would arrive on the evening of March 8 after nearly sinking twice on the harrowing sea journey south.

Meanwhile, the *Merrimack*, renamed CSS *Virginia*, was undergoing hurried completion at Norfolk. Loaded with workers until sailing time, the 310-foot-long ironclad steamed out of the shipyard to meet the blockading Union Navy at Hampton Roads at noon on March 8. Prior to departure, none of her guns had been fired and her engines had been tested hardly at all. At top speed of five knots it took thirty minutes to turn the cumbersome ship because of her length. The Federals feared that once clear of the Union Navy at Hampton Roads, the CSS *Virginia* would steam up the East Coast bombarding northern ports and then up the Potomac to Washington, DC, and bombard the nation's capitol. Caught completely unaware by the *Virginia* as she steamed out of the Elizabeth River to meet the Union blockading fleet, the Union frigates USS *Cumberland* and USS *Congress* were sunk in short order by the ironclad. By now the Union fleet was in complete disarray and the *Virginia* took full advantage of the confusion. Making for the frigate USS *Minnesota* as dusk fell the Confederate ironclad decided to withdraw to await dawn. As dusk came and the *Virginia* steamed back up the Elizabeth River, the USS *Monitor* steamed into Hampton Roads prepared to meet the Confederate threat.

Suffering its worst defeat the Union fleet at first did not recognize the *Monitor*. However, soon signals were passed throughout the fleet that the Union ironclad had arrived. The fleet waited uneasily throughout the night. More than one Union sailor wondered if this ship that looked like a water tank on a flat deck could possibly be successful in battle against the formidable *Virginia*? The following morning, its decks stripped of all gear except the gun turret and the pilot house, the *Monitor* was prepared for battle. At half-past seven in the morning of the 9th the *Virginia* got

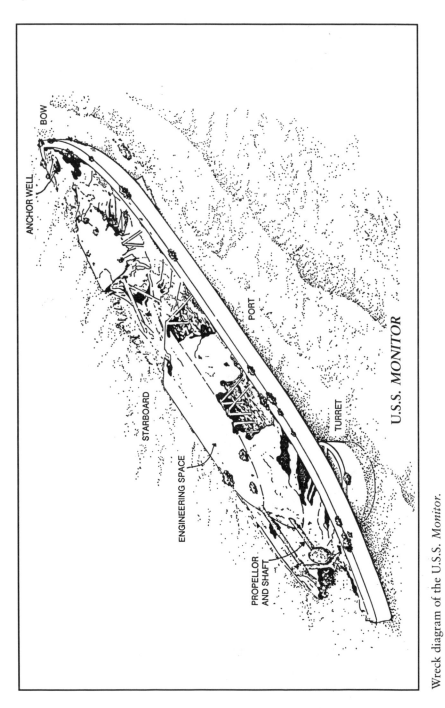

Wreck diagram of the U.S.S. *Monitor.*

underway and headed for the *Minnesota*. Positioning herself between the *Virginia* and the *Minnesota*, the *Monitor* steamed toward the Confederate ironclad. The *Virginia* started firing at the *Monitor* almost immediately but the Union gunboat held her fire until she was directly alongside the Confederate ship. For nearly five hours, the two ironclads shot at each other, often at point blank range. Although outgunned ten guns to two, the *Monitor* could easily outmaneuver the longer and more unwieldy *Virginia*. Since the *Monitor's* gun turret could revolve, the ship did not have to change course to change the aim of its two cannons. The *Virginia*, on the other hand, had to steer its 310-foot length where it wanted the ten guns on its gun deck to fire. After five hours of battle with neither side inflicting mortal wounds upon the other, a shot from the *Virginia* struck the *Monitor's* pilot house directly at the sight-slit and blinded Lt. Worden. In the twenty minutes or so it took to get Lt. Greene, the executive officer of the *Monitor* forward from the turret to the pilot house to take charge of the ship, the ironclad drifted aimlessly. The *Virginia*, leaking badly and perceiving that its adversary had withdrawn from the battle, turned and headed for the Elizabeth River and Norfolk. The *Monitor*, now under control again, fired a couple of shots at the departing *Virginia* and proceeded to come alongside the *Minnesota*. Thus ended the first naval battle between ironclads. From a tactical point of view the *Monitor* won the battle because it kept the *Virginia* from sinking the *Minnesota*. From a strategic point of view, the battle was a draw. However, the battle's influence on naval warfare and warship design was monumental. The French and British ships observing the battle were left with the knowledge that the day of wooden warships powered by sail and mast were over. The future of modern warships lay in iron armor and steam/propellor propulsion. Southern newspapers touted the battle as a victory for the South, while Northern newspapers gave the victory to the *Monitor*. Many believe that the *Monitor* singlehandedly saved the Union from defeat by preventing the *Virginia* from leaving Hampton Roads. If the *Virginia* had successfully routed Union forces on the eastern seaboard, European nations who had been holding back their support for the South because it could not win the war may have come to their aid after such significant victories.

The *Monitor* and the *Virginia* were never to meet again in battle to settle the question of who was the best. Later in 1862, the *Virginia* was burned by Confederates when Norfolk was captured by the Union. The *Monitor* returned to the Navy Yard in Washington and was repaired and refurbished for future battles. In November of 1862, the *Monitor* returned to Hampton Roads to await further orders. Other monitor-type ships were completed by the Union after the famous battle and eventually the U.S. Navy would commission thirty-three monitors of Ericsson's design.

On December 24, 1862, the *Monitor* was ordered to Beaufort, North Carolina under the tow of the USS *Rhode Island*. Departing Hampton Roads on December 29, the two ships had an uneventful trip south for the first day-and-a-half. South of Cape Henry, early on December 30, the sea condition worsened. By the afternoon they were nearing Cape Hatteras in the midst of a fierce storm. By now the storm had increased in intensity and the *Monitor* was taking on large amounts of water. Her pumps were barely able to keep up with the incoming water. Cutting her towing lines and later dropping anchor doomed the iron ship to a watery fate that the CSS *Virginia* with all of her guns had not been able to accomplish. As the water in the ship rose and reached the boilers and her pumps became ineffective it was clear the ironclad would sink. At about 9 PM, the *Monitor* signalled the USS *Rhode Island* to come to their assistance using a prearranged red signal lantern. At great risk to their own lives, crewmen in boats from the *Rhode Island* were able to save 47 of the 63 officers and men on board the ironclad. At 1:30 AM on December 31, the *Monitor* sank approximately 20 miles southeast of Cape Hatteras. The ship that singlehandedly saved the Union had perished.

For more than a century, the location of the *Monitor* would remain a mystery. In August of 1973, Duke University's research vessel, *Eastward*, sponsored by the National Geographic Society began a search for the ironclad. Using the navigational track of the *Rhode Island* as the basis for its search, the expedition discovered a wreck in 230 feet of water it believed to be that of the *Monitor*. It was to remain unclear as to whether it was really the *Monitor* until the following April of 1974. At that time another expedition funded by the National Geographic Society aboard the *Alcoa Sea Probe*, a high-tech, deep-ocean research vessel, returned to the site and positively identified the wreck as that of the *Monitor*.

In 1975, the site was nominated and placed on the National Register of Historic Places and on the 113th anniversary of the ship's launching the *Monitor* site was established as the nation's first Marine Sanctuary. The sanctuary is managed by the Department of Commerce through its National Oceanic and Atmospheric Administration (NOAA).

There have been several research expeditions to the *Monitor* site since its discovery. In 1977, the red lantern was recovered. In 1979, the Cousteaus tried to film the site but divers failed to reach the wreck because of extremely poor conditions. Later that year Harbor Branch Oceanographic Institution's R/V Johnson conducted the most extensive work by divers on the site. In 1983 its anchor was retrieved and is now on display at the Mariners Museum in Newport News, Virginia. Extensive videography and photography of the site has been done over the years but the results have been less than desirable because of the unpredictable conditions there and the inflexible schedules of the various expeditions doing work there.

In 1986, I submitted a proposal to NOAA to visit the *Monitor* site to do photography and videography of the site. The proposal was accepted but the dive plan using air for the dives ran counter to the NOAA Diving Office's regulations. These regulations do not permit diving deeper than 130 feet using air. At NOAA's suggestion, I resubmitted the dive plan using mixed gas (a mixture of helium and oxygen) for the dive, which was acceptable to NOAA.

Meanwhile, in December 1989, an Administrative Law Judge ruled that NOAA could not use its Diving Office regulations to forbid diving on the *Monitor*. This ruling opened the door to diving the *Monitor* using air. Not only are the logistics of using air simpler than mixed gas, air is much cheaper. Finally, in February 1990, I was awarded one of the first permits issued to a civilian diver to dive the *Monitor* site.

The Expedition

The Expedition received equipment support from many corporate sponsors. U.S. Divers supplied all of the diving equipment for the dives including the Monitor 2 dive computer. Other sponsors include IBM, Xerox Imaging, Hasselblad, Amphibico, Sony, Underwater Kinetics, Zodiac, Evinrude, Light and Motion, Orca Industries, Southern Nikonos, Probe Electronics, Equinox, Bio-Scan, Poseidon, and Helix.

Being the first civilian diver to dive the *Monitor* shipwreck came as a stroke of luck. It was ironic. My Expedition was scheduled by NOAA to be second to dive the wreck but in a tortoise-versus-hare chain of events we managed to be the first.

My permit ran from June 1 to August 31 and I scheduled four ten-day cruises to the *Monitor* during the period. I gave NOAA the first two days of my permit time so that they could dive the site in a four-person submarine, the *Johnson Sea-Link*. The submersible was launched from the R/V Johnson on contract from Harbor Branch Oceanographic Institution. The two days turned out to be perfect ones for their operation. The calm, clear-water dives yielded some of the best video of the wreck that NOAA had been able to achieve since they began managing the site in

1975. It was good luck for them but bad for me as I could have been diving there instead.

My first dive was scheduled for June 5 but a strong northeast wind prevented us from leaving the dock that day. On the positive side, we knew from our experience diving other deep wrecks in the area, that the day following cessation of a northeast wind is the optimal time to dive the *Monitor*. The water will be current-free and clear. Late in the evening on June 5, the winds stopped. Weather-wise, we were definitely on for the 6th. I was especially happy because the 6th was also my forty-fourth birthday.

Anticipation was at a fever pitch the next morning as we loaded the DV *Sea Fox*, a fifty-five foot vessel, moored at Teach's Lair Marina in Hatteras, North Carolina. The skipper is Captain Doogie Pledger, one of the best on the Carolina coast. John McKenney and the Jack McKenney Film Productions crew were on board to make a documentary film for television about the *Monitor* and this expedition. All of their equipment had to be loaded on board, including a large generator to power 3,000 watts of lights via 600 feet of heavy cable. Twenty-four sets of twin-80's, each equipped with a single 30 as a pony bottle, tanks containing five hundred cubic feet of oxygen for the final stage of decompression, four complete sets of decompression hoses, a large decompression platform, buoys, anchors, 600 feet of anchor line for the buoys, dive gear, ice chests, a sixteen-foot Zodiac inflatable, a twenty-five horse power Evinrude outboard motor, ten divers, six support personnel, the captain, two mates, and Lt. Ilene Byron, the NOAA observer, were placed aboard the nearly overloaded dive boat.

By 6:30 AM we were headed out from the marina for the 19-mile trip to the site. The water was flat calm with not a ripple in sight. Bright sunshine and a cloudless day. My birthday. Perfect so far. Two hours later we were three miles out from the site. The surface water temperature was 71 degrees. Within the next mile, the water temperature rose to 80 degrees and the water became azure blue. It was loaded with sargassum weed, a sure sign of clear Gulf Stream water. One mile from the site, we stopped to call the Coast Guard at Hatteras to tell them we were entering the Sanctuary and that we were about to begin diving operations. A short while later we arrived at the site. The loran numbers that NOAA provided were not correct. It took Captain Doogie about twenty minutes of searching to locate the wreck. There was absolutely no current on the site. Unbelievable! My forty-fourth birthday, the *Monitor* wreck site, flat calm seas, crystal clear and 80 degree water, and no current. We could scarcely believe our luck.

For months we had worked out the details of the first dive. A dive to the *Monitor* was complicated by the fact that NOAA did not permit a boat to anchor within 500 feet of the wreck. We devised a plan and had it approved whereby the captain of the *Sea Fox* would keep the vessel directly over the wreck while support crew lowered a single 200-pound anchor, specially built for the purpose, to within 20 feet above the wreck. Equinox provided their Dolphin underwater communication system for this phase of the operation. We had to sight-in the anchor to the bottom to make sure neither the wreck nor any artifacts were hit by the anchor. Camerman, John McKenney, soundman, Peter Manchee, and I were to descend the line to the anchor. If it was clear below, we would signal the boat, via the Equinox system, to lower the anchor to the bottom and give us slack in the line. Then, my means of a 250-pound lift bag and a tank of air provided for the purpose, we could move and place the anchor at the approved 75-foot distance from the turret on the northeast side of the wreck. The current on the *Monitor* site comes from the Gulf Stream which flows basically southwest to northeast. Positioning the anchor off the northeast end of the wreck would place it down current and out of harm's way.

Now that we were at the site under perfect conditions, we began to put our plan into effect. Before starting the anchoring operation, we had to launch the Zodiac. This done we loaded it with the Evinrude outboard motor, a large 330-cubic-foot oxygen cylinder, the generator, 600 feet of cable, the cable lights, decompression platform, decompression hoses, and a cylinder with 100 cubic feet of air which was to be hung at 60 fsw for out-of-air emergencies. Once loaded, and all of the lines, air cylinder, and decompression platform deployed into position, the Zodiac slowly motored a few feet away from the *Sea Fox* to await the lowering of the first anchor.

The anchor line was attached to the first 200-pound anchor and marked at the 210-foot length. The crew quickly lowered the anchor, a lift bag, and scuba cylinder to the appropriate depth. McKenney, Manchee, and I rapidly descended through crystal clear water on the way to the anchor. I had the Sony housing with the Hi-Band video camera, McKenney had the 16mm film camera, and Manchee had the Equinox signalling device. I was in the lead and at 180 feet I began to see the wreck. The site was undulating, dancing around. I blinked and kept descending. I knew about how I deal with narcosis. I do deep dives regularly and although narcosis is there I always function just fine. I had never seen undulating wrecks before. What was going on? As I passed the 200-foot barrier, I saw what was happening. The wreck, sitting in 75–100 feet of visibility, was completely shrouded by bait fish so thick that you had to pass through the layer of fish to see the wreck. The shimmering mass of fish took the shape of the wreck site and was definitely undulating. I was relieved and had to stifle a laugh. At 210 feet I had an unobstructed view of the wreck and of our anchor. Captain Doogie had placed the *Sea Fox* forty feet off the port side of the wreck and the anchor hung in perfect position. Nothing was below it. While waiting for McKenney and Manchee to arrive, I dropped down to the wreck and began videotaping the site. I was stunned. At a depth of 235 feet, it was beautiful; like a tropical oasis in a desert of ocean bottom. A living reef. My video light illuminated the most beautiful, colorful scene I had ever witnessed. Narcosis made it even more vivid. Yellows, reds, pinks, browns, greens, and blues of many hues colored the wreckage. McKenney had arrived by then and began filming me videotaping the wreck. With clenched fists raised over our heads, we signalled victory. The first on the site since Cousteau. I never wanted to be first. It just happened that way. It was without a doubt, the finest birthday present I had ever received in my life.

McKenney signalled me back to the anchor. After all, we made this dive to film the lowering and placement of the anchor. What seemed like the passing of hours had actually been only a matter of minutes. We looked up and there was Manchee patiently waiting for us to get back to him and signal the boat. After what seemed like an eternity, the anchor was lowered to the sand and Pete effortlessly moved it into position without the lift bag.

On the surface we knew that by now the crew had handed over the anchorline to the Zodiac where other crew made it secure to the large buoy that one of the diver, John Renfro, had built for the purpose. McKenney filmed Manchee swimming around the turret and more of the wreck. By now our time was up. We ascended to the surface and prepared for an hour or so of decompression. We were ecstatic that everything had gone as planned. Our plan had worked perfectly.

After we got back to the *Sea Fox*, the second dive team, John Renfro, Charles Capps, and Karen Rogers prepared the second 200-pound anchor and sent it down the anchorline to join the first. They went down and secured both anchors together and did a quick survey of the wreck. With the anchoring chore complete, the first day's operation was a tremendous success. By virtue of her dive to the site, Rogers became the first woman in history, to dive the *Monitor*. The entire team was very happy for her and the accomplishment. She had trained for the dive for months and had become one of our strongest divers.

Over the next few days we would make six more dives to the wreck.

Sometimes we made two dives a day to 235 feet with a three-and-a-half hour surface interval. The *Monitor* 2 dive computer, which all divers used, worked flawlessly.

Oxygen decompression at 20 fsw was essential for this kind of diving because it is safer to use than air.

For the most part, all of the dives went well. But, we did have problems. On one dive, we had a minor incident when one of the film crew, who was handling McKenney's light cable, became entangled at 200 feet and ran out of air before he could be freed. In a moment of panic, he made a rapid ascent using his buddy's air and went directly to the surface without any decompression. Luckily, his time at depth was short. He came through the episode without any problems although he clearly had a bad scare. We changed the way the film crew handled the cable underwater after that. Then there were problems with anglers stealing our buoy and having to dive for the anchorline and refit another buoy. But, we managed to overcome all of the obstacles and make the dives.

During June, I led two cruises to dive the *Monitor* and the dives went very well. All of the divers were pleased to be a part of the first two groups to dive the famous shipwreck.

The Wreck

The USS *Monitor* lies about ten miles inshore of the western edge of the Gulf Stream. By virtue of the close proximity to its tropical Caribbean waters, the wreck is a living reef that teems with marine life ordinarily associated with the Caribbean and the Florida Keys. Colorful corals and sponges grow in abundance on its collapsed structure.

When the ironclad sank, it turned upside down; the impact sheared the turret from the deck and it went sliding to the port side of the stern. Initially, the lower hull, which was elevated, probably reached fifteen feet or so above the sand after the ship went down. Immersed in corrosive salt water for over 128 years, degraded by marine organisms, battered by hurricanes and ocean storms, raked by incessant strong currents and, most likely, blown up by depth charges during World War II, the venerable ironclad has all but collapsed to the bottom in a pile of hull plates, iron ribs, machinery, and the like. The tilt to the starboard has buried the armor belt on that side but the turret still provides support for the armor belt on the port side.

From above the site, the remains possess irregular features of a ship larger than one would have imagined the ironclad to have been. At 173 feet in length, the USS *Monitor* was a large iron ship. It was no wonder that so many people of the day doubted its ability to float when the iron-clad was first launched.

The stern is mostly gone and there may still be seen the remains of the propeller shaft and the framing for the rudder. The propeller and pro-peller shaft have been displaced from their original position but are still present. The bottom of the hull is intact aft of the single amidships bulkhead that supported the turret. This part of the hull is supported by the engine, two boilers, pumps, machinery and equipment in the engine room and boiler area, the so-called engineering space. In the engineering space, the engine, boilers, pumps, and other machinery are still intact. The sides of the hull in this area have deteriorated and only hull frame members survive. Several of the hull plates along each side of the engineering space and a few on its upper surface are missing, exposing several hull ribs. The standing portion runs forward only a short distance of forty feet or less. Today, the engineering space is succumbing to the effect of years under the sea. Corrosion and the force of gravity is tilting the hull around the engineering space downhill to the starboard. Its ribs are buckling as well, indicating that the structure is settling downward. The tilt has caused a few of the hull plates on the upper surface to shear their retaining rivets and to be displaced. This process will accelerate over the next few years and soon the lower hull and ribs of the engineering space will collapse and settle around the engine and boilers. The degradation of the lower hull will be complete then. Forward of the main bulkhead, the hull has collapsed extensively into the interior of the ship. There are a number of artifacts visible near the pilot house which is thought to be equipment and fittings stored in the crew's quarters and wardroom.

The port side armor belt is intact and visible from the stern to the bow. There is significant separation between the armor belt and the hull to which it was attached. At the sand it is possible to swim all the way around the turret under what was the deck of the ship. There are what appear to be two hatches visible on the deck in this area but these may be the ventilator openings or the smokestack exhausts.

Much of the port side hull remains standing from the turret forward to the bow. The portion of the vessel which is bounded between the port and starboard sides and forward of the engineering spaces lies in rubble. In this area, hull plates, hull ribs, pipes, broken machinery and the like are piled upon each other in a helter-skelter fashion common to all broken-up iron ships.

At the bow, the anchor well is visible but has lost much of its symmetry. Rounding the bow and proceeding to the stern along the starboard side, there is seen a manifest difference in the condition of the wreck from that seen on the port side. No armor belt is visible and there is a remarkable loss of structure along this side all the way to the stern. The ribs of the lower hull containing the engineering space run into the sand on this side and several of the hull plates are missing. At the stern, sand has filled in the wreck from starboard to port.

Throughout the site, wreckage is covered with calcareous material several inches thick and with corals and sponges. Large amberjacks patrol the wreckage and curious black sea bass move in and out of nooks and crannies with ease. Butterflyfish and blue angelfish appear unexpectedly and small baitfish, mackerel scad, often obscure a view of the site.

During expedition dives, we made extensive 16mm film footage, videotape, 35mm, and Hasselblad images of the wreckage. Free swimming scuba divers are able to get to virtually every nook and cranny on the site. Divers inspected the wreck within inches. One of the divers, Ed Soellner, found a perfectly intact, coral-encrusted glass kerosene lamp chimney lying on the stern. He could not recover it under the terms of the permit. This may very well be the chimney for the lamp base on exhibit at the Cape Hatteras Lighthouse. NOAA personnel had seen the chimney during the submarine dive early in June but could not maneuver over and pick it up with the sub's robot arm. Herein lies one of the problems with NOAA's observations of the *Monitor* site. NOAA must survey the site with a small manned submarine or remote drone. The closest they can get to the wreck under these conditions is about ten feet. The submarine must stay on the north side (port, turret side) of the site as it is the down-current side, or they must stay above the site. The submarine cannot be maneuvered into the middle of the site nor can it survey the wreck's south side (starboard). The south side of the wreck is the up-current side and there is the danger of the submarine being pushed into the wreckage in a current. The advantage of free swimming scuba divers is obvious. With advances in video technology, underwater video housings, video lights, still cameras, and strobes, scuba divers can make images of the wreck that are superior to those that NOAA can accomplish with drones or submarines. If there are any lessons that NOAA will come away with after the Expedition, it is that properly equipped scuba divers, using air and state-of-the-art dive computers, cameras, and video equipment, can perform surveys of the *Monitor* site safely and for a fraction of the cost of a manned submersible operation. Divers can make high quality still, film and video images of the wreck. If artifacts are discovered, divers can make on-the-spot decisions regarding recovery and bring the artifact to the surface. NOAA should take advantage of this inexhaustible resource in this day of budgetary restraints.

The Expedition is to make recommendations to NOAA about many aspects of the *Monitor* site. We recommend that the site be better protected from unauthorized visits by divers. Such visits are now easy since the Coast Guard informed me that they do not patrol here at all. Boats regularly fish within yards of the site and there are fishing lures on the wreck.

We recommend that the site be open for visits by scuba divers for reasons other than scientific ones. Currently, there must be a scientific purpose for each visit. Permits should still be applied for and a NOAA observer should be aboard any dive boat on the site. A fee could be charged to defray the cost of the permitting process and to pay for the NOAA observer. NOAA should install an unbuoyed, permanent mooring anchor within sight of the wreck so that divers may dive down and attach an anchorline for diving.

The hull has deteriorated since its discovery in 1973 and the wreck is beyond recovery. We recommend that artifacts be collected immediately, conserved, and displayed to the American public. That the *Monitor* is one of the most historically significant shipwrecks in American waters is well recognized. It played such a crucial role in American maritime history and in the development of the world's navies that its artifacts must be saved. NOAA has collected only a few of the ship's artifacts since its discovery in 1973 and must now begin to recover what remains before the ocean makes recovery impossible or they are stolen.

And finally, if any part of the wreck is recovered, the turret remains the best possibility. It weighed 120 tons at construction and could be lifted out with a crane. Its 20 foot diameter and 9 foot high wall would make a remarkable display and monument to the ironclad. However, any large scale recovery of *Monitor* remains must be balanced against the fact that the site, besides being a shipwreck and living reef, is also a tomb for the brave, dead sailors who may have gone down with the ship. It is a war memorial like the USS *Arizona* in Pearl Harbor and others around the world. For this reason alone, we recommend that nothing of large scale be brought up from the site.

For over fifteen years, NOAA has debated about what to do with the *Monitor* site. To date, NOAA has not reached a decision and one is not expected until 1991. Recovery of the entire wreck has been ruled out but the question of significant artifact recovery has not been decided. If the debate goes on much longer, the unrelenting ocean will render any decision moot.

Though the depth to the *Monitor* is beyond recreational diving limits, any sport diver with deep diving experience and a valid reason for visiting the site, may do so by writing an acceptable proposal and submitting it to NOAA. Like other historic sites on land—Gettysburg, Jamestown, Williamsburg, Yorktown—the USS *Monitor* should be accessible to those wishing to visit the site. Nothing should ever be disturbed by visitors, but divers should be allowed to come to see and pay their respects, firsthand, to the ship and the gallant men who served her and to reflect upon the significant role they played in American history.

Empire Gem

THE TANKER *Empire Gem*, 8,139 tons and 463 feet long, was built in 1941 at Glasgow, Scotland, by Harland and Wolff, Ltd., as a British Ministry of War Transport to help Britain keep its vital supply lines open early in WWII. On January 23, 1942, at about 7:30 P.M., the tanker was headed north under clear, moderate seas and westerly winds 18 miles east of the Diamond Shoals lightship, cruising at full speed, 11.5 knots, when a single torpedo struck the after tank on the starboard side and caused a tremendous explosion. The torpedo had been fired by *U-66*, which was under the command of Frigattenkapitän Richard Zapp. At the time of the attack, the SS *Venore* was about two miles away and her side lights were visible to the captain of the *Empire Gem*. The *Venore* had been torpedoed by the *U-66* just prior to the attack on the *Empire Gem*, and the radio operator on the latter ship heard the *Venore*'s SOS when he was sending his own. (It was only the day before that the *U-66* had sunk the *Norvana* north of this area.) The SOS's from the *Empire Gem* were sent from an emergency set in the lifeboat because the regular ship's radio had been damaged by the explosion. Though the ship was able to continue at full speed for three hours after the attack, no more torpedoes were fired. The *Empire Gem* broke into two sections and the bow was anchored in position by two of the surviving crew. Both bow and stern sank in 120 feet of water about 100 yards apart 14 miles south of Cape Hatteras.

The wreck still leaks a small amount of its raw petroleum cargo into the water and, rising to the surface, the material emits a foul odor that can be easily detected near the site. Hence, the wreck site is known locally as the "smell wreck." The *Empire Gem* lies 25 miles east of Ocracoke Inlet on a course of 95 degrees and 17 miles southeast of Hatteras Inlet on a course of 125 degrees. One section settled upright at a depth of 140 fsw and the site is broken up with a jumble of machinery, pipes, valves, portholes, and other artifacts. The bottom slopes downhill in this area and the second section lies downhill of the shallower section about one-half mile away. The second section is upside down in 180 feet of water with its keel at 135 fsw. This section is much longer than the other and the wreck is oriented with its keel pointing downhill. This section is believed to contain the bow of the ship and an anchor may be seen where it was placed in 1942. The visibility is usually approximately 50 feet, but, on occasion, it may be 70 to 100 feet. During the summer, water temperatures are in the low to upper 70s. Currents will sometimes be encountered on the wreck. Because of the condition of each section, there are few areas to penetrate.

However, because the sites are not visited often by divers, there are a lot of portholes and other brass artifacts scattered about. Corals, sponges, sea urchins, sea bass, grouper, and other marine life may be seen at the site. Mike McKay (*Saltshaker*) is the only dive charter boat captain who runs to this wreck. He carries divers out from Hatteras or Ocracoke.

City of New York

THE *City of New York* was a 574-ton, wooden hull passenger and freight ship built in Hoboken, New Jersey, in 1851. The small ship was 166 feet long with a beam of 27 feet and a depth-in-hold of 18 feet. It was powered by two masts and sails and a single propeller driven by a two-cylinder vertical direct-acting Hogg and Delamater engine. Mailler and Lord Shipping Company of New York ordered Capes and Allison Shipbuilders to construct the ship to carry passengers and cargo to ports along the East Coast.

After the builders turned over the ship to the owners, the *City of New York* made a single trip in February of 1851 to Chagres, Panama, and returned to New York in April. The ship sat idle for months afterward. When Cornelius Vanderbilt organized his new Independent Line steamship company in 1852, he needed new ships. He offered to purchase the freighter from Mailler and Lord and a deal was struck. In January of 1852, the freighter sailed to San Juan del Norte, Nicarauga, to Chagres, and back to New York. Later that year the Boston and Philadelphia Steamship Company was founded and Vanderbilt sold the *City of New York* to his competitors for a nice profit. For the next nine years, the *City of New York* carried passengers and freight between Boston and New York.

In 1861, shortly after the outbreak of the Civil War, the U.S. War Department chartered the ship from the steamship company for $10,000 per month. In May, the *City of New York* was loaded at Philadelphia with stores bound for the Union army at Alexandria, Virginia. Arriving at Alexandria on May 24, the supplies were quickly off-loaded and the *City of New York* returned to Philadelphia to await orders. Because the ship was not in continuous use during this time, the war department renegotiated their contract with the steamship company and paid $4,500 per job thereafter. In August, the ship was ordered south to resupply the Atlantic Blockading Squadron at Charleston, South Carolina. The transport arrived safely in mid-August. While there, the *City of New York* was ordered to transport prisoners, captured from two blockade runners caught trying to enter the harbor at Charleston, to Fort Lafayette, New York. The ship arrived in New York with a load of prisoners in early September. After that trip the freighter was inactive for nearly a month. In October, the transport was sent to Halifax, Nova Scotia, to pick up supplies bound for New York. There, the American vice consul sent an American, William Rose, to the ship for transport to New York. Rose had traveled to England as a seaman twelve years before and had, upon

1873 ENDICOTT LITHO.   CITY OF NEW YORK   F. ALEXANDRE 4 SONS

2.4 *City of New York.* Courtesy of Erik Heyl.

his arrival, been pressed into service in the British army in India. He had spent the past eleven years there before he was finally discharged and sent to Nova Scotia aboard a British ship. He wanted to return to the United States and agreed to enlist in the U.S. Army if the vice consul could arrange transportation home. Thus, Rose gratefully returned to New York aboard the *City of New York*. Upon its return to the United States, the freighter was laid up for about a month before its next contract with the Union military.

In January 1862, the large Burnside Expedition was a combined navy and army expedition organized to capture several objectives in North Carolina including Roanoke Island, New Bern, Beaufort, Fort Macon, Goldsboro, Raleigh, and Wilmington. General Ambrose E. Burnside commanded the army troops and Rear Admiral Louis M. Goldsborough was in command of the naval vessels. This was the first major amphibious force in the history of the United States. The fleet would begin the assault at Hatteras Inlet, North Carolina.

The *City of New York* was chartered as a water and food carrier for the expedition at a cost of $300 per day. Loaded with large urns filled with water and food, the transport joined the rest of the fleet assembled at Hampton Roads, Virginia. On January 11, the fleet set sail and headed south to Hatteras Inlet. Two days later the fleet was off Cape Hatteras in the midst of a violent storm that tested the seaworthiness of every ship passing through it. Making for Hatteras Inlet and the relative safety of Pamlico Sound, many of the ships were forced to anchor outside the inlet and ride out the gale force storm. Those that were anchored near the Hatteras Bar and all of the smaller ships took a severe battering. The *City of New York* was anchored near the bar and could barely hold her position under full steam power. Suddenly her engine broke down under the strain and the ill-fated ship raised the distress signal. None of the other ships could come to her aid because they were all trying to save themselves in the midst of the storm. With no engine to hold her off the bar and with her anchor inadequate for the task, the *City of New York* grounded hard on the outer bar of Hatteras Inlet. The officers and crew immediately abandoned ship while huge waves battered the unfortunate vessel to pieces. Miraculously, no one lost their life making their way to shore through the murderous surf. The *City of New York* was broken apart within thirty minutes of grounding. It was one of thirty vessels lost to the storm by the Burnside Expedition on that fateful January 13.

Known also as the "Urn Wreck", the *City of New York* is located nine miles southeast of Hatteras Inlet on a heading of 102 degrees and 20.5 miles northeast of Ocracoke Inlet on a heading of 68 degrees. The wreck lies in 70 feet of water and is often difficult to locate. Mike McKay is the only dive charter boat captain who visits this site regularly, and he makes several trips a year carrying divers to the *City of New York* via Hatteras and Ocracoke Inlets. The vessel's remains are broken up and completely covered with coral. A hold full of large, coral-encrusted ceramic urns, used originally to transport food and water, is located in the middle of the site. Several years ago, a copper lantern stamped with the date 1801 was recovered from the wreck. The visibility on the site is usually five feet or less because of the close proximity to shore but may be more than 60 feet when clear Gulf Stream water moves in close to shore. Occasionally, surge and currents are present. The water temperature at the site is usually in the upper 70s or low 80s during the summer. In spite of the warm water, a wet suit is advisable for this dive to protect against being cut or scraped by the pervasive coral, especially during surge conditions. The shallow depth and short boat ride to the site make this a good dive for inexperienced wreck divers if they are accompanied by an experienced diver who can guide them in the low visibility. A compass, cross-wreck line, and bright dive light are useful for navigating around the relatively small wreck site. This dive is usually the second dive after a deeper off-shore dive.

Malchace

ORIGINALLY NAMED THE *Chickamauga*, the freighter *Malchace* was built in 1920 by the Stevens Shipbuilding Company at Jacksonville, Florida; it was 334 feet long and 3,516 tons (2,125 net tons). Owned by the Marine Transport Lines of New York, the *Malchace* was in Baton Rouge, Louisiana, on the first of April, 1942 loading over 3,600 tons of soda ash bound for Hopewell, New Jersey. After an uneventful trip across the Gulf of Mexico and up the East Coast, the *Malchace* was about 25 miles east of Cape Lookout at around 2:00 A.M. on April 9 when torpedo from the German submarine *U-160* struck the port side just below the waterline forward of amidships. The soda ash in the hold where the torpedo struck absorbed much of the explosion and the ship was relatively undamaged. Uncertain as to the extent of the damage, Captain Henry F. Magnusdal ordered the engines stopped in preparation for lowering the lifeboats. Captain Magnusdal and the 29 crewmen aboard stood by as the *U-160*, under the command of Kapitänleutnant Georg Lassen, surfaced and fired a second torpedo into the port side at the engine room. Lifeboat #1 was demolished in the second explosion and the engine

2.5   *Malchace*. Courtesy of The Mariners' Museum, Newport News, Virginia.

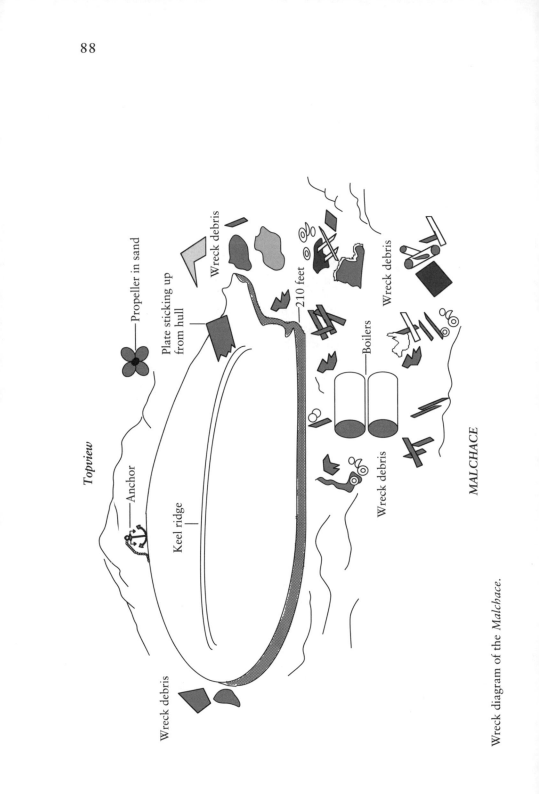

Topview

Anchor

Keel ridge

Propeller in sand

Plate sticking up
from hull

Wreck debris

210 feet

Boilers

Wreck debris

Wreck debris

Wreck debris

MALCHACE

Wreck diagram of the *Malchace.*

room was flooded. The ship was still making headway after the second torpedo struck, and Captain Magnusdal ordered the engines reversed to slow the vessel down. Immediately, he gave the order to abandon ship and the only remaining lifeboat was filled with crewmen and lowered. Others leaped into the water to await rescue, and one crewman subsequently drowned. The lifeboat picked up the rest of the crew and the captain, and the 28 survivors began rowing to safety. The *Malchace* sank around 4:00 A.M. nearly two hours after the attack, and Captain Magnusdal and the crewmen were rescued by a Mexican tanker, the *Faja de Oro*, four-and-a-half hours later.   [From Arthur R. Moore, 1983]

The Malchace sank in 210 feet of water. The wreck is located 33 miles from Hatteras Inlet on a heading of 194 degrees and 25 miles from Ocracoke Inlet on a heading of 163 degrees. The Malchace turned upside down and broke apart upon sinking. The hull is intact to aft of amidships where the boilers and engine were located. The keel of the intact portion may be reached at 180 fsw. That portion of the ship, including the engine, boiler rooms, and everything else aft of there, is extensively broken up. The remains are located in the large debris area on the starboard side of the inverted hull. Wreckage is scattered over a large area on the starboard side from about amidships to well aft of where the stern area would be located if the hull were intact. A large propeller lies in the sand off stern on the port side and is probably the spare propeller. The boilers are located in wreck debris on the starboard side of the hull. The ship must have broken up severely when it sank because many pieces of wreck are missing from the site including its engine. The wreck is a deep dive and should be attempted by only the most experienced deep wreck divers.

E. M. Clark

THE E. M. Clark was a tanker built in 1921 at Kearny, New Jersey, by the Federal Shipbuilding Company. The vessel, 516 feet long and 9,647 tons (6,020 net tons), carried a crew of 41 and was commanded by Captain Hubert L. Hassell. The ship's owner, Standard Oil of New Jersey, frequently shipped large quantities of fuel oil from the Gulf Coast to New York aboard the E. M. Clark. Early in the morning of March 18, 1942, loaded with nearly 120,000 barrels of heating oil, the E. M. Clark was travelling alone 25 miles southwest of Diamond Shoals when a torpedo struck the port side just forward of amidships below the midship house. The torpedo had been fired by the German submarine U-124, which was under the command of Korvettenkapitän Johann Mohr. The ensuing explosion killed a crewman who was near the spot where the torpedo struck, destroyed the #2 lifeboat, and severely damaged the bridge. Moments later a second torpedo struck the port side to the aft of amidships and the ship began sinking bow first with a port list. Captain Hassell gave the order to abandon ship, and he and the 40 remaining crewmen boarded and launched the #1 and #4 lifeboats. The 14 men in the #1 lifeboat were picked up several hours later by the USS Dickerson and taken to Ocracoke Lifeboat Station. The 26 survivors in lifeboat #4 were rescued and transported to Norfolk, Virginia. [From Arthur R. Moore, 1983]

The E. M. Clark sank 10 miles past the wreck of the Dixie Arrow in 230 feet of water 23.5 miles from Hatteras Inlet on a bearing of 145 degrees. The wreck is upside-down and relatively intact on the bottom, with her deck at 190 feet. This is a deep dive, and currents are often a

2.6   E. M. Clark. U.S. Coast Guard.   Courtesy of The Mariners' Museum, Newport News, Virginia.

problem. For those reasons, it is a dive for experienced divers only. The water temperature during the summer is in the 70s and the visibility is usually 50 feet or less. Marine life and artifacts abound on this wreck because it is seldom visited by divers. Mike McKay (*Saltshaker*) takes experienced divers out to this wreck.

Keshena

THE OCEAN TUG *Keshena*, 142 feet long and 427 tons, was built in 1919 at Superior, Wisconsin, for the Southern Transportation Company of Philadelphia, Pennsylvania. Chartered by the U.S. Navy, the tug was skippered by Captain Oscar Johnson and had 17 crewmen aboard. On July 19, 1942, the *Keshena* was located about 10 miles south of Ocracoke Island in a U.S. minefield where her crew was working to move the tanker *J. A. Mowinckel* out of the area. At about 5:00 P.M., the tug moved underneath the stern of the tanker to begin pushing operations when an explosion blew up the after part of her engine room, killing a member of the crew. Captain Johnson immediately ordered the ship abandoned, and the remaining crewmen leaped overboard. One of the crewmen drowned. The captain and the 15 survivors were picked up by a nearby boat and taken to the Ocracoke Coast Guard station. The *Keshena* sank stern first within ten minutes.   [From Arthur R. Moore, 1983]

The wreck now lies upright in 85 feet of water 10.5 miles southeast of Hatteras Inlet on a heading of 169 degrees and 12.5 miles from Ocracoke Inlet on a heading of 103 degrees. Mike McKay (*Saltshaker*) and George Harper (*Jaws*) run out of Ocracoke and Hatteras and visit the *Keshena* on a regular basis. The wreck lies in three sections which are located close together in a straight line. The bow portion is intact on the port and starboard sides to just slightly astern of amidships and provides 15–20 feet of relief. A diver can see where the row of portholes used to be along each side before earlier divers salvaged them. There is a large net caught on the port side forward of amidships with several floats still attached. From the boiler sternward the wreck is broken up and scattered about in the sand. The boiler and condenser lie in the sand at the end of the "structured" part of the wreck. From this point to the stern care must be taken not to get lost. If the visibility is 20 feet on this wreck, it is very good; visibility can range from nothing to about 70–80 feet. With 20 feet of visibility or less the lack of any consistent pattern of debris to the stern of the boilers makes it difficult to navigate to the actual stern. The stern is damaged extensively and is hardly intact at all. The jumbled debris of the stern area provides 10–15 feet of relief.

The *Keshena* lies within a mile or so of the much larger *F. W. Abrams*. The wreck of the *Abrams* was depth-charged extensively during WWII and is quite broken up. I believe its close proximity to the *Keshena* "protected" the *Keshena* from a similar fate. Navy crews were sent out to demolish the *Keshena* with depth charges because she was a hindrance to

2.7   *Keshena*. Charles C. Paul.   Courtesy of The Mariners' Museum, Newport News, Virginia.

navigation, and I suspect that the large size of the nearby *Abrams* masked detection of the *Keshena* and consequently the *Abrams* was repeatedly depth-charged by the Navy. The *Keshena* is too intact to have been depth-charged. Current is seldom a problem, and water temperatures are slightly cooler than 10 miles further offshore. Temperatures range in the 70s and 80s during the summer. There is plentiful marine life on the wreck. However, corals and sponges are covered with sediment, much as on the wrecks of the *Hutton* and the *Suloide*, apparently due to the wave action and surge that are common around shallow wrecks.

F. W. Abrams

THE TANKER *F. W. Abrams*, 485 feet long and 9,310 tons (6,896 net tons), was built in 1920 by the New York Ship Building Company of Camden, New Jersey, for Standard Oil of New Jersey and was originally named the *Nora*. The vessel carried a crew of 36 and was commanded by Captain Anthony J. Coumelis when, in early June of 1942, it departed Aruba bound for New York loaded with 90,000 barrels of oil. As was the custom, upon loading the fuel oil in Aruba, the captain of the *Abrams* received instructions from a British naval officer on the route the ship should take to New York. However, the U.S. Navy had failed to inform British officials in the Caribbean area about a new minefield established around Cape Hatteras. Captain Coumelis was ordered to stop at the Cape Lookout anchorage to avoid passing Cape Hatteras at night; under no circumstances, though, was he to enter the anchorage without escort. On the evening of June 10 the *Abrams* was off Cape Lookout waiting for an escort to guide her to the anchorage south of Ocracoke for the night. The Coast Guard patrol boat CG-484 arrived and escorted the vessel to her berth without incident. Early in the morning of June 11, in a driving rain, the CG-484 began guiding the *Abrams* out of anchorage. The visibility was extremely poor and within a short while the CG-484 was nowhere to be seen. The *Abrams* had lost her escort. Unaware of the minefield, Captain Coumelis continued on course, but at a slow speed due to the limited visibility. Two-and-a-half hours after the *Abrams* had left the anchorage, an explosion rocked the starboard bow of the ship causing the bow to sink about 10 feet. Captain Coumelis thought his ship had been torpedoed and attempted to drop anchor. The explosion had damaged the anchor such that it was not operable, and the ship drifted

2.8   *F. W. Abrams*. U.S. Coast Guard.   Courtesy of The Mariners' Museum, Newport News, Virginia.

2.9 *F. W. Abrams.* Ladder among debris.

for about 30 more minutes until she struck a second mine on her starboard side causing the ship to sink even further by the bow. Soon after the second explosion, Captain Coumelis ordered the ship abandoned. Its four lifeboats were then boarded and lowered, and the captain and his crew were able to land near the Ocracoke Lifeboat Station. The *Abrams* struck yet another mine on the port side forward of the bridge and slowly began to sink. By June 14, having drifted to within 10 miles of Ocracoke Inlet, the tanker could barely be seen above the water. Heavy seas battered her until she sank in 85 feet of water. [From Arthur R. Moore, 1983]

Because the large vessel was a hazard to navigation, the Navy wire-dragged and depth-charged the hulk. Consequently, most of the *Abrams* is scattered over the bottom, much like the *W. E. Hutton* and the *Suloide*, and the greatest relief on the wreck is only about 30 feet. There are, however, bulkheads and other areas to penetrate, and a large mast complete with crow's nest still attached rises 25–30 feet off the sand. Amid the wreckage, many brass artifacts can still be found. The remains of the ship are covered with beautiful corals, sponges, sea whips, fishes, and other marine life. When the visibility is very good, around 70–90 feet, the beauty of the wreck is undeniable. Sand fills in a lot of gaps between pieces of the wreck, and the reds and yellows of the corals and sponges illuminate the environment. During the summer, the water temperature is 70–75 degrees on the bottom and 80–85 degrees on the surface. Visibility can be as poor as 10–15 feet or less and as good as 70–90 feet, but on average one can expect it to be 20 feet. While current is not a big problem, I have occasionally experienced a gentle surge on the wreck. For divers wishing to see good wrecks in the Ocracoke area, this would be an excellent choice. Mike McKay (*Saltshaker*), George Purifoy (*Olympus*), Buck Wilde (*Sea Wife IV*), and Terry Leonard (*Outrageous IV*), run trips to the *F. W. Abrams*.

Dixie Arrow

THE *Dixie Arrow*, 468 feet long and 8,046 tons, was a crude oil tanker built in Camden, New Jersey, in 1921 for Socony-Vacuum Oil Company of New York. March of 1942 found the *Dixie Arrow* on a voyage from Texas City, Texas, bound for Paulsboro, New Jersey, loaded with oil. One-third of the ship's complement of 33 crewmen were not to survive the normally routine trip. Under clear skies, the *Dixie Arrow*, commanded by Anders M. Johanson, steamed well offshore of North Carolina because the men on board were aware of the shallow depths of the treacherous shoals along the coast's three capes. The waters beyond the shoals became shooting galleries for U-boats stalking Allied shipping. Knowing that ships rounding the shoals would not venture too far out to sea, the submarines would wait until an unsuspecting vessel appeared and spring an ambush.

Around 9:00 A.M. on March 26, after an uneventful trip around Cape Fear and Cape Lookout, the *Dixie Arrow* was steaming past the Diamond Shoals Light Buoy, 15 miles south of Cape Hatteras, when she was struck amidships by three torpedoes fired by Korvettenkapitän Walter Flachsenberg of the *U-71*. The first blew up the forward deck house killing all of the deck officers, including Captain Johanson, a radio operator, and several other crewmen. Seconds later the other two torpedoes exploded, setting the ship ablaze and causing it to buckle amidships. The *Dixie Arrow* was burning from amidships to her stern, and the fire had spread over the ocean surrounding the ship. The raging inferno destroyed two of the ships's four lifeboats before they could be launched. A third lifeboat swung violently on its davits, smashing up against the deck and

2.10   *Dixie Arrow*. U.S. Coast Guard.   Courtesy of The Mariners' Museum, Newport News, Virginia.

2.11   *Dixie Arrow* in flames.   Courtesy of The Mariners'
Museum, Newport News, Virginia.

crushing one crewman. The last lifeboat, however, was successfully
lowered and with eight on board made its way clear of the flames. As the
sole surviving lifeboat pulled away from the stricken vessel two men
jumped from the *Dixie Arrow*'s deck and perished in the flames below. A
floating raft became engulfed in a sea of flames as tanks aboard the vessel
ruptured, sending large quantities of burning crude over the raft and killing everyone on board.

By this time the only person left alive amidships was the helmsman,
Oscar G. Chappel. Seriously injured by the explosions and covered with
blood from severe wounds to his head and shoulders, Chappel stayed at
the helm, even though the wheelhouse was in flames. He was aware that
seven of the crew who were forward when the torpedoes struck were
trapped on the forecastle head, cut off from the lifeboats by the flaming
deck house and surrounded by the burning fuel around the bow. Seeing
the trapped men about to be engulfed by the wind-driven flames moving
toward them over the deck, Chappel threw himself against the wheel,
thereby putting the helm hard right, and held the ship into the wind. Although the flames were now directed at himself he managed to give the
trapped men time to jump overboard clear of the burning sea of oil at the
expense of his own chance to escape. With his ship still blazing and broken in two, Oscar Chappel went down with the *Dixie Arrow* within an
hour after it had been torpedoed. A half-hour before the *Dixie Arrow*
sank, the USS *Tarbell* picked up the men in the sole lifeboat as well as the

14 men who were in the water. Seven of those 14 were the men saved by
Oscar Chappel, who was posthumously awarded the Merchant Marine
Distinguished Service Medal for heroism.   [From T. R. Strobridge, 1956,
and Arthur R. Moore, 1983]

The *Dixie Arrow* lies in 90 feet of water 16 miles south of Hatteras
Inlet on a heading of 169 degrees and 15 miles southeast of Ocracoke
Inlet on a heading of 116 degrees. The site is visited by charterboats from
Nags Head, Hatteras, Ocracoke, Beaufort, and Morehead City. It is a
two-hour boat ride from Hatteras/Ocracoke and a four- to six-hour ride
from Beaufort and Morehead City. Captains from Morehead City, Beaufort, and Emerald Isle will move their boats to Ocracoke and Hatteras for
three-day to week-long trips to visit the *Dixie Arrow* and other wrecks in
the area.

Because of the close proximity to shore the visibility on the wreck is
usually 30–50 feet, but it may reach 100 feet on occasion. Current is
sometimes encountered, and under such conditions the visibility drops to
five feet or less. The wreck site is large, measuring 450 feet long and 75
feet wide. The tanker sits upright on the bottom. The bow deck is still
relatively intact and divers can view the remains of several portholes on
the port side of the bow. The anchor chain locker is located on the starboard side of the bow just after where the bow deck collapses to the sand.
A pile of anchor chain may be seen here. Aft of the bow, in the amidships
section, the decks have collapsed to the bottom leaving piles of rubble
and debris scattered amid the remains of machinery such as windlasses,
pumps, and the like. The amidships portion of the wreck is bounded by

2.12   *Dixie Arrow*. Below decks amidships.

2.13   Hull members of tanker *Dixie Arrow*.

2.14   Diver investigating remains of tanker *Dixie Arrow*.

2.15   Engine part lying in sand beside remains of the tanker
Dixie Arrow.

hull walls that vary in height above the sand from three to ten feet. The port and starboard hull walls run all the way back to the stern. There are large hull beams that stand with crossmembers still attached. Bulkhead plates still cover some of the beams giving the appearance of a bombed out building with few walls and no ceiling. There is an incredible jumble of broken machinery, pipes, windlasses, pumps, bulkheads, plates, masts, and other ship's parts piled throughout the amidships area. The height of the piles of rubble vary from sand level to eight feet above the sand. The keel is visible in some parts of this area. Several athwartships bulkheads are encountered when proceeding from bow to stern. The remains of a large net hung on the wreck several years ago may still be seen in the amidships section of the wreck.

The *Dixie Arrow's* two large boilers provide some of the largest relief on the site, reaching nearly fifteen feet above the sand. The stern section of the site is also broken up. The deck has collapsed to the bottom creating a jumble of wreckage in this area. Aft of the boilers is the large engine towering above the site. The engine shaft can be followed back to the large propeller that marks the end of the wreck site. The stern rises to about 20 feet above the sand in this area but is extensively broken up. There are large sections of the stern hull structure to investigate here. Machinery, bollards, windlasses, pipes, pumps, plates, bulkheads, and the

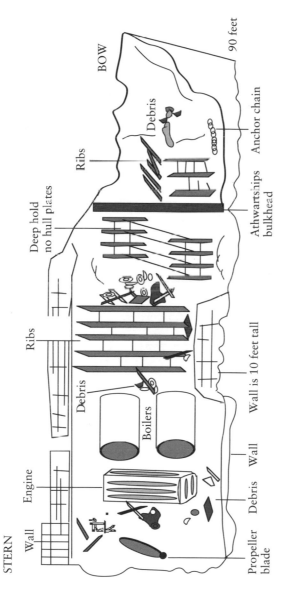

STERN

BOW

90 feet

DIXIE ARROW

Debris

Ribs

Deep hold
no hull plates

Athwartships
bulkhead

Anchor chain

Ribs

Debris

Boilers

Wall is 10 feet tall

Wall

Engine

Wall

Debris

Propeller
blade

Wreck diagram of the *Dixie Arrow*.

like are piled up and scattered about the stern. Deck plates lie at 45 degrees to the bottom creating nooks and crannies for investigation.

Marine life on the *Dixie Arrow* is one of the site's biggest attractions. In the spring, there are many Atlantic sand tiger sharks on the site. For the most part the sharks are gone by the middle of May, although the occasional straggler may be seen anytime during the summer. The *Dixie Arrow* is an excellent habitat for bottom dwelling fish because it is so broken up. Barracuda, grouper, hogfish, flounder, triggerfish, butterfly fish, amberjack, colorful corals and sponges, snapper, wrasses, filefish, damselfish, arrow crabs, and many other species ordinarily associated with the Florida Keys and the Caribbean Basin may be seen here. Over the years, divers have removed a number of brass portholes and other brass fixtures, but there are still quite a few nice brass artifacts remaining. The water temperature is in the lower 70s in May and the upper 70s and low 80s in the summer. The wreck may be dived without a wet suit in the summer, but care must be taken to avoid being cut or scratched by the coral or the sharp jagged edges of protruding metal pieces of the wreck, especially in a current. Some wreck-diving experience would be good before diving this wreck, although it is really not a particularly difficult dive. The relatively short boat ride from Hatteras and the moderate depth of the *Dixie Arrow* makes this a dive for new wreck divers with good supervision.

Proteus

IN THE FIRST DECADES of the twentieth century, travelling to the East Coast from the western United States was usually an arduous journey, but one of the most pleasant ways to travel coast-to-coast for those who could afford it was by rail to New Orleans and then by steamship from New Orleans to New York. The Southern Pacific Railroad Company offered the trip via its fine rail coach service from San Francisco and other western cities to New Orleans and from there to New York on one of five high-class ocean passenger steamers. One of those vessels was the 4,828-ton, 406-foot-long, steel-screw steamer, *Proteus*. She was named after one of the mystic society organizations that take part in Mardi Gras in New Orleans. In mythology, Proteus was the son of Neptune, one of the gods of the sea. The *Proteus* was built for the Cromwell Steamship Company by the Newport News Shipbuilding and Dry Dock Company at Newport News, Virginia, and was launched on December 16, 1899. The Cromwell Steamship Company was purchased by the Southern Pacific Railroad in July 1902 because the railroad sought to offer first-class sea service for West Coast travellers. Her identical sister ship, the *Comus*, had been launched a month before the *Proteus* and was another Southern Pacific passenger steamer that made the trip between New York and New Orleans. In their day, the *Proteus* and the *Comus* were the largest coastal passenger vessels, and newspapers reported them to be "models of design and build for ocean steamers . . . without peer in comfort and elegance."

These vessels were considered to be the safest of their time for modern travelers, and reviews and advertisements of the day proclaimed the *Proteus* and her sister ship to be virtually unsinkable and endowed with all

2.16   *Proteus.*   Courtesy of The Mariners' Museum, Newport News, Virginia.

the comforts of a private yacht. The charge for these accommodations was slightly higher than that for a first-class hotel on land: $35 one way, $60 round trip, first-class; $27.50 either way, second-class; and $20, steerage. In the American Bureau of Shipping's "Record of American and Foreign Shipping," the ships were rated "A1 for twenty years." That was the top rating and was commanded only by those vessels which met the rigorous requirements of the ABS. Because of their great comfort, spacious accommodations, large size, strength, and seaworthiness, the *Proteus* and the *Comus* were considered the finest coastal passenger ships sailing from New York and on many points were considered better than even the latest of the transatlantic liners.

The *Proteus* had 46 staterooms, accommodating 78 first-class passengers, 30 staterooms for 50 second-class passengers, and 108 berths in steerage. The dining saloons were large, elegant "apartments," equipped with electric fans, electric lights, comfortable chairs, and lounges with enough seating for the full company of passengers at one sitting. The main dining room accommodated 56 passengers with great comfort. The cabins, staterooms, and saloons were fitted with round or square air ports—the round portholes being around two feet in diameter and the rectangular ones much larger and all containing heavy glass plate lights. The rectangular ports had small stained-glass panels over them and were said to give staterooms and saloons a regal effect. Her deck space was large (12.5 laps of the deck equal one mile), and there were many promenades for first- and second-class passengers.

The *Proteus* was powered by a vertical triple-expansion engine having cylinders of 32, 52, and 84 inches in diameter and a 54-inch piston stroke. Steam was supplied by three double-ended boilers, 13 feet 10 inches in diameter and 20.5 feet long, which provided power to turn her large propeller, which was 18 feet in diameter. The *Proteus* could cruise at 14–16 knots and made the 2,000-mile trip between New York and New Orleans carrying passengers and freight in five days. These trips were not always uneventful, and one particularly memorable trip occurred early in 1916. On January 27, 1916, carrying 95 passengers and crew, the *Proteus* left her pier in New Orleans at noon bound for New York under dreary skies. Within two hours the ship was enveloped in a heavy fog and the visibility was extremely poor as Captain John Nelson commanded the ship at reduced speed down the Mississippi River towards the Gulf of Mexico. As the *Proteus* made her way through the fog, Captain Nelson was unaware of another ship ahead of him, also outward bound but moving more slowly than the *Proteus*. Captain Peterson of the oil tanker *Brabant* was also unaware of the approaching *Proteus* as he ordered his ship slowed even more as the fog became thicker. Then, without warning, the *Proteus* rammed the stern of the *Brabant*, gouging

2.17 The dining salon, *Proteus.*

2.18 The grand stairway, *Proteus.*

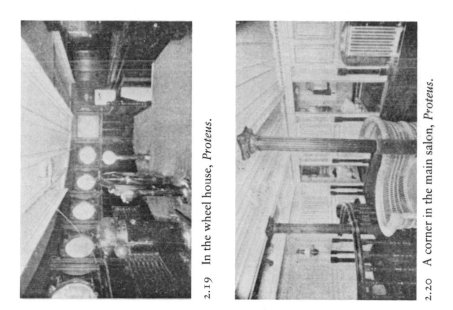

2.19 In the wheel house, *Proteus.*

2.20 A corner in the main salon, *Proteus.*

Illus. 2.17–2.20 courtesy of the Steamship Historical Society Collection, University of Baltimore Library.

a large hole above the waterline. Captain Nelson ordered the *Proteus* stopped; but finding that his ship was undamaged and the *Brabant* safely afloat, he had the *Proteus* continue out to sea and on to New York. No one was injured in the collision, and the *Brabant* was towed by tug back to New Orleans for repairs.

Nelson was soon replaced as skipper of the *Proteus* by Captain H. C. Boyd. Boyd had been in charge of the steamer *Antilles*, a Morgan Line ship, when she sailed to England at the outbreak of WWI to bring American war refugees home. On a later trip across the Atlantic, the *Antilles* was sunk in the European war zone, but Boyd and his crew were safely rescued.

On August 14, 1918, Captain Boyd directed the *Proteus*, carrying 75 passengers and crew, away from the Southern Pacific dock at the head of St. Louis Street in New Orleans, and by 4:30 P.M. was proceeding out of the mouth of the Mississppi River near Southpass, Louisiana. Turning southeast, then east, the *Proteus* headed toward Florida, where she would pass Tampa nearly 175 miles offshore about 5:00 P.M. the next day on her way to Tortugas Light, Florida. After passing Tampa, she reached the Tortugas Light about 11:00 P.M. that evening, and continuing cautiously through the Florida Keys she was within eight miles of Alligator Reef Light, Florida, by 8:00 A.M., headed for Miami, four hours away, where she would pass only 14 miles offshore. The trip close to Miami was the nearest the *Proteus* would be to shore until reaching Diamond Shoals, North Carolina. By Saturday, August 17, the ship had moved nearly 100 miles offshore passing Jacksonville, Florida, and would be over 200 miles offshore of Savannah, Georgia, by 11:00 A.M. Around three o'clock that afternoon the *Proteus* was off Charleston, South Carolina, on her way toward Diamond Shoals Lightship off Hatteras which would take her until 4:00 A.M. to reach. Fog created poor visibility on this leg of the trip, and Boyd ordered the *Proteus*'s speed cut from 15 knots to 12 as conditions became worse. Around 2:00 A.M., Sunday morning, about 34 miles southwest of Diamond Shoals Lightship, unaware that a Standard Oil tanker, the SS *Cushing*, was on a collision course with them, the crew of the *Proteus* guided their ship cautiously toward the edge of the treacherous shoals. Without warning the *Cushing* appeared out of the fog and collided with the *Proteus* amidships, creating a gaping hole beneath her waterline. A fireman, in a moment of panic, leaped overboard moments after the collision and was drowned. For the second time in as many years Captain Boyd was forced to give the order to abandon ship. An orderly evacuation of the *Proteus* was accomplished, and within an hour all were rescued by the undamaged *Cushing*. The only fatality of the collision was that of the drowned fireman. Six hours later on August 19, 1918, 25 miles

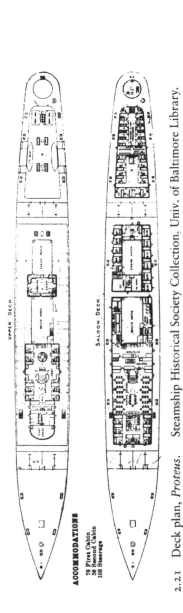

ACCOMMODATIONS

78 First Cabin
50 Second Cabin
108 Steerage

2.21   Deck plan, *Proteus*.   Steamship Historical Society Collection. Univ. of Baltimore Library.

2.23   *Proteus.* Bow anchor next to steam windlass.

2.22   *Proteus.* Stern rudder steering wheel.

south of Hatteras Inlet, the *Proteus* sank to the bottom—125 feet beneath the surface. Southern Pacific had had the *Proteus* and her cargo insured for $600,000, a figure hotly contested by the cargo owners. A lower court originally set the value of the *Proteus* at $725,000, but on appeal the Second Circuit Court of Appeals had the value raised to $1,225,000, substantially increasing the sum of money to be paid the cargo owners by Southern Pacific.

The *Proteus* lies 20 miles from Ocracoke Inlet on a heading of 147 degrees and 24.5 miles from Hatteras Inlet on a heading of 174 degrees. Several boats from the Beaufort–Morehead City–Emerald Isle area visit the wreck. Mike McKay (*Saltshaker*), Buck Wilde (*Sea Wife IV*), George Harper (*Jaws*), Terry Leonard (*Outrageous IV*), and George Purifoy (*Olympus*) make the long trip out of Beaufort Inlet. All of the boats run up to the *Proteus* in six hours except for the *Outrageous* and *Olympus,* which make the journey in four hours. McKay, Harper, and Purifoy frequently move their boats up to Ocracoke if they can get several days of charters to the *Proteus* or other nearby wrecks. Captain Art LePage of Wanchese was the first to put me on the *Proteus* and has known her location for years, but he had only taken one group of divers to visit her (in 1977) before he took me and a group out early in the summer of 1983.

The *Proteus* and its cargo now lie scattered across the bottom south of Hatteras, with the stern section of the ship towering 25 feet or so above the wreckage. A large brass wheel attached to a long shaft may be seen on the stern deck which is at 45 degrees to the bottom. The portion of the stern remaining uncollapsed is a small section, perhaps only 30 to 40 feet long, containing the round aft wheel house and including the dead-end of the stern. The brass wheel and shaft probably were part of the ship's rudder steering device which included a Williamson steering engine. Partially buried in the sand is the four-blade propeller nearly 18 feet in diameter, so large you may miss it at first, mistaking it for a large piece of bulkhead. Two of the four blades are completely buried in the sand. One can also see the remains of an automobile complete with brass radiator cap. Moving forward along the starboard side of the wreck near the stern, relief approaches 10–15 feet off the bottom and bulkheads and iron beams lie everywhere. The wreck lies 15–20 degrees on its port side and much of that side is buried in the sand.

All the large relief is along the starboard side, where, astern of amidships, it rises to 25–50 feet off the sand. The vessel's three huge boilers and its slightly smaller condensor tower above the wreckage near the keel slightly astern of amidships. The debris on the bottom between the starboard side and the keel comprises 60–70 percent of the type of wreckage

2.24 *Proteus*. Rectangular port (window).

to be seen on the site. This area is covered with large beams and twisted steel lying in a jumbled fashion amid the ship's machinery forming clusters of small "caverns." Collapsed and disintegrating after nearly 70 years under the sea, the amidships portion of wreckage contains much more of the ship's machinery, portholes (round and rectangular), and other large and small remnants spilled across the bottom. The boilers, condensor, and engine provide the greatest relief in the midsection of the wreck, and windlasses, compressors, generators, and winches may be seen throughout the wreckage. The boilers are the largest I have ever seen underwater, and swimming up to them made me feel as if I were an insignificant particle drifting in the water. Moving toward the bow portion, the amount of wreck debris gradually diminishes to the point where patches of sand may be seen between large pieces of the wreckage. Not much remains of the bow, but around the bow section may be found one of the two large three-ton anchors with one fluke pointing up and the other buried in the sand, a porthole stuck edgewise into the sand, and the large SEE freight hatches which were made in parts and were designed to fold up and lie on the deck. The cargo-hoisting engine which manipulated these freight hatches is nearby. Buried amidships beneath tons of twisted iron are the china and silverware required for over 200 passengers and many other brass artifacts. No steam engine has ever been found on or near the site. The fate of the engine remains a mystery.

Tropical marine life abounds on this wreck. Beautiful soft corals, sea whips, and sponges grow on every piece of metal, and angelfish, moray eels, sea turtles, sea cucumbers, blennies, butterflyfish, sea urchins, squir-

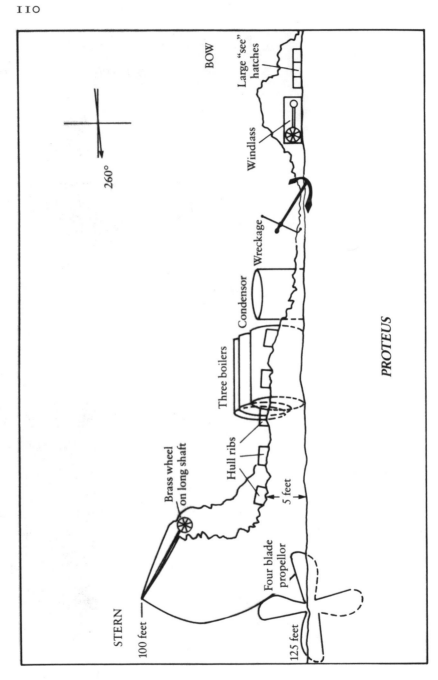

STERN

100 feet

125 feet

Four blade
propellor

Brass wheel
on long shaft

Hull ribs

5 feet

Three boilers

Condensor

Wreckage

260°

Windlass

Large "see"
hatches

BOW

PROTEUS

Wreck diagram of the *Proteus*.

2.25   Lyle gun recovered from the passenger ship, *Proteus*, by Danny Campbell.

rel fish, African pompanos, and slipper lobsters may be seen. One especially interesting group of large sea creatures seems to be attracted to this particular wreck. I don't know why, but on seven of eight dives I have made on the *Proteus* I have seen sharks. I have seen only sand tiger sharks, ranging from four to eight feet, and have seen them from May through October. Over the past few years, I have met divers who have told me this wreck or that wreck is a "shark-wreck" because they saw a shark there once or twice. The *Dixie Arrow* has that reputation. I have visited these so-called shark-wrecks more than once, including the *Dixie Arrow*, and have never seen a shark. However, I must admit that if I had to call a wreck a "shark-wreck," the *Proteus* would certainly qualify. I have never seen just one shark on this wreck per dive; there have always been two or more. On one memorable dive I watched three sharks cruising nearby along the wreckage headed toward the stern and then looked down toward the propeller and saw seven large sand tiger sharks lying on the bottom, 30 feet below me. I watched the 10 sharks for a while and then turned nervously back toward the anchor line to ascend. Other divers have reported similar sightings on the *Proteus*, but the sharks are only curious and have never caused any problems.

Many portholes, round and rectangular, have been recovered from the wreck, and the stained-glass portion of the large rectangular windows gloriously enhances an already beautiful brass artifact. Visibility, in my experience, has ranged from 40 feet to 150 feet, and the water temperature ranges from 75 to 80 degrees during the summer. Under clear tropical conditions the wreck is spectacular and rates as one of the top five wrecks for divers off the North Carolina coast.

An earlier version of this chapter was published in *Skin Diver* magazine, January 1985, 34(1): 110–116.

USS *Tarpon*

T HE *Tarpon* (SS-175) was one of two submarines built by the Electric Boat Company of Groton, Connecticut, during the 1936 U.S. shipbuilding program. The construction of the two vessels marked a major change in hull fabrication because they were the first all-welded submarines in the U.S. Navy. The *Tarpon*'s keel was laid on December 22, 1933, and she was launched on September 4, 1935. Lieutenant Leo L. Pace was at the command of the *Tarpon* when she was commissioned on March 12, 1936. The *Tarpon* was 298 feet long, approximately 25 feet wide, and displaced 1,316 tons surfaced and 1,968 tons submerged. She carried a crew of five officers and 45 men, and was designed to operate at a depth of 250 feet. Constructed with seven water-tight compartments plus the conning tower and propelled by diesel-electric engines, her maximum speed was 18 knots on the surface and eight knots submerged. The submarine had a cruising range of about 11,000 miles at 10 knots (she carried 85,000 gallons of fuel) and could run submerged for 10 hours at five knots and for 36 hours at minimum speed. The *Tarpon* was usually out on patrol for 75 days.

A Shark class submarine, the *Tarpon* carried the identification designation P4 and her hull number was 175. The outline plan for the *Tarpon* shown below incorporated many of the basic features that became standard in U.S. Navy submarines of WWII. The *Tarpon* was outfitted with one 50-caliber deck gun, and carried 18 torpedoes for her four bow tubes, two stern tubes, and two bow deck tubes.

From 1936 through October of 1939 the *Tarpon* operated out of San Diego and Pearl Harbor. From Pearl Harbor, the submarine was transferred to the Philippines in late 1939 where she joined other submarines in Manila to form a new squadron of 29 boats which composed the new Asian force replacing the old force of six S-type submarines.

On December 9, 1941, two days after the Japanese surprise attack on Pearl Harbor, the *Tarpon* and 17 other U.S. submarines left Manila for their first war patrol. Cruising an area southeast of Luzon the *Tarpon* identified several Japanese ships but could not get a shot at any of them, and when she ended her first patrol on January 11, 1942, at Darwin, Australia, she had not fired a torpedo. After two weeks in port, the *Tarpon* began her second patrol which took her to the Moluccas where, after five days at sea, she spotted a convoy of Japanese ships but did not attack because they were so well protected by escort vessels. Finally, on February 1, 1942, a freighter was apparently sunk by the *Tarpon* after she fired several torpedoes resulting in one hit. Crippled in the water, the freighter

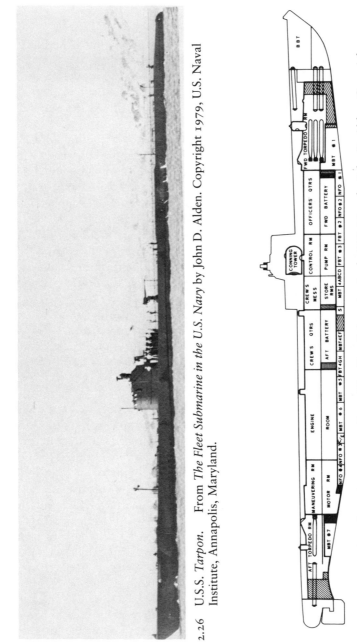

2.26   U.S.S. *Tarpon*.   From *The Fleet Submarine in the U.S. Navy* by John D. Alden. Copyright 1979, U.S. Naval Institute, Annapolis, Maryland.

2.27   Outline plan of U.S.S. *Tarpon*.   From *The Fleet Submarine in the U.S. Navy* by John D. Alden. Copyright 1979, U.S. Naval Institute, Annapolis, Maryland.

received two more hits from the *Tarpon* before the submarine left the area. After the war, however, there was no confirmation of the sinking in Japanese war records.

The evening of February 11, 1942, proved nearly fatal to the *Tarpon*. She was running on the surface, checking a radar contact, when suddenly she was illuminated by a Japanese navy ship's searchlight. The *Tarpon*, designed as a large boat for good seahandling qualities, had a slow diving time (more than 60 seconds). Although she managed to submerge, four depth charges severely damaged her bow planes, port annunciator, and rudder angle indicator. Lt. Commander Lewis Wallace, the *Tarpon's* commanding officer, ordered the boat to Fremantle. On the return trip, while west of Flores Island, near Adunara Island, in the Boling Strait, the *Tarpon* ran aground. Wallace ordered ammunition, fuel, torpedoes, and fresh water overboard to lighten the submarine, but it was not enough. She was firmly stuck. After the crew signalled a native boat from Adunara Island, an officer was taken ashore and returned with the only white man on the island, Pastor H. von Den Rulst, a Dutch missionary. The pastor told Wallace that high tide would occur between 4:00 and 6:00 P.M. that evening and that during each of the past four days Japanese planes had been over the island. At high tide, however, the submarine easily backed off the sand bar and continued her journey to Fremantle, arriving March 5 without further incident. The *Tarpon* was repaired and returned to service two weeks later, and her third and fourth patrols were routine, without any sightings of enemy shipping. She was sent to San Francisco in mid-June of 1942 for an engine overhaul and installation of new surface bow torpedo tubes. Work was completed at the end of September and she returned to Pearl Harbor.

In mid-January 1943, after an unsuccessful fifth patrol lasting nearly two months, the *Tarpon* spotted the *Fushima Maru*, an 11,000-ton passenger-cargo ship, while patrolling in Japanese home waters south of Honshu. Firing four torpedoes and following with two more, the *Tarpon* sank the Japanese vessel, which broke in half. Four days later while patrolling near Truk, the sub detected on radar a large ship. After firing a spread of four torpedoes, the *Tarpon* was forced to dive deep by Japanese escort ships, and so the crew of the submarine did not see all four of the torpedoes hit the 17,000-ton *Tatsuta Maru*, which was headed for Truk loaded with soldiers. The transport sank within minutes.

The *Tarpon* sighted no ships on her seventh patrol but did bombard a radio station at Taroa with her deck gun before she was forced to leave by shelling from shore guns. On returning to Japanese home waters for her eighth war patrol she damaged a freighter and sank a patrol boat. She then headed back to Midway in September 1943.

2.28   U.S.S. *Tarpon*.   Courtesy of the National Archives.

2.29   U.S.S. *Tarpon*, stern view.
Courtesy of the National
Archives.

2.30   U.S.S. *Tarpon*. Conning
tower.

2.31   U.S.S. *Tarpon*. Diver at entrance of forward escape hatch.

Her ninth patrol proved to be very interesting. On the night of October 16, patrolling the approaches to Yokohama, she made contact with a large unidentified ship. The *Tarpon* followed the vessel until nearly 2:00 A.M. the next morning and attacked with four torpedoes; although only one hit, it appeared to stop the vessel dead in the water. However, after a short time, the vessel turned and started toward the *Tarpon*. The submarine submerged under the ship and fired three more torpedoes, one of which struck the stern but did not sink the ship. The *Tarpon* fired again and struck the ship once more. This time the vessel blew up and disappeared. After the war, it was found that the vessel was a German raider, the *Michel*, which had been operating in both the Atlantic and the Pacific; the raider was the first such ship to be sunk by an American submarine in the Pacific. During the next couple of weeks, the *Tarpon* fired a total of nine torpedoes at enemy vessels, but did not hit anything and returned to Pearl Harbor.

The *Tarpon*'s tenth war patrol sent her on a mission to photograph atolls in the Marshall Islands and was uneventful, unlike her eleventh war patrol back to the Truk area where she nearly ended her war career. On July 14, 1944, the submarine spotted what was identified as an inter-island freighter, but was in fact a disguised anti-submarine ship. She fired three torpedoes at the vessel, missed, and was forced to dive quickly. Bombarded by depth charges the *Tarpon* managed to run deep and escape the area. Eleven days later she fired her last torpedoes at a small convoy but all missed their targets. The submarine approached closely to fire her deck gun only to have it jam. The convoy returned heavy fire and the *Tarpon* was forced to retreat. Her twelfth and final patrol in the Pacific

2.32   U.S.S. *Tarpon*. Deck aft of conning tower.

took her back to the Truk area for six weeks of uneventful duty, and she returned to Pearl Harbor in mid-October of 1944, whereupon she was ordered to sail to New London, Connecticut. The *Tarpon* left Pearl Harbor on Christmas Eve of 1944 and arrived at New London in mid-January 1945. After routine patrol duty along the East Coast, she was decommissioned on November 15, 1945, at Boston. The *Tarpon* received seven battle stars for WWII service. Her sister ship, the *Shark* (SS-174), did not survive the war, having been sunk by enemy action in 1942.

Leaving Boston under tow at the end of March 1947, the *Tarpon* was bound for New Orleans as a dockside Naval Reserve training ship where she would remain until placed out of service and struck from the Navy list on September 5, 1956. The *Tarpon* was sold for scrap to the Boston Metals Company of Baltimore, Maryland, in June 1957. In August of that year her hatches were closed up tight for the final time and she was taken under tow from New Orleans. On August 26, 1957, in a violent storm off Cape Hatteras, the *Tarpon* foundered and sank in 140 feet of water, a far more fitting final resting place for a venerable submarine than under a welder's torch. Her location remained a mystery for over twenty-five years.

In October 1983, I was fortunate to be one of the first divers to find and visit the remains of the *Tarpon*. The *Tarpon* lies in 140 feet of water 22 miles from Ocracoke Inlet on a heading of 147 degrees and 25 miles from Hatteras Inlet on a heading of 183 degrees. She is listing about 30 degrees to port, and her two propellers and deck gun barrel are missing, apparently having been removed before the vessel was sold. When I first visited the submarine all of her hatches were sealed. Since then, several hatches have been opened, and initially, small amounts of diesel fuel leaking from inside prevented penetration. Today all of the hatches have been open for

2.33   U.S.S. *Tarpon*. Stern torpedo
loading hatch.

quite some time and divers have penetrated the conning tower, crew's quarters, and control room.

The submarine's wooden decking has disappeared and much of the outer shell is missing, leaving many of the pumps, valves, pipes, and other machinery visible on the outside of the intact pressure hull. Torpedo loading hatches are clearly visible and are inclined at a 45-degree angle to the hull. The wheel that is turned to open these hatches has four spokes, whereas the *Tarpon's* other hatches, which are perpendicular to the hull, are opened with a wheel having six spokes. The deck of the *Tarpon* lies just below a depth of 130 feet. Until the winter of 1986, her conning rose to 110–115 fsw; and the top of her radar antenna on the conning tower rose to about 105 fsw. The periscope also stood nearly 20 feet above the deck. In 1986, a severe winter storm tore the conning tower from the deck and it now lies on the sand at 140 fsw on the port side and perpendicular to the hull. The periscopes are still present but the radar dish has been salvaged. The removal of the conning tower from the hull exposed the control room hatch. The hatch was opened in the summer of 1989 and divers have been entering the control room ever since. The depth to the sand varies depending on where you are with respect to the submarine. On the port side amidships, the sand is at 140 feet, while near the bow on the starboard or port side it may be 145 feet deep.

The wreck of the *Tarpon* lies about 0.4 mile from the wreck of the *Proteus*, and the diving conditions at the two sites are similar. The visibility on the first day I visited the submarine was about 40–50 feet with absolutely no current. However, over the years I have made over 200 dives on

2.34   U.S.S. *Tarpon*. Starboard bow anchor.

the *Tarpon*. The visibility may be in excess of 100 feet several times during the summer and current is sometimes a problem. At times there may
be a surface current running and no current on the wreck. I have seen
currents as strong as two or more knots here, and under those conditions
diving is impossible. On most occasions during the summer, current is
usually less than one-half knot and often there is no current. The average
visibility is 75 feet. The water temperature during the diving season is in
the upper 70s to mid 80s, and the wreck may be easily dived without a
wet suit. However, the use of a wet suit is advised to prevent cuts and
abrasions from corals and sharp metal on the wreck.

The submarine is covered with brass artifacts and other collectibles including shark's teeth, which are scattered in abundance on the deck. The
submarine lies along the western edge of what is now known to be a mating and aggregation area of the Atlantic sand tiger shark. Sand tiger
sharks are often seen on the wreck. During the early summer, dozens of
the sharks, some as large as 14 feet long, hover about the sub. They have
never bothered anyone and will move away from the hull and out into the
sand after a few divers arrive at the site.

The winter storm of 1986 tore the tip of the *Tarpon's* bow and pulled it
to the starboard and at a right angle to the hull. It is still attached to the
starboard hull. The removal of the bow tip exposed the bulkhead containing the four bow outer torpedo tube doors. This bulkhead is the furthermost point on the sub's hull today. The deck gun forward of the conning tower was a prominent feature of the forward part of the sub even
though it contained only the recoil mechanism, elevation controls, and
was missing its gun barrel. Most of the remains of the deck gun was lost
when the bow was torn away from the hull. Some of the elevation control
gears are still present on the deck. The *Tarpon's* two bow anchors could
be seen on the port and starboard sides until the winter of 1986. With the

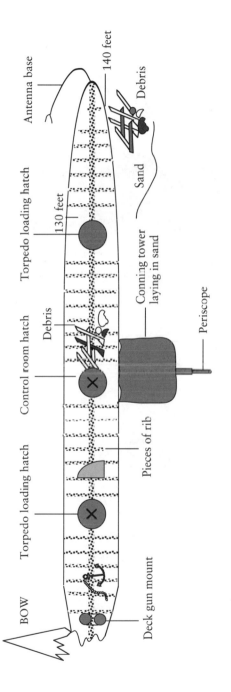

Antenna base

140 feet

Debris

Sand

Torpedo loading hatch

130 feet

Conning tower
laying in sand

Control room hatch

Debris

Periscope

Torpedo loading hatch

Pieces of rib

BOW

Deck gun mount

TARPON

Wreck diagram of the U.S.S. *Tarpon*.

2.35   U.S.S. *Tarpon*, American submarine.

2.36   U.S.S. *Tarpon*, American submarine.

destruction of the bow, only the starboard anchor remains in place on the hull. The port anchor is nowhere to be seen.

The stern of the *Tarpon* has remained unscathed by winter storms. The large curved metal attachment for the sub's radio antenna is still visible. The rudder may be seen under the stern hull at the sand. Viewing the submarine from a distance of 20 feet directly aft of the stern, divers can see that the *Tarpon* lies in a trough created by currents that sweep the length of its hull.

The calcareous growth found on many shipwrecks also covers the wreckage of the *Tarpon*. Corals, sponges, arrow crabs, blennies, Atlantic spadefish, barracuda, fireworms, butterflyfish, sea cucumbers, sea urchins, amberjack, grouper, and many other species of marine life may be seen on the wreck. On several occasions large schools of African pompanos have been seen swimming around the wreck.

Because of the distance to the wreck site, the depth, and the possibility of strong currents, the *Tarpon* is recommended for experienced wreck divers. It is quite an impressive wreck, 50 percent longer and wider than the *U-352* or the *U-85*. The *Tarpon* is visited by charter boats from Nags Head, Hatteras, Ocracoke, Beaufort, Morehead City, and Emerald Isle. Occasionally, charter boats will move from Nags Head, Morehead City, and Emerald Isle to Hatteras and Ocracoke over long weekends and run charters to the sub. The main dive charter boats carrying divers round-trip from Beaufort and Morehead City are the *Olympus*, *Saltshaker*, *Outrageous*, and *Sea Wife IV*. Mike McKay (*Saltshaker*), George Harper (*Jaws*), Scot Whitfield (*Gale Anne*), and George Purifoy (*Olympus*) occasionally move their boats to Ocracoke for three-to-four-day dive trips to area wrecks including the *Tarpon*. They carry portable air compressors on board so air fills are no problem.

[An earlier version of this chapter was published in *Skin Diver* magazine, March, 1985, 34(3): 122–123.]

British Splendour

THE TANKER *British Spendour*, 7,138 tons (4,172 net tons) and 441 feet long, was built in 1931 for the British Tanker Company by Palmers' Company, Ltd. at Newcastle, England. The tanker was powered by Doxford diesel engines with four cylinders, built by Wm. Doxford & Sons, Ltd., and cruised at 10 knots when fully loaded with liquid cargo. Early in April 1942, the *British Splendour*, leased to the British Ministry of Shipping to aid Britain's war effort, departed Houston, Texas, bound for England with 53 men aboard and loaded with 10,000 gallons of gasoline. She was to join a convoy being formed at Halifax, Nova Scotia, for the trip across the Atlantic, but coming up the eastern seaboard of the United States she was travelling with only the HMS *St. Zeno* for protection from marauding U-boats. Headed north on a course of three degrees at 10 knots under clear weather, smooth seas, and good visibility, the *British Splendour* ran with no lights showing, not zigzagging and under complete radio silence for the trip past Cape Hatteras late in the evening of April 6, 1942. Aproaching offshore of the tip of Diamond Shoals at about 10:15 P.M., with the *St. Zeno* a half-mile off her starboard bow and under the watch of seven lookouts including two gunners manning the defensive guns on her sterm, the *British Splendour* was struck on the port side aft of the engine room by a single torpedo fired from the *U-552* under the command of Korvettenkapitän Erich Topp. The ensuing explosion blew off the engine room skylight, severely damaged the poop deck and after deck, and killed 12 crewmen who were below in the engine room and aft. The gunners on the stern were unable to see the U-boat at any time and thus were unable to use their guns to counterattack. The ship began to sink stern first, and the order to abandon ship was given immediately. The captain and the remaining 40 crew members left the sinking ship by three lifeboats and one raft. The HMS *St. Zeno* picked up the 41 survivors, who were taken to Norfolk, Virginia. When last seen by the survivors, the bridge, bow, and six feet of funnel were above water, and the ship drifted for several hours before finally sinking. Aircraft searching for the vessel on April 7 could find no signs of her.

The *British Splendour* lies upside down in 110 feet of water 14 miles southeast of Ocracoke Inlet on a course of 153 degrees and 22 miles southwest of Hatteras Inlet on a course of 190 degrees. The site is about eight miles northwest of the *Proteus* and around 10 miles southwest of the *Dixie Arrow*. Though several portions of the ship are relatively intact,

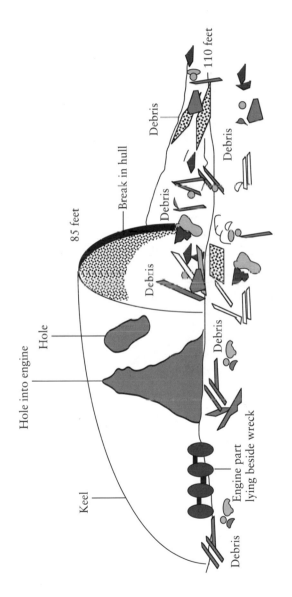

Wreck diagram of the *British Splendour*.

Within the diagram:

110 feet

Debris

Break in hull

85 feet

Debris

Debris

Hole

Hole into engine

Debris

Keel

Debris

Engine part
lying beside wreck

Debris

BRITISH SPLENDOUR

2.37 *British Splendour.*   Courtesy of the Peabody Museum of
Salem, Salem, Massachusetts.

the ship is split open at the engine room on its starboard side and several
large pieces of machinery have spilled out onto the sand. On the port side,
there is a gaping hole where the torpedo struck which allows divers to
swim through the ship and out the engine room on the other side. The
highest point on the keel is at 75 fsw and the keel tapers down toward the
bow to a depth of 100 fsw. The wreck is broken near the stern section
such that a large cross-section of the ship with 25 feet of relief can be
seen. Portions of the wreck amidships are intact except for the large holes
in the engine room, while other parts are broken up quite a bit and provide many areas for investigation. A good dive light is recommended.
Water temperatures in the summer are around 75–80 degrees, comfortable enough for only a wet suit top or "Farmer John" pants. Corals,
sponges, and other tropical marine life abound on the wreck, as do brass
artifacts. The site provides relatively shallow wreck diving for beginning
divers and provides experienced divers with longer bottom time for serious artifact collecting. Nevertheless, the site is seldom visited by divers.

   In the summer of 1983, divers entered the engine room area of the
wreck and determined the manufacturer of the engines to be Wm. Doxford and Sons, Ltd. Very few ships sunk off the coast of North Carolina
during WWII were powered by diesel engines, and only the *British Splendour* was powered by Doxford engines. Dave Bluett, a diver from Washington, D.C., recovered an engine plate from the wreck which was identified by the manufacturer as having come from the *British Splendour.*

   Mike McKay (*Saltshaker*), Buck Wilde (*Sea Wife IV*), George Harper
(*Jaws*), Terry Leonard (*Outrageous IV*), and George Purifoy (*Olympus*)
make the long trip to the wreck out of Beaufort Inlet. All of the boats run
up to the *British Splendour* in six hours except for the *Outrageous* and
Olympus, which make the journey in four hours. McKay, Harper, and

Purifoy frequently move their boats up to Ocracoke if they can get several days of charters to the *British Splendour* or other nearby wrecks. By docking the boat at Ocracoke Island for these long weekend charters, divers are treated to a short two-hour ride to the wreck. This is usually the second dive of the day, after a deeper, offshore dive.

Manuela

THE FREIGHTER *Manuela*, 394 feet long and 4,772 tons, was built in 1934 by the Newport News Shipbuilding and Dry Dock Company, Newport News, Virginia. Captain Conrad G. Nilsen commanded his ship with its 37 crewmen and six Naval Armed Guards as she joined a convoy bound from San Juan, Puerto Rico, to New York in late June of 1942. Loaded with nearly 100,000 bags of raw and refined sugar, the *Manuela* was proceeding northeast about 75 miles east of Cape Lookout when, early in the morning of June 24, 1942, a torpedo from the *U-404* struck amidships on the starboard side between the engine room and boilers killing two crewmen who were on watch in the engine room and flooding the area amidships. The starboard lifeboat was destroyed in the explosion, but 23 crewmen managed to escape in the port side #2 lifeboat while seventeen others leaped overboard and swam to liferafts. The *Manuela*'s distress call was answered by several vessels in the convoy, and she did not appear in danger of sinking during the time members of the crew were being rescued. The *U-404*, which was under the command of Korvettenkapitän Otto von Bulow, escaped the area after the attack and was never able to fire more than just the single torpedo. Within a half-hour after lifeboat #2 was launched, Coast Guard Cutter #408 came to the rescue and towed the lifeboat to the British armed trawler *Norwich City*. Coast Guard Cutter #483 picked up all of the crewmen who had swum to liferafts and took them to Norfolk, Virginia. At noon the next day, the *Manuela* was still afloat and a boarding party from Coast Guard Cutter #252 found a seriously injured crewman on the deck of the ship and transported him to Morehead City. He was the last of the crew to be accounted for. Captain Nilsen, the six Naval Armed Guards, and all hands

2.38 *Manuela.* Steamship Historical Society Collection, University of Baltimore Library.

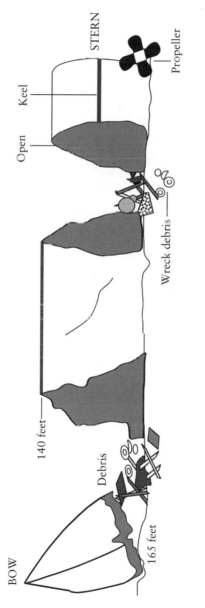

BOW

165 feet

Debris

140 feet

Wreck debris

Open

Keel

STERN

Propeller

MANUELA

Wreck diagram of the *Manuela*.

but the two crewmen killed in the engine room survived the attack. Late in the afternoon of June 25, the *Manuela* was taken to tow headed for Morehead City. During the night, the *Manuela* sank in 180 feet of water. The wreck is located 33 miles from Hatteras Inlet on a heading of 194 degrees and 25 miles from Ocracoke Inlet on a heading of 163 degrees.

[From Arthur R. Moore, 1983]

The *Manuela* lies broken into two sections at a depth of 165 fsw. The bow section sits upright on the bottom and points up toward the surface at an angle of about 65 degrees. The tip of the bow reaches about 150 fsw and provides the highest relief on the entire site. The bow section comprises less than 10 percent of the total remains of the vessel on the site. On the upturned bow deck is a windlass and some bollards. Down at sand level where the bow rests, the wreck site is strewn with large debris. The ship's bell, which positively identified this wreck as that of the *Manuela*, was found in June of 1987 by a group of divers led by Captain Larry Keen of Delaware. The bell was found in the debris at the base of the bow section on the deck side. The debris area extends aft from the bow to about 150 feet beyond the stern section. The bow sits off at an angle of 30 degrees to the stern section, which accounts for the wide arc of dispersal of wreck debris between the bow and stern pieces. This large area is where most of the brass artifacts have been recovered from the site. Although there are a few pieces of machinery in the debris area that have greater than five feet of relief, there is less relief throughout the majority of the area.

The stern section is lying on its starboard side and is located about 100 feet from the bow. This section is huge and comprises more than 60 percent of the ship's remains. The hull of this section comes up to a depth of 150 fsw and is relatively free of much marine growth. Sea urchins are, however, plentiful on the hull surface and divers should beware of landing hands and knees upon these spiny creatures. The deck gun that pointed upward from its mount on the stern section may no longer be seen, as it fell off into the sand during the winter of 1986.

This dive is deep and for very experienced divers only. The water temperature is in the mid-70s to 80s during the summer, and the visibility ranges from 50 to 150 feet. Divers have seldom visited the wreck of the *Manuela* because of the extreme depth, and as a result the marine life and artifacts are quite abundant at the site. Groupers, blue angelfish, barracudas and other marine life are plentiful. At times, current is a problem on this wreck, which lies only 10 miles from the *USS Tarpon*.

3. *Ocracoke to Cape Lookout*

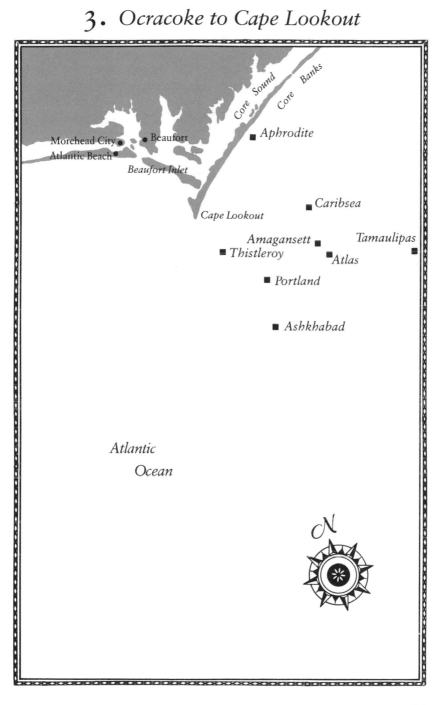

Core Sound

Core Banks

Aphrodite

Morehead City

Beaufort

Atlantic Beach

Beaufort Inlet

Cape Lookout

Caribsea

Amagansett

Tamaulipas

Thistleroy

Atlas

Portland

Ashkhabad

Atlantic

Ocean

Aphrodite

THE 206-foot-long, 1,098-ton ship, named for the Greek goddess of love and beauty, was built at Mystic, Connecticut, in 1864. The *Aphrodite* was a wooden vessel that was powered by steam and a propeller screw. Built at a cost of $160,000, the steamer began and ended life as part of Federal forces during the Civil War. Soon after its construction was completed in May 1864, the vessel was chartered by the U.S. government to transport men and material from the northeast to the blockading squadrons stationed along the East Coast and the Gulf of Mexico.

Not much is known about the transport steamer during the early months of its life, but on September 1, 1864, Rear-Admiral David Farragut, aboard his flagship, U.S.S. *Hartford*, wrote of the ship in a letter he drafted to Gideon Wells, secretary of the navy. He reported that the U.S. chartered steamer, *Aphrodite*, had arrived in Mobile, Alabama, on August 27, loaded with ice, provisions, and men for his West Gulf Blockading Squadron. The group of recruits were under the command of Lieutenant Bunce.

The Battle of Mobile Bay had been won by Farragut and his squadron three weeks earlier after a ferocious battle with Confederate forces near the mouth of the bay. In addition to ships and supplies that were lost, Farragut had lost a considerable number of his men during the fighting so the *Aphrodite* with her provisions and men were welcomed.

Following a short stay in Mobile, the *Aphrodite* proceeded east to Pensacola, Florida, where she arrived on September 1 and discharged her cargo for Farragut's squadron. Farragut noted in his report to the secretary that the ice was especially welcome as the supply there had been depleted. Shortly thereafter, the *Aphrodite* departed Florida and headed for New York to pick up more recruits for the Atlantic and Gulf blockading squadrons.

In New York, U.S. Navy Commander A. G. Clary had taken command of a group of 510 recruits and was awaiting immediate transport south. Clary was to rejoin his command, the U.S.S. *Seminole*, at Mobile after distributing the men among the blockading squadrons as he made his way south. The *Seminole* was one of the West Gulf Blockading Squadron fleet that had survived the Battle of Mobile Bay.

On September 30, Commander Clary was ordered aboard the *Aphrodite* with his charge of men and told to head to Mobile. He gave orders to the master of the vessel, Captain Morgan, to proceed south. The ship and her passengers left New York at 5 P.M. on the thirtieth and headed for the

North Atlantic Blockading Squadron. On Sunday, October 2, the *Aphrodite* was due east of Cape Hatteras when Assistant Surgeon Charles Gaylord reported that one of the men on board had measles. Gaylord advised Clary to put the sick man on shore as soon as possible to avoid an outbreak among all those on board. Clary then ordered Captain Morgan to change course and head for Beaufort, North Carolina, where they would put the sick recruit ashore. Clary suggested a course for the ship as it approached Cape Lookout shoals and the Beaufort bar. As evening approached, the U.S.S. *Powhatan* approached the *Aphrodite* and Clary went aboard the other vessel at the request of her commander. After a short visit, Clary left the *Powhatan* and the *Aphrodite* continued her trip to Beaufort. The weather was clear and the seas calm throughout the night as the ship made its way toward Cape Lookout. At around 5 A.M. on the morning of October 3, Clary was awakened by Captain Morgan who informed him that the *Aphrodite* had run aground. By this time the noise of the ship scraping across the sand bottom had already alerted Clary as to the nature of the frantic early morning visit. Rushing up to the deck, Clary could clearly see the shore and he began to understand the enormity of the situation. The *Aphrodite* was parallel to the shore, stuck hard and fast, and being pounded by broadside waves. Captain Morgan tried but was unable to back his vessel off the sand. He then set the ship's anchor, preventing her from moving further onto the beach. As daylight approached, Clary estimated they were beached about twelve miles from Cape Lookout.

Clary ordered two officers on board to launch two small boats and make their way to Beaufort, one by the Pamlico Sound and the other by the ocean. At Beaufort, they were to get help from Admiral Lee who was headquartered there. Both men arrived safely at Beaufort later that evening and told Admiral Lee about the *Aphrodite's* dire situation. At the time, neither of the officers knew that their ship had irrevocably lost its battle with the crashing waves. Admiral Lee immediately ordered the U.S. steamers *Keystone State*, under the command of Commander Cosby, and the *Shokokon*, under the command of Acting Master Sheldon, to head for the *Aphrodite* and pull her off the sand and assess the damage. Within hours, the two ships headed up the coast traveling slowly in the darkness.

Meanwhile, at the *Aphrodite*, Clary had begun moving the recruits and ship's crew to shore. He directed the safe landing of all of his recruits but two of the *Aphrodite's* crew were drowned while trying to swim to shore through the rough surf. They had been too impatient to await transport in one of the boats. While the men were being moved to shore, Morgan was trying unsuccessfully to free his ship. The hapless vessel was continually taking on water during this time from the relentless pounding of breakers against the ship. As more time passed, he realized the futility of his effort to free the ship. With each successive wave the vessel was driven harder aground. By 4 P.M. in the afternoon there was nine feet of water in the bilge, and with the fires in the boilers extinguished, her pumps had quit. At this point, Morgan realized with certainty that his ship was lost.

Early the next morning, the *Keystone State* and the *Shokokon* arrived and anchored nearby the *Aphrodite*. The crews began to hastily remove the government stores on board and transfer them to the rescue ships. Dozens of lead bars weighing 150 pounds each and engraved with the name *SAN ANDRES* were left on board the ill-fated ship.

While rescue operations were taking place aboard the *Aphrodite*, Admiral Lee was taking further measures to bring the several hundred recruits back to Beaufort. He sent nine Beaufort lighters via the Pamlico Sound to pick up the men. These boats were small, flat-bottomed schooners designed to draw little water and able to safely navigate the shallow waters of the sound. The lighters arrived on the scene to find most of the recruits waiting for transport. A few of them had taken advantage of the confusion to desert but the rest of the men were brought back safely to Beaufort. Two of the men that had contracted measles were put into a hospital in Beaufort. By October 7, the *Aphrodite* had broken in two and was a total loss.

Today, the remains of the *Aphrodite* lie about 12 miles northeast of Cape Lookout, a few miles below Drum Inlet in eighteen feet of water about 100 yards offshore. There are two sections of the wreck located about 100 yards from each other. Most of the wreckage lies beneath the sand. The portion of the larger section that is above the sand is about forty feet long and twenty feet wide. All of this section is heavily encrusted with coral and it is difficult to recognize the features of the ship.

At one end of the site there is a large overhang piece that rises about five feet above the sand and provides the greatest relief on the site. One side of the overhang is walled off and the other side is open. From the overhang, relief on the wreck gradually tapers down to the sand as it reaches the other end. The overhang covers an opening about six feet deep that a diver can enter. Once inside, it is possible to reach farther back into the opening. Inside this area was stacked the *SAN ANDRES* lead bars that were left behind in 1864. Under here may be seen the remains of timber and metal portions of the ship. Also found in this area were pieces of English china plates. No intact plates have been recovered yet, but some of the pieces have the crest of the manufacturer embossed on the back of them. The overhang area was probably a cargo hold. Forward of the high overhang out in the sand is an anchor and anchor chain. Between the overhang and the anchor are a number of lead bars scattered about in the sand. Brushing away the sand reveals other lead bars. A number of the bars have been salvaged by local divers. It is not clear what the lead was used for but perhaps they were going to be melted down into bullets or they may have been ballast of some sort. Pieces of dinner plates, a brass spike, a brass chisel, and parts of the ship's machinery have also been recovered.

Down the wreck is a shallow trough about three feet deep and just large enough for a diver to swim through. It is not clear what part of the ship this represents. There is a small boiler or condenser about three feet in diameter and five feet long on the site. There is not much else remaining of the ship on the two sites as most of the wreckage is covered with sand.

Besides the abundance of coral on the site, there are other marine creatures present. Anemones, arrow crabs, starfish, sea urchins, black bass, flounder, Atlantic spadefish, and sheephead are found here.

The visibility on the site is poor at best. Ten feet of visibility would be exceptional and it is usually less than three to five feet. Its shallow depth means long bottom time. But, because of the shallow depth and the fact that the wreck lies in the surf zone, surge is a big problem. Gloves and a wet suit should be worn to protect from cuts and abrasions from the coral and metal when being pushed around the site by the surge. It is best to dive the *Aphrodite* when the wind is blowing out of the northeast as under these conditions the surge is minimal.

Current is sometimes a problem here, and with the poor visibility it is easy to get lost on the site. However, the shallow depth makes it easy to surface and get bearings. A cross-wreck line should be deployed to help divers return to the dive boat. Strong rip currents can carry a diver long distances; however, don't panic, inflate your bouyancy compensator and wait to be picked up by the dive boat. Although the dive is shallow, conditions of low visibility, surge, and current make it a difficult dive at times. Inexperienced divers should be accompanied by an experienced guide when they make this dive.

Tamaulipas

THE *Tamaulipas*, 6,943 tons (4,267 net tons) and 435 feet long, was built in 1919 at Sparrows Point, Maryland, for the Mexican Trading and Shipping Company of New York. The tanker was originally called the *Hugoton*. Operating out of Wilmington, Delaware, the *Tamaulipas* carried fuel oil between Tampico, Mexico, and New York. In early April 1942, the ship departed Mexico with 70,000 gallons of fuel oil bound for the East Coast of the United States. As she passed Cape Lookout late on April 9, 1942, the captain of the *Tamaulipas* had no intention of waiting until daylight to go past Cape Hatteras in accordance with wartime Navy regulations; so he continued to guide his ship northeast on the way to New York. The *U-552*, with Korvettenkapitän Erich Topp in command, was also cruising the waters off Cape Lookout and spotted the tanker shortly before midnight about 20 miles northeast of the cape. Without warning, the *U-552* fired a single torpedo which struck the *Tamaulipas* amidships on the starboard side, igniting the fuel oil with a tremendous explosion. With both regular and emergency radio transmitters destroyed and his ship broken in two by the torpedo, Captain A. Falkenberg ordered the crew of 37 to abandon ship. Within a few minutes, the #1 and #3 lifeboats were loaded, and all but two crewmen, who were killed in the blast, were aboard rowing away from the sinking vessel. Three hours later the broken tanker could be seen with the bow and stern sticking out of the water and the midship portion sinking. The captain and surviving crew members were picked up by the HMS *Norwich City* and carried to Morehead City, where they arrived less than two hours after the sinking.
[From Arthur R. Moore, 1983]

The *Tamaulipas* sank April 10 in 155 feet of water on the northeast side of the shoals off Cape Lookout 38.1 miles from Beaufort Inlet, and 23.3 miles from the East Slough buoy on a heading of 87 degrees. (The buoy marks the east end of the cut across the shoals.) The vessel sank in two pieces, and the stern section, comprising about 40 percent of the wreckage, lies about two miles away from the larger bow section. The bow section is upside down and the keel is at 130 feet with the bottom at around 155 feet. Strong currents have been experienced on this wreck (up to 1.5 knots), and this factor as well as the depth makes the *Tamaulipas* a dive for only the most experienced wreck divers. From above the wreck reminds one of a watermelon lying in the sand with one end cracked open. There are several gaping cracks in the starboard side of the ship at a depth of around 140 feet. The keel is sparsely covered with marine life

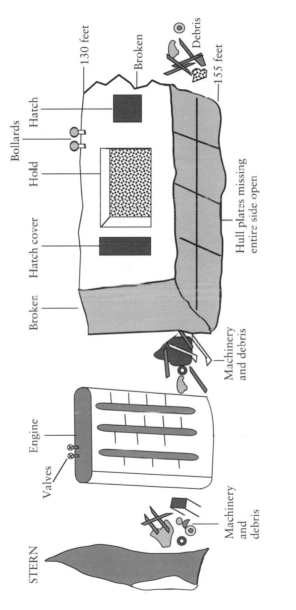

STERN

Engine

Valves

Machinery
and
debris

Broken

Hatch cover

Bollards

Hold

Hatch

130 feet

Broken

Debris

155 feet

Machinery
and debris

Hull plates missing
entire side open

TAMAULIPAS

Wreck diagram of the *Tamaulipas.*

3.1 *Tamaulipas.*   Courtesy of the Peabody Museum of Salem, Salem, Massachusetts.

such as sea urchins, soft corals, sponges, and the like. Visibility on the wreck ranges from 50 to 150 feet, and water temperatures during the summer months are in the upper 70s to 80s. The wreck is located east of the *Atlas* and is good diving throughout the diving season. The stern section is the best part of the *Tamaulipas* to dive. The stern sits upright at 155 fsw and is relatively intact. The deck is at 130 fsw and contains a large open hold, which is easily penetrated. The port side is missing large pieces of its side plates, making viewing and penetration from the side quite easy. The remaining 100 feet of the wreck is broken up all the way to the stern proper. The large triple-expansion engine provides the greatest relief in the rubble section, where it rises to 130 fsw. The remains of the wheel house are also located in the rubble of the stern section.

Diving on this wreck must be done with care. A diver wishing to spend any time at all on the wreck will need to make a decompression dive. The *Sea Wife IV, Jaws, Saltshaker IV* and the *Gale Anne* carry divers to this wreck.

The *Tamaulipas* is now also referred to as the "Far East Tanker."

3.2 Deck of the tanker *Tamaulipas.*

Atlas

THE TANKER *Atlas*, 7,139 tons (4,368 net tons) and 430 feet long, was built in 1916 at Philadelphia, Pennsylvania, by W. Cramp and Sons Shipbuilding Co. for Socony-Vacuum Oil Co. She departed Houston, Texas, on April 1, 1942, with Captain Hamilton Gray and 33 men on board and was bound for Sewaren, New Jersey, loaded with a cargo of gasoline. Early in the morning of April 9, 1942, after an uneventful trip, the *Atlas* was steaming past Cape Lookout; the weather was clear with a light southerly wind and gentle sea swells. The ship was following the nine-fathom curve and was approximately 1.5 miles inside the Cape Lookout Shoals Outer Buoy when the watch officer reported the sound of a diesel engine off the starboard bow. Although nothing was sighted, the *Atlas* was immediately turned to present her stern toward the sound. The maneuver was belated, however, as moments before the *U-552*, commanded by Korvettenkapitän Erich Topp, fired torpedoes toward the tanker. As the *Atlas* began her turn a torpedo struck the ship on the starboard side nearly amidships. Gasoline poured throughout the ship and into the sea, and the fumes were so strong that Captain Gray ordered the *Atlas* abandoned. He and 33 men boarded and lowered three lifeboats and began moving away from the ship. When the lifeboat carrying the captain was about 100 feet from the *Atlas*, a second torpedo struck and the blast set the ship and surrounding sea on fire. Realizing that his lifeboat was surrounded by gasoline on the sea, Captain Gray ordered his lifeboat party into the water while the fire swept over them. When the fire had burned out, the men returned to the smoldering lifeboat, extinguished the flames that were destroying the craft, and reboarded it. Two of the men died in the water and several were badly burned. The captain could

3.3 *Atlas.* U.S. Coast Guard. Courtesy of The Mariners' Museum, Newport News, Virginia.

see by the light of the blazing ship that the other two boats had made it to safety away from the gasoline before the fire. After a few hours the three lifeboats joined together and began the long journey to the Cape Lookout Lighthouse, which was visible at the time of the torpedoing. By dawn, a Navy patrol plane spotted the survivors and directed the Coast Guard to the rescue. The 31 remaining crewmen and the captain were taken to Morehead City where five of the crew were hospitalized for burns. The burned hulk of the *Atlas* tanker sank about 8:00 P.M. on April 9, 1942, in 130 feet of water, another casualty of the U-boat war.

The wreck of the *Atlas* tanker is located 28.1 miles from Beaufort Inlet, and 12.5 miles from Knuckle Buoy on a heading of 60 degrees. The site is visited frequently during the diving season by dive charter boats from Beaufort and Morehead City. The wreck sits upright on the bottom at 120–130 feet depending on where you are on the wreck. The tanker was constructed with two decks and these lie at approximately 80 and 105 feet. Portions of the vessel are broken up, and the deck areas are mostly in disarray. The amidships section is extensively broken up and the boilers are easily seen. There is a very large fishing net hanging on the wreck forward of amidships. Although the net is rotting away, care must still be taken while diving in this area to avoid entanglement. The best portion of the tanker to investigate lies away from the net, so you really haven't missed a lot if you stay away from it altogether and see the rest of the wreck. Divers have recovered a number of artifacts from the site including brass portholes, valves, gauges, and one of the *Atlas*'s large anchors. Pipes, machinery, and brass artifacts are scattered about the wreck

3.4   *Atlas.* Ladder leading into hold.

3.5 *Atlas.* Deck.

site, and divers do not have to go all the way to the sand to find a souvenir. The tanker sits only about five miles from the eastern edge of Cape Lookout Shoals, so the visibility is usually 30–50 feet, although occasionally it may reach 70–80 feet. Strong currents are frequently a problem on this wreck, and when the current is running the visibility drops considerably. The *Atlas* is covered with beautiful corals, sponges, slipper lobsters, anemones, sea fans, sea whips, blue angelfish, butterflyfish, blennies, and other tropical marine life. Seen in reasonable visibility, it is one of the prettiest and most interesting wrecks off the coast of North Carolina; it ranks as one of the top five North Carolina shipwrecks. The decks have two or three hatchways which allow entry into the holds below, but penetration into these areas would be dangerous and take divers much deeper than 130 feet. Because of the relatively long boat trip (about three hours at 10 knots), the depth of the wreck, and occasional strong current, this wreck is for experienced wreck divers.

Amagansett

THE MENHADEN FISHING BOAT *Amagansett*, 226 tons and 135 feet long, was built in 1954 as a deep-ocean fishing vessel. Caught in a violent storm on November 20, 1964, the vessel foundered and sank on the east side of Cape Lookout Shoals off Cove Banks between Drum Inlet and the Cape Lookout Lighthouse in 130 feet of water approximately a half-mile northwest of the *Atlas* tanker wreck. The wreck site is 12 miles from the Knuckle Buoy on a heading of 55 degrees and 27.6 miles from Beaufort Inlet.

A small, completely intact wreck, the *Amagansett* lies on her starboard side. A host for some corals, sponges, and much calcareous growth, the wreck is also a haven for bait and game fish. The vessel's large propeller is visible at the stern. Water temperatures on the wreck range from the mid-70s to low 80s during the summer, and the visibility is similar to that found on the *Atlas* tanker, around 30 to 50 feet, and occasionally 70 plus feet. Currents are frequently encountered on the wreck, and they can reduce visibility to less than 20 feet. Because of the *Amagansett*'s proximity to the much larger and more beautiful wreck of the *Atlas*, divers prefer to by-pass the "Shad Boat," as it is sometimes called, in favor of the more interesting tanker. However, the fishing vessel is interesting to visit at least once to see an intact wreck in clear water.

The extreme depth of the wreck, the presence of strong currents, and the long boat ride make this a dive for experienced wreck divers. Though the *Amagansett* is infrequently visited by dive charter boats, the *Saltshaker*, *Sea Wife IV*, *Olympus*, *Easystep II*, and *Jaws* will all carry divers to this wreck.

Caribsea

ORIGINALLY NAMED *Lake Flattery*, the *Caribsea* was a Great Lakes freighter built in 1919 at Duluth, Minnesota, for Stockard Steamship Company of New York. At 2,609 tons (1,610 net tons), the 251-foot-long vessel carried freight along the East Coast from Caribbean ports to New York and Philadelphia. At the beginning of March 1942, the *Caribsea* departed Santiago, Cuba, bound for Norfolk, Virginia. Early in the morning on March 11, she was running at a slow speed 12 miles east of Cape Lookout to comply with U.S. Navy orders for all vessels to pass Cape Hatteras during daylight hours. Offshore Hatteras was a virtual "torpedo alley," and U-boats were taking a toll of shipping passing outside Diamond Shoals, especially among those ships running at night. The *U-158*, under the command of Kapitänleutnant Erich Rostin, spotted the small freighter, and—according to German naval reports—Rostin mistook her for a Coast Guard cutter. The *U-158* fired two torpedoes from her bow tubes at the *Caribsea* and both struck the freighter's starboard side simultaneously. One struck the #2 hold just forward of amidships and the other struck amidships. The small ship sank within three minutes, and there was no time to launch any lifeboats. Twenty-one members of the crew perished in the attack, and the seven survivors leaped overboard and clung to whatever was floating nearby. The survivors were picked up by the SS *Norlindo* and put aboard a Coast Guard cutter off Cape Henry, Virginia. [From Arthur R. Moore, 1983]

The *Caribsea* lies in 85 feet of water east of Cape Lookout Shoals and only around 10 miles from shore as the crow flies; the site of the wreck is 12.5 miles from the Knuckle Buoy on a heading of 31 degrees.

3.6 *Caribsea*. U.S. Coast Guard.   Courtesy of The Mariners' Museum, Newport News, Virginia.

3.7   *Caribsea*. Windlass on the bow.

3.8   *Caribsea*. Bow section below deck.

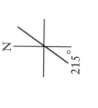

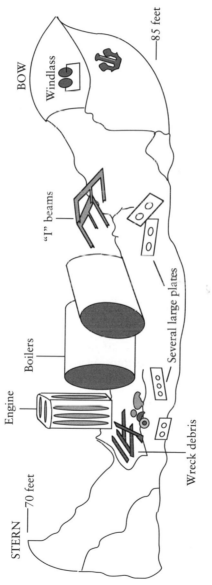

Wreck diagram of the *Caribsea*.

Because it lies so close to the shoals, the visibility on the wreck is usually less than 40 feet or so, but during the summer 80–100 feet of visibility may be encountered. Current is sometimes a problem on the wreck, but generally it is of little consequence. Water temperatures early or late in the diving season may be five or 10 degrees cooler than in offshore waters, but in the summer water temperatures in the mid-70s and 80s are the rule.

The wreck has been wire-dragged to prevent the wreckage from obstructing navigation, and during WWII the Navy and the Coast Guard depth-charged the wreck as a precaution because U-boats would often hide near sunken wrecks to prevent detection by surface ships. Consequently, not much remains of the original ship's structure. A portion of the bow is intact and rises to nearly 70 fsw, and a section of the forward hold, including the anchor chain locker, remains. Her two bow anchors may still be seen hanging on the port and starboard sides of the bow. A large windlass can be seen on the deck of the bow, and the bow can be penetrated easily through gaping openings in the sides which lead to several levels below the bow deck at a depth of 80 fsw and deeper. The anchor chain locker lies at the second level below the bow deck. The *Caribsea*'s triple expansion engine and two large boilers provide the greatest relief on the wreckage, rising to 70 fsw. The keel and various iron girders and large iron plates lie on the bottom in a helter-skelter fashion. Corals, sponges, urchins, sea bass, angelfish, butterflyfish, blennies, an occasional shark or two, manta rays, and a variety of crustaceans and mollusks may be seen. Because the *Caribsea* is visited often, most of the prime artifacts, like portholes, have been recovered. However, each diving season brings a new discovery or two when winter storms shift the sand covering the wreckage, thus exposing new areas. In the summer of 1983, Jim Pickard found a beautiful brass hull plate bearing the original name of the vessel, hull number, name and location of the builder, and other information. Scores of divers over the years probably swam right over the plate and never realized it. Occasionally, another porthole is uncovered from the sand by a lucky diver and adds another tale to the many stories of diving the *Caribsea*.

The trip out to the site is about 24 miles from Beaufort Inlet and across Lookout Shoals. Most charterboats from Beaufort, Morehead City, and Emerald Isle visit the wreck. The *Outrageous, Olympus,* and *Sea Wife IV* gets you to the site the fastest. *Saltshaker* and *Jaws* do not get there quite as fast but are comfortable boats for the longer ride.

Ario

THE TANKER *Ario*, 435 feet long and 6,952 tons (4,271 net tons), was built in 1920 at Sparrows Point, Maryland, by the Bethlehem Shipbuilding Company. Owned by the Mobil Oil Corporation, the *Ario* frequently made the trip from Texas to New York loaded with fuel oil. Early in the morning on March 15, 1942, while on the return trip from New York to Corpus Christi, Texas, with Captain T. R. Hannevig and 36 crewmen aboard and no cargo in its hold, the *Ario* was struck on the starboard side by a torpedo fired from the *U-158* under the command of Kapitänleutnant Erich Rostin. Captain Hannerig gave the order to abandon ship, but before the crew could begin lowering lifeboats a second U-boat appeared on the *Ario*'s port side and joined the *U-158* in shelling the sinking tanker. Twelve crewmen were in lifeboat #3 when a shell struck while it was being lowered. Eight of the crew in the lifeboat were killed and the other four fell into the water and waited for rescue. The #1 lifeboat was the only lifeboat to be successfully launched. Although the shell-fire smashed one of its lifeboat falls while the boat was still about ten feet above the water, the craft landed upright and no one was injured. The men in the #1 lifeboat rowed around picking up survivors who had leaped overboard or fallen from the #3 lifeboat when it was destroyed. The *Ario* continued to float for some time after the attack and the two submarines departed the area. The captain, chief mate, chief engineer, and two other crewmen reboarded the vessel to determine if she could be salvaged. The ship was found to be a loss, unsalvageable and slowly sinking. An engineer remained on board the *Ario* while the lifeboat stood close by waiting for rescue ships to reach them. Around 8:00 A.M., nearly eight hours after the attack, the USS *Dupont* arrived on the scene and

3.9   *Ario*. U.S. Coast Guard.   Courtesy of The Mariners' Museum, Newport News, Virginia.

picked up all the survivors and took them to Charleston, South Carolina. The *Ario* was kept under observation until 12:30 P.M. on March 15 when she was seen still afloat on her side. She finally sank in shallow water 10 miles east of Cape Lookout near the *Caribsea*. [From Arthur R. Moore, 1983]

No one has ever found this wreck. Interestingly, the *Ario* and the *Tamaulipas* are identical ships. Built eight months apart by the same shipbuilder, both tankers are 451 feet (length) by 56 feet (breadth) by 32 feet (depth), both have two decks, both are 6,950 gross tons (4,270 net tons), and both have identical triple-expansion engines. They were sunk within three weeks of each other less than 18 miles apart. The search for this wreck still continues. It is entirely possible that the wreck site of the *Tamaulipas* is really that of the *Ario* and that the *Tamaulipas* sank further offshore in deeper water. Positive identification of the wreck currently assumed to be that of the *Tamaulipas* will help resolve the mystery.

Ashkhabad

THE RUSSIAN FREIGHTER *Ashkhabad*, 401 feet long and 5,284 tons (3,164 net tons), was built in 1917 by Harland and Wolff at Glasgow, Scotland. (During its seafaring history, the vessel was renamed several times and was known as the *Dneprostroi*, the *Kutais*, the *Mistley Hall*, the *Aldersgate*, the *Milazzo*, and the *War Hostage* before it was called *Ashkhabad*.) Owned by the USSR, the *Ashkhabad* had as her port of registry the city of Odessa. The Soviet vessel was torpedoed on April 30, 1942, about 100 miles off the coast of North Carolina by the *U-402* commanded by Korvettenkapitän Siegfried von Forstner. The *Ashkhabad* remained afloat but in a very waterlogged condition drifting toward Cape Lookout until May 3, when she was sunk by U.S. Navy gunfire at the very tip of Cape Lookout Shoals.

Lying in 55 feet of water, the Soviet vessel was depth-charged and wire-dragged as a hazard to navigation and is consequently very broken up on the bottom. Her two boilers, engine, and bulkheads present the greatest amount of relief on the wreck site. However, the wreckage consists mainly of twisted beams, plates, broken machinery, bulkheads, and the like, and in this regard the *Ashkhabad* is quite similar to the *Hutton* and the *Suloide*. Deck railings are intact and some are attached to steel deck plates that were blown outward. Many artifacts have been removed from the wreck site over the years—such as portholes, brass valves and fittings, and gauges. A bell was found a few years ago by Mike Sheen with the name "Kylushkenets" engraved on it.

3.10   *Ashkhabad*. U.S. Coast Guard.   Courtesy of The Mariners' Museum, Newport News, Virginia.

3.11   Bell recovered from Russian freighter, *Ashkhabad*, by Mike Sheen.   Photograph courtesy of Mike Sheen.

The wreck lies 22.1 miles from Beaufort Inlet at the tip of Cape Lookout Shoals, and 6.5 miles from Knuckle Buoy on a heading of 121 dedegrees. During diving season, the site is infrequently visited by dive charter boats from Beaufort and Morehead City. The water temperature on the site is in the 70s during the summer, and the very close proximity of the wreck to the shoals means that the visibility will usually be very limited. On most occasions, the visibility is less than 15 feet, although 40–50 feet of visibility may be encountered. Currents and surge are a constant problem because of the relatively shallow depth and the closeness to the shoals. The wreck is covered with corals and sponges and is a good habitat for numerous types of fish life, including flounders and large groupers. The shallow depth means longer bottom time to investigate the wreck, but on the negative side it also means there will be greater effects of vigorous surface sea conditions on divers below—i.e., lots of surge if there is a rolling sea surface. A cross-wreck line and compass are recommended for navigation under the prevailing limited visibility conditions to prevent extreme disorientation on this wreck. A bright dive light is also useful for illuminating beneath collapsed areas of the wreckage. Poor visibility nothwithstanding, the dive is a good one for inexperienced wreck divers when accompanied by an experienced guide. The wreck is usually the second dive of the day, after a deeper offshore dive.

Portland

THE FREIGHTER *Portland*, 2,648 tons (1,621 net tons) and 289 feet long, was built in 1919 by Albina Engine and Machine Works at Portland, Oregon, and was originally named the *Jacox*. Acquired in 1940 by the Compania Columbus de Vapores of Panama, the ship was operated under Panamanian registry. Powered by triple expansion engines built by Ellicott Machine Corporation of Baltimore, Maryland, the vessel cruised at 10 knots. In mid-February 1943, the Panamanian ship left Philadelphia bound for Havana. On February 11, 1943, in the midst of a violent storm, the *Portland* ran aground on the northeast side of Cape Lookout Shoals.

Battered and broken up by violent seas the unfortunate vessel sank in only 55 feet of water 18 miles southeast of Beaufort Inlet. The navigational buoy "2" now marks the wreck site, which is six miles from the East Slough Buoy on a heading of 146 degrees. At one time, the site was marked by a buoy designated "P" and consequently many boat captains refer to the *Portland* as the "P Wreck." Previous reports of the ship being torpedoed or striking a mine are false. The wreck site is not large, and the remains are scattered across the sand bottom more or less in a straight line, with the bow section separated from the mid and stern sections by a short stretch of sand. The bow is pointed up toward the surface and reaches up to a depth of 25 fsw. There are two anchors on the bow. There are masts on the midsection, which, if followed along their length, will lead to the bow and stern sections. The stern section, which lies on its port side, is quite large and still relatively intact, even though it has broken up considerably over the last few years. There is a compartment in the stern that contains 50-caliber machine-gun ammunition and a number of two-inch rounds. A fire extinguisher found on the site a few years ago had the name "Portland" stamped on it. Because of the wreck's close proximity to the shoals, visibility is usually poor, being less than 10 feet, and currents and surge are sometimes encountered. A compass and cross-wreck line are recommended for navigation on the site, and a bright dive light is useful for illuminating dark recesses. The water temperature is in the mid-70s to low 80s during the summer, and the wreck may be dived without a wet suit. However, some protection is needed against scrapes and cuts from coral and other sharp objects, especially if there is any rolling or rough surface sea conditions, which are readily transmitted to divers below at the shallow depth.

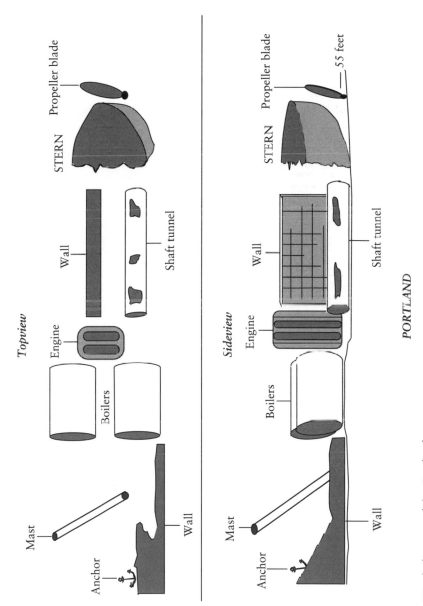

Wreck diagram of the *Portland*.

In the mid-1970s, commercial salvage divers plundered the wreck, which accounts for a great deal of its deteriorated condition. Sport divers have removed numerous brass artifacts from the site, including portholes, valves, gauges, wheels, and various fittings. The three-inch deck gun which sat on the fantail on the stern was also recovered several years ago. Occasionally, winter storms uncover new sections of the wreck, and new artifact finds are made each year. Corals, sponges, sea anemones, sea urchins, flounders, groupers, sheepheads, and a variety of other marine life abound at the site.

The shallow depth of the wreck, the infrequent presence of currents, and the relatively short boat ride out to the site make the *Portland* a good wreck dive for inexperienced divers in spite of the usually poor visibility. Long bottom times give divers ample opportunity to thoroughly investigate the remains of the wreck. Dive charter boats from Beaufort and Morehead City visit the *Portland* frequently during the dive season since it makes a convenient shallow second dive after diving the deeper wrecks of the *Tamaulipas, Atlas, Amagansett,* and *Caribsea.*

Thistleroy

THE FREIGHTER *Thistleroy*, 4,027 tons (2,008 net tons) and 345 feet long, was built in 1902 by Irvines' Shipbuilding and Dry Dock Company at West Hartlepool, England, for the Albyn Line of Sunderland, England, and was originally named the *W. E. Johnson*. Loaded with a cargo of cotton and phosphate bound for Cork, Ireland, and Liverpool, England, the *Thistleroy* departed Galveston, Texas, in late December 1911. On December 28, the freighter was approaching Cape Lookout Shoals from the southwest during a violent storm. She ran aground on the southwest edge of the shoals and was battered into the shoals where she broke up and sank in 20 feet of water between what is now the East and West Slough buoys marking a channel through Cape Lookout Shoals.

The visibility on the wreck is usually less than five feet because the *Thistleroy* lies in the middle of the shoals. The best time to dive the wreck is at slack high tide; otherwise, strong currents and almost zero visibility will be encountered. Although the bow is pointed up, much of the wreck is buried beneath the sand. Winter storms typically expose new portions of the wreckage and cover over previously exposed portions. The stern section has collapsed to the sand, but several bulkheads are often exposed and twisted beams, plates, and the ship's partially buried boiler are still visible. The site is covered with corals, sponges, sheep-

3.12 *Thistleroy*. Photograph from the Paul C. Morris Collection, Nantucket, Massachusetts. Courtesy of Paul C. Morris.

heads, flounders, groupers, and other marine life, but the very limited visibility makes it difficult to appreciate the wreck. During the diving season, the water temperature ranges in the upper 70s to mid-80s, and a wet suit is usually not necessary except to protect against scrapes and cuts in the prevalent surge and current. The shallow depth means a lot of bottom time, but it also means that rough surface sea conditions are transmitted quite readily to the bottom, often creating a problem for the diver. A compass and cross-wreck line are essential for exploring this wreck. The quite readily to the bottom, often creating a problem for the diver. A compass and cross-wreck line are essential for exploring this wreck. The *Thistleroy* is visited very infrequently by Captain Bob Eastep; he is one of the few boat captains in the area who will take divers to the wreck. Even with poor visibility, dived at slack high tide, the wreck is a good one for inexperienced wreck divers accompanied by an experienced guide.

Central America

ORIGINALLY CALLED THE *George Law*, the 272-foot-long, 2,141-ton *Central America* was a Pacific Mail Steamer which ran between New York and the Isthmus of Panama carrying passengers, mail, and freight from 1855 to 1857. At the time, all ships that had a government subsidy to carry United States mail were commanded by U.S. Naval officers. Thus the ill-fated *Central America* was commanded by 44-year-old Captain William Louis Herndon.

A veteran naval officer, Herndon had seen considerable sea duty in the Pacific Ocean as well as in the Caribbean. While commander of the USS *Vandalia*, he had made a complete exploration of the whole 4,000-mile-long Amazon River from its headwaters in Peru to its outlet in the South Atlantic. He and his crew were the first Americans to make the journey, and his book, *Exploration of the Valley of the Amazon*, described their explorations of this little-known portion of South America in great detail. Captain Herndon had also seen sea duty in the Atlantic for two years as master of the *Central America*. During those two years of voyages, Herndon often passed the dangerous Diamond Shoals off Cape Hatteras and was well aware of the fate of ships that had run into the shoals. His two years of Atlantic Ocean duty came at a time when the California gold rush brought fortunes to hundreds of men who had struck it rich in mining areas of the West. Such men travelled to their homes in the East by way of the Isthmus of Panama on ships like the *Central America*.

In early September 1857, the *Central America* set a course for the return trip to New York from Panama. In addition to her crew of 101, she had taken on 474 passengers; among them were miners fresh from the

3.13   *George Law (Central America)*.   Erik Heyl. Courtesy of The Mariners' Museum, Newport News, Virginia.

157

California gold fields carrying more than two million dollars worth of gold on board. On September 9, after an uneventful trip, the steamer ran into a gale off of Cape Hatteras blowing out of the northwest. The storm continued to build throughout the night to hurricane force and battered the ship for two-and-a-half days. Her auxiliary sails were torn to shreds, and she was leaking in several places from the battering by huge waves as they crashed against her sides. Passengers and crew worked to bail the tons of water the ship took on when her pumps failed, but the damage was too great. As the storm roared throughout the night and the ship wallowed out of control in mountains of seas, Captain Herndon ordered red rockets sent up as distress signals.

By daylight the ship was heavy in the water. She continued to take on water in the tremendous seas and, according to reports of the day, looked as though she would go under at any moment. By mid-morning, the New England brig *Maine* out of Boston, having seen the distress flares, raced to the rescue. The *Central America*, however, had only two lifeboats remaining after the terrible battering during the night, so there was little hope that all of the 575 on board could make the trip over the boiling seas to safety. Throughout the day and night, Herndon directed two rescue trips to the *Maine* with lifeboats filled with women and children. On their third trip to the sinking vessel, though, Herndon ordered the life-

WRECK OF THE STEAMSHIP CENTRAL AMERICA.

APPALLING DISASTER.

On Saturday, September 12th, 1857, Capt. Herndon, bound to New York, from California, with the Pacific Mails, Passengers and Crew, to the number of 592 persons, and treasure to the amount of over $2,000,000, foundered in a hurricane, off Cape Hatteras.

Whole number on board, 592.   Number saved, 166.   Number on board whose names are known, 134.   Names unknown, 292.

3.14   Wreck of the *Central America*.   Courtesy of The Mariners' Museum, Newport News, Virginia.

boats to stand off because the ship was going to sink at any moment. He ordered part of the decking cut up to use as rafts when the ship finally went under. Then, Herndon put his first officer in charge of the ship while he went below to his flooded cabin and put on his full-dress uniform complete with sword. Returning to the bridge, he could see that the ship was slowly sinking, trapping him and 423 passengers and crew on board. The 152 rescued women and children on board the *Maine* watched the *Central America* sink and reported that Captain Herndon's final moments of life, "for sheer majesty, have seldom been equalled in naval history." With his cap raised in a salute, standing at attention in his full-dress uniform, he disappeared as the *Central America* sank beneath the waves.

The ship went down about 8:00 P.M. on the night of September 12, 1857, on the outer edge of the Gulf Stream directly off of Cape Hatteras (35° 13.6N; 75° 26.9W) in a little over 100 feet of water. Forty-nine passengers and crewmen who survived the fatal plunge were picked up by a passing ship, and several others were rescued a few days later. Four hundred and twenty passengers and crewmen died.

Neither the ship nor its treasure of several million dollars in newly mined gold—nor even Captain Herndon's sword—has ever been found. Not that no one is looking. A Florida company, Expeditions Unlimited, announced in 1979 that it was beginning a search for the ship and cargo. Members of the company claimed that their research showed that the ship carried gold, gold dust, gold bullion, gold coins, and 13 silver bars. However, not a single word has been heard from that group since 1979.

Although most records record 35° 13.6N and 75° 26.9W as the spot closest to the sinking of the *Central America*, a rescue ship reported, in an obscure reference, that 31° 25N and 77° 10W was where she sank. The former location is off Cape Hatteras while the latter is 300 miles to the south, off the coast of Georgia.

Early in 1984, a group of divers claimed to have found a golden-laden vessel off Hatteras which, at first report, was believed to be the *Central America*. Later, however, it was believed not to be the wreck of the mail ship, and no clue as to the actual identity of the wreck that was discovered has been forthcoming. As late as the fall of 1984, no work had yet been started on salvaging this mysterious wreck. The location of the *Central America* remained a mystery until the summer of 1986. At that time a group of salvors, the Columbus-America Discovery Group, using computer maps and sophisticated sonar search and remotely-operated recovery technologies, discovered a wreck in 7,000 feet of water 200 miles offshore of the North Carolina–South Carolina border that they believed was the *Central America*. In the summer of 1988, using a deep submergence remotely-operated vehicle named Nemo, the group recovered the *Central America*'s bronze bell thus confirming the identity of their find. In August and September of 1989, excavation of the site began with the help of Nemo, and more than three tons of gold were raised to the surface and put on board the research ship, *Artic Explorer*. The value of the gold aboard the *Central America* when it sunk is believed to be worth over $400 million dollars at today's prices.

4. Cape Lookout

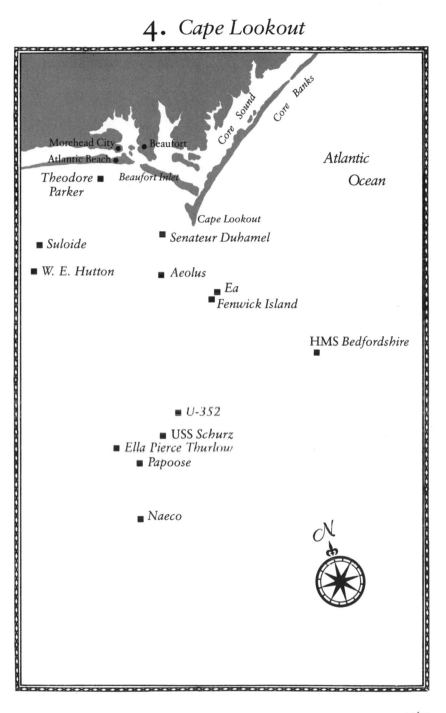

Morehead City • Beaufort
Atlantic Beach •

Theodore ■   *Beaufort Inlet*
Parker

Core Sound

Core Banks

*Atlantic
Ocean*

Cape Lookout
■ *Senateur Duhamel*

■ *Suloide*

■ *W. E. Hutton*   ■ *Aeolus*

■ *Ea*
■ *Fenwick Island*

HMS *Bedfordshire*
■

■ *U-352*

■ USS *Schurz*
■ *Ella Pierce Thurlow*
■ *Papoose*

■ *Naeco*

N

HMS *Bedfordshire*

JANUARY 18, 1942 MARKED the beginning of the U-boat war off the North Carolina coast. On that date the tanker *Allan Jackson* was sunk 60 miles off Cape Hatteras by the *U-66*, which was under the command of Frigattenkapitän Erich Zapp. Two more ships were sunk later the same day by U-boats in the Cape Hatteras area. All together 13 ships would be sunk off the North Carolina coast during January 1942. The toll would rise weekly, with nine sinkings in February, 25 in March, and 20 in April. The U.S. Navy and Coast Guard did not have enough patrol vessels and aircraft to fight the U-boat war, so they took hundreds of private yachts into service and converted them into poorly armed patrol craft. About this time, 40 PBY Catalina Flying Boats built for the British were at Elizabeth City, North Carolina, set to be delivered to England. The American government asked the British if they would release the planes to the U.S., but the request was denied as the British felt they had a greater need for the craft than the Americans. However, they were willing to loan the U.S. 24 antisubmarine trawlers for coastal patrol, and one of those trawlers was the HMS *Bedfordshire*.

Built as an ocean-going fishing vessel in 1935 at Middlesborough, England, the *Bedfordshire* had been taken into the Royal Navy along with hundreds of other trawlers and outfitted for antisubmarine duty off England's shores. Measuring 170 feet in length and displacing 900 tons, the trawler was armed with a 0.303-caliber Lewis machine gun, a four-inch quick-fire deck gun on a platform raised above her bow, depth-charge launchers on her stern, and 80–100 depth charges. Supplied also with ASDIC, an antisubmarine detection device, the *Bedfordshire* was ready for duty off the Atlantic coast of America. Her biggest problem was speed, as she could only make about 12 knots, which was considerably slower than a U-boat. Under the command of Lieutenant R. B. Davis, and with three additional officers and a crew of 33 men aboard, the *Bedfordshire* left England bound for the U.S. in early March 1942. On the way across the North Atlantic in convoy with two other trawlers, the *Bedfordshire* stopped to pick up the survivors of the Norwegian vessel *Tyr*, which had been torpedoed off Nova Scotia by the *U-196*. When the *Bedfordshire* arrived at Halifax on March 11, the rescued were put ashore, and the ship went on to join three other armed trawlers in escorting a damaged armed merchant cruiser, the HMS *Queen of Bermuda*, which was being towed to New York for repairs. On March 31, the convoy reached the Brooklyn Naval Yard, where the *Bedfordshire* was docked for some repairs before continuing south.

4.1   H.M.S. *Bedfordshire*.   Courtesy of L. VanLoan Naisawald.

The British trawler's first assignment off the coast of North Carolina was to relieve the USS *Roper* at the site where the American vessel had sunk the *U-85*. From April 14, 1942, the day after the *U-85* had been sunk, until April 22, the *Bedfordshire* remained at the site to provide security for the U.S. Navy's diving operations. When that duty was completed, the *Bedfordshire* proceeded to Morehead City, which was to be her base of operations during patrols of various areas between Cape Lookout and Norfolk, Virginia.

On May 8, two days after a sister armed trawler, the *Senateur Duhamel*, was struck by the destroyer USS *Semmes* and sank in the Morehead City shipping lanes, the *Bedfordshire* arrived back in port for refueling after a long patrol. Three days later, on Sunday, May 11, the trawler left Morehead City for the final time, with the crew aboard aware that two days earlier the *U-352* had been sunk by the Coast Guard cutter *Icarus* 20 miles offshore of Morehead City. At the time the *Bedfordshire* headed out to sea, another U-boat, the *U-558*, was on station southeast of Cape Lookout, having returned from an unsuccessful hunt off Cape Fear. While no prey was at hand, the skipper of the *U-558*, Kapitänleutnant Gunther Kretch, and the 43 officers and crewmen on board often practiced rapid dives in preparation for the hasty departures that were occasionally required of U-boats operating on the surface. As the U-boat surfaced from a practice dive on the afternoon of May 11, two patrol boats were spotted on the horizon, forcing the *U-558* to dive to the bottom where she remained for nearly six anxious hours as the patrol boats looked for her. On returning to periscope depth, Kretch could still see patrol boats, so he decided to stay submerged for an hour longer, then surface and make a run for it at the U-boat's top speed of 18 knots, far faster than the patrol boats could go. At 8:00 P.M. the U-boat surfaced, pointed its bow south, and ran for it under a moonless, overcast night. About two hours later, Kretch spotted the silhouette of a patrol boat off of his stern. Not having sunk anything in a month, Kretch pressed the attack. His target was the HMS *Bedfordshire* cruising at six knots. At 11:26 P.M., when the *U-558* was within 1,000 yards of the trawler, Kretch fired two torpedoes at his target and missed. There was no indication that the men on board the *Bedfordshire* knew they were under attack. Moving to a new position only 600 yards away, Kretch ordered a third torpedo fired at the trawler, and 36 seconds later, at 11:40 P.M., the torpedo struck amidships, blowing the trawler out of the water and sinking her immediately. All on board were killed, and the *U-558* continued her journey south seeking more prey.

On May 14, two bodies washed ashore some distance from each other on Ocracoke Island and were recovered by the Coast Guard. One was identified as an officer from the *Bedfordshire*, Sub-Lieutenant Thomas Cunningham, and the other as Stanley Craig, Ordinary Telegraphist, also from the trawler. Ironically, a few weeks before the *Bedfordshire* was sunk, Sub-Lieutenant Cunningham provided Aycock Brown, special investigator for the Office of Naval Intelligence, with six British flags for use in the burial of four British seamen whose bodies had been recovered from the surf near Nags Head after their ship, the tanker *San Delfino*, had been torpedoed off Nags Head in April. One of the Union Jacks that Cunningham provided was to grace his own coffin after his identity was confirmed by Aycock Brown. Two other bodies were recovered a week later near Ocracoke Inlet in badly decomposed condition and were believed to have come from the *Bedfordshire*. All four men were interred with military honors on a private piece of land donated by a local family next to their own family cemetery on Ocracoke Island. The British Cemetery is located east of the National Park Service Visitor's Center on a winding road which runs northeast from Silver Lake. Though maintained by local citizens, it is under the jurisdiction of the Commonwealth War Graves Commission in London.   [From L. VanLoan Naisawald, 1972]

The *Bedfordshire* lies approximately 25 miles southeast of Beaufort Inlet on a heading of 155 degrees and two-and-one-half miles due west of Buoy 14. Her scattered remains rest in 105 feet of water southeast of Cape Lookout Shoals and attest to the complete devastation of the small vessel by the single torpedo. Strewn across the sand with little or no relief on the site, the wreckage consists of I-beams, large plates, pipes, pieces of machinery, and twisted portions of bulkheads. This wreck is one of the

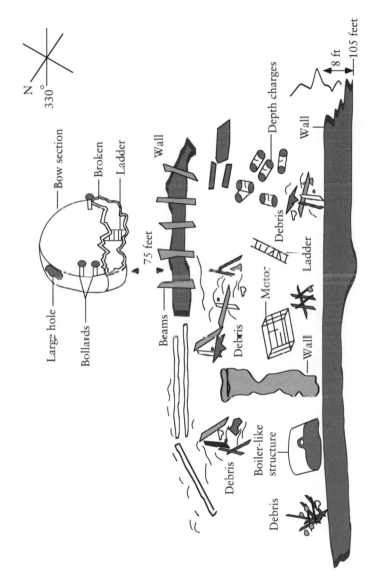

Wreck diagram of the H.M.S. *Bedfordshire*.

smallest offshore sites that divers will encounter off the North Carolina coast. The wreck lies in three separate pieces, two of which are within 75 feet of each other and the third is about two hundred feet away from the other two sections. The largest piece consists of the remains of the amidships portion of the vessel. The bow, stern, and cabin are missing from this piece. The bow end of the largest piece lies on a heading of 330 degrees. At the end of this section closest to where the bow used to be, the port side hull is standing to a height of about two feet. There is a large unidentified boilerlike structure with a smaller cylindrical device attached on top, located just inside the port side wall, that provides the largest relief on the site, about six feet. Aft of this boilerlike structure is a large motor. The port hull runs aft for 40 feet or more and rises at the sternmost end to about five feet above the sand. Throughout the area bounded by the remains of the port hull are piles of debris, hatch covers, bollards, a windlass, broken bulkhead plates, a large ladder, a mast, an athwartships bulkhead, pieces of machinery, and pipes. At the end of the site farthest from the boilerlike structure are six unexploded depth charges. These are gray, cylindrical objects about the size of a thirty-gallon drum lying in a relatively uncluttered part of the wreck field near where the stern broke off. The depth charges are alternately covered by sand and uncovered by currents and winter storms. Occasionally all six may be visible but two, one on top of the other, are always visible. Although thought to be unarmed, these are dangerous devices and should not be touched. On the starboard side across from the depth charges are several hull ribs sticking up out of the sand to a height of about five feet. In this area, several large hull plates have collapsed upon each other providing nooks and crannies for marine life to dwell. A resident nurse shark may be seen on the site.

Approximately 75 feet off the starboard side of the largest section and almost directly across from the hull ribs and perpendicular to it, is the bow. The bow piece is quite small and its tip points away from the largest piece. Bollards may be seen on the port side on the deck of the bow. At the sternmost end of the bow piece is an athwartships bulkhead about two feet high and to which is attached a short ladder and porthole. The port side near the tip of the bow has a gaping hole in it. The relief on the entire bow is less than four feet.

Approximately 200 feet away from the starboard side of the largest piece is a section of the cabin. Heavily damaged in the explosion when the *Bedfordshire* was torpedoed, relief here is only about three feet. This is the smallest section of the *Bedfordshire's* remains that have been located to date. George Purifoy of Morehead City discovered the location of the wreck a few years ago, and he has recovered several artifacts from the remains, including brass portholes and the ship's binnacle. The remains are covered with corals, sponges, and other marine life, and bottom-dwelling fish as well as ocean-ranging fish abound. The water temperature ranges in the upper 70s to low 80s during the summer, and the dive can easily be made without a wet suit. The visibility during the summer is 50–70 feet and occasionally may exceed 100 feet. Current is usually not a problem. Several charter boats make the two-and-a-half-hour trip from Beaufort, Morehead City, Atlantic Beach, and Emerald Isle infrequently during the summer. Because it is such a small site, the *Bedfordshire* is often the second dive after a deeper offshore dive. Because of the depth of the dive and the relatively long boat ride out to the site, this dive is recommended for experienced wreck divers.

Ea

A SMALL FREIGHTER OF SPANISH registry, the *Ea* was built in 1896 by
S. P. Austin and Son of Sunderland, England. The vessel, 235 feet
long and 1,269 tons (758 net tons), was off the coast of North Carolina
near Cape Lookout Shoals in March of 1902, loaded with rosin and
phosphate rock. The wind was blowing moderately out of the southeast,
and the crew was preparing for bad weather off Cape Lookout, even
though there had been clear weather on the voyage since the *Ea's* departure from Fernandina, Florida. On March 15, the sky was gray and overcast as the *Ea* approached the Cape Lookout Shoals through very rough
seas. Around 2:00 P.M., the *Ea* was about 12 miles from the Cape Lookout Lighthouse when she struck the tip of the shoals, having ventured too
close to shore because of the bad weather. Soon the freighter with her
crew of 27 Spaniards on board was being dashed into the shoals and completely surrounded by huge breakers. The *Ea* was not going to finish her
northward trip to New York and Hamburg, Germany, but rather was
being broken apart by the raging sea and would remain forever on the
Cape Lookout Shoals. Lifesavers from the Cape Lookout Station spotted
the ship about 3:00 P.M. and immediately sent a surfboat to the rescue.
The seas were so rough, however, that rescuers were turned back in their
efforts to reach the stricken crewmen. The weather deteriorated to such
an extent that it wasn't until March 18, three days later, that the surfboat
finally was able to reach the *Ea*. By this time the ship had broken in half,
with the bow and the stern underwater. The captain and 26 crewmen
gathered on the bridge to await rescue, and after two trips to the *Ea* the
lifesavers in the surfboat managed to rescue everyone aboard the wrecked
freighter. The rescuers were aided by several vessels that answered the
Ea's distress signal.

The *Ea* broke apart and lies in three sections in 40 feet of water.
Located 18 miles from Beaufort Inlet on a heading of 151 degrees, the
wreckage covers an area around 200 feet long. Because of the close proximity to the shoals, visibility on the wreck is limited to less than 20 feet.
Most often, the visibility is 5–10 feet. Currents are frequently a problem
and contribute in large measure to the poor visibility. During the summer,
the water temperature is usually 75–80 degrees. Except for the bow section, which sticks straight up, there is little relief on the wreck. Most of
the wreckage is scattered across the sand, with the boilers and the steam
engine providing the greatest relief on the sternmost section. There are a
few open holds which are accessible. A dive light, compass, and cross-

wreck line are recommended as the lack of visibility and the lack of recognizable structure in many areas of the wreck make it easy to get lost.

The wreck is frequently visited by dive charter boats from Beaufort and Morehead City and makes a good second dive after a deep offshore dive. The best time to dive the *Ea* is at slack high tide. Interesting artifacts are still being recovered from the wreck site, and small chunks of beautiful, clear, yellow rosin may be broken off larger pieces of the cargo in a hold located near the bow. This is a good dive, in spite of poor visibility, for divers who are new to North Carolina wreck diving and want to experience a shallow inshore dive that requires only a short boat trip to reach.

Fenwick Island

THE MENHADEN FISHING TRAWLER *Fenwick Island*, 230 tons and 125 feet long, foundered and sank in a violent storm at the southern tip of Cape Lookout Shoals on December 7, 1968. The small vessel lies completely intact on her port side in 65 feet of water 14.6 miles southeast of Beaufort Inlet on a heading of 135 degrees, 32.4 miles southeast of Bogue Inlet on a heading of 104 degrees, and a little over one mile southwest of the Knuckle Buoy, which marks the end of the shoals.

Over the years, the wreck has been dived by numerous divers, and several interesting artifacts have been recovered from the site, including the mahogany ship's wheel, an electric toaster, light fixtures, and coffee mugs and saucers. Recently, George Purifoy recovered the ship's telegraph. The wreck has about 30 feet of relief rising to about 35 fsw. A prominent feature is a large metal "S" welded onto the smokestack and offset by small metal pegs. Because of the shallow depth, the wreck is a good dive for inexperienced wreck divers, although visibility is usually less than 15 feet due to the close proximity to the shoals. Under the right conditions, visibility can reach 40–50 feet. Currents are sometimes encountered, particularly in the afternoon when divers go to the site for a shallow second dive after a deeper offshore dive; at that time of day, ingoing or outgoing tides can cause problems. When there is current, the visibility on the wreck is reduced considerably. During the summer, the water temperature at the site ranges in the mid-70s to low 80s. Marine life is plentiful on the wreck, and divers will see groupers, flounders, sheepheads, sea bass, and bait fish, as well as corals, sponges, calcareous growth, and other invertebrates. A cross-wreck line and compass are recommended for navigation at the site, and a bright dive light is useful for illuminating much of the wreck. Dive charter boats from Morehead City and Beaufort frequently visit the *Fenwick Island* during diving season.

Senateur Duhamel

ORIGINALLY A FRENCH OCEAN TRAWLER, the *Senateur Duhamel* was 165 feet long and 739 tons. After the fall of France during WWII, she was confiscated by the British and put to use as an antisubmarine vessel in the Royal Navy to fight the U-boat menace. As an armed trawler, the *Senateur Duhamel* was equipped with four-inch guns and 303-caliber machine guns and carried dozens of depth charges on her stern. When it became clear that supplies bound for Britain and Allied forces in Europe from the United States were also threatened by the U-boat blockade of the East Coast shortly after the U.S. entered the war, several British armed trawlers were sent across the Atlantic for antisubmarine duty. The *Senateur Duhamel* arrived off the coast of North Carolina late in the spring of 1942 and was based at Morehead City. However, she was not to see much action against the German U-boats. On May 6, 1942, as she was approaching Beaufort Inlet in the shipping lanes leading to Morehead City under conditions of limited visibility, she was rammed by the destroyer USS *Semmes* and sank. Because the *Senateur Duhamel* sank in 65 feet of water very close to the main shipping lanes in the vicinity of Morehead City, she was depth-charged and wire-dragged to prevent any obstruction to shipping.

The trawler lies 25.6 miles east of Bogue Inlet on a heading of 91 degrees and 6.7 miles southeast of Beaufort Inlet on a heading of 138 degrees. A buoy designated "8" marks the site. The wreck is extensively

4.2   *Senateur Duhamel.*   Steamship Historical Society Collection, University of Baltimore Library.

broken up, and the remains are scattered across the bottom, with the ship's two boilers and her engine providing the greatest relief on the site. The *Senateur Duhamel* was carrying a considerable amount of munitions when she went down, and divers over the years have brought up quantities of small-caliber ammunition as well as large shell casings. The wreck is dived nearly every weekend during the diving season, and hundreds of divers have scoured her remains for artifacts. In the early 1970s her intact binnacle and compass were recovered, and through the succeeding years many brass artifacts have been retrieved as well—including portholes, the propeller, valves, fittings, light fixtures, and the like. The wreckage of the trawler lies basically at sand level with the exception of the boilers which rise to about 40 fsw, the engine which rises to about 50 fsw, the small remains of her bow which rise about eight feet off the bottom, and other bits and pieces which have two to three feet of relief.

The wreck site lies in more or less a straight line, with the stern on a heading of approximately 135 degrees and the bow at 315 degrees. Proceeding from the stern forward, there are large plates in the sand and a shaft tunnel or conduit on the starboard side. Reaching the engine, which is fairly large, divers will see the propeller drive shaft sticking out one end of it, a ladder or walkway lying in the sand, and the two large boilers directly ahead. Off to the right forward end of the starboard boiler lie several large concrete slabs which were used to protect the ship's ammunition magazine. Some of the ship's hull ribs lie exposed on the starboard side directly opposite the boilers. Moving around the boilers and proceeding further forward, one will see the amidships portion of the vessel where there are several pipes, another large conduit, and several battery boxes and plates scattered about the bottom. A large area of concrete slabs, lying as though they were dominoes which had fallen over, can be found to the starboard side and forward of the amidships area. Still fur-

4.3   *Senateur Duhamel.* Portion of condenser.

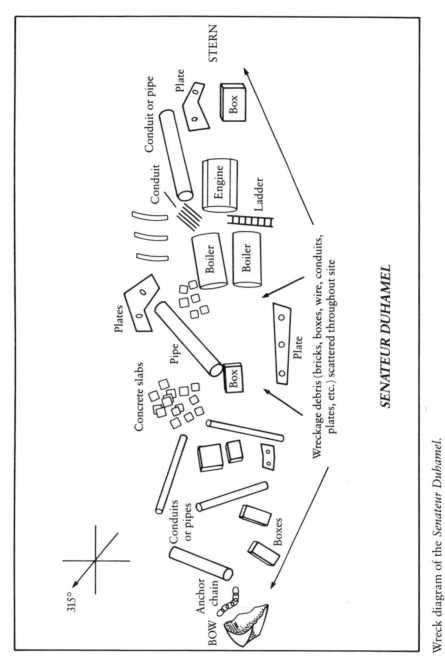

Wreck diagram of the *Senateur Duhamel.*

ther forward are located more boxes, pipes, conduits, plates, twisted metal, debris, and a large piece of pipe, which is a portion of the mast lying across the bow section with its tip near the starboard edge of the wreck site. As one then approaches the bow, the wreck site narrows considerably and there are bricks, pipes, wires, boxes, and the anchor chain scattered about. The bow looms directly ahead and is the tallest object visible forward of the boilers. Though most of the desirable artifacts have already been removed from this oft-dived wreck, each year winter storms uncover new portions of it and divers can find portholes and other artifacts each season.

The visibility is usually less than 10–15 feet because of the proximity to shore, but occasionally it may be 40 feet or more. Currents are frequently encountered on the site because it lies near Beaufort Inlet where it is subject to strong tide fluctuations, especially in the afternoon when it is dived a lot as a shallow second dive after a deeper offshore dive. When the tide is running, the visibility drops considerably. Although the water temperature reaches the mid-70s during the summer, a wet suit is recommended to prevent cuts and scrapes during currents or surges. The wreck remains are covered with coral and other calcareous growth, but sponges, sea urchins, sea anemones, flounders, sheepheads, and other marine life also abound. In addition, the wreckage is covered with silt material because sediment stirred up by the semi-diurnal tide fluctuations settles out over everything. The frequent visits of divers each week of the dive season have had a very negative environmental impact. The wreck site has become virtually a garbage pile littered with beer and soft drink cans and the like deposited by divers during their surface interval sit time. Some recent attempts to clean up the site and educate divers about the problem may alleviate the situation. A compass and cross-wreck line are recommended for navigating the site, and a bright dive light is useful for illuminating the dark recesses of the wreck.

Dive charter boats from Beaufort and Morehead City regularly take divers to the *Senateur Duhamel*, and because of its proximity to shore and the presence of the "8" buoy, many small private boats travel to the wreck as well. On any pretty weekend afternoon as many as a dozen boats may be anchored on the wreck. In spite of the poor visibility and the chance of currents, the wreck is a good one for inexperienced divers, especially when accompanied by an experienced guide, and scuba classes frequently use the site for their checkout dives. The *Senateur Duhamel* can often be dived when weather prevents diving further offshore.

Aeolus

L IFE IS A TRANSITION of events and things. So it is with ocean-going ships. In the beginning, a water-borne vessel is created for one purpose, later modified for another, and in the end serves a different one. The passing of one structure marks the beginning of another. The life of the *Aeolus* was no different. Originally named *Turandot*, construction of the attack cargo vessel began at the end of March 1945, by the Walsh-Kaiser Company of Providence, Rhode Island, under a Maritime Commission contract. Designed as a troop transport vessel to bring American GI's home from the Pacific at the end of World War II, the 426-foot-long, 4,087-ton ship was launched on May 20, 1945, and commissioned on June 18, 1945. Within a month, the *Turandot* was on her way to the Canal Zone, loaded with passengers and cargo, for what was to be the first of many trips through the Panama Canal. Arriving on the Pacific side of the Canal, the ship was escorted west to the Hawaiian Islands by the American submarine, U.S.S. *Barbero*. Arriving at Pearl Harbor in mid-August, her stay in Oahu was a short one. The exigencies of a war effort that was winding down in the Pacific demanded that the troop transport continue further west to New Hebrides, the Marshall Islands, Wake Island, and back to Eniwetok. In mid-October, the *Turandot* departed Eniwetok with more than 600 American troops who had survived the Pacific warfare and were headed home to the States. Arriving in California after a two-week voyage, the ship barely had time to make necessary repairs before being sent out to the Marianas to pick up another one thousand American troops. Arriving back in California in mid-December with the newly liberated troops, the *Turandot* spent the rest of the year being repaired and outfitted. With the war in the Pacific now over, the demand for the services of an attack cargo ship dwindled. Early in 1946, the *Turandot* returned to Hampton Roads, Virginia, where she was decommissioned in March of that year. She was struck from the navy list one year later and would spend the next seven years in mothballs as part of the Reserve Fleet.

In the fall of 1954, the *Turandot* was called back into service by the navy and converted into a cable-laying ship at Baltimore, Maryland. In May of 1955, the ship was renamed *Aeolus*, after the Greek god of the winds, and recommissioned into the navy. And god of the winds she became. For eight months after her commission, she served in the Atlantic laying cable and performing surveys in the West Indies, the Bahamas, and off Charleston, South Carolina. Following this tour, the *Aeolus* was

4.4   *Aeolus*. Photograph courtesy of Eddie Hill.

transferred to San Francisco where she performed similar duties off the West Coast until 1986. Age and the sea had taken their toll of the *Aeolus*, having logged 249,114 nautical miles in her 42-year career. The old ship was acquired by the Maritime Administration and, again, dockbound as part of the James River Reserve Fleet in Virginia.

In 1987, ownership of the *Aeolus* was transferred to the state of North Carolina for use as an artificial reef. Taken to Wilmington, North Carolina, the *Aeolus* began the long and expensive process to prepare her for her final duty on the ocean bottom. After six months of hard work and an expenditure of nearly one hundred thousand dollars for cleaning and scouring the ship's fuel tanks, stripping off all of her doors, and removing small, loose objects throughout the ship, the *Aeolus* was ready for tow to her final resting place 22 miles south of Beaufort Inlet off Morehead City, North Carolina. Tens of thousands of dollars of nautical equipment was left on board the ship because it was not cost effective to remove them. Besides, it meant divers would have treasures to recover from the vessel once it settled to the bottom. On July 29, 1988, after several weeks of delays, the *Aeolus* was towed by the Wilmington towing tug, *WalRow*, to its appointed resting place eight miles from the site of the World War II sinking of the German U-boat, *U-352*, a popular North Carolina wreck dive. At the site, 38 pounds of high explosive was attached to the inside of her hull about fifteen feet below the waterline. Twenty minutes later, the charges blew four, two-foot holes in her hull and the mighty ship began to sink. Unfortunately, two of the charges on the port side became dislodged by the water in her hold before detonation leaving only the starboard charges to do their necessary work. The result was an immediate list to starboard. The *Aeolus* took about 20 minutes to sink to the bottom 105 feet beneath the surface where she came to rest on her starboard side. Divers and fishermen have been visiting the site continuously since its sinking. The ship is huge on the bottom. On weekends, a dozen dive boats may be seen anchored on the site. The *Aeolus* has been steadily settling in the sand and the depth to the hull is now 50 fsw. The visibility on the site is in excess of 100 feet during the dive season. Marine life has already begun to grow on the ship's surfaces. Divers may be tempted to enter the ship to investigate its many rooms and passageways but such endeavors should be undertaken with extreme caution as there is much debris inside which could present serious problems. There is more than enough ship to see from the outside and its relatively shallow depth makes a good introduction to North Carolina wreck diving.

Transition from troop ship to cable ship to artificial reef was part of this ship's life. Some ships are torched into history at the end of their maritime lives, some sink ignominiously into water too deep to be seen by anyone again, while others sink and live again. Forty-three years ago, the ocean carried the *Aeolus* home along with the lives of many soldiers who had survived the battlefields of the Pacific. Today, their descendants and others may visit the *Aeolus* in its new home on the bottom of the ocean where it is once again bringing forth new life.

Dive charter operators from Beaufort, Morehead City, Atlantic Beach, Emerald Isle, Swansboro, and Jacksonville run trips to the *Aeolus*. The loran C coordinates are 27081.0, 39490.0.

U-352

A UNIQUE SHIPWRECK for at least two reasons, the *U-352* was the first German U-boat to be sunk by the U.S. Coast Guard in World War II. The location of its demise was to play a large role in the later history of the submarine.

By virtue of its relatively shallow depth and the presence of the warm, clear tropical waters of the Gulf Stream bathing it, the *U-352* is the most popular wreck off of the North Carolina coast. The preserved remains of a German war-machine killed in the battle for the Atlantic, lying where it fell 40-odd years ago, has attracted thousands of divers over the past decade. A stark reminder of the futility of war as well as of the proximity of combat in WWII to the American coast, the submarine has been the center of controversy several times since its location was discovered in the mid-1970s.

The desecration of a German war memorial and the sub's live torpedoes focused the attention of the nation on the *U-352* in recent years. These controversies have been since settled, but much widespread interest has been generated about this vessel. The commander of the *U-352*, Kaptiänleutnant Hellmut Rathke, who was captured after the sinking, now lives in West Germany; many of his crewman on board the U-boat also survived the war and now live in the United States and West Germany. Through these men and the official record, the history of the *U-352* in the battle for the Atlantic has been documented in detail. Because of its prominence among North Carolina shipwrecks and its extreme popularity, the complete story of this submarine's final battle is presented in its entirety to the reader.

The Sinking of the U-352

[The account of the U-352 presented here was written by Homer Hickam, Jr., and first appeared under the title "Day of Anger, Day of Pride" in the January 1983 issue of American History Illustrated. It is reprinted by permission of the author.]

The German Naval High Command acted quickly after Pearl Harbor. Admiral Karl Doenitz, commander of the U-boat fleet, immediately dispatched five U-boats to destroy shipping along the American coast as part of his long-planned Operation *Paukenschlag* ("the roll of drums"). The first U-boat commanders who arrived were startled at what they found. In Europe, war had become routine. Navigational lights, lighthouses, even house lamps on shore had been extinguished for years. Entire cities were blacked out. Ships did not use radios except in emergencies. But in America, city lights, buoy lights, even ship running lights lit up the sky. Freighters and tankers wallowed alone down familiar trade routes, their radios filled with idle chatter about every subject, including destinations and cargoes. Even American naval forces routinely radioed their positions and sailing dates.

The Germans, like wolves, pounced on the herd of sheep they found. Their tactical doctrine was to rest on the bottom during the day and rise at night to catch their prey silhouetted against the bright lights of shore. In bloody testimonial to the effectiveness of this doctrine, on a single night, March 18, 1942, five ships went down off Cape Hatteras.

All up and down the East Coast, pieces of ships and bodies of American merchant sailors drifted in on every tide. The U-boat crews referred to the period as their "second happy time," the first being their brief flurry of success against the British at the beginning of the war. More accurately, the Royal Navy caustically referred to the latest U-boat campaign as the "American Shooting Gallery" and dispatched several corvettes across the Atlantic to help.

Against this backdrop of destruction, the stage was set for one of the most dramatic encounters of the war, the battle between the U-boat 352 and the U.S. Coast Guard cutter *Icarus*. When they met, no help came to either of them. The battle was a fight to the finish. Today, the loser sits on a sandy bottom, 115 feet deep, 20 miles off Morehead City, North Carolina. Scuba divers visit it occasionally and are gradually stripping the hulk. Very few of the divers know its history, but the wreck they plunder was once a gallant ship, as was the ship that put it down.

On the morning of April 4, 1942, Kapitänleutnant Hellmut Rathke signaled his crew to cast off all lines. They obediently sprang to their stations, and the *U-352* edged out into the St. Nazaire harbor. No band disturbed the misty quiet of the French port city. Rathke had not wanted one. The less attention given his departure the better. All too many of his comrades in the U-boat force were dead, victims of British aircraft and destroyers who always seemed to know when a U-boat took to sea.

Rathke was glad to get away from the city. The entire German occupation force in St. Nazaire was edgy. Only a week before a British commando raid had thrown the port into confusion and much of the city's carefree charm had disappeared. Rathke had orders to proceed to America, take up a position off the North Carolina coast, and disrupt as much shipping as possible. He was pleased with the assignment and considered it a compliment to him and his crew.

An East Prussian by birth, Hellmut Rathke was 32 years old and considered a rising star in the U-boat arm of the German navy. Courteous

4.5   U-352.   Courtesy of WZ-Bilddienst, Wilhelmshaven, West Germany.

4.6   Kapitänleutnant Hellmut Rathke standing on the conning tower
of the U-352 conducting christening ceremonies in August 1941.

4.7   Kapitänleutnant Hellmut Rathke coming aboard the U-352
during christening ceremonies in August 1941. Illus. 4.6 and
4.7 courtesy of Korvettenkapitän Hellmut Rathke, Ret.

and cultivated, he was nonetheless a strict disciplinarian. Before this mission, the U-352's second, he had refused leave to one of his crew who had become drunk and "adrift" in the fleshpots of St. Nazaire. U-boat crews considered this leave just before a mission their right, but Rathke would not bend. Despite his toughness, the crew liked their commander. They felt safe with him because he had brought them back alive from their first war cruise.

As the U-352 cleared the small St. Nazaire lock, Rathke's thoughts focused on his boat and that first war cruise. He had followed his *Unterseeboot 352* from the moment its keel was laid. It was a powerful Type VII−C submarine, a 750-ton, 220-foot-long craft armed with an 88-millimeter gun positioned at the head of the conning tower and with two 20-millimeter anti-aircraft guns mounted on the bridge. Below, there were four torpedo tubes in the bow and one in the stern. For all its firepower, however, the U-352 had never sunk a ship. On the first war cruise Rathke had taken his boat to sea for five weeks, nearing Iceland at one point. Twice he had attacked, once boldly sending a spread of four torpedoes at a British destroyer. All of his torpedoes either missed their target or were duds. Repeatedly, corvettes and aircraft attacked the U-352, some of them badly shaking up both the boat and the crew. Whenever Rathke attacked in return, he only succeeded in disclosing his position. He did not know whether the torpedoes he had been issued were from a defective lot, or whether all German torpedoes were defective. Whatever the truth, he no longer trusted the fourteen "fish" his U-boat carried.

Rathke looked over the side at a blotch of black paint on the conning tower. It covered the spot where the Flensburg coat of arms had once been displayed. The German coastal city had adopted his U-boat, and Rathke's wife and small daughter lived there at the time. He wondered when and if he would see them again. After reaching the open sea safely, the commander ordered "*langsame Fahrt*," slow speed, for the trip across the Atlantic. He would try to conserve as much fuel as possible on the crossing. Rathke knew he would need every drop he could get once the U-352 went into action against the Americans.

Gunner's Mate 2d Class John Bruce liked his assignment aboard the USGC cutter *Icarus*. It was a relatively small craft, only 165 feet long with a 25-foot, three-inch beam displacing 334 tons. This produced a necessary closeness and cooperative spirit among the seventy-five men aboard. Although it was early in the war, the *Icarus* had already attacked submarines off the Ambrose Channel and Atlantic City. Once, pieces of decking and patches of oil rose to the surface after a depth charge attack, and the *Icarus* crew was sure it had cornered the U-boat. The wily Germans, however, slipped away before the *Icarus* could line up for another attack.

The *Icarus's* effectiveness was extremely limited by its obsolete sound detection gear. This created an undercurrent of frustration among the crew. Too often the *Icarus* attacked schools of fish or rocks or even the wrecks of U-boat victims. Sometimes it seemed as they were fighting ghosts.

Though also frustrated by its lack of success, 24-year-old Bruce believed the *Icarus* would eventually do well. Toward that end, he kept the guns clean and well oiled on the quarterdeck, and it was also his job to keep everything in the way of ordnance functioning on the stern. Aft of the midship, the *Icarus* was armed with depth charge racks, a World War I vintage Y-gun, and two .50 Browning water-cooled machine guns mounted port and starboard a few points toward the beam. The forward armament consisted of two more .50 guns and a three-inch, .23 deck gun mounted halfway from the bridge to the bow. On the flying bridge were two .30 Lewis machine guns, and locked up in the armory were two .45 pistols, two Thompson submachine guns, a number of .30 Springfields, and several hand grenades. The *Icarus* carried no other armament. Moreover, because of ammunition restrictions, the gun crews had had no target practice for over a year. The ship's commander, Lieutenant Maurice D. Jester, knew the men needed practice but had not as yet allowed it.

Lieutenant Jester was something of an enigma to the young crew under his command. The native of Chincoteague, Virginia, had entered the Coast Guard as a surfman in 1917 and worked his way up the ranks until he was commissioned in 1941. By the time he took command of the *Icarus* he was 52 years old. The crew respected his knowledge of the sea but thought him somewhat aloof. His only contact with them seemed to be

4.8 U.S.C.G. *Icarus.* Courtesy of the National Archives.

when they served him coffee or when he meted out punishment for minor infractions.

In late April 1942, the *Icarus* received startling orders. Jester was to take his ship and proceed to Key West, Florida, where further orders would be provided. The *Icarus* had been built in Bath, Maine, in 1932 and since then had patrolled no farther south than Norfolk, Virginia. Her permanent station was the town of Stapleton, Staten Island, New York, and her crew had established themselves in the community. Reluctantly, they prepared the *Icarus* for the trip. All leaves and passes were cancelled, and early on May 8 the *Icarus* pulled away from its berth. As it cleared the harbor, a passing tug signaled G-O-O-D-L-U-C-K. After thinking for a moment, the *Icarus* signalman flashed back T-H-A-N-K-S-W-E-W-I-L-L-D-O-O-K.

The *U-352* eased into American waters on the morning of May 2, 1942. Kapitänleutnant Rathke had made the four-week crossing as productive as possible. The average crewman on board his U-boat was 22 years old and 10 of them were only 19. Few among them were professional seamen, and Rathke knew they could use all the training he could give them. He simulated attacks both on the surface and underwater, periodically ordering crash dives, timing how long it took to submerge until he was satisfied with the results. He also held evacuation drills. At the order, his men pulled on their life-jackets and escape lungs and lined up to practice their escape. Only one man could pass through the control room and conning tower hatches at a time, making speed and order critical.

To soften the training, Rathke allowed short sunbathing periods for three or four men at a time while they were in mid-ocean and out of aircraft range. As the U-boat neared the United States, Rathke even permitted the radiomen to tune in American jazz programs. By the time the *U-352* took up its station, Rathke was satisfied with the training, spirit, and morale of his crew. He began to look for targets, but soon discovered that he was the hunted as well as the hunter. On the first day, several patrol planes harassed him into crash diving.

Rathke did not find a ship to attack until May 5. His second-in-command, Leutnant Joseph Ernst, identified it as a refrigerator ship. Rathke did not wait for darkness. He lined up and fired two torpedoes and then watched expectantly through his periscope. Nothing happened. Frustrated, he surfaced so that he could speed ahead for another attempt. Almost immediately one of the tower watchmen sang out. Rathke whirled and looked where the watch was pointing. Four miles away at 600 feet a two-engined plane was barreling in on a direct course for the *U-352*.

Rathke pushed the watch in ahead of him and then jumped through the hatch to the deck seven feet below. The U-boat began its crash dive.

Seconds that seemed as long as minutes ticked by. Finally, Ernst announced that the U-boat was submerged. Rathke expected to be bombed, but when no explosion came after an hour, he surfaced, looked around, and saw that the refrigerator ship was gone.

Three more times he attacked freighters with no hits. On May 7, an airplane coming out of the sun almost caught him. His ship was barely submerged when the bombs struck, doing no damage but leaving Rathke pessimistic about the entire mission. He decided to try to change his luck.

Moving out from the twenty-meter line, Rathke sailed the U-352 into slightly deeper water. He waited there for two days without seeing anything. Finally, late on the afternoon of May 9, he watched a single mast rise above the horizon. Rathke ordered a crash dive and maneuvered toward the sighting. He ordered the attack periscope up, but wasted no time on identification. He meant to sink that ship. He ordered numbers one and two torpedo tubes flooded and fired in quick succession. They were loaded with electric torpedoes of the latest design. The U 352 shuddered and then began to rise with a sudden buoyancy caused by the departure of the torpedoes. Leutnant Ernst adjusted the submarine's trim, but the adjustment was too severe, and Rathke lost sight of his target as the periscope dipped under the sea. He thought that just as well and ordered his boat down. Suddenly the U-boat shook from the recoil of a distant explosion. Rathke ordered the boat brought up to periscope depth so he could observe the target. He believed it to be a small freighter. It was, however, the U.S. Coast Guard cutter *Icarus*.

The *Icarus*'s crew felt very much alone. Once they had left their home district, they felt like intruders wherever they sailed. When Ensign Charles Pool, the communications officer, sent a message to the commandant of the Sixth Naval District advising him of the *Icarus*'s entry into the area, the response had been a cold, noncommital "Received." This was not their first snub of the day. Earlier, off the Virginia coast, a convoy of three freighters and an escorting destroyer going north sailed into view. The officer of the bridge had the *Icarus* swing closer to see if anyone recognized the ships. Instantly the destroyer charged the small cutter, swerved in front of it, and angrily blinked a warning to stay away. The *Icarus* plowed doggedly along, running across the next convoy just south of Wimble Shoals. This time the crew had learned its lesson and kept its distance.

Gunner's Mate John Bruce spent the day doing a number of small sailor's chores. He had checked the guns under this control and was satisfied with their readiness. He wanted to test them one time, but no order for target practice had come. The day was warm and overcast, the sea almost flat, and many of the men had spent some time on deck speculating on their duty in Key West and on how to win the war. When the air cooled late in the afternoon many of the crew, including Bruce, drifted off to their quarters. Soon the *Icarus* was quiet except for the constant muffled roar of her two Winton diesel engines.

At 4:15 P.M. Lieutenant Edward D. Howard, the executive officer, had the bridge. Jester had retired to his quarters. Howard kept the course steady at a speed of 14 knots. Below, in the sound room, soundman William L. Rabich listened intently into his earphones. Through the normal clutter he heard something unusual. The only word he could think of to describe the sound was "mushy." He called crewman Santiago Quinones to listen in. Quinones immediately called Howard and told him that he believed there was a submarine nearby, probably no more than a hundred yards away.

Howard considered calling general quarters but decided to summon Jester to the bridge instead. He ordered Quinones to keep listening. Another soundman, Arthur Laskowski, joined Rabich and Quinones. They could not understand why the *Icarus* did not attack. The contact began to fade. Quinones now placed the object at 2,000 yards off the port bow. At 4:25 the contact suddenly improved. Still the *Icarus* plowed ahead. Howard wanted to be absolutely sure of his target. He did not want to waste precious depth charges on any more rocks or wrecks.

At 4:29, almost 10 minutes after Rabich had made his first contact, Jester was still not on the bridge.

Quinones was now convinced that the contact was a submarine and that it was maneuvering parallel to the *Icarus*, probably to line up for an attack. Just as he picked up the phone to call the bridge, a tremendous explosion rocked the ship. Quinones reeled against the shock. What he feared had already occurred.

Below, John Bruce was relaxing in his bunk when the *Icarus* suddenly shook as if it had grounded. Deck plates were jarred and lights flickered. Bruce was out of his bed and running to the deck even before general quarters was called. Once there, he saw a huge swirl of mud and water 200 yards off the port quarter.

Lieutenant Howard kept the bridge calm while he analyzed the situation. He suspected that a torpedo or mine had missed his ship but struck the sea bottom and exploded. From the information Quinones gave to him, he placed the U-boat still off the port beam and reported this to Jester as the commanding officer puffed onto the bridge. Jester immediately ordered the *Icarus* hard aport and called down to Warrant Machinist Henry Cookson to stand by with his mechanics in the engine room. He knew they were about to be shaken up badly by the explosions of the *Icarus*'s own depth charges in the shallow water. Every man braced himself. The *Icarus* was on the attack.

When the *U-352*'s periscope rose above the water's surface, Hellmut Rathke expected to see a burning freighter. Instead he saw a boiling brown sea and a fast, armed cutter maneuvering in front of him. Certain that his periscope had been seen, Rathke ordered an order to dive. He realized one of his torpedoes had struck the ocean floor and exploded. His initial response was to move behind the cutter to try to hide in its wake. Rathke began to do this and then remembered the muddy turmoil he had seen in his periscope. What better place to hide?

The *U-352* sank quickly to the bottom where its nose pushed gently into the soft mud churned up by the torpedo. Rathke planned to wait for one pass from the cutter and then either surface to periscope depth for another salvo of torpedoes or, if he could maneuver into position, rise all the way and attack with his 88-millimeter deck gun. Either way he believed he could destroy his adversary.

It was now 4:30. Only two minutes had elapsed since the torpedo exploded, but the *Icarus* had already completed its turn with all hands at battle stations. Lieutenant Jester set his ship on the course his soundmen and Lieutenant Howard estimated the submarine was following and lined the bow directly over the still churning explosion. At 180 yards the soundmen lost contact. Jester calculated what he thought to be a proper interval and ordered a diamond pattern of five depth charges laid. First the crew dropped one charge by the rack, followed by two from the Y-gun, then one from the rack, and later, another from the rack. The depth charges splashed into the muddy water of the torpedo swirl. Their explosive mechanisms were set for 100 feet. Jester ordered the *Icarus* into another sharp turn.

The crew of the *U-352* heard the *Icarus* and cringed as the cutter roared directly overhead. Rathke listened intently, trying to gauge his attacker's course so he could surface and finish it off quickly. Outside, the first depth charge from the *Icarus* dropped toward the submarine's deck gun. Two other charges drifted down next to the conning tower. Another plummeted directly for the U-boat's engine room, while the last charge passed about fifty feet behind the stern.

The *Icarus* trembled under the impact of its own explosives. Fuses blew and deck plates heaved. The "black gang" in the engine room held on to anything they could grab and then raced to the diesels to check for damage.

On board the *U-352*, every gauge in the control room and in the tower shattered and sharp glass flew through the air. Leutnant Ernst was flung headfirst into a control panel, crushing his skull. Lights flickered through-out the U-boat and then died. Rathke gradually forced himself out of a red haze. He dragged himself up by hanging onto the attack periscope, now bent and ruined. The tower floor was slick with Ernst's blood. The emergency lights burned dimly.

Rathke called for a damage report from the engine room. Could he still maneuver? The reply was negative. Both electric motors had been knocked off their mounts, although one machine was operating intermittently. Rathke reviewed his situation. His second-in-command was dead, he had lost most of his instruments, and he could not maneuver. Nevertheless, he believed there was a chance to get away. Perhaps the American ship did not know it had hit his U-boat. Perhaps if he played dead, stayed right where he was, he might yet get his boat through. What he did not know, what he could not tell without his instruments, was that the U-352 was already on the move. Rathke's boat had lost the heavy deck gun plus a good portion of the sheet metal surrounding the tower, altering the sub-marine's buoyancy. The U-352 drifted, bow up, stern slightly dragging, toward the west.

Aboard the *Icarus* the three soundmen knew by the strong signal they were getting from the U-boat that it was moving. They relayed the infor-mation to the bridge. Jester began to turn the *Icarus* around, heading to-ward the contact. He made several passes trying to line up exactly. At 4:45 he ordered a second attack with the depth charges to be thrown out at his command.

The U-352 was a dead boat. Rathke ordered silence and every man sat or stood absolutely still. The only sound to be heard was their breathing and a constant dripping from one of the torpedo tubes. When the drip-ping became a spurt, one of the torpedomen called out. Rathke sent a runner back to stop the talking. Obermaschinist Grandke came forward from the engine room requesting permission to work on the one electric motor not completely destroyed. Rathke turned Grandke down, putting his finger to his lips. He could still hear the American ship patrolling above, but no depth charges had fallen for fifteen minutes. The Germans might still escape as long as they could remain undetected. The *Icarus*'s engine noises faded and then grew ominously strong.

The *Icarus* had been cruising in patterns, question marks on the sea, but now it lined up for its second attack. Jester gave the command and a "V" pattern, one charge from the rack and two from the Y-gun, splashed into the water. The rack charge fell toward the submarine's bow, while the Y-gun explosives fell to one side.

The charges slammed into the U-352. It keeled over on its port side and then settled to the bottom, one of its buoyancy tanks ruptured.

Rathke called for a damage report. His pressure hull had held, but he was not sure it could withstand another such attack. The *Icarus*, already on its way back for another round, quickly provided the answer. This time a single depth charge was dropped on the spot where the bubbles rose from the split buoyancy tank. The pressure hull held, but the crew reported numerous leaks in the buoyancy control system.

At 5:08 the *Icarus* dropped another charge on the bubbles. This one missed but came close enough to force a decision on Rathke. He ordered his men into their life-vests and escape lungs. Finally out of options, Rathke ordered all remaining tanks blown and his gun crews to stand by. The *U-352* was coming up.

The *Icarus* was coming around for yet another pass. The gun crews on the cutter had been at their battle stations for 39 minutes with a spectacular view, but they had little to do. Once during the attack a patrol plane flew in from the southwest over the port bow, waggling its wings and exchanging recognition signals with the *Icarus*. The men at their guns waved, but it did not stop or seem to realize a battle was going on. The gun crews settled back, not expecting to go into action until the submarine attempted to slip away.

On the bridge, Lieutenant Howard spotted signs of the *U-352* first. A thousand yards to starboard a huge bubble burst up from the sea, leaving a wake of spreading white foam. Howard thought he could see a dark shape underneath and called it to Jester's attention just as the submarine's bow broke the surface. It was 5:09 P.M. The bow, at a 45 degree angle, pushed farther out of the water until the conning tower became visible. The submarine immediately settled with all of the deck awash except for about eight feet of the bow. No order came to the gunners, but the men on the starboard side and the flying bridge opened fire. Jester sent word to the gunners to keep firing. He believed if the Germans reached their deck gun, the *Icarus* could be blown out of the water with one shot. There is no evidence that anyone on board the *Icarus* realized the U-boat's deck gun had been blown off during the first attack. One crewman later reported seeing the gun, but he was alone in his observation.

Rathke threw open the conning tower hatch and saw a horrifying sight. The tower bridge was a jumble of twisted steel and grotesquely bent equipment. Moreover, his U-boat was barely afloat, the calm water level only four inches below the rim of the hatch. He threw his secret codes out of the hatch and gave the order to abandon ship. The quartermaster ran from the control room to the stern yelling, "All men out!" As the men of the *U-352* lined up, Obermaschinist Grandke, unaware of the situation's hopelessness, roared, "You crazy dogs! We can still run for it on our diesels!"

The first few German crewmen who crawled out on the conning tower deck were raked by the *Icarus*'s machine guns and fell, screaming. Rathke kept the men going. He believed his attackers would soon stop firing after they saw he was surrendering. Instead the *Icarus* was lining up to put its three-inch gun into action. Jester meant to have this submarine.

Charles E. Mueller was manning the three-inch gun. He had not had much in the way of practice, but he was an excellent shot. The first shell hit in front of the U-boat's tower and ricocheted through it. The second shell landed behind the tower. The third hit it dead center.

Maschinemaat Gerhard Reussel was climbing out of the *U-352* tower hatch just as the shell struck. He was thrown high in the air and then fell into the sea, blood spurting from his severed leg. Rathke ordered the last of his men out, but the engineering officer, Oberleutnant Heinz Tretz, refused, disappearing back into the boat to ensure scuttling was complete. Amidst a hail of three-inch shells and machine gun fire, Rathke jumped.

There was chaos aboard the *Icarus*. The three-inch gun was punching out shells as fast as it could be loaded, and every gun was blazing. One pointer on a .50 gun became so anxious he bent the restraining frame with brute force and shot up his own bulkhead. John Bruce was in the middle of the frenzy, jumping from gun to gun, clearing jams and solving problems. When one of the .30 guns on the flying bridge jammed, they called for him. By the time he was able to make his way there, the gunner had field stripped the gun completely and parts were strewn all over the deck. Bruce cursed the man and then began gathering up the parts. At least he had a good view from the flying bridge. He could see tracers soaring out at the U-boat, hitting the tower and hull and ricocheting off into space. He was impressed at the continued orderliness of the submarine's evacuation in the face of such intense fire.

The men of the *U-352* swam away from their boat. Rathke looked for Reussel and found him in a sea of blood. Pulling off his belt, he tried to tie a tourniquet around the stump of the young man's leg, but there was little left to keep the belt from slipping off. Rathke looked up and saw his U-boat suddenly sink. He called to his men to have courage, but still the firing continued from the *Icarus*. Helplessly, he watched them being shot to death in the water. Rathke screamed at the Americans to stop, and his men picked up the cry for mercy. Rathke was certain he heard the Americans reply through a megaphone, "Damn Germans. Go to Hell!"

John Bruce saw the U-boat go down. From his station aft he saw the gunners still firing. "For God's sake!" he yelled. "Don't shoot them in the water!" The gunners on the stern stopped, but the forward gunners kept shooting. One of the aft crewmen derided Bruce. "That could have been us in the water," Bruce replied. Everyone understood what he meant. Three minutes after the *U-352* went down, a runner from the bridge went to each gun ordering a cease fire. The time was 5:17. The soundmen were still getting contacts from the U-boat, so Jester ordered one last attack. Running over the bubbles, one depth charge was dropped. No more sounds came from below. Jester, concerned that other U-boats might be in the area, ordered the *Icarus* on a course away from the scene.

Rathke watched incredulously as the *Icarus* began to steam away. Apparently the Americans intended to let them drown. Actually Jester was unsure of his authority to do anything other than sink submarines. He had to ask permission to rescue survivors. Ensign Pool began a series of frustrating radio calls. First he called Norfolk with the message, "Have sunk submarine. 30–40 men in the water. Shall *Icarus* pick up any of the men?" There was no reply.

Next he tried Charleston with the same message. The message was received but again there was no answer. Pool waited ten minutes and sent, "Have you any message for us?" A minute later a coded message came back. After decoding, it read, "No."

Eight minutes later, at 5:40 P.M., Pool tried the commandant of the Sixth Naval District with the message, "Shall *Icarus* pick up prisoners?" No answer. He desperately tried again. The *Icarus* was drawing farther and farther away from the U-boat crew. "32 German submarine men in the water," he radioed. "Shall we pick them up?" Finally, at 5:49 a message came back. "Pick up survivors. Bring to Charleston." Pool snatched the message and rushed it to the bridge. Jester immediately ordered the *Icarus* around, flank speed.

Rathke saw the *Icarus* returning. He called to his men to stay together and to help support the wounded. He had held Reussel in his arms the entire time he was in the water. The crewman was very weak but still alive. Rathke spoke to the men around him. "Remember your duty," he counseled. "Do not tell the enemy anything."

The *Icarus* came closer. Using his limited English, Rathke asked that his wounded be taken aboard first. This was done. John Bruce helped position a 55-gallon drum beside the gangway on which the prisoners deposited their belongings as they came aboard. Rathke was the last man out of the water. Bruce and crewman John Freda reached down to help him, but he shrugged their hands away and climbed aboard on his own power. Limping, he pushed his way through to where Reussel lay and took the boy's hand. "It was all for the Fatherland," he said. Reussel died four hours later.

Of what significance was May 9, 1942, and the battle of the *U-352* and the *Icarus*? The battle did result in the first enemy submarine sunk by an American Coast Guard vessel in World War II. And the victory did deny Hitler one more submarine and a trained crew and captain. Coast Guard

4.9   Meal for captured U-352 crew at the U.S. Navy Yard, Charleston, South Carolina.   Courtesy of the National Archives.

4.10   With Kapitänleutnant Hellmut Rathke in the lead, captured officers and crew of the U-352 march under guard at the U.S. Navy Yard, Charleston, South Carolina, shortly after the sinking of their submarine.   Courtesy of the National Archives.

ships received extra armament at Lieutenant Jester's suggestion, and the morale of the Coast Guard and all American naval forces improved.

Still, to military historians, the impact of the battle in the huge, sprawling world war was minimal. Naval intelligence received very little hard information as a result of the sinking. Rathke gathered his men during the night aboard the *Icarus* and gave them a little speech, reminding them of their duty to their country. When he learned this, Jester separated the Kapitänleutnant from his crew, but Rathke had already made his point. It did not really matter. There was nothing about the *U-352* that British Intelligence did not already know. The ship was exactly like the *U-570* captured intact by the Royal Navy almost a year before.

The importance, then, of the *U-352–Icarus* encounter must be in purely human terms. To Kapitänleutnant Hellmut Rathke and his command, the battle was devastating. With 14 of their comrades dead and their U-boat destroyed, the German crew felt as if they had failed their country and their friends. Although they exhibited high morale after they were picked up, they were actually struggling with a great sense of failure and guilt compounded by the shock of the battle.

The men of the *Icarus* did what they could to heighten their captives' spirits. Trays of sandwiches from the galley and boxes of cigarettes from the ship's stores found their way to the Germans' compartment. Pharmacist's Mate Kahn did all he could do for the injured in almost heroic

4.11 U-352 commander Kapitänleutnant Hellmut Rathke (second from left) and Leutnant Oskar Bernhard (center) with American navy officers at the U.S. Navy Yard, Charleston, S.C. Courtesy of the National Archives.

fashion, but his tiny medicine chest offered little help to the several severely wounded men, one of whom had lost an arm and one, Reussel, who died. The German sailors recognized the effort when they left the *Icarus*. They relayed their thanks to Jester for the crew's many kindnesses. Rathke and many of the others, however, remained embittered at Jester because they had been machine-gunned in the water. This was something they believed no U-boat commander would ever allow. Despite the propaganda of the day, they were correct. Except for a single incident late in the war, U-boat crews did not machine-gun survivors.

The pride that the crew of the *Icarus* felt at their accomplishment was tempered only by the respect many of them came to feel toward their prisoners. After being crammed together for 17 hours, the coastguardsmen found that their German prisoners were fellow sailors not much different from themselves. The two crews began to talk to each other, and soon the Americans who could speak German and the Germans who could speak English were swapping jokes and war stories. Even Rathke joined in, laughing as he chided a German crewman for an enamel pin he wore, given him by a "cute little French girl."

By the time the *Icarus* tied up at Charleston harbor on May 10, 1942, the crew felt concern for the Germans and expressed hope that they would be treated well. Marines with fixed bayonets and scores of American and British intelligence officers met them. John Bruce watched the Germans, most of them barefooted, march in perfect order off the *Icarus*. He winced when he saw them forced to stand on the hot concrete and railroad tracks next to the dock. But neither he nor anyone on board could help them. The Germans marched away and no one on the *Icarus* ever heard of them again.

Diving the U-352 Today

The *U-352*, 218 feet long and 769 tons surfaced (871 tons submerged), lies in 115 feet of water 25.6 miles southeast of Beaufort Inlet on a heading of 159 degrees and 36 miles southeast of Bogue Inlet on a heading of 123 degrees. Probably the most visited wreck off the coast of North Carolina, the *U-352* has been a controversial wreck almost from the time its location was discovered by local divers in the mid-1970s.

For several years after the discovery of the wreck, live torpedoes, depth charges, and several rounds from the sub's 88mm deck gun lay on or near the wreck, creating a great deal of public concern about the safety of diving the *U-352*. Reports from sport divers began circulating that the submarine was a bomb waiting to blow sky high. Over the years since the location of the U-boat was discovered by Captain George Purifoy of Morehead City, divers have penetrated the sub and recovered numerous arti-

4.12   U-352. Outer shell decay.

facts including the captain's log, two sextants, a brass alcohol burner, pistols, belt buckles, a brass propeller, a lamp, a first-aid manual, a brass whistle, goggles, communication equipment, a brass plaque inscribed with the Morse code alphabet, and numerous other brass artifacts. In addition, in 1976 and 1977 divers were entering the U-352 and removing the remains of German submariners who went down with the vessel. Several skulls and various bones were exhibited to the public by a now defunct dive shop in Jacksonville, North Carolina, to promote the shop's trips out to the wreck. That display of human remains set in motion the first of many controversies surrounding the sub. The removal of remains from the submarine raised a public outcry from both sides of the Atlantic, and the West German government issued a formal protest to the United States in 1978. The West German government claimed jurisdiction over all sunken warships of the Third Reich and considered the site an unmarked war cemetery and the removal of the remains a desecration. The German government gave the U.S. Navy permission to inspect and destroy the U-352 after the remains of any sailors were removed to a German soldiers' cemetery in the United States.

Although the bones had disappeared by the summer of 1977, public outrage of the desecration of a German war memorial was still strong. About this time concern surfaced about the live torpedoes, depth charges, and 88mm ammunition on and near the submarine. In July 1978, in response to public concern about the explosives on the site and the pilfering of the dead Germans' remains, U.S. Senator Lowell P. Weicker, Jr., of Connecticut, personally visited the wreck site to determine the extent of the danger posed by the unexploded ordnance. He found several tor-

4.13   U-352. Conning tower with open hatch.

pedoes and other ordnance on and around the submarine and reported his findings as well as his fears for the safety of divers and fishermen to President Carter's secretary of defense, Harold Brown. Brown ordered the Navy to conduct an on-site investigation into the possible dangers of the live ordnance. In spite of the Navy's finding that indeed there was substantial danger to divers present at the site, it was not until May 1980 that the Navy began ordnance disposal operations. Much of the Navy's reluctance to do anything was seen to be a result of the controversy concerning what should be done with the U-boat itself. Divers were afraid the Navy would destroy their unique wreck site, and local communities feared that tampering with the vessel would hurt the local U-boat "cottage industry" which sprang up after the sub's discovery. From the end of May through July 6, Navy divers made nearly 140 dives on the U-352, accumulating more than 361 hours of bottom time, and discovered seven torpedoes, including two inside the forward torpedo tubes, one in the galley, one wedged under the starboard side, and one protruding from the stern torpedo tube. In addition, they recovered several 88mm rounds from the sand around the vessel. The Navy divers burned or disarmed all the torpedoes except one in the galley and the two in the forward room, which the Navy said "posed no hazard as long as they were left undisturbed." To prevent access to the torpedoes and seal the vessel from intruding divers, the Navy bolted plates over all the hatches. That was meant to serve as a compromise between sport divers and those who wished to see the sub destroyed. Nevertheless, soon after the Navy departed, sport divers removed the plates. During its inspection of the U-352, the Navy found no

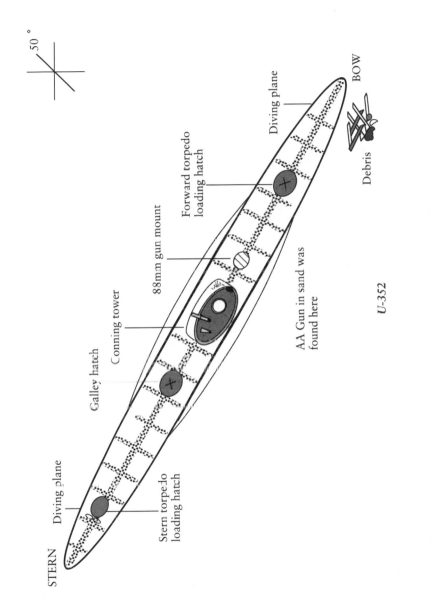

50°

STERN

Diving plane

Galley hatch

Conning tower

88mm gun mount

Forward torpedo
loading hatch

Diving plane

BOW

Debris

Stern torpedo
loading hatch

AA Gun in sand was
found here

U-352

Wreck diagram of the *U-352*.

human remains, and—with the removal of unexploded ordnance around the sub—the controversy over the ordnance and human remains has died down since 1980. Most, if not all, available artifacts have been removed from the *U-352*.

Today all the hatches are open to the public, and—with the exception of the torpedoes well inside the sub—there is little or no danger of explosion to divers who still flock to the site by the hundreds each year. Most divers are content to stay on the outside and swim the length of the submarine viewing and photographing the remains of a German U-boat. One of the most popular offshore dive sites, the wreck is visited nearly every weekend by dive charter boats from Beaufort, Morehead City, Swansboro, and Jacksonville, and divers come from all over the world to visit the *U-352*. The usual running time to the site is two to three-and-a-half hours depending upon the charter boat. The *U-352* lies with its bow pointed on a heading of 50 degrees and lists to the starboard about 40 degrees. Both her exposed propeller and her deck gun are gone. The deck gun was blown off the *U-352* when she was sunk. One of her two 20-millimeter anti-aircraft guns was recovered in 1983 from the sand directly below the deck gun mount by George Purifoy; it now stands on his dock at the foot of 8th Street in Morehead City. One of her two propellers was salvaged in September 1979 by a group of Virginia sport divers led by Dave Bluett and now is located in Washington, D.C. Much of the decking and the outer shell is gone, exposing the supporting frame members, but the inner pressure hull behind which the crew had its quarters is still intact. The conning tower rises to about 10 feet above the hull, but much of its metal covering has been removed. The conning tower hatch, forward and stern torpedo loading hatches, and the galley hatch are all open, despite having once been sealed by the Navy, and their hatch covers have been removed by salvage divers.

The water temperature ranges in the upper 70s to low 80s during the summer, and the dive can be easily accomplished without the use of a wet suit. Visibility on the wreck is usually 50 feet or so and is quite often 70–100 feet. On really clear days, the sub can sometimes be seen from the surface. The many divers who visit the site each summer have removed most of the corals, sponges, and other marine species that used to grow on the wreck. However, the wreck provides a nice habitat for bait fish which attract many game fish as well as bottom-dwelling fish such as groupers, flounders, sheepheads, and spade fish. Because currents are frequently encountered at the site and because the depth and the distance from shore are considerable, the *U-352* should be dived by experienced wreck divers. Novice divers who go to the site should be under the strict supervision of an experienced guide.

USS *Schurz*

THE WRECK OF THE USS *Schurz* is sometimes referred to as the "WWI Destroyer," but it was not a destroyer at all; it was actually an unprotected cruiser. Built in 1894 and originally named the *Geier*, the cruiser was one of four ships of this class built about the same time for the German navy, and these were the last warships in the fleet designed to take rigging. The 1,630-ton *Geier* was 295 feet long and propelled by both steam and sail, reaching a maximum speed of 15–17 knots. She carried two 14-inch torpedo tubes on her bow and was lightly armed with eight 4.1-inch guns which fired a 105mm, 31-pound projectile, as well as with five one-pounders and several machine guns. She also had gun turrets on her bow and stern.

In October 1914, the *Geier* left Tsingtao, China, to escort the German steamer *Lockson* to Honolulu. At the outbreak of WWI, Japan and Germany found themselves on opposite sides of the conflict, and by late 1914 most of the Pacific had been cleared of German naval bases. America had not yet entered the war and was a declared neutral. On their way to the neutral port of Honolulu, the *Geier* and the *Lockson* were chased across the Pacific by two Japanese cruisers, the *Rizon* and the *Asama*. Not knowing the destination of the *Geier*, the Japanese ships were aided by the Marconi station at Honolulu, which flashed word of the German gunboat's arrival when it docked on October 15. While the *Geier* took many days to take on coal and many more days to make engine repairs, the *Rizon* and the *Asama* waited outside the harbor for the German ship to emerge. The day after the *Geier* docked, the United States threatened to close the Marconi station at Honolulu for flashing word of her arrival and thus violating U.S. neutrality. The Japanese embassy in Washington requested that the *Geier* be forced to leave the harbor or submit to internment, and the U.S. did subsequently order the *Geier* to leave, but to no avail. On November 8, after the Germans refused to leave the harbor, the vessel was interned at Honolulu and all the officers and crew were ordered to remain on board.

During the internment of the *Geier*, the men on board telegraphed messages from German agents in America to German agents in Japan while the ship's band played lively tunes to drown out the static of the Morse code. Sometime later on, it was discovered what the Germans were doing when American officials obtained the diary of Karl Grasshof, the captain of the *Geier*. The diary revealed that while Grasshof and his subordinates were enjoying the protection of the United States, they had violated U.S. neutrality by assisting Count von Bernstorff, the German

4.14   U.S.S. *Schurz*.   Courtesy of WZ-Bilddienst, Wilhelmshaven, West Germany.

ambassador to the U.S., in plotting to get sailors and officers from the *Geier* back to Germany, by transmitting spy messages, and by attempting to stir up ill feeling with stories that the U.S. was planning to invade Canada. [From *Philadelphia Press*, 1918]

On January 1, 1916, the *Geier* was ordered to San Francisco after the captain and crew had repeatedly complained about the unbearable Hawaiian tropical heat. A few days later, when American naval officers took charge of the vessel, it was found that her engines had been wrecked by a fire started by her crew. A few days after that it was discovered that the crew had hidden machine guns and ammunition on board even though they had been ordered to turn over all of their arms when the *Geier* had been interned. American officials looked upon these acts with great dismay, and in June 1917, two months after the U.S. declared war on Germany, it was announced that the *Geier* was to be used by the U.S. Navy. Her name was then changed to the USS *Schurz*. In December 1917, six months after the ship had been commissioned into the U.S. Navy, officials made public what the Germans on board the *Geier* had been doing during the ship's internment in Hawaii, and her confiscation was therefore looked upon with great pride by most Americans. Re-outfitted, the USS *Schurz* sailed for the East Coast to do battle with her previous owners. In command was Captain W. D. Wells, who had a crew of 215 men.

Early on the morning of June 18, 1918, the *Schurz* was in a dense fog

10 miles off Cape Lookout. German submarines had been active off the East Coast and had sunk several ships during the year. Even in a fog, it was not unusual for ships to be running without lights to avoid detection by the submarines. Shortly before 4:00 A.M. that June morning, everything appeared normal and the fog was beginning to lift. Suddenly, out of the gloom, the American tanker *Florida* was seen to be a few hundred yards away, running without lights and headed directly toward the *Schurz*. The watch officer sounded the alarm, but by the time the *Florida* turned her lights on it was too late. The one fatality in the crash was a crewman on the *Schurz* who had rushed to the side to see what was happening.

At 4:00 A.M., an immediate SOS was sent out from the *Schurz*. The SS *Saramacca*, an American steamship sailing from the West Indies, answered the call. When passengers from the *Saramacca* arrived on deck, they saw the *Schurz* with a deep gash in her side lying low in the water while the *Florida* stood nearby apparently undamaged. Scores of sailors were bobbing in the water while others were clinging to life-rafts. The rescue ship picked up survivors from the sea and also received those rescued by the *Florida*. Just as the last survivors were taken from the water the *Schurz* disappeared beneath the seas to rest on the bottom, 110 feet below. Robert McLean of Chicago, a world champion figure skater who was a passenger on the rescue ship, took the only photograph of the *Schurz* sinking. The ship's safe, containing a large amount of gold and still believed by some to have been on board when she went down, was actually transferred to the rescue ship before the *Schurz* sank. The *Florida* continued her northward journey, and Captain Wells and the 214 crewmen were brought ashore.

The location of the remains of the *Schurz* was a mystery until the early 1970s when George Purifoy and associates of his from Morehead

4.15   U.S.S. *Schurz*. Anchor chain.

City discovered the whereabouts of the wreck. Probably no diver has had as much experience diving the *Schurz* as George, and on his boat, the *Olympus,* he has, over the years, taken hundreds of divers to visit the wreck. The *Schurz* lies 36.5 miles from Bogue Inlet on a heading of 128 degrees and 27.7 miles from Beaufort Inlet on a heading of 164 degrees. Many dive charter boats visit this wreck, most departing from Morehead City and Beaufort and a few from Swansboro and points south. The trav-

4.16   U.S.S. *Schurz.* Port side wall.

4.17   U.S.S. *Schurz.* Anchor chain capstan.

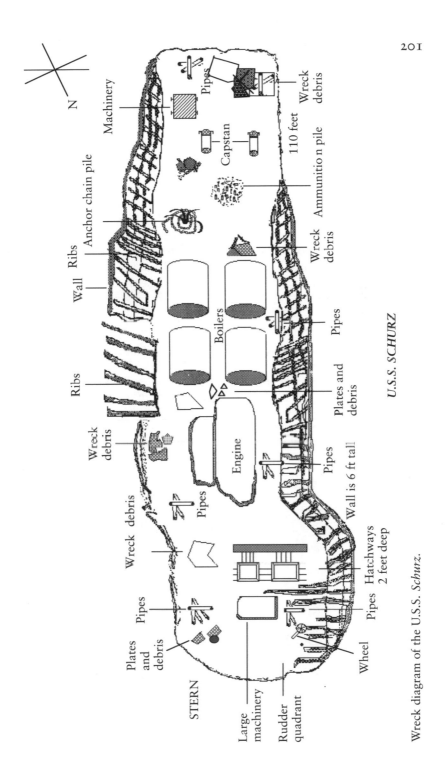

Wreck diagram of the U.S.S. *Schurz*.

elling time to the wreck varies from two to three-and-a-half hours, depending on the boat and weather conditions. At a boat speed of 10 knots, the trip will be a little under three hours. This wreck is one of the most popular offshore dive sites and is visited nearly every weekend during the diving season.

Water temperatures from June through September range in the mid-70s to the 80s, and the visibility varies from 30 to 150 feet. A few times during the summer the visibility is such that the wreck is easily visible from the surface, as on the occasion some years ago when a short section of white plastic pipe was inadvertently dropped overboard from the boat that had taken me out to the site. After a few minutes the pipe could easily be seen lying on the wreck 110 feet below by divers on our boat. On an average diving day, the visibility will be more than 70 feet, the water temperature around 80 degrees or so, with little or no current present at the site.

Not much of the *Schurz*'s original structure remains intact, and the wreckage lies scattered over a large area of the bottom. Upon descending to the wreck, divers are treated to an array of visual delights ranging from an abundance and density of tropical marine life to brass artifacts, three boilers, a condenser, machinery, ammunition, anchor chains, portholes, and other remnants of the German warship. Although on any trip to the wreck a diver can always find a brass trophy, the prime artifacts have already been recovered over the past few years. The ship's chronometer was brought up by Joe Harris of Durham in the summer of 1983, and George Purifoy recovered another large clock a year earlier. The ship's binnacle,

4.18   Clock recovered from the U.S.S. *Schurz* by George Purifoy.

two of her four telegraphs, brass cleats, a large circular brass platform, a silver dogtag bearing its owner's name, and the coral-encrusted remains of a brass-jacketed, water-cooled machine gun have also been retrieved by George Purifoy. Many other brass artifacts—such as portholes, fittings, light fixtures, valves, kitchen utensils, and tableware—have also been recovered. There is a large pile of live rifle and pistol ammunition located near the anchor capstan on the stern. If you feel you have to collect such souvenirs, be careful.

The wreck is also a photographer's paradise. Besides the remnants of the wreck itself, the marine life provides subject matter for many hours of diving. Blue angelfish, parrotfish, moray eels, sea turtles, flame scallops, spiny lobsters, filefish, anemones, sea urchins, sponges, butterflyfish, corals, snappers, groupers, black bass, and amberjacks are but a few of the creatures that inhabit this wreck.

A visit to the shipwrecks off the coast of North Carolina must certainly include a trip to the *Schurz*, one of the last nineteenth-century steam sailing ships built for the German navy.

Ella Pierce Thurlow

BUILT IN 1918 at Rockland, Maine, by the Francis Cobb Company, the 1,509-ton, 221-foot-long, four-masted schooner was originally named *R. B. Drisko* by its owners, the Atlantic Coast Company. The name was changed to *Ella Pierce Thurlow* when the vessel was sold to the New England Maritime Company of Boston, Massachusetts. Built of oak hardwood, yellow pine decking, and iron and copper fastenings, the vessel was a freighter designed like a barge with four masts. It was designated a schooner barge. The *Ella Pierce Thurlow* plied the eastern seaboard of the United States carrying cargo of raw materials for industry from the south to the industrial north.

In late March 1932, the *Ella Pierce Thurlow* was in Savannah, Georgia, being loaded with nitrate to be transported to New York. On March 23, the schooner encountered a storm off the North Carolina coast that battered the ship. The eleven crew members managed to escape in liferafts as the ship foundered and sank in 125 feet of water 30 miles south of Beaufort Inlet near Morehead City, North Carolina.

The wreck site is about one-quarter mile from the *Papoose* so the diving conditions are similar for both sites. The water temperature is in the upper 70s and the low 80s during the summer. The visibility is usually around 75 feet but may be in excess of 100 feet several times during the summer. Current is seldom a problem although occasionally it may be present on the site. The depth of the dive is slightly deeper than 120 feet. The relief on the site is less than four feet as the wreck is very broken up. The ship sank directly to the bottom and the sides collapsed to the sand. By hovering 10 feet or so above the wreck and looking from one end or the other, the outline of the ship is visible. The keel is filled with sand and the sides, with a few ribs, stick up out of the sand and run the length of the ship. There is no discernible bow or stern. The bow area, however, is easy to identify by the large anchor still in its hawse hole and attached to anchor chain, which is still wrapped around the anchor windlass. There are two small condensers nearby and a large mast with a crow's nest. The centerline of the site is composed of sand and is about the width of a narrow highway. Beneath the sand lies the ship's keel. On either edge of the sand are hull ribs and planks which have become covered with calcareous material. Beautiful corals, sponges, sea fans, sea whips, moray eels, butterflyfish, wrasses, filefish, triggerfish, blue angelfish, arrow crabs, anemones, grouper, snapper, african pompano, spadefish, sea turtles, sea cucumbers, rays, and other marine life are found on the site. It is a small

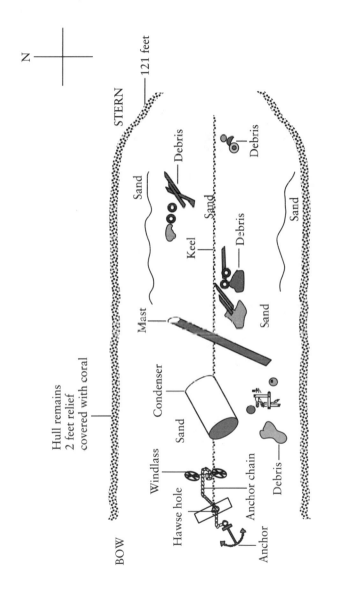

ELLA PIERCE THURLOW

Wreck diagram of the *Ella Pierce Thurlow*.

4.19   Condenser from the schooner-barge *Ella Pierce Thurlow*.

4.20   Hull remains of schooner-barge *Ella Pierce Thurlow*.

site and the abundance of marine life on it gives it the appearance of an oasis in a desert of sandy ocean bottom.

Because the wreck lies at sand level, it must be dived at its maximum depth. Although the maximum depth is 121 fsw, unless a diver is using a dive computer, the wreck must be dived using 130 fsw tables. It is a deep dive and should be done only after having gained deep ocean diving experience. The *Gale Anne* docked at Atlantic Beach is currently the only charter boat to take divers out to the site.

Papoose

THE *Papoose* was built in 1921 at San Pedro, California, for the Petroleum Navigation Company of Houston, Texas, and was originally named the *Silvanus*. The tanker, 412 feet long and 5,939 tons (3,636 net tons), carried fuel oil and gasoline from Texas to New York. In mid-March 1942, Captain Roger Zalnick and a crew of 34 men departed Providence, Rhode Island, and headed south to New York. After a brief stop, the *Papoose* proceeded down the Eastern Seaboard on her way to Port Arthur, Texas, to pick up another load of oil. Late in the evening of March 18, 1942, the *Papoose* was about 18 miles south of Cape Lookout when suddenly a torpedo struck her port side amidships, flooding the engine and fire rooms and killing two crewmen. The torpedo had been fired from the *U-124*, which was under the command of Korvettenkapitän Johann Mohr. With the *Papoose* dead in the water, Captain Zalnick radioed for help and gave the order to abandon ship. Lifeboats #2 and #4 on the port side had been destroyed in the blast, so lifeboats #1 and #3 on the starboard side were lowered and the crew began to evacuate the sinking ship. Finding the *Papoose* immobilized, Mohr moved the *U-124* around to the starboard side of his target for the final blow. Fifteen minutes after the first torpedo struck, the *U-124* fired a second into the starboard side of the crippled and unarmed ship. The torpedo, nearly hitting lifeboat #3, struck just aft of amidships, and within minutes the *Papoose* rolled over. However, several hours passed before the vessel sank in 130 feet of water. As they rowed toward shore, the survivors found their way lit by another of the *U-124*'s victims, the *W. E. Hutton*, a fully laden oil tanker attacked an hour after the *Papoose* had been torpedoed. At 7:30

4.21   *Papoose*. U.S. Coast Guard.   Courtesy of The
Mariners' Museum, Newport News, Virginia.

A.M. the next morning, the survivors of the *Papoose* were picked up by the USS *Stringham* and taken to Norfolk, Virginia. [From Arthur R. Moore, 1983]

The *Papoose* lies upside down in 130 feet of water 36.7 miles from Bogue Inlet on a heading of 134 degrees and 30 miles from Beaufort Inlet on a heading of 170 degrees. Located far offshore, the wreck sits in very clear, warm water. However, divers should have a few North Carolina wreck dives under their belt before they undertake to dive the *Papoose*. Though the dive itself is not arduous, divers need to have a little experience to deal with such factors as the depth, the currents, and the long boat ride out to the site. Dive charter boats out of Morehead City (*Olympus, Sea Wife IV,* and *Saltshaker*), Beaufort (*Easystep II,* and *Outrageous*), and from Emerald Isle, (*Jaws*) visit the wreck a few times each summer, and, depending on the boat, the trip takes about four-and-a-half to five-and-a-half hours. In the deep water at the site, current ranging from slight (less than a half-knot) to moderate is frequently encountered. The visibility is usually between 50 and 150 feet, and several times a summer a diver on the stern may easily watch divers at the other end of the wreck. When visibility is particularly good, a diver on the sand can look up and see the bottom of the dive boat 130 feet above.

Because the *Papoose* lies slightly on her port side and upside down, it is difficult to get to a lot of the interesting features located on her port hull near the sand. On the starboard side of the ship, it is quite easy to swim under the slightly elevated side and see passageways and rows of portholes which are accessible. At a depth of 110 feet or so, there are large,

4.22 *Papoose.* Looking up starboard side from 130 feet.

gaping cracks in the hull on the starboard side which allow penetration into various hull compartments. Take a bright dive light or two with you on this dive because some additional illumination is needed to see under the inverted portions on the edge of the ship and especially inside the wreck. Due to the inverted position of the wreck, many of the features that are interesting to see are located near the sand; but to spend any time on the wreck at that depth requires decompression diving. However, the large, flat keel lies at 85 feet, and there are several openings into the hull at depths less than 120 feet that are quite interesting for those divers not wanting to dive too deep. For example, there are large openings at around 110 to 115 feet that allow access to the engine room. A diver should remember, however, to never penetrate a wreck alone and to have two or three lights available for each member of a buddy team.

While the engine room is interesting to visit, it is dangerous because all the machinery is hanging from above and some of it may fall. The rudder looms tall above the keel and is the highest point on the wreck. The shaft for the large propeller (18 feet in diameter) is visible, but the propeller itself was salvaged in 1974 by Skippy Winner. About 150 feet from the stern is a huge crack in the hull full of rubble, iron girders, twisted hull plates, and other wreckage. This crack is 50–75 feet wide and makes a nice area to visit while it also permits access to the wreck through a large cross-section opening rather than a simple hole in the side. Care must be taken diving in this area because of the possibility of ocean surge. Surging bottom currents may pitch and pull the unwary diver into sharp or coral-encrusted objects that could at the very least tear and cut up exposed skin or wet-suit material.

4.23   *Papoose.* Light fixture inside engine room.
Courtesy of Jim Pickard.

4.24 *Papoose*. Opening on starboard side.

The exquisite marine life on the wreck and the usually excellent visibility make the site a photographer's paradise. With its location so far offshore and close to the Gulf Stream, the *Papoose* provides a habitat for a variety of tropical marine life. Sea urchins, moray eels, blue angelfish, African pompanos, barracudas, butterflyfish, amberjacks, soft and hard corals, sponges, lobsters, and groupers are but a few of the sea-dwelling species a diver may encounter on this wreck.

For brass artifact collectors, there are still many portholes, valves, gauges, pulleys, and other items remaining throughout the wreck site.

Naeco

THE *Naeco*, 412 feet long and 5,373 tons (3,238 net tons), was built in 1918 by the Bethlehem Ship Building Corporation of Wilmington, Delaware, for the Pennsylvania Shipping Company of Philadelphia. Originally called the *Charles M. Everest*, the three-deck tanker transported fuel oil, kerosene, and gasoline from Texas to the East Coast. Powering the tanker was a triple expansion engine with piston diameters of 27.5, 45, and 74 inches and a 48-inch piston stroke.

In late March 1942, the *Naeco* left Houston, Texas, loaded with kerosene and #2 fuel oil bound for Sewaren, New Jersey. The captain of the ship was Emil H. Engelbrecht, and a crew of 38 was on board. The captain timed the ship's arrival off the coast of North Carolina such that the *Naeco* would pass the treacherous torpedo alley off Cape Hatteras during the early morning hours of March 23, 1942. Unbeknownst to Captain Engelbrecht and his crew, however, the tanker had been watched by the *U-124*, under the command of Korvettenkapitän Erich Mohr, from the time the *Naeco* passed 65 miles southeast of Cape Lookout. The *U-124* had already sunk the *Papoose*, the *W. E. Hutton*, and the *E. M. Clark* five days earlier and had damaged the *Esso Nashville* two days before off Cape Fear. The morning of March 23 would be equally rewarding for Korvettenkapitän Mohr, as the *U-124* fired a single torpedo into the starboard side of the *Naeco* just forward of amidships. The explosion set the fuel oil on fire and soon the entire ship forward of amidships was ablaze. All of the crew who were forward when the torpedo struck were killed, and Captain Engelbrecht died in the inferno that engulfed the midship house. All lifeboats forward were destroyed in the blast, but lifeboat #3 on the

4.25   *Naeco.*   Courtesy of The Mariners' Museum, Newport News, Virginia.

port side and lifeboat #4 on the starboard side were not damaged and were boarded and lowered immediately after the torpedo struck. Lifeboat #4 was swamped when it hit the water because the ship was still moving forward at around 14 knots. The chief engineer managed to get the engines shut down after about 10 minutes, and lifeboat #3 was safely launched with 10 crewmen on board. Four crewmen aboard lifeboat #4 when it was swamped found themselves in the ocean swimming for their lives. One of the men swam back to the *Naeco* and managed to get back aboard. Another found a small raft floating nearby and managed to pull himself onto it. The other two men from lifeboat #4, unaware of what had happened to their companions, continued swimming. The U.S. Coast Guard vessel *Dione* picked up the 10 survivors in lifeboat #3 four hours after the attack and rescued the two crewmen who had started swimming when lifeboat #4 was swamped. The USS *Umpqua* picked up the seamen who had returned to the *Naeco*, and the USS *Osprey* picked up the fourth survivor from the life-raft. The *Naeco* stayed afloat for about another hour before she broke into two sections and sank in 140 feet of water 37 miles south of Cape Lookout.   [From Arthur R. Moore, 1983]

The *Naeco*'s bow and stern sections sank about two miles apart and are infrequently visited by divers. Fishermen, however, have known the location of the two wreck sites and fished them for years. The general area of the wreck is 37.4 miles from Beaufort Inlet on a heading of 170 degrees.

In the early 1970s a few divers made the lengthy boat trip (five to six hours one-way) out to the stern section of the *Naeco*, but the great distance from the shore and the extreme depth of the wreck generally deterred divers from going to the site. In the summer of 1982, after searching for a captain who knew the loran C coordinates for the stern section and would be willing to take out divers, I found Don Huneycutt, a boat captain and diver who operated the *Donna J III* out of Swansboro. Although not too enthusiastic about going that far offshore to try to find a wreck he had never been to before and whose coordinates were given to him by a commercial fisherman who had only fished the wreck, Don agreed to take me and a small group of divers out to try to find the wreck. After travelling six hours on a relatively calm and beautiful day we arrived at the site where the *Naeco* was supposed to be. Don threw out a buoy to mark the spot and began to search the area. This is the most nerve-wracking part of this type of dive trip because you never know how reliable the coordinates are and whether or not the captain has the ability to find the wreck site. I wasn't worried so much about Don's ability as a captain because he is one of the best navigators I've met. My concern had

4.26   *Naeco.* Hatch.

more to do with whether a commercial fisherman would really be truth-
ful about the location of a prime fishing site or would simply give an approximate location. After about 15 minutes of searching, the *Donna J*'s
depth recorder detected a large metal object directly below. We anchored
into the object, which was roughly 140 feet below, and prepared to descend to whatever it was.

The water was very warm, about 80 degrees, and quite clear, around
100 feet of visibility. As I descended to about 85 feet I could see the entire
wreck below me. From the point where the bow broke off to the stern, the
wreck loomed larger and larger as I settled onto a portion of a mast at
110 feet. I inspected the wreck below and noted its "stair-step" structure.
I could see hatchways leading below deck and twisted steel and pipes
lying all over the deck. The perch I was on is the tallest structure on the
wreck; located at 110 fsw, it is at the minimum depth from the surface to
the wreck. The majority of the wreck lies at 130 feet, and the sand bottom is at 140–45 feet. I descended to the deck below and swam the
length of the wreck, which is around 300 feet. The stern section is more
or less intact, and the lack of diver visitations was evident. The wreck was
covered with silver snappers, one species that has found great favor
among spearfishermen and consequently is not found to any extent at all
on wrecks frequented by divers. I also saw many brass artifacts on the

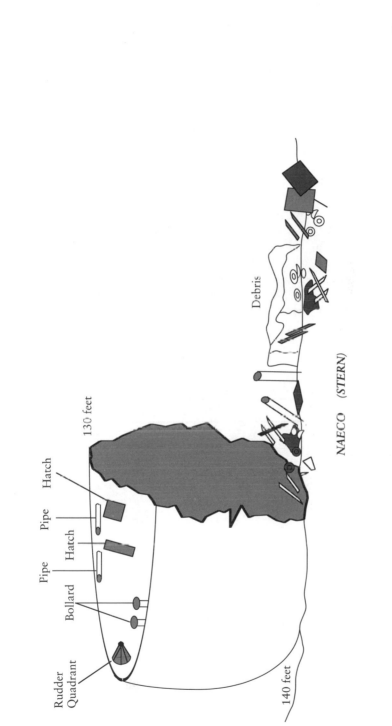

Wreck diagram of the *Naeco*.

decks where they have lain openly for these many years. Portholes, valves, handles, and a variety of other brass objects were scattered everywhere. On the half-dozen trips out to the *Naeco* I have made since that first one, several divers have recovered intact portholes from the wreck, as well as other artifacts. As I swam around the wreck on my first visit, I saw an abundance of tropical marine life not equalled at the site of any other wreck I had yet dived. Lying so far offshore and well into the eddies of the Gulf Stream, the *Naeco* is covered with beautiful corals, sponges, anemones, butterflyfish, blennies, African pompanos, blue angelfish, barracudas, snappers, lobsters, moray eels, trigger fishes, fanworms, octopuses, arrow crabs, groupers, and many other species usually found in the Caribbean. Surfacing after that first dive, we were overwhelmed by the unique nature of the wreck, its intactness, the artifacts, the water quality, its depth, and the fact that we were the first divers to visit the *Naeco* in nearly a dozen years and probably were some of the very few divers who had ever seen the tanker after its tragic encounter with the *U-124* in March 1942. The wreck of the *Naeco* must certainly rate as one of the top five wrecks to visit off the North Carolina coast.

On subsequent trips to the wreck I have seen visibility as little as 40 feet (once, out of seven trips) and as great as 150 feet plus, with the average being in excess of 80 or so feet. More than once, I have experienced currents up to a half-knot, but usually there is only a slight current. On one trip there was a considerable surface current of about a half-knot but absolutely no current below. However, because of its depth and the length of the boat trip to the site, this wreck should be attempted only after a diver has had experience on wrecks like the *Schurz*, the *Papoose*, and the *Atlas*. It is a rewarding goal to strive for and definitely worth the effort spent on gaining the experience needed to see this wreck. Dive boats from Beaufort, Morehead City, and Emerald Isle visit the *Naeco*.

Theodore Parker

THE LIBERTY SHIP *Theodore Parker*, 7,176 tons (4,380 net tons) and 441 feet long, was built in March 1943 by the California Shipbuilding Corporation at Terminal Island, Los Angeles, California. Powered by an engine built by Joshua Henry Ironworks at Sunnyvale, California, with two large boilers and a four-blade propellor (18 feet six inches in diameter), the *Theodore Parker* cruised at 11 knots. Owned by the U.S. government and operated by Angwilines, Inc., of New York, the Liberty ship made several uneventful Atlantic Ocean crossings carrying food and materiel for the Allied war effort during WWII. Departing Hull, England, on November 16, 1944, bound for New York in ballast, the vessel struck a mine off the east coast of England about 75 miles from the entrance to the Humber River. She was severely damaged and returned to Hull where repairs were made over the next three months. Repairs completed, she left England on February 23, 1945, arriving in New York on March 9, 1945. After the war, she was consigned to the Merchant Marine Reserve Fleet on the James River near Newport News, Virginia.

In 1974, the *Theodore Parker* was purchased by the State of North Carolina for use as an artificial reef and on June 4, 1974, was sunk in 50 feet of water 1.5 miles off Bogue Banks, three miles west of Fort Macon,

4.27 *Theodore Parker*. U.S. Army. Courtesy of The Mariners' Museum, Newport News, Virginia.

4.28   *Theodore Parker*. Below deck.

18 miles east of Bogue Inlet on a heading of 72 degrees, and four miles southwest of Beaufort Inlet on a heading of 245 degrees. Before the vessel was sunk, her superstructure was cut and removed down to the second deck, giving her a 30-foot-high profile; thus her deck lies at 20 fsw. The deck has several large open holds which allow divers and considerable sunlight to penetrate below decks into a myriad of pipes, machinery, ladders, catwalks, and bulkheads, which are interesting to explore. The deck is perfectly flat and resembles a narrow football field which is covered with marine life. Flounders, groupers, sheepheads, and other bottom- and wreck-dwelling fish are plentiful, and the wreck also attracts ocean-ranging fish. Visibility on the site is usually less than 10–15 feet because of the very close proximity to shore, but on occasion it may reach 40–50 feet. The water temperature is in the mid-70s during the summer, and the wreck can be dived without a wet suit. Surge is sometimes a problem if surface sea conditions are rolling or rough.

Because of the extremely shallow depth of the deck, this wreck is a good one for inexperienced wreck divers, and many scuba classes use this site for their checkout dives. The *Theodore Parker* can often be dived when weather prevents diving on wrecks offshore. The wreck is also often used as a shallow second dive after a deeper offshore dive, and as such is

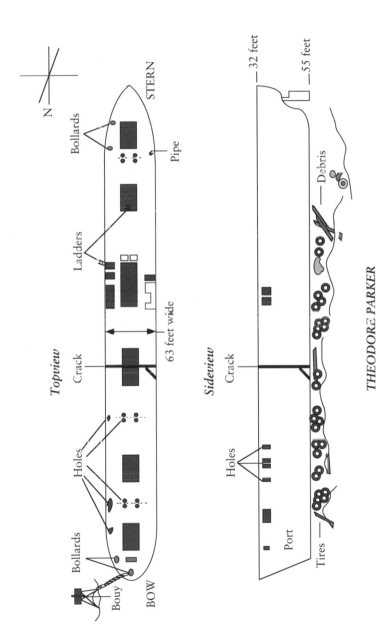

Topview

STERN

Bollards

Pipe

Ladders

63 feet wide

N

Crack

Holes

Bollards

Bouy

BOW

Sideview

Crack

Holes

Port

Tires

Debris

32 feet

55 feet

THEODORE PARKER

Wreck diagram of the *Theodore Parker.*

usually dived in the afternoon when currents are prevalent because of incoming or outgoing tides. Under these conditions, the visibility drops drastically, as does the diver's enjoyment of the dive. Dive charter boats from Beaufort and Morehead City visit this site frequently during the diving season.

Suloide

THE *Suloide*, 3,235 tons (1,870 net tons) and 338 feet long, was built in 1920 at Rostock, in what is now East Germany. The freighter was originally named the *Maceio* and then bore the name *Amassia*. Acquired by Lloyd Brasileiro in 1941, she was registered in Rio de Janeiro and re-named the *Suloide*. In late March 1943, the *Suloide* departed Trinidad, loaded with manganese ore bound for New York. After an uneventful trip up the East Coast, the freighter was approximately seven miles offshore of Bogue Banks on March 26, when she struck the partially submerged hull of the tanker *W. E. Hutton*, which had been torpedoed almost exactly one year earlier by the *U-124*. The *Suloide* drifted inshore about one mile north of the *Hutton* before sinking in 65 feet of water.

Located 11.5 miles southeast of Bogue Inlet on a heading of 103 degrees and 11.9 miles southwest of Beaufort Inlet on a heading of 235 degrees, the site of the *Suloide* is marked by a buoy designated WR-13. Nearly every weekend, dive charter boats from Beaufort and Morehead City go out to the wreck, and because it is such a short run from Bogue and Beaufort inlets, the site is also frequently visited by small private pleasure boats. The relatively shallow depth and the short boat ride to the site make this an excellent dive for inexperienced divers to become ac-quainted with offshore North Carolina wreck diving, and many scuba classes use the wreck of the *Suloide* as their open water checkout dive.

4.29   *Suloide*.   Courtesy of The Mariners' Museum, Newport News, Virginia.

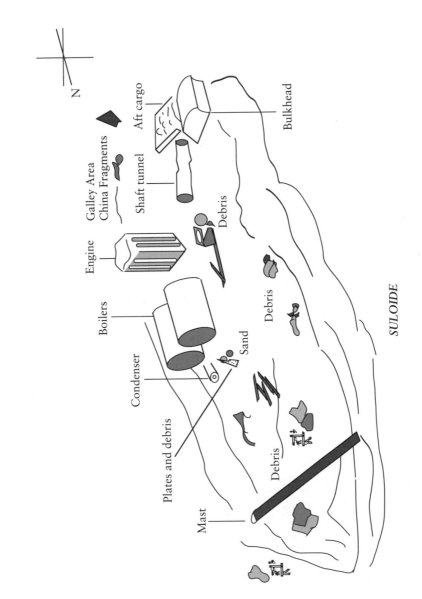

Wreck diagram of the *Suloide*.

4.30 *Suloide*. Shaft tunnel.

Ranging in the 70s during the summer, water temperatures here are cooler than on wrecks further offshore. The visibility is usually about 15 feet or less because of the proximity to shore, but on occasion it may exceed 70 feet. Under conditions of good visibility, the entire wreck site may be seen to be rather small and dominated by two large boilers which provide the greatest relief on the site. The Navy depth-charged and wire-dragged the *Suloide* because it was a hindrance to navigation, and consequently the remains of the ship are extensively broken up and scattered over the bottom. The wreckage consists mainly of twisted beams, plates, pipes, machinery, and bulkheads, with the *Suloide*'s two large boilers, her engine, and several large twisted bulkheads standing above the sand. The anchor chain is visible near the bow, and the long drive-shaft tunnel behind the boilers near the engine is a prominent feature.

Over the years, the wreck has been visited by countless divers who have recovered many artifacts, including brass portholes, valves, gauges, a silver cream pitcher, a silver condiment tray, and various silver knives, forks, and spoons. Occasionally, winter storms will uncover previously unexposed areas of the wreck site, and new artifacts are discovered each season. The wreck remains are covered with corals, sponges, sea anemones, sea cucumbers, bait and game fish, and many more species of tropical marine life. Flounders are plentiful in the sand around the wreck, and spearfishermen are often rewarded with a good catch of these fish as well as of the large groupers which inhabit the wreck.

A compass and a cross-wreck line are recommended for navigation on the site because disorientation is frequently a problem under the low visibility conditions often encountered. A bright dive light is useful for

4.31   Silver cream pitcher and condiment tray recovered from the freighter, *Suloide*, by Mike Sheen.   Photograph courtesy of Mike Sheen.

illuminating the numerous nooks and crannies created by the jumble of wreck debris. The relatively shallow depth permits long bottom times to investigate the site, but it also accounts for the frequent presence of surge, especially when there is a rolling sea on the surface. A wet suit is recommended for diving the *Suloide* since surge and currents may cause divers to scrape across corals and sharp, jagged pieces of the wreckage. The *Suloide* may often be dived when weather prevents diving on offshore wrecks.

W. E. Hutton

THE *W. E. Hutton*, 7,076 tons (4,359 net tons) and 435 feet long, was built for the Pure Oil Company of Netherland, Texas, by the Bethlehem Ship Building Company of Alameda, California, in 1920. (The tanker was originally named the *Portola Plumas*.) With her home port in Baltimore, Maryland, the *Hutton* was most of the time transporting fuel oil from Texas to the northeastern United States. Powered by a triple expansion engine with cylinders of 27, 47, and 78 inches in diameter and a 48-inch piston stroke, the tanker cruised at around 14 knots.

In mid-March 1942, the *Hutton* was travelling alone from Smith's Bluff, Texas, carrying 65,000 barrels of #2 heating oil to Marcus Hook, Pennsylvania. Late at night on March 18, 1942, the tanker had reached a point about 20 miles south of Cape Lookout when she came under the observation of the *U-124*, which was commanded by Korvettenkapitän Johann Mohr. Shortly before midnight a torpedo struck the *Hutton*'s starboard bow, blowing away both anchors along with a portion of the bow. Captain Carl Flaathen promptly ordered the ship abandoned because he knew that the U-boat would fire again and that he and his crew of 36 were sitting on a huge bomb. Less than ten minutes later, the *U-124* fired a second torpedo into the port side of the ship, igniting the fuel oil cargo with a tremendous explosion that set ablaze the *Hutton*'s midship section and killed 13 men. Of the 23 surviving crewmen, 12 escaped in one lifeboat, three in another, and eight on two life-rafts. Thirty-five minutes after the first torpedo struck, the *Hutton* sank in about 70 feet of water. The survivors stayed together in their separate crafts until daylight when they transferred to one lifeboat and headed toward shore. After rowing for a few hours, they were picked up by a British ship, the *Fort Halifax*, and taken to Savannah, Georgia.   [From Arthur R. Moore, 1983]

4.32   *W. E. Hutton*. U.S. Coast Guard.   Courtesy of The
Mariners' Museum, Newport News, Virginia.

Because of its proximity to shore and shallow depth, the *Hutton* is visited frequently by charter boats from Morehead City and Beaufort. The wreck lies 12.5 miles from Bogue Inlet on a heading of 115 degrees and 13.8 miles from Beaufort Inlet on a heading of 226 degrees, and most boats in the area can find it without too much trouble. During the war years, the large tanker presented a hazard to navigation in the shallow waters where she sank. It was nearly one year to the day after the *Hutton* went down that a Brazilian freighter, the *Suloide*, struck the wreck and sank about one mile away. After WWII, the *Hutton* was substantially broken up and reduced to twisted steel and rubble. Her remains are now scattered over a large area.

Given the location of the wreckage, close to shore and in shallow water, there is always the possibility of surge and some turbulence. However, current is seldom a problem. As a rule, poor visibility—less than 10 feet—will be encountered for a few days after coastal storms. Water temperature on the wreck is cooler by a few degrees than on offshore wrecks. The *Hutton* is used for checkout dives by local scuba classes and makes a nice shallow second dive after a deeper offshore dive. In good weather, the wreck can be reached by small, fast boats that either have their own loran C units or are guided to the *Hutton* by other boats already anchored at the site.

4.33   *W. E. Hutton.* Doorway.

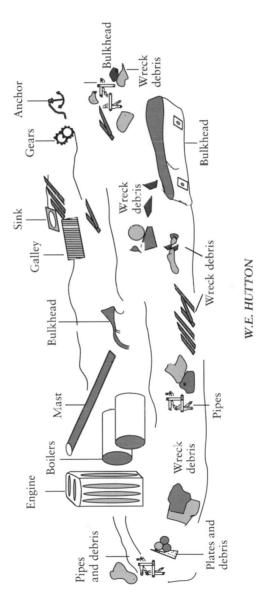

W.E. HUTTON

N

Anchor

Gears

Sink

Galley

Bulkhead

Mast

Boilers

Engine

Pipes and debris

Plates and debris

Wreck debris

Pipes

Wreck debris

Bulkhead

Bulkhead

Wreck debris

Wreck debris

Wreck debris

Wreck diagram of the *W. E. Hutton.*

As with any wreck that is visited every weekend, brass artifacts are scarce, but occasionally a diver will find another porthole or brass valve. The relief on the wreck is greatest around the *Hutton*'s two boilers where it reaches 15 feet. Many pieces of twisted steel are scattered among huge pieces of bulkheads lying helter-skelter over quite a large area of the bottom. The wreck site is probably 100 feet or more wide and several hundred feet long and presents many large nooks and crannies for the diver to explore. Each winter, storms batter the shallow wreck, and as a result divers are treated to newly exposed wreckage each season. The wreck is covered with beautiful marine life; sea urchins, anemones, flounders, corals, sponges, slipper lobsters, snails, eels, sea cucumbers, starfish, sheepheads, butterflyfish, and spadefish are but a few of the species the diver will encounter on the *Hutton*.

This wreck is a good one for the novice or inexperienced diver, and on a day when visibility underwater is 40 feet or more a diver will be rewarded with a superb dive. The *Hutton* may be dived when weather prevents diving wrecks that are further offshore.

5. New River Inlet

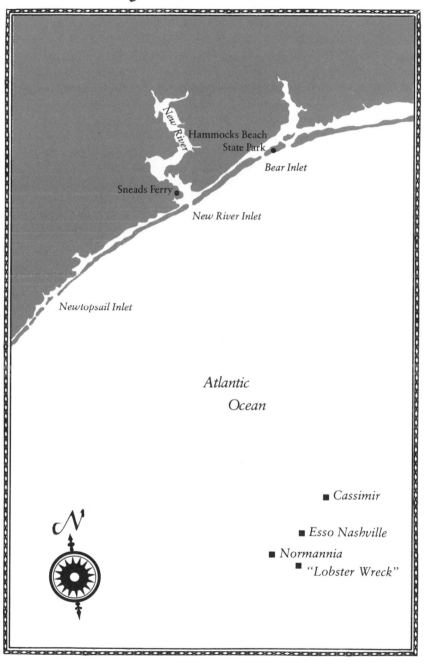

New River

Hammocks Beach
State Park

Bear Inlet

Sneads Ferry

New River Inlet

Newtopsail Inlet

Atlantic
Ocean

■ Cassimir

■ Esso Nashville

■ Normannia
■ "Lobster Wreck"

Cassimir

BUILT IN 1920 BY THE International Shipbuilding Corp. of Hog Island, Pennsylvania, the *Cassimir*, 5,030 tons (3,105 net tons) and 390 feet long, was powered by a General Electric geared steam turbine engine. The Cuba Distilling Company of New York, which owned the tanker, ran the ship between Cuba and Baltimore, Maryland, to transport molasses to be used in the manufacture of rum. In February 1942, Captain J. A. Bodman and a crew of 36 guided the loaded ship out of the harbor at Santiago, Cuba, and began the long journey to Maryland. Passing Frying Pan Shoals early in the morning of February 26, 1942, the *Cassimir* proceeded northeast slowly in a dense fog about 50 miles east of the tip of the shoals, headed on a collision course with the Grace Line freighter *Lara*. When the *Cassimir* became visible dead ahead, the crew of the *Lara* were unable to alter their ship's course, and the *Lara* knifed into the *Cassimir* just forward of amidships tearing a large hole beneath the waterline. As the *Cassimir* began listing to the starboard, Captain Bodman ordered that the ship be abandoned, and all but five of the crew were rescued by the *Lara*, which had not been damaged in the collision. The survivors were taken ashore at Charleston, South Carolina, several hours after the collision. The *Cassimir* remained afloat for a few hours, drifting in a northerly direction, before she sank approximately 47 miles southeast of Masonboro Inlet on a heading of 108 degrees in 120 feet of water. [From Arthur R. Moore, 1983]

The site of what is presumed to be the wreck of the *Cassimir* is 46 miles from Bogue Inlet on a heading of 176 degrees. WR-2 is the designation of the buoy that marks this wreck, and "WR-2" is also a name used

5.1 *Cassimir*. U.S. Coast Guard.   Courtesy of The Mariners' Museum, Newport News, Virginia.

5.2 *Cassimir*. Porthole inside stern section.
Courtesy of Jim Pickard.

for the wreck. While the wreck still has not been positively identified, there are several good pieces of evidence indicating that it is the *Cassimir*. The wreck is a tanker, built quite similarly to and around the same time (1910–1920s) as the *Cassimir*, and it is the right size for the *Cassimir*. Like the *Cassimir*, which had two decks, the wreck has multiple decks. Also, the location of the wreck corresponds well with the location of the *Cassimir* as reported by the *Lara*. And, finally, several years ago Mike Sheen of Dynamo Dive Shop in College Park, Maryland, dived the WR-2 with some other divers, and they reported seeing the welded letters "CASS . . ." on the stern of the wreck. Although I have made several dives on the stern section, I have never seen any large letters welded on the stern, nor has any other diver who has been on the wreck in the past few years. There are so many corals and sponges and so much calcareous growth on the stern that it would be impossible to find a name now. Nevertheless, the general belief is that the wreck is indeed the *Cassimir*.

The wreck lies in two sections, the smaller bow section being about 50 yards from the much larger and far more interesting stern section. The bow points upward at an angle of 50–60 degrees and comprises only about 10–15 percent of the wreck. Aside from the beautiful corals, sponges, and other interesting marine life growing on the bow, that section of the wreck is relatively uninteresting. There is a large anchor windlass present on the deck of the bow, and a diver can get a good look at the remarkably small sides (bulwarks) of the ship around the forecastle deck at the very tip of the bow. The sides here cannot be more than two feet high off the deck, and obviously, when the ship was afloat, the deck on this part was quite a distance above the surface of the ocean. The operator of the windlass or the lookout on the forecastle must have had to take care in rough weather not to get swept over the short sides on the

5.3   *Cassimir*. Commodes inside stern section.   Courtesy of
Jim Pickard.

bow. The tip of the bow is 85 feet deep and the sand below is at 115 feet.

The stern section has been demolished as a menace to navigation from the bowmost end to aft of amidships where the stern proper (poop deck) remains intact. After leaving the bow, the forwardmost part of the stern encountered by divers consists of I-beams standing more-or-less upright and outlining the hold in which they once made up the structural support. The hull plates in this part have long ago fallen into the ship's interior. Within the area bounded by the beams lies a mass of twisted plates, machinery, and pipes that at one time bound the vessel together and gave it life.

Directly aft of this area is a large bulkhead supporting the uncollapsed deck which is relatively intact for a short distance. On the deck is large machinery including a windlass, transverse pipes, and valves. Proceeding toward the stern past this portion of deck is a large section of the ship which has collapsed fifteen feet carving out a pit that resembles a large hold. Piled upon each other in here are large beams, pipes, plates, machinery, cables, and other debris. Passing out of this area and moving aft, the deck becomes intact again for a short distance. Scattered on the deck are broken pieces of machinery. It is possible to penetrate the *Cassimir* in the amidships portion of the wreck but it is not recommended because of the need for a guideline to get back out, the need for lights, and because of the fragile nature of the deck above. Inside are large dark rooms with pumps, transverse pipes, gauges, and other liquid handling machinery. Aft of this area, the deck collapses again to the bottom. At the far end of the collapsed area is the stern proper. The intact portion of the stern lists

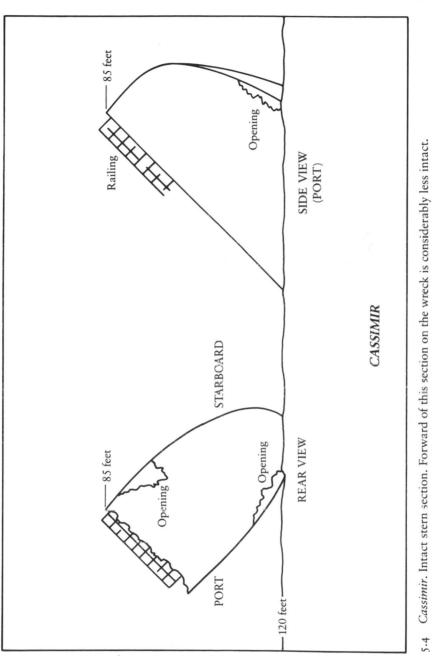

5.4 *Cassimir*. Intact stern section. Forward of this section on the wreck is considerably less intact.

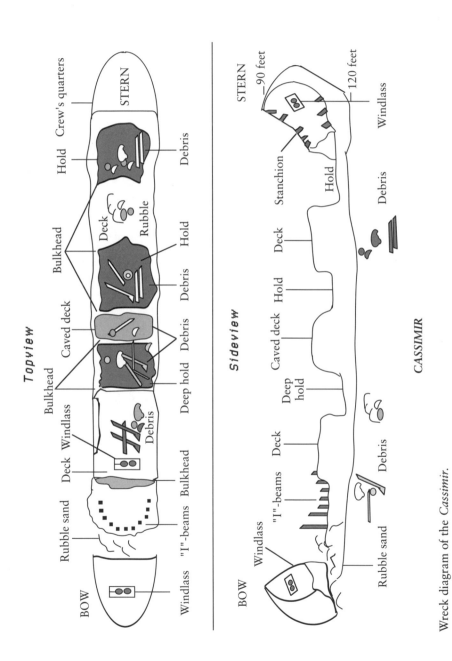

Topview

BOW

Rubble sand — Deck — Windlass

Windlass — "I"-beams — Bulkhead

Bulkhead

Bulkhead — Caved deck

Deck — Rubble

Hold — Crew's quarters — STERN

STERN

Debris

Hold

Debris

Debris

Deep hold — Debris

Debris

Sideview

BOW

Windlass

"I"-beams — Deck — Caved deck — Hold — Deck

Deep hold

Debris

Rubble sand

Debris

Stanchion

Hold

STERN

90 feet

Windlass

120 feet

Debris

Wreck diagram of the *Cassimir*.

about 30 degrees to port, and the stern proper is jutted upward at an angle of about 45 degrees. The uppermost portion of the stern lies at a depth of about 90 fsw and has coral-encrusted posts spaced around the edge of the stern deck. Most likely, the posts held a chain which served as the stern railing around the poop deck. From a hole in the stern at a depth of around 100 fsw, the head or bathroom may be seen below at 120 fsw. Two commodes are clearly visible, and by swimming around the stern to the sand, a diver may enter this compartment which also contains portholes and other brass artifacts. Close inspection of the commode seats reveals very little marine growth on them, suggesting that the paint used would be excellent antifouling material for the bottom of boats. The decks further forward on the stern section are a jumble of twisted steel, I-beams, catwalks, pipes, winches, and other material. The boiler and engine rooms are located in this area and are interesting but difficult to penetrate. A dive is useful for penetration into this area and into "caverns" formed by collapsed bulkheads and beams. There is, surprisingly enough, quite a bit of structure remaining in isolated sections of the collapsed portion of the stern.

The wreck is quite beautiful and stretches several hundred feet across the bottom. The marine life in and around the wreck is extraordinary: blue angelfish, butterflyfish, African pompanos, blennies, slipper lobsters, spiney lobsters, spotted moray eels, corals, and sponges abound. Bait and game fish usually can be found in large numbers around the wreck as well. Because of the generally good visibility and the wide variety of tropical marine life, the *Cassimir* is a photographer's dream. Brass collectors will find quite a few artifacts remaining on the wreck because it is so infrequently visited by divers.

Water temperatures on the site range in the mid-70s to mid-80s, and the visibility is generally in excess of 80–100 feet. However, on one out of the eight dives I have made on the *Cassimir*, the visibility was only 30 feet and there was a half-knot current running across the wreck. Current is often a problem on the *Cassimir*, and I have seen it run one-half to one knot on more than one occasion. The wreck is deep: 120 feet to the sand on the outside and deeper if you penetrate the interior of the wreck.

Boat captains from Beaufort, Morehead City, and Emerald Isle will take divers to the *Cassimir*. It is a three-and-one-half hour trip with George Harper running *Jaws* out of Bogue Inlet near Emerald Isle. It takes about an hour longer on the *Olympus, Saltshaker, Sea Wife IV*, and the *Outrageous* running out of Beaufort Inlet near Morehead City and Beaufort.

The deep dive, the occasional strong currents, and the long boat ride make this dive one for experienced divers. It must, however, rank as one of the top five dives off the North Carolina coast and is certainly worth accumulating the wreck-diving experience needed to see it.

The "Lobster Wreck"

ONE OF THE MOST FASCINATING wrecks to visit off the coast of North Carolina is the mysterious "Lobster Wreck." It is one of those rare seldom-visited sites divers and maritime enthusiasts dream about. Basking in 120 feet of warm, very clear, tropical water nearly 45 miles off Bogue Inlet, the "Lobster Wreck" was first introduced to divers in 1985. Captain Ed Wolfe, who operates the dive charterboat *Whipsaw* out of Wrightsville Beach, had fished over the wreck for several years but it was not until the summer of 1985 that he began to carry divers out to the site. For a few seasons, Captain Wolfe was the only ride to the site but after a while word leaked out about its location and now dive boats from Emerald Isle, Morehead City, and Beaufort make the trip to the wreck.

I was on the first two trips that the *Whipsaw* made carrying divers out to the site and the images of those dives will be forever etched in my memory. Spiny lobsters (*Panulirus argus*) more abundant than I had ever seen anywhere before were everywhere and many were as big as your leg. Lobsters were sitting on top of the boilers, in and on top of the engine, and within and around every piece of machinery and debris on the site. They were all sizes from adult to young. Specimens that weighed fifteen to eighteen pounds were not uncommon. Marine scientists explain that these lobsters migrate to the site each year carried by eddies of the nearby Gulf Stream. Other marine life is present as well. Groupers that are as large as a diver are abundant. Beautiful, colorful corals and sponges are found throughout the wreckage, some even appearing to grow directly out of the expanse of sand surrounding the site indicating portions of the wreck are covered and remain to be seen. In addition to the lobsters and groupers, many other species are regularly seen on the "Lobster Wreck." Blue angelfish, hogfish, African pompano, Atlantic spadefish, blennies, anemones, sea fans, sea whips, sea turtles, barracuda, amberjacks, Atlantic sand tiger sharks, arrow crabs, triggerfish, butterflyfish, moray eels, starfish, and sea urchins are abundant on the site. These and other sea life, like the lobsters, are carried up from the Caribbean basin by the Gulf Stream which passes close by the North Carolina coast. At times bait fish are so plentiful on the site that they actually block a good view of the wreck. Ocean-ranging game fish are attracted to this site for good reason.

Visibility averages 75 feet during the dive season and may often exceed 100 feet. Current is seldom a problem on the site but it does occasionally occur. At times, current of a knot or more may be experienced here.

The vessel's identity and vintage are unknown but each trip out brings

5.4   Hull ribs of the "Lobster Wreck."

5.5   Mast located in bow area of "Lobster Wreck."

back a little more information. The visible portion of the wreck occupies an area of about 75 by 250 feet and includes four large boilers whose diameter is about 12 feet, coal scattered around the boilers, a large engine, port and starboard iron bulkheads up to 7 feet tall, a 25–30-foot-long iron mast, an old naval anchor, and much broken-up wreckage in between. The entire area is apparently the midship and bow sections of the vessel and the remains of the stern are not visible. The large mast, the top of which looks like a light fixture, is so covered with corals and other

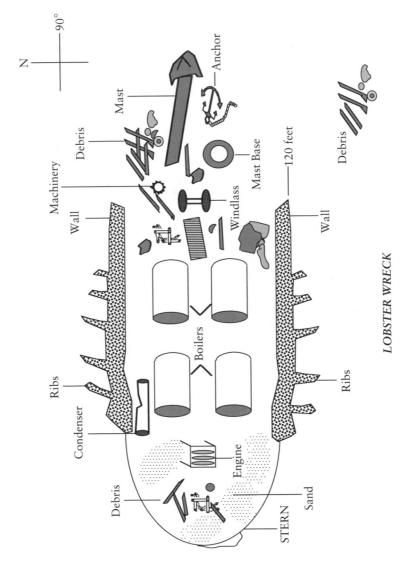

LOBSTER WRECK

Wreck diagram of The "Lobster Wreck".

5.6   Diver with lobster and porthole on "Lobster Wreck."

5.7   Spiny lobster on "Lobster Wreck."

marine growth as to obscure its identity, lies in the wreckage straight back from the engine and points toward what is presumed to be the direction of the stern. Near the tip of the mast and to one side is a large old anchor stuck upright by a fluke in the sand. Notwithstanding the presence of an anchor, this is believed to be the stern because of the order in which the boilers and engine present themselves with respect to this area. The boiler-end of the engine is usually in the direction of the bow and the opposite end of the engine is in the direction of the stern. The tip of the mast and the nearby anchor lie off the end of the engine that is opposite the boilers and thus, should be situated toward the stern end of the site.

The extent of marine life growth on the wreckage, the old anchor, the presence of coal around the boilers, and other features of the wreck suggest the vintage of the vessel to be late nineteenth century. There are some features of the wreck including the anchor that are similar to the *Proteus*, a passenger vessel built in 1899 and sunk in 1918 off the Carolina coast in about the same depth of water. The marine growth is thicker and more extensive on the lobster wreck, however. A few divers have recovered portholes and other artifacts which might prove helpful in identifying this wreck. A twelve-inch in diameter brass bourdon gauge recovered near the boilers had the name *American Steam Gauge and Valve, Boston, Mass.* and *Pat'd March 24, 03* inscribed on it so it is likely that the ship was American and built in the late nineteenth century.

Photographing the wreck site is usually easy because the visibility is good. This fact and the abundance of subject matter makes this wreck site a prime location for underwater photographers. However, limited bottom time and seemingly limitless lobsters combine to focus a diver's attention away from photography, shipwreck identification, and artifact collection toward a more gastronomic endeavor.

Esso Nashville

THE *Esso Nashville* was a 445-foot-long, 7,943-ton tanker (4,697 net tons) which was built in 1940 by the Bethlehem Steel Company for Standard Oil of New Jersey. With 38 crewmen on board, Captain Edward V. Peters commanded the tanker as she departed Port Arthur, Texas, on March 16, 1942, loaded with 7,800 barrels of fuel oil bound for New Haven, Connecticut.

After five uneventful days at sea, the *Esso Nashville* was just off Frying Pan Shoals shortly before midnight on March 20. The weather was rainy and there was a moderate sea as the tanker passed 16 miles northeast of the shoals shortly after 1:00 A.M. on March 21. For about an hour, the *U-124* under the command of Korvettenkapitän Johann Mohr had been following the tanker; then, two torpedoes were fired from the German submarine. On board the *Esso Nashville* a heavy impact was felt as the first torpedo crashed into the starboard side without exploding. About a minute later the second torpedo struck just aft of the wheel house and did explode, showering the deck with fuel oil.

Although unable to communicate with the engine room, Captain Peters had given the crew standing orders to stop engines in the event of an attack, and within a few minutes the engines were quieted. The blast broke the ship's back, and the bow and the stern were lifted into the air. Fire did not break out, but it was clear that the tanker was an imminent danger of sinking, so Captain Peters gave the order to abandon ship. All four lifeboats were lowered. Shortly after they were launched, two of the lifeboats were sighted by the USS *McKean*, and the eight crewmen in the boats were rescued. Twenty-one crewmen in a third lifeboat were picked up after dawn by the USCGC *Tallapoosa*. While trying to enter the fourth lifeboat, Captain Peters fell into the water, breaking his leg, and

5.8   *Esso Nashville*. U.S. Coast Guard.   Courtesy of The Mariners' Museum, Newport News, Virginia.

was unable to reach the lifeboat. He managed to pull himself back aboard the *Esso Nashville* and remained there until after daylight when he was rescued by the USCGC *Agassiz*, which also picked up the other eight crewmen in the fourth lifeboat. All hands had been safely rescued.

The bow section of the *Esso Nashville* broke off and sank later in the day on March 21. However, the stern section, comprising two-thirds of the vessel, remained floating on an even keel and was towed to Morehead City by the USS *Empqua*. Towed later to Baltimore, Maryland, the partially damaged ship was fitted with a new bow section, and the renovated *Esso Nashville* returned to service almost exactly a year after the *U-124*'s attack. The *U-124* sank the *Papoose*, *W. E. Hutton*, and the *E. M. Clark* off the North Carolina coast three days before attacking the *Esso Nashville*.

The bow section of the *Esso Nashville* lies in 115 feet of water 40 miles southeast of Masonboro Inlet on a bearing of 108 degrees and is approximately 5 miles southwest of the *Cassimir* (WR-2). The bow section is oriented to the east and is upside down extending up off the bottom at its easternmost point 25–30 feet, reaching 85–90 fsw. From its maximum point of relief, the hull slopes down towards the sand, reaching the bottom approximately 100 feet from the eastern end of the bow. The rest of the wreck extends to the west about 100–150 feet and is very broken up, consisting of a jumble of I-beams, plates, and machinery, with only about two to three feet of relief above the sand.

There is a large cavernous hole on the north and south sides of the inverted bow portion, and divers may enter this section with ease and swim all the way through and out the other side. Holes in the hull overhead allow shafts of bright light to penetrate the interior of the hull, giving it a cathedral-like appearance. With the aid of a bright dive light, a diver may swim around inside the large bow section exploring nooks and crannies while always in sight of an exit. Inside the hull is a maze of beams and bulkheads scattered about in the high volume of space created inside the bow section. Leaving the relatively intact inverted bow and proceeding toward the stern end of the wreck site, divers will come upon a large amount of twisted and broken wreckage lying about in the sand.

The wreck is covered with beautiful corals, sponges, sea anemones, blue angelfish, sea urchins, sea cucumbers, starfish, and large spiney lobsters. A myriad of bait fish and large ocean-ranging fish can also be seen at the site. During the summer, the water temperature on the wreck is in the upper 70s and low 80s. The visibility ranges from 70 to 100 feet, although it occasionally drops to 50 feet or less. Current is seldom a problem on the site.

Divers did not visit the *Esso Nashville* until the summer of 1984 when

5.9   *Esso Nashville.* Ladder inside bow.

Captain Ed Wolfe began taking dive charter trips out to the site from Wrightsville Beach. Captain Wolfe's *Whipsaw* is the only dive charter boat carrying divers on the four-hour trip to the wreck. Many brass artifacts have been recovered from the wreck, including several portholes, a brass running light, and the gyro-rudder steering device. Because of the long boat trip and the depth of the dive, only divers with wreck-diving experience should make the trip. One of the prettiest of wrecks, in terms of marine life present at the site, and one of the most interesting, because of the access into the voluminous bow, the *Esso Nashville* is well worth a novice diver's effort to gain the wreck-diving experience necessary for visiting the wreck.

Normannia

THE *Normannia* was a 2,681-ton (1,717 net tons) steel steam freighter, 312 feet long, built in 1897 by Howaldtswerke in Kiel, Germany, for the Peter Brown Company of Copenhagen, Denmark. In early January of 1924, the *Normannia* was docked in Black River Bay, Jamaica, where her holds were being loaded with recently cut mahogany logwood destined for Charleston and Philadelphia. The ship, commanded by Captain Blom, carried a crew of 26; but on this trip Blom was also accompanied by his wife Anna and their two dogs. Departing Jamaica with her holds filled, the *Normannia* started the trip north to Charleston.

The morning of Wednesday, January 16, 1924, found the ship in building seas and winds about 24 hours away from her destination. By noon the winds had reached gale force as the *Normannia* continued to move slowly up the coast, her progress being slowed by the battering of heavy seas and high winds. By mid-afternoon she had been driven far off course and was now located 30 miles east of Cape Fear with the storm showing no signs of subsiding. By this time the seas were too much for her, and she began leaking through worn plates in the hull. By 3:00 P.M., six feet of water had gotten into her holds and the fires in the boiler room had been extinguished. Captain Blom sent out the first SOS at 5:30 P.M., and it was received by Naval wireless in Charleston. Two Coast Guard cutters,

5.10   *Normannia.*   Courtesy of the Peabody Museum of Salem, Salem, Massachusetts.

5.11   *Normannia*. Lead battery cases.

the *Modoc* and the *Yamacraw*, were dispatched to the aid of the stricken vessel.

Meanwhile, the steamship *H. R. Mallory* picked up the distress signal and replied that she was only 10 miles northeast of the *Normannia*'s position, which she could reach in an hour. On arriving at the scene, Captain H. W. Barstow of the *Mallory* could see nothing of the distressed ship and began searching the area when a crewman spotted a light flashing off their starboard bow. Barstow radioed Captain Blom to set off two rocket flares. When the *Normannia*'s exact position was determined, the *Mallory*'s spotlight was directed at the stern of the foundering vessel so that Barstow could maneuver the rescue ship as close as was safely possible to the *Normannia*, which was only a quarter mile. About 8:30 P.M. a yawl from the *Normannia* was sent through the gale carrying Iwulhman Hausen, the second mate, and three seamen, who braved the murderous seas and winds to reach the *Mallory*. Upon arriving, they said they were bound from Jamaica to Charleston with a load of mahogany and that the hold and engine room were full of water. Captain Blom requested through Hausen that the *Mallory* tow the *Normannia* to safety, but Captain Barstow refused, saying he would only take off the crew. Barstow then sent W. P. Dunkin, his third officer, and a small crew aboard a lifeboat to bring back the remainder of the crew from the sinking *Normannia*. By midnight, after four terrifying hours, Anna Blom and all but the captain and six crewmen had been transferred to the *Mallory*. Anna tried to remain aboard the *Normannia* with her husband, but he insisted she leave and threatened to drop her down into the lifeboat if she did not go on her

5.12 *Normannia*. Two boilers and engine. View towards the stern.

own. Before departing, Mrs. Blom managed to save their two dogs and to round up tobacco and cigarettes for the men and some clothes for herself.

Captain Blom and the six crewmen who remained with him rode out the storm through the night. But on Thursday, January 17, when it was clear the *Normannia* was doomed to sink, the captain and the six crewmen abandoned ship and were picked up immediately by the freighter *Charles E. Hargood*. On Friday, January 18, Captain Blom, his wife, and all of the members of the crew were safely reunited in Charleston, having survived one of the fiercest winter storms to hit the East Coast.

The *Normannia* now lies in 110 feet of water approximately 28 miles east of Frying Pan Shoals, and 35 miles southeast of Masonboro Inlet on a bearing of approximately 125 degrees. Nearly every other weekend of the summer, divers visit the site. Ed Wolfe, on the *Whipsaw*, runs to the *Normannia* out of Wrightsville Beach. George Harper on *Jaws* regularly visits the site out of Emerald Isle. Boats running out of Beaufort and Morehead City (*Outrageous*, *Saltshaker*, and *Olympus*), infrequently visit the site. The wreck is one of the top five off the coast of North Carolina. Over the years, it has become a beautiful habitat for corals, sponges, spiny and slipper lobsters, sea anemones, sea urchins, sea cucumbers, butterflyfish, blennies, blue angelfish, amberjacks, large manta rays, sea turtles, and a variety of other tropical marine life. Spiny lobsters weighing 8–10 pounds have been taken off this wreck. Many

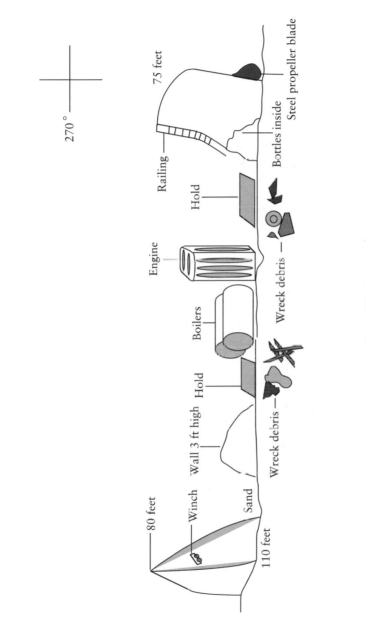

NORMANNIA

Wreck diagram of the *Normannia*.

brass artifacts have been recovered from the *Normannia*, including a number of portholes.

The wreck site lies in a straight line about 300 feet long running east to west. The bow (west) and stern (east) sections are intact, while the amidships portion is broken up at sand level with little or no relief. The bow section is about 40–50 feet long and sticks up at a 45-degree angle to the bottom, rising to about 80 fsw. A large windlass is attached to the deck of the bow, and there is a large opening in the deck near the sand where you can enter this section for about 5–10 feet. The bow is separated from the rest of the vessel by a patch of sand approximately 20–25 feet wide. From this point to the stern, the *Normannia*'s hull ribs and sides rise 5–10 feet off the bottom and provide the most relief on the site, excluding her engine, condensor, and boilers which are located midway between the bow and the stern.

Swimming from the bow to the stern, one first encounters a large hold with machinery and remnants of what appears to be petrified logwood trapped inside the hold. Past this section are the *Normannia*'s engine and two boilers, another large hold with more logwood, and finally the stern section and its large iron four-blade propeller at the rear. The stern is also pointed up at a 45-degree angle to the bottom and rises to about 70 fsw. The edge of the deck of the stern is lined with a coral-encrusted railing and has a few pieces of machinery lying about. At the base of the stern section on the port side near the sand facing forward is a large opening that allows access to a small room (steering engine room) which housed a rudder steering device. There are geared pieces of machinery attached to the ceiling and walls of this room, and a number of antique beer bottles have been recovered from beneath the sand floor of the room. Most of the bottles are green, with and without mold seams, and were originally sealed with a cork, the remains of which have been found in a number of bottles. One brown beer bottle has been recovered with the words "Cerveceria, La Tropical, Habana" embossed in the glass. La Tropical was apparently the brand name of a beer produced in Havana, Cuba, and the bottle must have been taken on board the *Normannia* during the ship's voyage through the Caribbean.

A slight to moderate current, usually running from stern to bow, is frequently encountered on the wreck. The visibility is most often 50–60 feet, but visibility of 80–100 feet during the summer is not uncommon. Water temperatures range from the mid-70s to the 80s during the summer, and the wreck can be dived without a wet suit, though care must be taken to avoid scrapes, scratches, and abrasions. Divers should have a few ocean wreck dives under their belt before visiting the *Normannia*, but the dive is not a difficult to one to make. It is worth gaining the experience needed to dive the wreck because the sights are absolutely exquisite.

6. Cape Fear

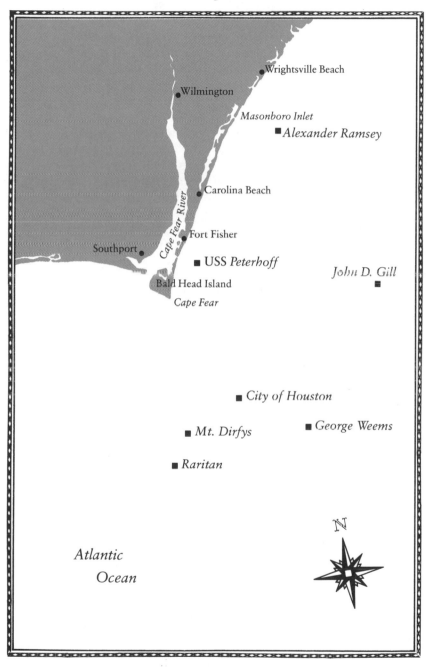

Wrightsville Beach

Wilmington

Masonboro Inlet

■ *Alexander Ramsey*

Carolina Beach

Cape Fear River

Fort Fisher

Southport

■ USS *Peterhoff*

John D. Gill

Bald Head Island

Cape Fear

■ *City of Houston*

■ *Mt. Dirfys*

■ *George Weems*

■ *Raritan*

N

Atlantic
Ocean

Alexander Ramsey

THE LIBERTY SHIP *Alexander Ramsey*, 441 feet long and 7,176 tons (4,380 net tons), was built in December 1942 by the Permanente Metals Corporation at Richmond, California. Powered by a 2,500-horsepower engine made by the General Machinery Corp. of Hamilton, Ohio, and a four-blade, 18.5-feet-in-diameter propeller, the ship cruised at 11 knots. After service in WWII, the *Alexander Ramsey* was consigned to the U.S. Merchant Fleet Reserve at the James River site near Newport News, Virginia. Purchased in 1974 by the State of North Carolina for use as an artificial reef, the vessel was cut down to the second deck, giving it a 30-foot-high profile. The *Alexander Ramsey* was sunk 3.5 miles east of Masonboro Inlet on a heading of 110 degrees in 50 feet of water on August 26, 1974.

With her deck at 20 fsw, the wreck is ideal for inexperienced wreck divers to learn wreck-diving techniques, and the site is frequently used for scuba class checkout dives. Dive charter boats from Wrightsville Beach visit the wreck frequently during the summer.

The relatively shallow depth permits long bottom times, but the proximity to shore results in low visibility and occasional surge when there is a rolling sea. The visibility is usually 5−10 feet, but on occasion it may reach 40−50 feet. Water temperatures during the summer are in the mid-70s to the 80s. The deck is covered with marine life, and there are large holds which allow easy penetration below decks where one can investigate a variety of machinery, catwalks, and other interesting structures. The site is an excellent habitat for bottom-dwelling fish, and ocean-ranging fish are attracted as well. Current is frequently encountered, and even the most sluggish current diminishes the visibility considerably. The *Alexander Ramsey* can often be dived when weather conditions prevent diving further offshore.

6.1   *Alexander Ramsey*. U.S. Army.   Courtesy of The Mariners'
Museum, Newport News, Virginia.

USS *Peterhoff*

THE *Peterhoff* was 210 feet long with a beam of 28 feet and a depth in the hold of 15 feet. Built at Petrodvorets on the Gulf of Finland in 1852 as a yacht for Czar Nicholas I of Russia, the 800-ton screw propelled, iron steamer vessel was confiscated by the British during the Crimean War and used as a British merchant ship prior to its days as a blockade runner for the Confederacy.

In 1862, the American consul in London, Francis H. Morse, obtained a letter drafted by the Bennett and Wake Shipping Company of London describing the shipper's detailed plans for sending a vessel to the Rio Grande. There the ship's cargo would be exchanged for cotton at Matamoros, Mexico, across the Rio Grande from Brownsville, Texas. Although the cargo was bound for the South, large profits appear to have been the motive for arranging the shipment rather than sympathy for the Confederacy. Morse was able to identify the vessel to be used as the *Peterhoff*, a screw-propeller steamer which had recently run the Union blockade at Charleston, South Carolina, and had returned to England with a valuable load of cotton. Morse notified the U.S. secretary of state, William H. Seward, of these facts, and the *Peterhoff* was placed on the Union blacklist of ships suspected of carrying goods into Southern ports.

The *Peterhoff* sailed from England late in January 1863 toward her destination, Matamoros, Mexico, as was indicated by her manifest, shipping list, clearance, bills of lading, and other papers. Because she was too heavy to cross the bar at the mouth of the Rio Grande, the *Peterhoff* was to anchor off the river and lighters would take her cargo up the river to Matamoros. Her freight, which was valued at $650,000, included 36 cases of artillery harnesses, 14,450 pairs of army boots, 5,580 pairs of gray blankets, 95 casks of large horseshoes, 52,000 horseshoe nails, iron, steel shovels, morphine, codeine, and quinine. The *Peterhoff* stopped briefly at St. Thomas in the Danish West Indies late in February after an uneventful trip across the Atlantic. On February 25, a Union ship-of-war, the *Vanderbilt*, captured the *Peterhoff* after a brief chase that was prompted by the suspicion that the *Peterhoff* was carrying "war-like" goods, which according to the laws of war a neutral ship was prohibited from transporting to either side.

The *Peterhoff*'s captain, Stephen Jarman, ordered papers burned and a package thrown overboard when it became clear that his ship would be captured. Jarman then allowed Union officers to come aboard and examine the ship's papers. However, when the officers became suspicious about

6.2   U.S.S. *Peterhoff.*   Courtesy of the Peabody Museum of Salem, Salem, Massachusetts.

the nature of the cargo and the ship's destination, they ordered the vessel seized.

A crew from the *Vanderbilt* took the *Peterhoff* to Key West, Florida, and then north for a prize court to decide whether or not the U.S. was justified in capturing a British vessel. When news of the *Peterhoff*'s capture reached England, the British press reacted with vehemence. Fear of war with the U.S. caused the stock market prices to fall, and British exchanges closed. Marine insurance rates skyrocketed, and shipping companies argued to no avail to get the British government to increase the number of British warships in the West Indies to protect legitimate trade with neutral nations.

Finally, on July 24, 1863, Judge Samuel R. Betts of the U.S. District Court, Southern District of New York, ruled that the ship was laden with contraband and that her papers were false with regard to her true destination. The court's finding was that the *Peterhoff* was not really bound for Matamoros but rather for a port in Confederate territory. Betts therefore condemned both the ship and her cargo, and in February 1864 the court sold the cargo at public auction for $273,628.99. At the same time, the Navy Department bought the steamer for $80,000, converted her to a warship at Hampton Roads Navy Yard and commissioned her immediately into the Union navy. In late February 1864, Act. Vol. Lieutenant Thomas Pickering took command of the *Peterhoff,* and the ship was assigned to the North Atlantic Blockading Squadron.

The USS *Peterhoff* departed Hampton Roads, Virginia, on February 28 for Wilmington, North Carolina, and on March 6, while stationed off New Inlet the ship collided with the USS *Monticello*, a 665-ton, 185-foot Union warship, and sank. The next day the USS *Mount Vernon* destroyed the *Peterhoff*'s hulk to prevent possible salvage by the Confederates.

The international dispute over the legality of the seizure was to continue for over four years. Even though the ship and her cargo had been sold, an appeal of Judge Betts's decision was made to the U.S. Supreme Court. On April 15, 1867, Chief Justice Salmon P. Chase made the long-awaited verdict, announcing that the *Peterhoff* was not engaged in dissimulation, that she was in fact on a "proper course from England to Matamoros." In the chief justice's view, "the ship's manifest, shipping list, clearance and other customs papers all indicated this." That either the ship or the cargo was ultimately destined for a blockaded Southern port was not considered relevant in his decision. Chase's opinion stated "that it was impossible to hold, that inland trade from Matamoros to Brownsville was affected by the blockade of the Texas coast. . . . Neutral trade with Matamoros, even with the intent to eventually supply goods to Texas by way of the Mexican port, could not be declared unlawful. . . . Though it was clearly inconvenient to the U.S. if the destination was Texas, nothing could be done about it." The court ruled therefore that both ship and cargo were "free from liability for violation of the blockade."   [From Stuart L. Bernath, 1968]

The *Peterhoff* lies in 30 feet of water, two miles offshore of the radar dome near Fort Fisher, approximately eight miles southwest of Masonboro Inlet. Dive charter boats from Wrightsville Beach travel to the site via Masonboro Inlet. The best time to dive the wreck is at slack high tide when the visibility may be 10–12 feet. Visibility at any other time will be less than three to five feet. The wreck covers a large area of the bottom, and the boiler, the engine, many valves, pipes and fittings, hull ribs, cannons, cannon carriages, leather or rubber gaskets, and other artifacts are visible but heavily encrusted with marine growth. Three smooth cannons, a 30-pound Parrott Rifle and a porcelain bowl bearing the name "Peterhoff" have been recovered. A large portion of the wreck remains intact, and the areas fore and aft of the boiler and around the engine provide the diver with a variety of nooks and crannies to investigate. Although the bow and stern sections have broken from the main body of the wreck, they are still properly aligned. Much of the upper deck structure remains. The engine area of the site is littered with coal, and most of the remains are covered with heavy coral growth. Two cannons and a variety of ship's equipment may be seen on the site. Surge is sometimes a problem on this wreck because of its shallow depth, but bottom times can be long, allowing for extensive underwater activities. The water temperature during May through October is in the 70s to mid-80s. Early and late in the diving season, water temperatures will be colder here compared to further offshore. A hood may be necessary when diving the *Peterhoff* in the spring or fall.

The wreck of the USS *Peterhoff* still belongs to the U.S. Navy because the vessel was never decommissioned after it sank in 1864. Although permission is not required to dive on the wreck site, a permit from the Navy is required before artifacts can be removed. The wreck site is listed in the National Register of Historic Places, and so it falls under the jurisdiction of the National Park Service of the U.S. Department of Interior. The wreck is also part of the Cape Fear Civil War Shipwreck District.

For diving and permit information, contact one of the following: Underwater Archaeology Branch, Division of Archives and History, P.O. Box 58, Kure Beach, NC 28449; or a National Park Service archaeologist at (202) 343-4113.

John D. Gill

THE TANKER *John D. Gill*, 528 feet long and 11,641 tons (7,217 net tons), was built in 1941 by the Sun Shipbuilding and Dry Dock Company of Chester, Pennsylvania, for the Atlantic Refining Company. In March 1942, making only its second voyage in service, the *Gill* departed Atreco, Texas, loaded with fuel oil bound for her home port of Philadelphia, Pennsylvania. Captain Allen Tucker pushed his new ship, which was powered by a single steam turbine engine, across the Gulf of Mexico, around the Florida Keys, and up the East Coast. On March 11, the *Gill* was ordered into Charleston, South Carolina, by the Coast Guard because of German submarine activity in the area. With his crew of 42 plus seven Navy gunners to man the five-inch guns mounted on the *Gill's* bow and stern, Captain Tucker waited anxiously in Charleston harbor for word that all was clear so that his ship could continue her journey north.

On March 12, however, the captain decided to have the *Gill* continue northward despite the threat of submarines and against the wishes of the Coast Guard. Shortly after noon, the tanker left Charleston, running in a calm sea with light southeast winds. That night, according to Coast Guard records, "the *Gill* proceeded with extreme caution past Cape Fear, travelling two-and-a-half miles inside the Frying Pan Shoals Lightship Buoy." Shortly after 10:00 P.M., she was about 25 miles east of Cape Fear when the #7 tank on the starboard side was struck by a torpedo fired from the *U-158*, which was under the command of Kapitänleutnant Erich Rostin.

The fuel oil that poured out of the *Gill's* tank floated on the surface of the sea, completely surrounding the ship. The *Gill* listed immediately, but not severely; even so, the order to abandon ship was given. A crewman threw over the side a life-ring fitted with a self-igniting carbide light

6.3 *John D. Gill.* Courtesy of The Mariners' Museum, Newport News, Virginia.

which ignited the fuel oil, and within a few minutes the entire ship was ablaze. The fire destroyed the starboard lifeboats, leaving only two port lifeboats, #2 and #4, and a life-raft available for the captain and crew. Lifeboat #2 was lowered safely and carried 15 crew members to safety. The crew members in lifeboat #4 were not as fortunate, however, because the boat jammed in her lifeboat-falls, dumping men into the water, some of whom were drawn into the *Gill*'s screw which was still turning. "The quartermaster was responsible for saving a number of lives when he re-leased a raft and, avoiding the blazing oil, swam to it and directed others in the water to safety, towing them when they were unable to help them-selves. A series of explosions marked the progress of the fire raging through the Gill, and at 3:00 A.M. on March 14 a terrific blast from the explosion of the powder magazine signaled the end of the tanker." [From T. R. Strobridge, 1956] A few hours later the burned-out ship broke in two pieces and sank in 90 feet of water 23 miles from Masonboro Inlet.

Survivors in the #2 lifeboat were rescued by the Atlantic Refining tanker *Robert H. Colley* and carried back to Charleston, South Carolina. The eight crew members and three Navy gunners on the raft were picked up about 7:00 A.M. by the Coast Guard patrol boat #4405, transferred to a Coast Guard cutter, the USCGA-186, and taken to Southport, North Carolina. The USCGA *Agassiz* and the Coast Guard picket boat USCGC-4342 carried 16 bodies to Southport, bringing the total of those who died in the sinking of the *Gill* to 19 crewmen and four Navy gunners. "Eyewitnesses on board the *Gill* later testified that the flame from the self-igniting carbide flare on the life-ring was responsible for setting fire to the escaping oil and enveloping the vessel in flames a few minutes after the explosion. As a result, the use of such flares was prohibited on all American ships."   [T. R. Strobridge, 1956. Material also from Arthur R. Moore, 1983]

Charter boats from Wrightsville Beach, Carolina Beach, and South-port frequently visit the *Gill*; when there is good weather, many small boats also go out to the site and anchor on the wreck. The site is 26 miles from Masonboro Inlet on a heading of 137 degrees, and it is marked by the "4" buoy which is maintained by the Coast Guard. The *Whipsaw*, *Pisces*, *Forego*, and *Lindy Lee*, all of Wrightsville Beach, take divers to the *Gill* on most weekends of the diving season. Divers may sleep aboard the *Whipsaw*, *Pisces*, and *Lindy Lee* on the night prior to a charter, thus allowing them to load their gear casually and sparing them the effort of having to travel to a charter boat for a 6:00 A.M. departure. It generally takes two-and-a-half hours to go from the sea buoy off Masonboro Inlet out to the wreck. Small, fast boats can reach the site in an hour, but there must be good weather for them to do so.

6.4   *John D. Gill.* Doorway to nowhere.

The *Gill's* bow section, which comprises 70 percent of the wreck, settled upright and is more or less intact. The deck is at 60 feet and is essentially a flat platform on which one can easily identify ventilation shafts, a single lifeboat davit, several large fuel transport pipes, cables, a solitary door standing in a portion of the cabin area, two anchors, an anchor chain, and a large bow hatch. The solitary "doorway to nowhere" was knocked down during a winter storm and may no longer be seen. The anchor on the starboard side of the bow deck is so large a diver may not recognize it at close distances. A large portion of the bow has caved in, and it is possible to swim into the wreck from the bow and proceed just below the deck all the way to the stern. Large pieces of the anchor chain are visible, as is a piece of the smaller chain formerly used to secure the "4" buoy to the wreck. A new crack was added to the wreck when the concrete anchor now used to hold the "4" buoy at a distance from the wreck was inadvertently dropped onto the rear starboard side of the wreck during an overhaul of the buoy by the Coast Guard. The tip of the bow is also beginning to crumble away. A gun platform may be seen off the starboard bow lying upside down in the sand about 25 feet away from the wreck, and on both sides of the wreck lie several piles of pieces of the superstructure. The port side of the bow has a large gaping hole left by a salvage crew that blasted through the superstructure to reach the

6.5   *John D. Gill.* Deck.

spare propeller. Over the last few years, the port side of the bow has caved in quite extensively. The stern end of the bow section is interesting because when the ship cracked it was broken cleanly in two.

A diver can swim into the wreck directly through the stern break, but care must be taken if current and surge are present. Before descending into the wreck through the break, a diver can check for surge by swimming over one of several ventilator shaft openings located on the deck. Surge is easily detected here, and even the mildest surge may push a diver several feet up above the deck; in heavy surge it is akin to a rocket ride toward the surface. Needless to say, the same rapid elevator-style ride will be experienced inside the wreck where the consequences would be more severe.

The stern section lies about 50 yards past the end of the bow section and is pretty broken up. Less frequently visited than the bow portion, the stern section still offers a few nice brass artifacts. Ten years ago the stern section was quite popular with commercial salvage divers, who removed the four-blade propeller and portions of the engine as well as other parts of the engine. At the very end of the stern lies the *Gill*'s large, round five-inch deck gun upside down in the sand with the gun barrel holding it up.

The visibility on the *Gill* ranges from 20 to 150 feet during the summer, with the average being about 50–60 feet. Water temperatures during the summer range in the mid-70s to the 80s. Surge is occasionally a prob-

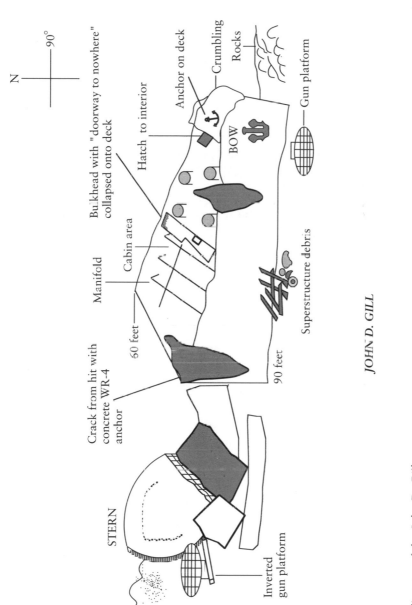

N — 90°

STERN

Crack from hit with
concrete WR-4
anchor

60 feet

Manifold

Cabin area

Bulkhead with "doorway to nowhere"
collapsed onto deck

Hatch to interior

Anchor on deck

Crumbling
Rocks

BOW

Gun platform

Superstructure debris

90 feet

Inverted
gun platform

JOHN D. GILL

Wreck diagram of the *John D. Gill.*

lem, and when there is much surge, the visibility usually drops. Currents are frequently encountered on the wreck but usually do not present a problem.

The tropical marine life on the ship is fantastic. Among the many species at the site are slipper lobsters, moray eels, blue angelfish, butterflyfish, anemones, corals, and sponges. Barracudas can be seen on just about any dive, and occasionally a sand tiger shark or two may be present. Amberjacks are often in the vicinity of the wreck, while sea turtles, manta rays, and mackerels are less common. The corals, sponges, sea fans, and sea whips make the *Gill* a naturalist's paradise. Their beautiful colors and exquisite shapes and textures provide a visual delight reminiscent of a terrestrial flower garden and perfect subject matter for photographers.

So much may be seen on the deck that a diver need not ever descend to the bottom—spending the whole dive, instead, at 60 feet. The wreck is an excellent dive for inexperienced divers because of the shallow depth of the deck, the usually good visibility, and the fact that the *Gill* looks like an intact ship sitting on the bottom. For the experienced diver, there are many areas of the ship below decks for penetration and exploration. And for all there is a myriad of Caribbean marine life to behold.

City of Houston

IN 1870, the U.S. Civil War had ended half a decade before. Reconstruction would not be over for another seven years or so. The physical, emotional, and financial recovery from the war would take even more years to complete. The financial crash of 1869 had added further woes to an already foundering economy. Many businesses were forced to close their doors. People in the war-ravaged South and the unemployed from the industrial North began to look west for an escape from their troubles. The expansion was on. Americans started to move west to the land of opportunity. Railroads began building westward only to be resisted by the Indians. Indian wars and the pacification of the west proceeded in earnest. The C. H. Mallory Company of New York saw another way to get goods from the east to the west without the railroads and the troublesome Indians. Steamships!

In 1870, despite a depressed economy, C. H. Mallory contacted Reaney, Son and Archbold Ironworks of Chester, Pennsylvania about constructing several iron steamships over the next four years for his new Texas Line. Mallory might have been less expansive in his plans had he known the country would enter an economic depression in 1872 before half of his order was ever completed. However, Mallory did know that the high tax on iron, which was imposed after the Civil War, would drive the costs of construction of such ships upward. He opposed the tax believing it had done almost as much as the *Alabama* to crush shipbuilding interest in the country. Nonetheless, after lengthy negotiations, he ordered four steamers to be built. The first ship of the four that was completed by Reaney Ironworks was the *City of Houston*, a 240-foot-long, 1,253-ton steamer. Completed in the summer of 1871, the vessel was designed to carry passengers and freight between Galveston, Texas, and New York.

On August 12, 1871, the *City of Houston* departed New York for its first trip to Galveston. Ironically, the maiden voyage would set the pattern of bad luck that would plague this ship for the remainder of her life. Four days into its first trip in service, with Captain Partridge at the helm, the vessel entered the Straits of Florida where it encountered the first of many severe storms which were to test its seaworthiness over the next few years. The storm struck with such force that her foremast was destroyed and one of her boilers was broken free, rupturing a steam pipe which disabled the ship. For three days and four nights passengers and crew worked unceasingly to keep the vessel afloat. Seven of the passengers were U.S. Navy sailors who had booked passage from New York. These men were awarded a special commendation from the secretary of navy, George

6.6   *City of Houston.*   Courtesy of the Peabody Museum of Salem, Salem, Massachusetts.

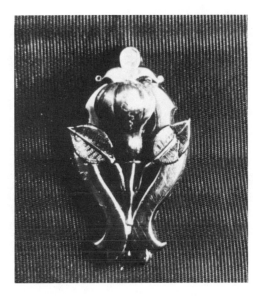

6.7 Gold brooch recovered from the passenger liner *City of Houston.*

M. Robeson, for their efforts to save the ship. The *City of Houston* limped into the port of Fernandia, Florida using power from its remaining boiler. The pride of the Texas Line would remain here for two weeks while repairs were being made. After repairs were completed and the ship determined to be sound, the *City of Houston* departed Florida for Galveston. Arriving three days later, the *City of Houston* finally completed her ill-fated maiden voyage.

In 1872 and 1873, the *City of Houston* completed several trips between New York and Galveston without incident averaging around 11 knots over the 2,000 mile journey. At that speed, the one-way trip south took seven days to complete.

In May of 1874, the *City of Houston* paid a visit to the port of New Orleans, Louisiana. On May 13, the vessel left New Orleans and was proceeding down the Mississippi River on its way to the Gulf of Mexico. About 45 miles below New Orleans, near Point a la Hache, the *City of Houston* collided with the tugboat *Tillie C. Jewett*. The smaller tugboat suffered a fatal gash in the side and sunk almost immediately. Two of the tugboat's crew were drowned. As a result of an investigation into the accident, Captain C. H. Andrews, pilot of the steamship, had his license suspended for 15 days. Captain John T. Davis, master and pilot of the tug

6.8   One of the anchors from the passenger liner *City of Houston*.

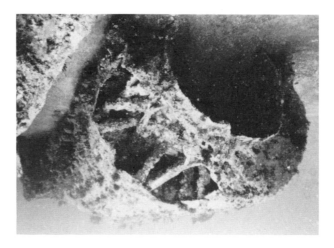

6.9   Condenser from the passenger liner *City of Houston*.

6.10 Shaft tunnel from the passenger liner *City of Houston*.

and the one who was on watch at the time of the collision, was fined $50 and had his license suspended for 15 days. The steamship suffered only minor damage as a result of the collision.

In March of 1876, the *City of Houston* was drydocked at Chester, Pennsylvania for alterations. A larger forward hold was added lengthening the vessel an additional 50 feet to 290 feet and increasing the ship's gross tonnage to 1,515 tons. The ship was placed back into service on the New York to Galveston run where it completed several round trips over the next two years without incident.

In New York in late October of 1878, the *City of Houston* began loading a cargo of miscellaneous merchandise bound for Galveston for the Christmas season. Among the ship's cargo were Singer® sewing machines, railroad wheels, English china and porcelain dinnerware, china dolls, tea sets, school slates, jars and bottles of medicine and foodstuffs, clocks, bullets and a wide variety of merchandise bound for general stores. On Sunday, October 20, the *City of Houston*, under the command of Captain Stevens, departed New York fully loaded with cargo and carrying thirty-three passengers. The weather could not have been better for the first couple of days of the southbound voyage. However, unknown to Captain Stevens, a severe storm had begun to develop in the Caribbean the day the ship left New York. Early in the morning of October 20, the Signal Service had ordered up storm signals at Key West, Florida. On the morning of October 21, the storm was located southeast of Key West where it was increasing in strength as it moved up the eastern seaboard. By the morning of the twenty-second the storm was located to the east of

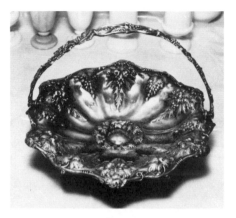

6.11   Silver serving bowl recovered
from the passenger liner *City of
Houston*.

southern Georgia packing winds of over 50 miles per hour. At midnight
on the twenty-second, the center of the storm was located near Cape Hatteras off the North Carolina coast. Winds had now reached over 60 miles
per hour.

Late in the afternoon on October 22, the *City of Houston* was located
off Cape Hatteras, North Carolina. The seas and the wind began to pick
up as the ship made its way southwest toward Cape Fear. As evening approached, extremely heavy seas set in and gale force winds buffeted the
ship with violence. By 9 P.M., an uncontrollable leak had developed in the
engine room that became so severe that much of the ship's machinery
soon became disabled. By 2 A.M. on Wednesday morning, October 23,
the boiler fires were extinguished by water which poured into the ship.
The vessel lost all power making her uncontrollable. Captain Stevens notified the passengers of the situation and ordered all to prepare the lifeboats for evacuation of the ship. He ordered signal flares to be burned
from the pilot house even though it was unlikely another ship could see
them through the pitch black night and driving rain. By 4 A.M. all of the
lifeboats were in readiness and the passengers were ordered to put on life-
jackets. At dawn, a ship was seen nearby but because of the wind was
unable to come to the rescue of the hapless vessel. At 8 A.M. there was ten
feet of water in the holds. A single pump powered by a small donkey en-

gine on the stern had not been able to keep up with the incoming water. The ship slowly began to sink. Captain Stevens was about to order the lifeboats lowered when a lookout spotted a steamship headed toward them. The steamer, *Margaret*, had seen the distress signals and headed to the rescue. Within an hour the *Margaret* had reached the stricken ship. The lifeboats were lowered and, although the sea was extremely rough, all passengers and crew were safely transferred to the *Margaret*. Within an hour, the *City of Houston* and all of its cargo sank to the ocean bottom. The passengers gave the Captain and crew of the *City of Houston* high marks for their courageous conduct throughout the ordeal. The *Margaret* continued on to her destination, Fernandia, Florida, with the rescued passengers and crew. After disembarking them at Fernandia, Captain Holmes ordered the *Margaret* back to New York. On the return trip, Captain Holmes reported seeing quantities of wreck material including furniture and boxes, some of which were marked *Galveston*, floating about 60 miles northeast of where the *City of Houston* had gone down. The *City of Houston* sank off the tip of Frying Pan Shoals off Cape Fear, North Carolina in 90 feet of water. The remains of the ship are extensively broken up on the bottom and there is less than six feet of relief over most of the site. The ship's two boilers are missing but the donkey boiler, engine, two anchors, condenser, shaft tunnel, rudder quadrant, and part of a propeller blade are present on the site. The keel and ship's ribs are visible in portions along the wreck field and there are many large bulkheads with portholes lying around the area. The bow of the wreck points toward the northeast and the rest of the wreckage lies in a straight line extending approximately 300 feet to the southwest. Visibility on the site may be more than 100 feet during the summer. Current is infrequently present on the wreck and when it occurs it is usually less than half a knot.

The wreck abounds with tropical marine normally associated with Caribbean diving. Blue angelfish, triggerfish, grouper, arrow crabs, hogfish, blennies, corals, sponges, sea fans, sea whips, Atlantic spade fish, sea turtles, manta rays, Atlantic sand tiger sharks, barracuda, and many other creatures may be seen here.

Artifacts salvaged from the wreck are the most interesting that have been recovered from an offshore North Carolina wreck site to date. They include a solid gold brooch, a large solid silver basket, English china dinnerware, porcelain figurines, assorted hand-blown bottles, china vases, china dolls, china tea sets, railroad wheels, ironstone dishes, sewing machines, bullets, jars of foodstuffs and medicines, and assorted general merchandise. Many of the artifacts are still packed in crates in the hold and some of the pieces of china are still in their original copper foil wrap-

6.12   Print of ambrotype photograph of "Louise" recovered from the passenger liner, *City of Houston*, by Wayne Strickland.   Photograph courtesy of Wayne Strickland.

pers. A wooden box has also been recovered from the hold which has *Galveston* stamped on it. A photograph, believed to be the oldest to have been recovered from a shipwreck, was discovered in one of the passenger's trunks. The ambrotype photograph that was found consists of a silver image made on a glass plate. The glass with image, when placed on a black background in a frame, produces a positive image for viewing.

Because of the good visibility and relatively shallow depth, this dive is a good one for divers of all skill levels. Captain Wayne Strickland, Southport, North Carolina and George Purifoy, Morehead City, North Carolina are the only boat captains taking divers to the site. It is a three-hour boat ride on Captain Strickland's charterboat, *Scuba South I*, from the dock at Southport, North Carolina. The trip takes six hours from Morehead City.

George Weems

THE *George Weems*, 416 tons (250 net tons) and 149 feet long, was built in 1874 at Baltimore, Maryland, as a Coast and Geodetic Survey boat and was originally named the *George S. Blake*. The small vessel, powered by sail and steam, was sold in 1905, converted to a freighter, and renamed the *George Weems*. On May 20, 1908, while travelling up the East Coast carrying a load of cotton and lumber, the ship caught fire, burned, and sank next to the old Frying Pan Lightship, which doesn't exist today and which has been replaced by Position Buoy "2 FP" ("2 Frying Pan"). The captain and all 19 crewmen were rescued safely.

Located within view of Frying Pan Light, the site of the wreck is 25 miles from the "2CF" Buoy off the mouth of the Cape Fear River and 35 miles from Masonboro Inlet on a heading of 168 degrees. Lying in 40 feet of water, the *George Weems* is missing much of her hull because of the fire. At the stern end of the wreck site is a large cast-iron, four-blade propeller, and forward of this area is the main body of the wreck. There is a large drive shaft visible, and much wreckage is scattered about. The engine may be seen lying over on its starboard side. The two boilers broke loose and now one lies on the port side and the other on the starboard side of the wreck site. Forward of the boilers is the cargo hold, the remains of which consist of keel and hull ribs. The wreck takes a slight turn to the right forward of the cargo hold, and here the remains of the ship's two anchors may be seen. Numerous brass artifacts have been recovered

6.13 *George Weems.* Steamship Historical Society Collection. University of Baltimore Library.

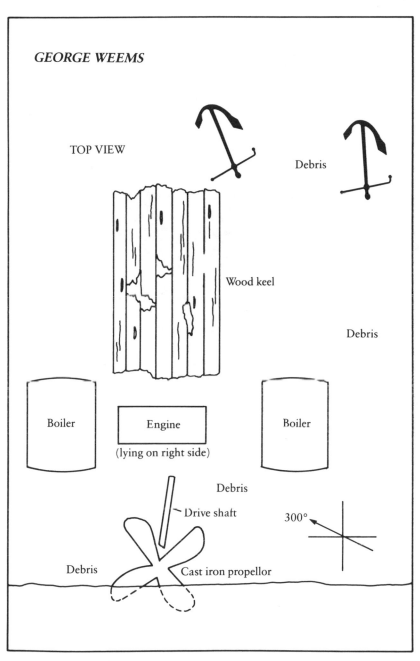

Wreck diagram of the *George Weems*.

6.14   Bell from *George Weems* (previously *George S. Blake*).   Photograph courtesy of Wayne Strickland.

from the site, including a brass plaque and an unusual octagonal porthole. There are supposed to be a dozen or more such portholes on either side of the wreck just below the sand.

The visibility is usually 20–30 feet, but one may occasionally encounter 60–70 feet of visibility. The water temperature ranges in the upper 70s to the low 80s during the summer, and the dive can be made without a wet suit. Current is seldom a problem on this dive, although on one occasion I experienced a current of about one knot. The shallow depth of the dive, the good visibility, and the lack of current make this an excellent dive for inexperienced wreck divers.

Captain Wayne Strickland's *Scuba South I* will carry divers on the four-hour trip to the wreck from Southport. He is the only boat captain I know of who visits the site with divers. In addition to being a knowledgeable boat captain with plenty of experience in commercial salvage work, Captain Strickland is a NAUI instructor and an active sport diver, and he has first-hand knowledge of the layout of each of the wrecks he visits.

Mount Dirfys

THE FREIGHTER *Mount Dirfys*, 5,242 tons (3,217 net tons) and 400 feet long, was built in 1918 by W. Dobson and Company at Newcastle, England, and was originally named the *Bernini* and then the *War Penguin*. In 1933, the ship was acquired by the Atlanticos Steamship Company of Piraeus, Greece, and was then operated under Greek registry. Departing Lourenco Marques, Mozambique, on the east coast of Africa, in mid-December 1936, the *Mount Dirfys* was loaded with chrome ore bound for Wilmington, North Carolina. During a storm on December 26, the freighter foundered off the southern coast of North Carolina and was driven onto the southwest tip of Frying Pan Shoals off Cape Fear where she sank in 30 feet of water.

The wreck lies 21 miles southwest of Southport on a heading of 160 degrees and 36 miles south of Masonboro Inlet on a heading of 183 degrees. Dive charter boats from Southport frequently make the two-hour trip carrying divers to the wreck site during the dive season, while very infrequently dive charter boats from Wrightsville Beach make the trip of four to five hours via Masonboro Inlet.

All the remains of the *Mount Dirfys* are present at the wreck site. The bow collapsed in 1982, and now all of the wreck lies at the sand in 30 feet of water. Aft of the bow is the forward cargo area followed by three boilers lying in a line across the wreck. Aft of the boilers is the blown-apart engine which is suspended on its port side by a piston rod. The wreck aft of the engine is lying in rubble to the stern where it is partially intact and where there is a steering post which comes up to within 10 feet of the surface. The propeller was salvaged years ago, and aft of the stern where the propeller should be is a large hole about 20 feet deep which collects shells sometimes to a depth of 4–5 inches. This area makes for excellent shell collecting, but the presence of shells in this hole is transitory: the currents and sea action that deposit the shells can take them away as well. The shells that are present one week may be gone the next.

Because of the wreck's proximity to shore, the visibility is usually 20–30 feet, although occasionally it may reach 60 feet, and strong currents are sometimes a problem. The water temperatures are in the mid-70s during the summer, but wearing a wet suit is nevertheless advised because of the presence of currents and surge which can buffet the diver into sharp corals or metal. The wreck is covered with corals, sponges, groupers, sheepheads, flounders, bait fish, sea anemones, sea urchins, and other marine life. Over the years, divers have recovered numerous brass artifacts from the site, including portholes, valves, fittings, gauges, and light fixtures. Commercial salvage divers have also worked the wreck for scrap copper and brass. A cross-wreck line and a compass are recommended for navigation on the wreck, and a bright dive light is very useful for exploring the jumble of wreckage.

The shallow depth of the wreck permits a lot of bottom time for exploration and makes the *Mount Dirfys* an excellent dive for beginning wreck divers to gain valuable experience.

Raritan

THE 251-FOOT-LONG, 2,649-ton (1,614 net tons) *Raritan* was built in 1919 at Wyandotte, Michigan, and was originally named the *Lake Fairton* and then the *Detroit-Wayne*. The small freighter plied the Great Lakes for several years before being acquired by the Raritan Steamship Corporation of New York. Subsequently, the *Raritan* made frequent trips from the Caribbean to New Orleans, her home port, as well as to other ports along the Gulf of Mexico and on the Eastern Seaboard.

In late February 1942, with Captain Otto Lohr in command and 29 crewmen on board, the *Raritan* departed Buenaventura, Columbia, carrying a full cargo of coffee bound for New York. Crossing the Gulf of Mexico and then continuing up the East Coast, the *Raritan* made good time to the North Carolina coast. Arriving off Frying Pan Shoals on February 25, the *Raritan* crept slowly through a thick fog which made navigation difficult for several hours. Captain Lohr had gotten too close to shore on his approach to Frying Pan Shoals, and slowly but surely the ship was headed for shallow water. By the time Lohr realized his mistake, the breakers on the shoals could be heard and the unmistakable grinding and slowing of the ship signalled the beginning of the end for the *Raritan*. Stranded and stuck fast in the shoals, Captain Lohr radioed a distress call, and he and all the crew were safely rescued. The *Raritan* broke up and was swept out off the shoals, ultimately resting in about 80 feet of water a few miles south of Frying Pan Shoals.   [From Arthur R. Moore, 1983]

The wreck site is 20 miles from the "2CF" Buoy off the mouth of the Cape Fear River on a heading of 163 degrees. Ed Wolfe, captain of the *Whipsaw*, will occasionally make the five-hour run from Wrightsville Beach. Some dive charter boats based in Southport, which is much closer to the wreck site, also run to the *Raritan*. Captain Wayne Strickland frequently makes the three-hour trip to the *Raritan* from Southport.

The water temperature at the site, which is close to shore, will be some-

6.15 *Raritan*. U.S. Coast Guard. Courtesy of The Mariners'
Museum, Newport News, Virginia.

what cooler than further out to sea. The visibility is in the 70-foot-range
when excellent, but it usually is 20 to 30 feet or less. Currents are occasionally a problem. One additional problem with this site is that it is located in the shipping lanes that lead to the harbor at Wilmington. Even
though a dive charter boat will have its dive flags flying, it may still pose a
navigational problem to the large ocean tankers that frequent the area.
For fear of being run over in the shipping lanes, once a dive captain
changed my dive charter trip from the *Raritan* to another offshore wreck
when the surface visibility was reduced by fog to a mile or so. Still, in
spite of the problems associated with the wreck site, the *Raritan* is an
interesting wreck to visit.

The wreck is broken into two sections which are about 80–100 yards
apart. On a given dive trip to the *Raritan*, divers generally dive one section or the other on a single dive rather than both because of the distance
between them. The bow section is intact back to the forward cargo
bulkhead and lists to the port side. To about 50 feet aft of the forward
cargo hold, the wreck is broken up and lying in the sand. The stern section also lists to port and is intact to the stern cargo section. Forward of
that cargo section, the wreckage—including the engine room area—
extends about 100 feet and is mostly reduced to rubble. The engine sits
upright, and there are two boilers forward of the engine. The bow and
stern sections rise up to about 30 feet above the sand to about 55 fsw.

There is not a lot of coral growth, but the wreck is covered with calcareous growth. An abundance of fish can be found at the site, including
sheepheads, flounders, groupers, sea bass, colorful tropicals such as blennies and blue angelfish, and a lot of bait fish.

This is a good dive for inexperienced wreck divers when they are accompanied by an experienced buddy.

PART TWO

Near Shore Wrecks

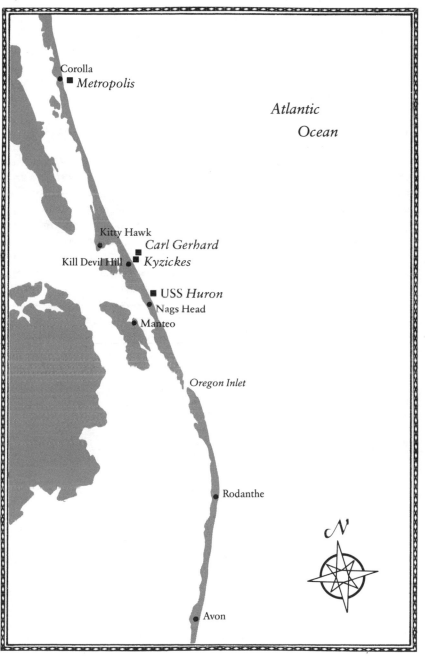

Corolla
■ *Metropolis*

Atlantic

Ocean

Kitty Hawk
■ *Carl Gerhard*
Kill Devil Hill ■ *Kyzickes*

■ USS *Huron*
Nags Head
Manteo

Oregon Inlet

Rodanthe

Avon

Metropolis

BUILT IN 1861 BY CHARLES MALLORY at Mystic, Connecticut, and originally named the *Star and Stripes*, the 878-ton, 200-foot-long *Metropolis* was sold to the United States Navy in mid-1861 to be used as a blockader off the North Carolina coast. During the course of the war, she captured several ships whose cargo was destined for the Confederacy. She also participated in expeditions against fortifications on Roanoke Island and along Pamlico Sound and helped capture New Bern. After the war she was sold to Thomas Watson and Sons of New York and was used for several years to carry passengers and cargo from New York to Havana.

In 1871, the *Metropolis* was lengthened and her engine refurbished, but other more critical repairs to her hull were neglected. She was then returned to the New York–Havana run and continued in good order for six years. In late November 1877, the *Metropolis* was chartered to transport cotton from Wilmington, North Carolina, by a railroad company whose service was temporarily stopped because rising flood waters had carried away the railroad bridge at Weldon. After departing New York for Wilmington on December 2, 1877, the *Metropolis* developed serious leaks a day out of port but continued to Hampton Roads where she limped into port with six inches of water in her engine room. Although she was soon repaired, the railroad company cancelled the charter because after inspection the *Metropolis* was found to be in unsuitable and unseaworthy condition.

In January 1878, the *Metropolis* was chartered to a company that was hired to build railroads in Brazil. Departing Philadelphia on January 29, 1878, bound for Para, Brazil, she carried over 500 tons of railway equipment and supplies and 248 passengers, most of whom were mechanics and laborers hired by the railroad contractor.

Off the coast of Delaware, the *Metropolis* encountered a fierce gale coming out of the southeast which continued to grow during the night. Early in the morning of January 30, her propeller well began to leak so badly that coal was jettisoned to lighten the ship as it made an emergency attempt to make Hampton Roads once again. All day and into the night the vessel made her way slowly toward land and safety, but late that night her pumps broke down and she began to take on a lot of water. With the force of the storm rising and the ship sitting low in the water, heavy seas pounded her with relentless fury, tearing away her smokestack and several lifeboats and flooding her decks. The rising water finally reached the boilers and put out the ship's fires on the afternoon of January 31. With

7.1   *Metropolis.*   Courtesy of The Mariners' Museum, Newport News, Virginia.

no power and at the mercy of high winds and seas, the *Metropolis* was pushed toward land where at 6:30 P.M. she ran aground on the outer bar off Currituck Beach about three miles south of the light. Swinging broadside to the raging surf which crashed across her hull and destroyed all the remaining lifeboats, the *Metropolis* was pounded apart. The vessel and her cargo were a total loss, and 102 passengers perished.

No one on land gave any assistance to the stricken vessel and its passengers and crew, even though the *Metropolis* foundered within 10 miles of the old Kitty Hawk lifesaving station. Many of the survivors reported that upon reaching the shore after their ordeal at sea, they were robbed of their remaining possessions by bands of marauding local inhabitants. Many died after reaching shore. The press of the day denounced the inefficiency of the newly formed lifesaving service and the laxity of government officials in allowing an unseaworthy vessel to sail with passengers on board. Charges of inhumanity, looting, and vandalism were levied against residents of Currituck Beach, and the first mate said that "the loss of the lives of over 100 men and two women may be partly attributed to the culpable negligence and inefficiency of the lifesaving station." Residents of the area said that they had never witnessed a more complete wreck, and inspection of the ship's timbers that had washed ashore showed them to be completely rotten. That the owners knew of her condition was evident in that they were unable to secure insurance for her because of her condition. The *Metropolis* made its mark in history as one of the worst maritime disasters along the North Carolina coast.

The wreck of the *Metropolis*, also known as the "Horsehead Wreck," lies in 15 feet of water, three miles south of Currituck Beach Light, about 100 yards offshore in the surf zone. Her boiler, an iron davit, and a portion of her hull are still visible above the sand. Visibility underwater is generally less than three feet.

Carl Gerhard

THE SWEDISH FREIGHTER *Carl Gerhard*, 244 feet long and 1,505 tons (870 net tons), was built in 1923 at Larvik, Norway, for F. Malmros of Trelleborg, Sweden. In command of the ship was Captain A. Ohlssen, a Scandinavian with 31 years of experience at sea. Twenty-three of those years were spent serving the owners of the *Gerhard*, so it came as no surprise when, in 1923, he was given command of the new ship and its 20 Swedish and Norwegian crew members. For six years he navigated the vessel without mishap in American waters up and down the East and Gulf coasts.

In September 1929, the *Carl Gerhard* began her last trip in service at Mabou, Cape Breton Island, Nova Scotia, where she took on a load of 1,825 tons of gypsum rock. Shortly after departing Marbou, headed south for Tampa, Florida, the freighter ran solidly aground. The dumping of nearly 200 tons of cargo failed to lighten the *Gerhard* sufficiently to get her off the mud bar, and it took a week for a tug to arrive from Halifax, Nova Scotia, to dislodge her.

In spite of the inauspicious beginning for the trip south, Captain Ohlssen decided to have the *Gerhard* proceed with the remaining cargo to Tampa. A gale wind began to blow on Tuesday night as the ship continued down the New England coast, and she began taking on water. In addition to the storm battering the ship, the overcast skies made it impossible for Captain Ohlssen to "shoot the stars" with his sextant to determine his position off the coast. For five days, he was unable to locate stars, the sun, or any lighthouse to fix the ship's position. Although lost, the small ship nevertheless fought its way south as the storm continued to batter her. Navigating by dead reckoning and his knowledge of the currents in the area, Captain Ohlssen estimated the *Gerhard*'s position on Sunday, September 22, 1929, to be about 55–60 miles offshore, a position that would put the ship 10–15 miles away from the treacherous Diamond Shoals. What he did not know was that the northeast storm had been blowing for several days and that the prevailing currents had temporarily changed and were driving his ship closer and closer to the shoals.

At 4:35 A.M., Monday morning, September 24, the *Carl Gerhard* struck the outer bar of the shoals about one mile north of Kill Devil Hills. The large crashing waves and violent winds pounded the stranded vessel further and further across the bar. Ironically, the *Gerhard* went ashore at the same spot another ship, the Greek tanker *Kyzickes*, had gone ashore two years earlier. The *Kyzickes* had also been driven shoreward until it straddled the bar and broke into pieces, the forward and aft sections lying about 100 yards apart. It was into the gap in the wreck of the *Kyzickes*

7.2   *Carl Gerhard* (left) and wreck of the *Kyzickes* (right).
Courtesy of The Mariners' Museum, Newport News,
Virginia.

that the *Gerhard* was slowly being pushed until she struck the bow section of the *Kyzickes*, swinging around and settling beside the stern of the
earlier wreck. Rescuers from the Kill Devil Hills Coast Guard station
sighted the *Gerhard* at dawn, and by afternoon they were able to get
safely on shore the captain, 21 crew members, the wife of the first mate,
two dogs, and a cat, with no injuries or loss of life.

The wreck of the *Carl Gerhard* is located off Kill Devil Hills just to
the north of the large stern section of the *Kyzickes* on the inner bar of two
sand bars, which are located 100 to 200 yards offshore. The bow section
of the *Kyzickes* rests on the outer bar further offshore than the *Gerhard*.
The *Gerhard* and the stern section of the *Kyzickes* lie so close to each
other that they actually touch along one section. The battered and rusty
hull of the *Gerhard* lies in around 15 feet water. Because of the close
proximity to shore, the presence of the sand bar and much wave action
and surging, the visibility on the wreck is usually limited to less than five
to eight feet. Spearfishing is generally good on the wreck as sheepheads,
spadefish, and other varieties live in and around the wreckage. The
Gerhard's proximity to shore has led many divers to visit the wreck, and
consequently most of the artifacts have been recovered. The water is usually cold in the summer, with temperatures at depth in the 60s. A full wet
suit is therefore advisable. Local dive shops in Nags Head and Wanchese
can give you up-to-the-minute information about diving conditions on
the *Gerhard*. The wreck of the *Gerhard* and the two sections of the
Kyzickes nearby make up what is known locally as the "Triangle Wrecks."
The *Irma*, a schooner which sank in 1925, is another nearby walk-in dive
site, located about 300 yards south of the *Kyzickes*.

Kyzickes

BUILT IN 1900 AT LORAIN, OHIO, the tanker *Paraguay*, 2,627 tons and 227 feet long, plied the Great Lakes under American registry for a number of years before she was sold, transferred to Greek registry, and renamed the *Kyzickes*. The tanker was commanded by Captain Nickolas Kantanlos as she departed Baltimore, Maryland, on November 28, 1927, with a crew of 28 and a full cargo of crude oil bound for Seville, Spain.

Three days out into the Atlantic the *Kyzickes* began taking water and Captain Kantanlos ordered the ship to return to Baltimore. On Friday, December 1, a day after setting out once again from the harbor, the vessel encountered a storm from out of the northeast. The crew fought furiously to pump water out of the foundering vessel, but the violence of the storm was too much for them.

By noon on Saturday, the first of a series of wireless messages from the stricken tanker was received by shore stations and other vessels at sea. She was about 200 miles east of the Virginia capes, being battered by a severe storm and leaking from bow to stern. Shortly thereafter, the messages ceased because the wireless antenna had been destroyed. Several ships altered course and headed for the *Kyzickes*, the closest being 60 miles away. By Saturday night, four of the crewmen had been washed overboard and lost, the ship's boilers were extinguished, and the engines had stopped. Without power and lights, the *Kyzickes* drifted at the mercy of the storm, unable to be seen by rescuers. Captain Kantanlos ordered signal flares to be set off, and one of the rescue vessels saw them but lost the ship's position in the storm.

The *Kyzickes* continued to be battered through the night, and by daybreak, Sunday, December 4, she struck Diamond Shoals. Through the stormy darkness, signal lights were seen nearby from the bridge of the tanker. Quickly, signals were returned by the men on the bridge, who received answering signals from the would-be rescue ship, which appeared to be nearly alongside by now. Signal lights brought relief to the men on board, who were enduring a terrible battering by the seas breaking over the shoals. The *Kyzickes* was slowly being torn apart. The terrible irony of what followed dashed all their hopes of a speedy rescue. By rising dawn the captain and crew on the bridge realized that the "rescue vessel" was in fact the stern end of their own ship which had broken off and had swung around alongside the bow portion; the signals received from the stern were from five of the crewmen who had been trapped there when that portion of the ship broke off. A large plank was laid across the gap between the parts of the *Kyzickes*, and the five crewmen on the stern

7.3   *Kyzickes.*   Courtesy of The Mariners' Museum, Newport News, Virginia.

crossed over to the bow to join the captain and the 19 other surviving crewmen. By daylight, the *Kyzickes* had been seen by lifesavers from Kill Devil Hills and Nags Head, and a rescue was undertaken immediately. By seven o'clock that night, Captain Kantanlos and the 24 crewmen on the bow section were safely rescued.

The bow of the *Kyzickes* lies a couple of hundred yards offshore on the outer shoal approximately one mile north of Kill Devil Hills in about fifteen feet of water. She is nearly covered with sand, but winter storms periodically uncover various portions of the wreck. The engine provides the biggest relief, reaching up almost fifteen feet to the surface. The water temperature is cool, even in the summer, and the visibility is usually not more than five feet, with one to three feet being the usual conditions. Currents, surging, and rough waves are sometimes encountered, but often conditions are mild enough for a diver to do serious spearfishing. Sheepheads, flounders, and other fish abound on the wreck. Closer to shore on the inner shoal lies the wreckage of the larger stern section, which is covered with the remains of pipes, cables, tanks, and machinery. The stern rests in about 15 feet of water partly buried in the sand, such that although she lies on her side all of her stern lies under water. Nearby the stern, and touching the *Kyzickes*, lie the remains of the *Carl Gerhard*, which was driven ashore exactly at the same spot two years after the *Kyzickes* struck the shoals. Care must be taken when making walk-in dives on either section of the *Kyzickes* because of surge and strong wave action. A wet suit and gloves are necessary protection to prevent scratches and abrasions while diving in the often turbulent shallow waters of what have become known as the "Triangle Wrecks." (The two sections of the *Kyzickes* and the *Carl Gerhard* nearby make up the triangle.) Local dive shops at Wanchese and Nags Head can guide divers to these beach wrecks.

USS *Huron*

THE FEDERAL GUNSHIP *Huron*, 541 tons and 175 feet long, was one of eight new sloops of war authorized to be built by the 42d Congress in February 1873. She was built by John Roach and Sons at Chester, Pennsylvania, in 1874, and was commissioned into service at the Philadelphia Navy Yard on November 15, 1875. The *Huron* carried four nine-inch guns and was powered by sail and steam; her boilers and engines alone weighed 118 tons.

Commander George P. Ryan commanded the ill-fated war ship and her crew of 116 men and 15 Marines when she left Hampton Roads on Friday, November 23, 1877, bound for the West Indies on a scientific expedition to the coast of Cuba. During the day and that evening, the sea was running from the southeast and there was a stiff breeze blowing as the vessel made its way south down the coast. When the *Huron* passed the Cape Henry Light near midnight, the seas and wind began to pick up force and the ship was rolling to leeward about 10 degrees, but the captain and crew evidently felt there was no cause for concern about the security of the ship.

By 1:00 A.M. on the 24th, most of the crew members were asleep and unaware of the impending danger. Though awakened by the order to take

7.4 U.S.S. *Huron.*   Courtesy of The Mariners' Museum, Newport News, Virginia.

soundings, those below decks immediately returned to sleep until a severe thumping was heard as the ship struck bottom. The subsequent order to go astern awakened all below decks, and 128 men piled out onto the deck in confusion. The night was dark, winds were now at gale force, and the ship was hitting bottom three or four times a minute.

Each time the ship hit bottom something on board would snap with a resounding crack as though the *Huron* would split apart at any moment. Below decks in the engine room, the starboard boiler had broken free and rolled across the fire room. Huge waves were breaking across the ship as all power was lost. Many of the crew who had lashed themselves in the rigging to await daylight could see the shore in the distance by the phosphorescence of the raging breakers. Other crewmen tried to bring down the sails, which were straining under the gale force winds, but their efforts were to no avail. Captain Ryan gave the order to throw the guns overboard, but by then the *Huron* was lying on her port side, with her deck inclined at 40 degrees to the raging sea which surged across and swept everything in its path away. Ryan ordered more signal flares lit, hoping someone on shore nearby would come to their rescue, but as soon as he gave the order a lifeboat broke loose from its davits and swept him over the side to his death.

Ensign Lucian Young made his way back to the cabin where the signals were stored and dragged two boxes to the deck. Igniting five rockets and 100 signal flares, Ensign Young waited for some sign of activity from the shore. Unfortunately for Ensign Young and the others on board the *Huron*, it was the inactive season and no lifesavers were at the Nags Head Station.

By dawn's early light, the scene on board became more gruesome. Fifty men were on the forecastle, and each time a sea would wash over them some would be washed overboard. One large mass of water crushed 20 men at once. By 8:00 A.M., the poop decks, lifeboats, main- and mizzen-masts, and rigging were being torn away with every sea that washed across the ship. By 8:30 A.M., the 13 people still on the *Huron* jumped overboard and tried to swim to shore—some being carried a mile or more up the shore before they could drag themselves out of the water. As daylight progressed, it became clear that there were only 34 survivors of one of the most tragic wrecks off the North Carolina coast. For days after the tragedy, bodies washed up on shore, some as far as thirty miles away from the wreck site. Ninety-eight officers and men, the pick of the United States Navy, had lost their lives on that cold November morning.

Ironically, the *Huron* was dashed onto shore three years after the government had established the Life Saving Service with such meager funds that the stations, which were located 20 miles apart along the coast,

290

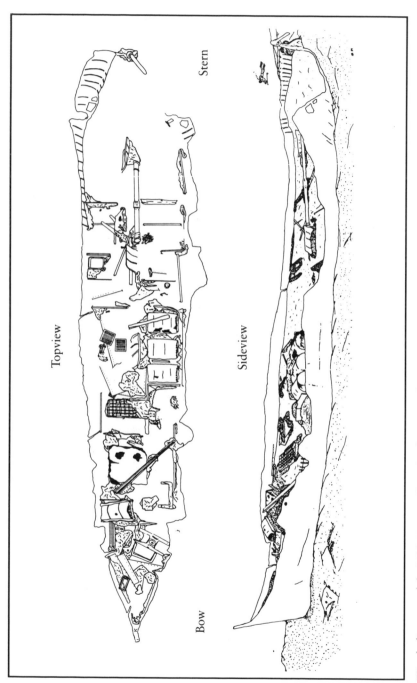

Wreck diagram of the USS *Huron*. Drawing by Joe Friday, Jr.

could only be manned during the winter months beginning December 1. Word of the wreck and deaths stunned the nation whose grief and sorrow at the needless loss of lives quickly turned to anger at the shortsighted government, and soon Congress made available funds to keep the stations open nine months of the year to ensure more adequate protection to mariners who braved the sea. North Carolina, with more Life Saving Stations than any other state, played a tragic part in the build-up of what eventually became the Coast Guard. As if to add salt to the wounds of an already taunted government, fate and the relentless ocean took the life of Lieutenant John J. Guthrie, superintendent of the Sixth Life Saving District, who had come from Norfolk two days after the disaster to view the remains of the *Huron*. While attempting to land through the surf in a boat launched from a wrecking tug, Lieutenant Guthrie and four oarsmen were thrown into the raging sea and drowned when their boat capsized, adding five more victims to the tragedy of the *Huron*. A court of Naval Inquiry investigating the circumstances of the *Huron*'s demise determined that the stranding occurred due to an error in the compass caused by the listing of the ship. In spite of this, however, Captain Ryan was found to be primarily responsible for the grounding and the loss of the *Huron* because of his failure to make certain navigational checks that would have determined that his vessel was too close to shore.

Today, most of the remains of the *Huron* lie 200 yards north of Nags Head Pier about 100 yards offshore in 20 feet of water. The sharp bow of the wreck rises from the sand nearly fifteen feet to within five feet of the surface. The hull is intact to the waterline. The bow lists to the port and there is debris strewn along the sides of the wreck. Inside the hull are collapsed bulkheads and decking from the forecastle covered with a carpet of barnacles. Swimming aft is the decking of the forward hold partially exposed on the starboard side. Underneath the decking lies a storage compartment where blocks and deadeyes were once stored for use in the *Huron*'s rigging.

A large iron cylinder, big enough to swim through, overshadows the forward hold area. This is what remains of one of the *Huron*'s starboard boilers. The position of the boiler is far away from the engine room where it was originally set. The *Huron*'s freshwater tanks lie aft of the boiler in their original position. The four tanks form a square eight feet wide by eight feet long. They are full of holes from corrosion, are partially filled with sand, and serve as home to several large sheepshead. Iron beams, possibly from the deck, sit across the water tanks and extend diagonally to the port side of the hull.

Further aft, beyond the water tanks and beams is the ship's magazine and shellroom area. Stray cartridges from the small arms locker lie a few inches under the sand, but it is illegal for divers to remove artifacts from the wreck. A wooden shell box sits exposed in the sand behind the magazine. It contains forty spaces where naval artillery shells were once stored for the *Huron*'s eleven-inch Dahlgren smoothbore cannon. Two or three shells remain in the box. Aft of the shell box, along the port side, lies the coal storage area and the three port side boilers. The boilers are usually covered with barnacles but are still easy to identify. The bulkheads that separate the coal storage area from the boilers still stand and can be identified by the presence of scattered coal around the area.

The remains of the engine compartment contain debris connected with the operation of the *Huron*'s steam engine. The engine itself has been destroyed and cannot be identified. The engine room area is the most disorienting part of the site. It is the widest part of the ship and there are few prominent features that can be used for reference points. Aft of the engine room is the remains of the ship's propeller shaft lying on the sand. It is broken apart near the engine compartment and sits between partial bulkheading that was once part of the shaft passage alley. Assorted pipes stick out of the sand and the remains of five separate storage areas are outlined in the sand by exposed bulkheads. These areas were once the food storage compartments, known as breadrooms, and the storage compartment for the paymaster stores.

The steering quadrant, rudder, and rudder post stand exposed and upright in the sand at the stern of the wreck. The rudder of the *Huron* is still connected to the post and is turned hard to port.

The remains of the *Huron*'s four-bladed iron propeller can be seen sticking out of the sand underneath the starboard side of the stern. This side of the wreck is broken and bent double for a distance of about thirty feet. The port side of the stern is completely blown away.

Outside of the hull lies the collapsed sides of the ship and parts of the *Huron*'s rigging. During the winter, storms change the formation of the sand bar surrounding the wreck site, which in turn covers up a portion of the wreck while uncovering another portion.

The wreckage is covered with corals, and it is the habitat for swarms of bottom and surf-dwelling fish such as flounders, sheepheads, spadefish, groupers, and black sea bass. The visibility on the wreck is one to five feet because of the surf action which keeps the bottom stirred up. The water temperature is usually quite cool even in the summer when it ranges in the mid- and upper 60s to low 70s. A full wet suit is recommended for warmth and for protection from cuts and abrasions which can be incurred when divers are knocked about the wreck site by currents and surge.

The site of the U.S.S. *Huron* will soon become the first underwater shipwreck state park in North Carolina.

[The description of the remains of the U.S.S. *Huron* and the map of the site was provided by Joe D. Friday, Jr., from his Master's thesis on the U.S.S. *Huron* and is used with permission.]

8. *Cape Fear Civil War Shipwreck District*

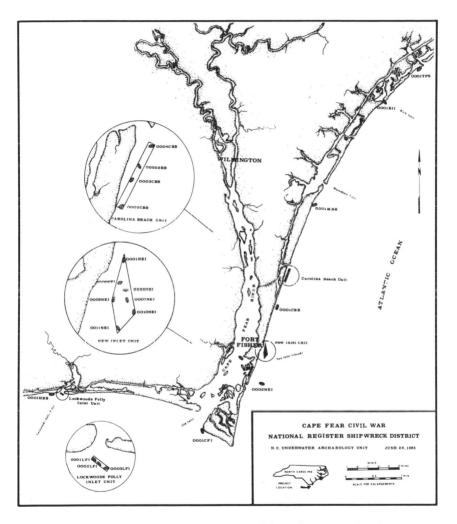

Cape Fear Civil War Shipwreck District. Courtesy of the Underwater Archaeology Unit, Fort Fisher, NC. Refer to the tables on pages 301–303 to key designation code to wreck name, date built, vessel type and date lost.

THROUGHOUT HISTORY ships have been one of man's most elaborate artifacts in which design and build reflect specific needs. Through the study of ships insight can be gained into the economic and social conditions of the society in which they were built and the industrial technology available at the time of construction. Shipping was of paramount importance during the Civil War since the vast majority of both raw materials and manufactured goods, necessary to sustain the Confederate War effort, were transported across the Atlantic.

Today the Cape Fear area boasts the largest collection of Civil War shipwrecks anywhere in the world. This group represents the full range of rapidly evolving merchant vessels used to elude the Union naval blockade, as well as a compliment of naval warships involved either in restricting or assisting merchant traffic. The physical remains of these vessels preserve important details concerning the transition in naval architecture and technology from sail to steam and wood to iron.

Artifacts collected from the Cape Fear Civil War shipwrecks are often well-preserved and closely dated. As a group these artifacts can shed light on military and civilian activities during the war. When conserved and placed in museums, these artifacts serve as tangible reminders which highlight historical awareness. With the popularity of sport diving, the educational potential of wreck sites themselves can be developed through the use of interpretive maps and underwater trails.

The Cape Fear Civil War Shipwreck District preserves a physical record of an important part of United States history. The shipwrecks within it provide the means to more fully understanding the Civil War period through the development and utilization of their historical, archaeological, educational, and recreational potential.

The Civil War came at a time in history when great technological changes were taking place in maritime construction. The two major innovations were the use of the steam turbine both as a primary means of propulsion and as a supplement to sail, and the use of iron in hull construction. Great Britain was the major country involved in developing these new techniques, though the United States and the other European powers were to a lesser extent also experimenting with and changing their ship designs. For many years British shipmakers had experienced increasing difficulty in procuring an adequate supply of high quality timber, particularly oak, with which to build ships. By the second decade of the nineteenth century iron manufacturing had developed to the point that it became economically and technologically feasible in England to use iron in the construction of ships.

In addition to this trend development of the steam engine and its use connected to a paddle wheel or screw to power ships continued. The first iron steamer was the *Aaron Manby* built in England in 1821. From that time on this was the trend in Great Britain and by 1860 there was no question in England that the new large iron screw steamers were more desirable than either American or British built wooden ones.

In the United States use of iron was not as widespread due primarily to its high cost and the still readily available supply of ship-building timber. Steam engines were in use, mainly on river boats and coastal ships, though of an inferior nature to the British-built steam engines. Few attempts were made in America to construct large ocean-going steamers, and those took place in the northeast.

The lack of marine facilities in the South forced the Confederacy to rely on the vessels which could be seized or those which could be purchased abroad, in order to carry on vital foreign trade. The fleet of available vessels was quickly exhausted with most being pressed into naval service. England's active shipbuilding industry and established transatlantic trade relations became the logical supplier of merchant vessels for Southern trade.

The most vital element in blockade running was acquiring a vessel capable of successfully eluding the Union blockade of Southern ports, which began in 1861. Sailing vessels carried the bulk of commerce early in the war. The 253 different sailing vessels known to have run the blockade off North and South Carolina dropped to 145 in 1862, 53 in 1863, and 14 in 1864. This reduction resulted from the realization that large sailing vessels were too slow to avoid the blockaders while the quicker schooners simply could not carry enough cargo. As Union strategists understood that steam vessels would form the best blockade, the South arrived at a similar counter solution, steamships were needed to successfully run that blockade.

In the beginning, almost any existing steamers were employed. Successful at first, they soon began failing in a similar manner as sailing vessels. What was needed was a vessel that combined the qualities of speed, low freeboard, large cargo capacities, and shallow draft. The answer to these specific needs was found in the side paddle wheel steamers, which were in use as packets on the Clyde River in Scotland by 1860. These sleek vessels known as "Clyde Steamers", combined long slender iron hulls and shallow drafts with powerful engines enabling them to achieve tremendous speeds. The freeboard was low enough to reduce the vessel's silhouette, but high enough to give them stability in high seas. The *Antonica*, ex *Herald*, was the first of these vessels to be employed as a blockade runner when it made its first of 24 successful runs in March 1862. By the end of that year similar vessels were being purchased and outfitted in Europe at a rapid pace.

In January 1863 the *Banshee I* was completed at British yards in Liverpool. This was the first vessel built from the keel up specifically for blockade running and served as the prototype for those built during the remainder of the war. Measuring 200 feet by 20 feet by 12 feet it had a flat bottom and was constructed of ⅓-inch thick steel plates. With a draft of 8 feet, the vessel had four water-tight compartments. The transatlantic crossing by *Banshee I*, her maiden voyage and the first by a steel vessel was beset with problems brought on by structural weaknesses. Basically the steel plates were too thin and badly fitted and the engines too powerful for her frame. Despite these problems, she succeeded in making fourteen runs in her eight month career before being captured off of Wilmington.

During the Civil War at least 31 steam and 22 sail blockade runners, as well as a wide assortment of Federal and Confederate military vessels were lost in the Cape Fear River. With the exception of the USS *Peterhoff*, which was lost in a collision, all wrecks were stranded along the beach or on inlet shoals and sank in less than thirty feet of water. Upon wrecking, a vessel became the focus of furious attempts to save it and its cargo. The Federals had the decided advantage in efforts to recover the total vessel since they could approach from sea with tugboats. The Confederates concentrated on a wreck's cargo, which was not only more important to their specific needs but could be unloaded with ease onto the beaches which they controlled.

Rough weather and artillery fire from the enemy hampered salvage attempts by either side. In only a few cases was a whole vessel refloated or the cargo of a wrecked vessel completely salvaged. In most cases, the Confederates would recover a small portion of the cargo before Union boarding parties would destroy both the vessel and cargo by setting it afire. Steam machinery was often rendered useless at the time of wrecking due to the removal of key parts by the vessel's crew.

Civil War wrecks were never as intensely salvaged as they might have been during peacetime. Time and conditions of the war did not permit major recovery of a wreck's machinery, cargo, or hull structure. After the war, when commercial salvors resumed normal activities, few of the Civil War wrecks were of interest. The raising of a portion of the hull of the *Venus* is one of the few confirmed salvage ventures.

Wreckers charged with removing or leveling sunken vessels which posed a threat to navigation did affect several Civil War wrecks. In the mouth of the Cape Fear River a Federal Gunboat, probably the USS *Violet*, and the *Georgianna McCaw* were partially destroyed as well as the CSS *Raleigh* in New Inlet. A number of the Confederate transports scuttled in the Cape Fear River to block the channel below Wilmington were reportedly removed immediately after the war.

On the whole, vessels lost during the Civil War have rested on the ocean or river bottom undisturbed by man's activities. However, the continuous pounding of waves, shifting sands, and marine fouling organisms have degraded their structural integrity over the years. The degree and nature of deterioration has been directly affected by the type of wreck.

Steamers, with their heavy metal power plants, support stanchions, and reinforced hulls have held up the best. Those with iron hulls have fared far better than their wooden counterparts and often remain intact to the upper deck level in the very stern and bow area. In the fore and aft cargo compartments the hull generally has broken near the turn of the bilge and fallen out exposing the inner portions of the vessel or fallen in on itself, offering some protection to remaining contents. While wooden hull sections are eventually swept off the site, metal sections seem to hold up in varying degrees, perhaps dependent on the quality of metal used.

Wooden sailing vessels generally break completely apart, often in large sections, which are widely scattered. Only heavy materials associated with the wreck, such as anchors, ballast, certain cargoes, and armament remain on a wreck site. Hull preservation is often limited to the keel/keelson, floor frames, and bottom planking which are weighted and covered by ballast.

Deterioration is also dependent on the type of nearshore environment within which a wreck exists. Wrecks lying on hard bottoms are exposed to the maximum force of currents while those that are entombed in sand can be greatly protected. The latter situation is most likely to occur in inlets where tons of sand may shift in a short period of time. Complete sections of hull, both metal and wood, have been found in North Carolina inlets.

Wrecks submerged in sea water are subject to deterioration by natural processes of decay, oxidation, and electrolysis that occur rapidly at first and gradually diminish as a heavy layer of encrustation forms. With time a delicate equilibrium is achieved which aids in a vessel's protection. Currently the Civil War wrecks lying in the lower Cape Fear area are in a relatively stable condition.

The most detrimental natural occurrence to Civil War wrecks is severe coastal storms, either hurricanes or northeasters. During these storms intense currents can break up wreck hulls and cast small artifacts upon the adjacent beaches.

Civil War wrecks act as artificial reefs which attract sea life and have served as prized fishing spots. To capitalize on the greater abundance of fish, ocean piers have been built out to the *Vesta, Modern Greece* and *Fanny and Jenny*.

Today, the locations of several wrecks such as the *Venus* and *Modern*

Greece have survived through oral tradition. Even stronger identifications have stuck with the *General Beauregard, Ranger,* and *Bendigo* since a portion of each has remained visible at low tide. However, most of the Civil War wrecks were forgotten soon after the war and their locations and identities were lost to the sea.

Over the years a number of these wreck sites have been located and recent site inspections by state archaeologists have produced needed information on nine additional shipwrecks and confirmed four suspected wreck sites. Presently there are twenty-one known Civil War wreck sites with basic documentation and there are at least twelve other sites in need of further investigation.

In November of 1985, twenty-one shipwrecks in the Cape Fear area were nominated to be placed in the National Register of Historic Places. The Cape Fear Civil War Shipwreck District was accepted and placed in the Register on December 23, 1985. The shipwreck district includes the wrecks of twenty-one Civil War vessels. As future survey and assessment activities are expanded that number may be nearly doubled. Fifteen of the wrecks are blockade running steamers. They each represent a key step in the evolution of the classic Civil War blockade runner. Furthermore, these fifteen wrecks represent nearly 20 percent of all steam blockade runners lost during the Civil War. Nowhere in the world is there a comparable concentration of vessel remains.

Four Union and one Confederate military vessels are also included in the district. Although not nearly as significant in terms of percent of overall Civil War naval losses, this group represents a good cross section of ships used in conjunction with blockade running activities. Two bar tenders, an ex-blockade runner and an ironclad are part of the military wreck assemblage.

The general area of the Cape Fear Civil War Shipwreck District is the same as those originally established by Union naval leaders for the Wilmington flotilla. Jurisdiction went as far south as Little River, at the North Carolina/South Carolina line and to New Topsail Inlet, North Carolina. Shipwrecks are most dense in the vicinity of the Cape Fear River Inlet where the most intensive naval activities took place. As distance up and down the coast increases, wreck occurrence progressively becomes more sparse as the historic boundaries are reached. All wrecks lie close to shore and within the present state three-mile limit.

The New Inlet Unit encompasses seven wrecks and includes 185.38 acres. At Lockwoods Folly Unit three wrecks are contained in 169.9 acres. The Carolina Beach Unit of 82.07 acres surrounds four wrecks.

The Wrecks

New Inlet Unit

Seven wrecks are located at the mouth of New Inlet off of Fort Fisher. An eighth can be found on the inside of the inlet where it meets the Cape Fear River channel. It was in the New Inlet vicinity where the most active blockade running of the entire Civil War took place.

Since the closing of New Inlet in the late 1800s, the wrecks in this Unit have been subjected to nearshore conditions. Here the currents running along the shore have kept the wrecks unsanded and exposed to storm surge, therefore reducing the inlet's protective sands that may have originally covered these wrecks. While the exposure of wrecks above the bottom is interesting to divers, the present New Inlet area seldom provides more than two feet of visibility, particularly on the shallower wrecks. Light easterly winds blowing for several days generally provide the best diving conditions. The wrecks in this unit are:

Name	Designation	Date Built	Vessel Type	Date Lost
Modern Greece	0001 NEI	1859	Iron Screw Steamer	6/27/1862
CSS *Raleigh*	0003 NEI	1863/64	Wood Screw Steamer/ Ironclad	5/7/1864
Condor	0006 NEI	1864	Iron Sidewheel Steamer	10/1/1864
USS *Louisiana*	0008 NEI	1860	Iron Screw Steamer/ Powder Ship	12/24/1864
Arabian	0009 NEI	1851	Wood Sidewheel Steamer	9/15/1863
USS *Aster*	0010 NEI	(?)	Wood Screw Steamer/ Bar Tender	10/8/1864
Stormy Petrel	0011 NEI	1864	Iron Sidewheel Steamer	12/15/1864
Unknown Vessel	0007 NEI			

Lockwood's Folly Inlet Unit

In Lockwood's Folly Inlet three wrecks have been located lying in a line across its mouth. All wrecks lie within the turbulent inlet and are subject to tidal currents and periods of sanding and unsanding. Although Lockwood's Folly Inlet has remained in its same general location since the Civil War, the inlet channel has moved back and forth across the wreck periodically. Water visibility is generally good at high tide on calm days. The wrecks in this unit are:

Name	Designation	Date Built	Vessel Type	Date Lost
Elizabeth	0003 LFI	1852	Wood Sidewheel Steamer	9/3/1863
Bendigo	0001 LFI	1863(?)	Iron Sidewheel Steamer	1/4/1864
USS *Iron Age*	0002 LFI	1862	Wood Screw Steamer/ Bar Tender	1/11/1864

Carolina Beach Unit

Four blockade runners were lost along the beach halfway between New Inlet and Masonboro Inlet. At the time of the Civil War this area was a long open stretch of beach which was sparsely populated. During the years since, Carolina Beach has grown into a sizable resort town and in the 1950's Carolina Beach Inlet was artificially opened to provide ocean access for recreational and commercial fishing boats. The new inlet now strongly influences the four wrecks particularly the northern two, which undergo rapid sanding and unsanding as the inlet channel drifts south. Tidal flow through the inlet generally insures that sea water with good visibility will be present over the sites at high tide on calm days. The wrecks in this unit are:

Name	Designation	Date Built	Vessel Type	Date Lost
Venus	0002 CBB	(?)	Iron Sidewheel Steamer	10/21/1863
Lynx	0005 CBB	1864	Steel Sidewheel Steamer	2/26/1864
Hebe	0003 CBB	1863	Iron Twin Screw Steamer	8/18/1863
Duoro	0004 CBB	1863	Iron Screw Steamer	10/11/1863

Individual wrecks not located within a unit:

Name	Designation	Date Built	Vessel Type	Date Lost
Phantom	0001 TPI	1863	Steel Screw Steamer	9/23/1863
Wild Dayrell	0001 RII	1863	Iron Sidewheel Steamer	2/1/1864
Sophia	0001 MBB	(?)	Wood Bark Sail	11/5/1862
General Beauregard	0001 CBB	1858	Iron Sidewheel Steamer	12/11/1863
USS *Peterhoff*	0002 NEI	prewar	Iron Screw Steamer/ ex-Blockade Runner	3/6/1864
Ella	0001 CFI	1864	Iron Sidewheel Steamer	12/3/1864
Ranger	0001 HBB	1863	Iron Sidewheel Steamer	1/11/1864

[This chapter is an edited version of material from the National Register of Historic Places Nomination Form for the Cape Fear Civil War Shipwreck District written by Mark Wilde-Ramsing, Archaeologist, Underwater Archaeology Unit, North Carolina Division of Archives and History and is used with permission.]

ALL OF THE CIVIL WAR-ERA WRECKS described in this chapter lie within 200 yards of shore in the surf zone and can be visited without a permit. Several of the shipwrecks are part of the Cape Fear Civil War Shipwreck District. However, the removal of any artifacts from these wrecks does require a permit. For more information and to obtain a permit, contact the Underwater Archaeology Branch, Division of Archives and History, P.O. Box 58, Kure Beach, NC 28449.

Because the wrecks are so close to shore, several factors must be taken into consideration before diving on them. Many of these wrecks can be reached directly from shore, while others are more accessible from a small boat. In either case, finding the wreck site on one's own is often difficult, if not impossible. Local dive shops, tackle and boat shops, sporting goods stores, surf fishermen, and charter boat captains are the best sources of information about finding a particular beach wreck. Quite often residents of the area near the site of the wreck can provided specific up-to-the-minute information about how to locate the wreck and what you should expect to find at the site. Surf fishermen know the wrecks near the shore because the wreck sites have become havens for marine life and hence are prime fishing spots. Some fishermen may be reluctant to give away the location of such fishing grounds to divers who might ruin a good thing for them. Go use alternative sources of information if fishermen show an unwillingness to share the wrecks with you.

Beach wreck dives have some advantages and disadvantages. One advantage is that shore dives are inexpensive. Even if you have to get someone to take you in a small boat, the cost is much less than for an offshore dive, and the running time to the wreck adds up to minutes rather than hours. Shore dives are also excellent sites for spearfishing—flounders, spadefish, and sheepheads abound on these wrecks. Because the depths involved are shallow, usually 30 feet or less, a diver can get a lot of bottom time on a dive. One major disadvantage of beach dives is that, due to the proximity to shore, visibility on the wrecks generally is poor, usually three to five feet or less. Carry a compass because the limited visibility may cause you to become disoriented without one. Surge and currents often encountered on these close-to-shore wrecks keep the water continuously churned up, which contributes to the poor visibility. Surge is a particular problem on shallow wrecks because sudden strong surface wave action is translated below to moderate to severe turbulence. A diver caught unaware might find himself dashed into the sharp, abrasive coral-encrusted wreck remains, resulting in scrapes, cuts, and torn or punctured dive gear. Gloves for hand protection are essential on these dives.

Remember, too, that entering the water from the beach requires swimming through the very turbulent surf zone where heavy water action is prevalent. Extreme care must be taken to avoid being knocked about by the surf.

The best time for a dive at a beach site is slack tide, preferably slack high tide. Accurate tide tables can be obtained locally. Divers should plan to enter the water about 30 minutes before slack high tide and be prepared to leave the wreck by about 30 minutes past high tide. Water movement around the wreck will be least during this period, and if you dive at slack high tide, somewhat clearer water will have moved into the wreck area, thus improving visibility somewhat. Just keep in mind that the visibility will usually never be great no matter when you dive these wrecks; occasionally, though, 20–30 feet of visibility is reported on some beach wrecks.

Be sure to fly a dive flag from an inner tube or float anchored to the wreck. People running the small motorboats that are often at these sites will then be aware that divers are below.

The water temperature close to shore will be warmest during June, July, August, and September, so plan your dives accordingly.

There are more Civil War-era wrecks in the surf off the North Carolina coast than I have listed here. The wrecks included in this chapter are easy to find and are the most often dived.

Oriental

The *Oriental* was a 210-foot-long, 1,202-ton, iron-hulled screw steamer built at Philadelphia by Neafie and Levy Shipbuilders. Her keel was laid on July 5, 1860, and the vessel was constructed with a beam of 32 feet and a depth of hold of 21 feet. Launched nearly a year later on June 29, 1861, the *Oriental* was propelled by a single four-bladed propeller driven by a single cylinder, low-pressure condensing marine steam engine that received power from a tubular box boiler. Completely outfitted during the summer of 1861, the *Oriental* underwent sea trials in the fall. The first of these trials began September 7 as the vessel slipped her moorings at the foot of Hanover Street in Philadelphia shortly before noon and headed down the Delaware River. By late afternoon it was clear the steamer was ready for service and she made the return trip to the dock at a top speed of slightly over eight knots. When plans for her construction were conceived, the *Oriental* was to operate between New York and Havana, Cuba. Thus, she was registered at the Port of New York. However, with the Confederate attack on Fort Sumter and the outbreak of hostilities of the American Civil War, the U.S. Army Quartermaster Corp

8.1   Steam engine of Union trans-
        port, *Oriental*.

8.2 *Oriental*.   Courtesy   of   the   Peabody   Museum   of   Salem,   Salem,
Massachusetts.

desperately needed troop transports. Seizing the opportunity for steady work and good money for their ship, the *Oriental*'s owners leased her to the army for $1,000 per day as a troop transport.

In late January 1862, the *Oriental* was sent to Annapolis, Maryland, where she picked up 1,200 men of the 47th Pennsylvania Volunteers. They were to be transported to Key West, Florida, where they would relieve the 1st U.S. Infantry. Departing for Florida on January 27, the steamer had an uneventful trip south arriving in Key West on February 4. No time was lost loading fuel and supplies for the return trip north as the ship was scheduled to depart for New York with Companies A and H of the 1st U.S. Infantry and a few civilian passengers. The return trip was made more pleasant by the presence of twenty women in spite of the old seaman's admonition against females on shipboard. Later, in April 1862, the government ordered the steamer south once again only this time carrying not troops but blacks being sent south to Port Royal, one of South Carolina's barrier islands near Charleston, where they formed a community known as the Gideonites. The steamer stayed in Port Royal until early May when she was ordered back to New York. Departing South Carolina with passengers and cargo, the transport headed north. Utilizing the northerly flowing Gulf Stream, the steamer made good time up the coast. Having successfully navigated past the tip of treacherous Diamond Shoals off Cape Hatteras, the *Oriental* adjusted her course to move closer to shore so she would not have to buck the southerly flowing Labrador Current that met the Gulf Stream here. In the evening of May 8, having approached too close to shore near Bodie Island three miles south of Oregon Inlet and thirty-three miles north of Cape Hatteras, the steamer struck the outer sandbar and went aground. Union troops stationed on shore nearby rescued all of the passengers and crew but the *Oriental* and its cargo were lost.

The wreck lies at a depth of twenty feet. Her boiler, engine, propeller, propeller shaft, and much of the hull remain above the sand. The visibility is less than five feet and the site is affected by currents and surge. At low tide, the engine protrudes above the surface of the water.

Phantom

The *Phantom* was a 322-ton, steel, single screw steamer built in Liverpool, England, in the summer of 1863. The vessel, measuring 192.6 feet in length by 22 feet by 12.4 feet, was a Clyde River steamer that was employed as a blockade runner when shortages of available merchant steamers occurred because demand for their services was so great. One of the original line of steamers ordered by the Confederate government, it made four runs before meeting its fate.

The blockade runner *Phantom* was loaded with arms, medicine, and general stores when she departed Bermuda bound for Wilmington in September 1863. On the morning of September 23, the *Phantom* was discovered by the USS *Connecticut* 50 miles off the coast east of New Inlet. Apparently the vessel had made a landfall earlier, but too far north of the Cape Fear River, and when she was discovered, she was heading back out to sea to make a closer approach to the mouth of the river under cover of darkness.

Clyde River steamers were fast, but very fragile, and often did not complete the arduous journey across the Atlantic.

When discovered by the USS *Connecticut*, the *Phantom* turned and ran for the Cape Fear River with the Federal navy ship in pursuit. Four hours later the chase was still hot, and the *Phantom* was not going to escape. She suddenly turned and ran in to shore near Rich's Inlet where she lies today. Captain S. G. Porter and his crew escaped to shore in boats after setting the *Phantom* on fire to prevent her from falling into Federal hands. The wreckage of the *Phantom* lies in about 30 feet of water a quarter mile south of New Topsail Inlet and 300 yards offshore. On the site, only the steam machinery and boilers are exposed, the rest of the wreck being sanded in. Much of the hull is apparently broken out at the turn of the bilge. Since the early 1960s sport divers have recovered many lead bars weighing 155 pounds each.

Nutfield

The *Nutfield* was a 531-ton, side-wheel steamer that measured 224 feet in length by 27 feet by 13 feet. The blockade runner was carrying ammunition to Wilmington along the "Bermuda line" or "track" from Bermuda in February 1864. By this time Union blockaders knew of the route and regularly patrolled it searching for blockade runners. So it was not surprising that at daylight on February 4 the *Nutfield* was sighted by the USS *Sassacus*. In fact, just the night before, the *Nutfield* had escaped blockaders at New Inlet and was off New River headed for the Cape Fear River at the time the *Sassacus* discovered her.

By noon the faster *Sassacus* had gotten within range of the *Nutfield* and proceeded to bombard her with such great accuracy that the steamer turned and then ran onto a bar near New River Inlet. Before escaping on small boats, the crew of the *Nutfield* set their ship on fire. One lifeboat capsized, and all but one of the crewmen in that boat drowned. The survivor was taken prisoner by the *Sassacus*. Meanwhile, the captain and the rest of the crew made land safely. The men on the *Sassacus* extinguished the fire and tried for two days to pull the *Nutfield* off the bar with no success. However, they did manage to take away much of the

Nutfield's cargo, which included merchandise, drugs, Enfield rifles, eight Whitworth guns, and a quantity of lead.

The *Nutfield* lies in 20 feet of water 200 yards offshore of New River Inlet, and all that remains visible are her boiler, her engine, and portions of her hulk. However, some divers do not believe that the remains of this wreck are really from the *Nutfield*.

Fanny and Jenny

The *Fanny and Jenny* was a side-wheel steamer used as a blockade runner on the Nassau-to-Wilmington run because of her speed; she could move through the water at up to 14 knots. Commanded by Captain Coxetter, the *Fanny and Jenny* reached the vicinity of Wrightsville Beach in five days, arriving on February 8, 1864. Wanting to land two miles north of Fort Fisher to make the short run down the beach to the Cape Fear River under cover of darkness, the captain needed to be sure of his location, so he ordered the steamer anchored while he took his bearings. Unhappily, he realized that he was further north than he had intended to be. He ordered the *Fanny and Jenny* down the beach in the dark. Unfortunately, she was running too close to shore, and around midnight she stranded on a shoal near Masonboro Inlet.

At daylight, on February 9, the *Fanny and Jenny* was discovered by the USS *Florida*, commanded by Captain Pierce Crosby. Crosby wanted to save the blockade runner for the prize money awarded for such captures and ran a line to the stranded vessel to pull her off the shoal. The Confederates from Fort Fisher, using long-range Whitworth guns, opened fire on the *Florida* from Masonboro Beach, damaging her paddle-wheel arms and seriously damaging the ship itself. The captain and crew aboard the *Fanny and Jenny* became very frightened when the *Florida* returned fire, and some of them, including Captain Coxetter, tried to reach shore in the lifeboats. Captain Coxetter and the ship's purser drowned in the surf, while the rest of those escaping made it safely to shore. Twenty-five of the crew who had remained on board were captured by the *Florida*.

Captain Coxetter had had in his keeping a valuable gold, jewelled sword which was to be delivered to General Robert E. Lee as a gesture of admiration from many prominent British sympathizers. It is still aboard the remains of the wreck.

The *Fanny and Jenny* lies about 100 yards north of Masonboro Inlet jetty and about 100 yards offshore in less than 12 feet of water. The visibility underwater is less than three to five feet. Most of the wreck is sanded over, but parts of the hull, the engine, and the boiler are still visible. Winter storms frequently uncover portions of the wreck. Several years ago, scuba divers recovered the *Fanny and Jenny*'s anchor.

Sophia

The *Sophia* is the only sailing blockade runner included in the Shipwreck Historic District. It was a 375-ton British bark operating out of Liverpool. Having made two successful runs through the blockade, it was detected on its third attempt to run the blockade. On November 4, 1862, while carrying three brass rifled field pieces with gun carriages and other military supplies bound for Confederate forces, the *Sophia* was chased by Union blockaders when she was spotted running close to shore near Masonboro Inlet headed toward the mouth of the Cape Fear River. She went aground near Masonboro Inlet, and the Captain and crew made shore safely in boats. The *Sophia* and its valuable cargo were destroyed by Union personnel before Confederates could transfer it to the beach.

The wrecking of the *Sophia* on November 4, 1862, forcefully drove home the dangerous nature of blockade running to all who tried it. It suddenly became very serious business since Union vessels disregarded a white surrender flag and fired on the hapless boat for the first time in the war.

The *Sophia* lies in 20 feet of water south of Masonboro Inlet, and a boat is needed to get to her as the wreck is located about three-and-a-half miles south and west of the inlet. Lying on the bottom just outside the surf zone in an area measuring 250 feet by 100 feet, the wreck site is covered by a thin layer of sand. Some features of the wreck include an anchor, anchor chain and winch, and several sets of wooden carriage wheels and hubs. The latter offers confirmation that the wreck represents the remains of the *Sophia*'s cargo of gun carriages. Other artifacts resemble that of a wooden sailing ship.

USS *Columbia*

The *Columbia* was captured on August 3, 1862 by the *Santiago de Cuba* off the coast of Florida attempting to run the blockade set up there. In November 1862, the U.S. Navy purchased the vessel from the Key West Prize Court and re-outfitted the vessel as a Navy blockader. She soon joined the North Atlantic Blockading Squadron off Wilmington, North Carolina, and began her blockading duties.

The newly commissioned USS *Columbia* met its fate through an error that should never have occurred. About 5:30 P.M. on January 14, 1863, the *Columbia* was headed toward land in calm seas and mild weather. The sailor assigned to throw the lead line used to determine the water depth was busy at his work as the vessel neared the shore. However, though he measured two-and-a-half fathoms, he called out "seven-and-a-half fathoms," and the ship continued to shore until she struck the bar near Masonboro Inlet.

On the second and third days after the stranding, the captain and crew of the *Columbia* were subjected to gale-force winds, and the ship began to break up. On day four, the weather had cleared enough to allow the USS *Cambridge* and the USS *Penobscot* to approach and rescue some of the officers and crew. Then, however, Confederate fire from shore drove the rescue ships away, while a Rebel force captured the *Columbia*. The Rebels stripped her, leaving nothing on board, and captured 40 of her officers and crew, including the captain. Before departing, the Rebels also set the ship on fire, and she burned extensively. The captured officers and crew members were imprisoned but were later exchanged for Rebel prisoners in the North.

The *Columbia* lies in less than 15 feet of water about 100 yards offshore from the end of Masonboro Inlet jetty. Because of strong currents around the jetty, it is difficult to dive at the site except at slack tide. Slack high tide is the best time to dive this wreck, although visibility is seldom better than three to five feet. When the tide is moving through the inlet, there is no visibility underwater. This wreck lies within sight of the *Fanny and Jenny*. All that remains of the *Columbia* are her boilers, her engine, and some portions of her hull.

Venus/Lynx

Presently there remains a question as to which of two wreck sites correspond to the blockade runners *Venus* and *Lynx*. One is located at the southernmost end of the Shipwreck Historic District's Carolina Beach Unit and the other is the Unit's next to most northern site. Both vessels were iron sidewheel steamers lost in the same general area between Masonboro and Fort Fisher (present day Carolina Beach), and archaeologists have not been able to solve the identification problem. Local tradition and sport divers maintain that the southernmost wreck in the Carolina Beach Unit is the remains of the *Venus* while recent visits by archaeologists studying Carolina Beach Inlet contend that it may be the remains of the *Lynx*. While the exact identification is unclear, the reported historical locations and general vessel characteristics provide a good deal of certainty that the *Venus* and *Lynx* lie at the two sites.

The *Venus*, 265 feet long and 1,000 tons, was a steamer that made the Bermuda-to-Wilmington run carrying arms and goods for the Confederates. Loaded with lead, bacon, coffee, and dry goods, the blockade runner was discovered early in the morning of October 21, 1863, off New Inlet by the USS *Nansemond*. Giving chase, the *Nansemond* opened fire on the *Venus*, destroying the steamer's mast and wardroom and killing several people on board. The *Venus* ran to shore and stranded on a bar near where the *Hebe* stranded a couple of months earlier. The captain of the *Venus* and 22 crewmen were captured by the crew of the *Nanse-mond*, who with the help of the USS *Niphon* tried to haul the stranded ship off the bar but failed. The Federals set fire to the ship as Confederate gunfire from the beach forced them to leave her, but the *Niphon* and the USS *Iron Age* blasted the *Venus's* boiler and riddled her hull with shot. The hull was set on fire once again, and the blockade runner was completely destroyed.

The *Venus* lies south of Carolina Beach Inlet in 15 feet of water. The wreckage consists of a portion of her hull and her engine and boilers.

The *Lynx* was built in Liverpool, England during the spring of 1864 along the lines of the typical, late-model blockade runners. Her steel hull measured 220 feet by 24 feet by 11.5 feet and was powered by sidewheels driven by powerful steam engines. After a successful career as a blockade runner, including nine runs into southern ports, chiefly Wilmington, the *Lynx* was chased ashore on September 25, 1864, above Fort Fisher. The vessel is one of few vessels wrecked on its outgoing voyage from Wilmington and carried a typical cargo of 600 bales of cotton as well as $50,000 in government gold. Upon grounding, the gold was removed and the vessel was burned to prevent capture. Much of the cotton had been thrown overboard during the *Lynx's* attempt to outrun Union steamers.

Both sites have been visited by sport divers since the 1960s. The southernmost wreck is an iron sidewheel steamer in excess of 200 feet in length with a beam measurement of 23 feet at the turn of the bilge. Well-preserved steel machinery rises twelve feet above the bottom. Poor visibility and a deteriorated hull have prevented positive identification of remains other than possibly those of a tubular boiler. The wreck rests nearly parallel to shore.

The remains of the next to northernmost site is covered in eight to ten feet of sand amidship with only paddle wheel shaft assembly, uppermost support beams and top of the forward boiler exposed. A small portion of the port stern with mooring bits attached may be seen. The vessel heading is northwest or angled in toward shore.

Hebe

During the last half of 1863, ten blockade runners were destroyed in the vicinity of Cape Fear. Among those ten was the *Hebe*, one of the South's best and fast blockade runners. The *Hebe* was an iron steamer driven by an experimental twin screw propulsion system. Built in London, England, in the spring of 1863, it measured 165 feet by 23 feet by 13 feet 6 inches. On her third run from Nassau, loaded with coffee, food, drugs, and clothing, the *Hebe* attempted to reach New Inlet on the morning of August 18, 1863. Having made a bad landfall eight miles from

New Inlet, she was spotted at daybreak and then chased by the Federal gunboat USS *Niphon*. Rather than be captured, the captain and crew on the *Hebe* turned their ship and ran her aground near Masonboro Inlet about nine miles from Fort Fisher; the men then escaped safely to shore in boats. The *Niphon* tried to pull the *Hebe* off the bar, but a Confederate battery of Whitworth guns and a force of riflemen drove the *Niphon* away. The Confederates then bombarded the *Hebe,* destroying her completely to prevent a rich prize from falling into Union hands. Salvage attempts took place for several days after its loss.

The *Hebe* lies near the Carolina Beach fishing pier about 150 yards offshore in 22 feet of water. Visibility is less than five feet. The wreck site is identified as the *Hebe* by its two propellers. The vessel's remains are lying diagonal to shore with its bow pointing in a northerly direction. The wreck length is approximately 169 feet by 22 feet. The hull is well-preserved in the extreme bow and stern. The length of hull is now exposed. In the fore and aft cargo holds the sides have broken out at the turn of the bilge, however, the hull floor beams remain in place. While the boiler is in good condition, the steam engine shows signs of heavy deterioration, most likely the result of partial salvage or destructive efforts at the time of sinking.

General Beauregard

The *General Beauregard*, built in Glasgow, Scotland, in 1858, was a 629-ton coastal ferry boat converted for blockade running in early 1863. She was an iron sidewheel steamer measuring 223 feet by 26 feet by 14 feet with a draft of 7 feet.

The *General Beauregard* was running the blockade into New Inlet for the seventeenth time when it was boxed in short of her destination. Around 7:00 P.M. on December 11, 1863, the *General Beauregard* was headed for New Inlet or the Cape Fear River when the Federal cruiser *Howaquah* spotted the blockade runner and gave chase. Hampered by heavy sea and coming under fire from the *Howaquah*, the *General Beauregard* turned and ran toward shore. The steamer was run ashore north of Fort Fisher off Carolina Beach. The next day, the *Howaquah* and the USS *Tuscarora* tried to pull the *General Beauregard* off the bar but were driven away by two Confederate batteries on shore located on either side of the stranded vessel. The Confederate forces destroyed the blockade runner. There was no report of salvage by either Federals or Confederates.

The wreck lies in less than 15 feet of water, 200 yards offshore, off the foot of Spartenburg Avenue in Carolina Beach. The visibility is less than three feet. Because it has remained exposed at low tide, the wreck site has

8.3   Hull remains of blockade runner, *General Beauregard*.

been known as the *General Beauregard* since the time of its sinking. Its steam machinery is intact with its paddle wheel shaft and hubs remaining in place. Cooling tanks, grated cargo hatches, water tanks, a large rectangular aft boiler, bollards, and a davit exist on the site. Both bow and stern sections are broken but not removed from the body of the wreck and are for the most part covered with sand. The *General Beauregard* was formerly known as the *Havelock*.

Modern Greece

The *Modern Greece* was a 200-foot-long, 750-ton English steamer used by Confederate sympathizers as a blockade runner during the Civil War. One of the earliest and largest steamers to attempt the blockade, the *Modern Greece* was running at full speed close to shore headed for Wilmington early on the morning of June 27, 1862. Blockaders spotted the ship as she approached Fort Fisher and gave chase, forcing the blockade runner aground only ¼ mile from the fort. The ship was loaded with 200 tons of black powder, clothing, four Whitworth breechloading rifles, whiskey, 12,000 Enfield rifles, lead ingots, and medical supplies desperately needed by the Confederacy. The crew of the *Modern Greece* managed to escape, and the Confederates in Fort Fisher fired solid shot into the vessel to flood the black powder so the blockaders would not be able to demolish her by detonating the explosive cargo. Later, troops from Fort Fisher were able to salvage a good deal of the cargo from the stranded ship, including all of the liquor.

The location of the *Modern Greece* has been known for many years, and underwater archaeologists have taken many artifacts from the wreck site. Several large portions of the wreck were uncovered from beneath the sands in 1962 when a storm struck the area, and in 1962 and 1963 state archaeologists removed and preserved thousands of artifacts. Their content along with the general wreck characteristics confirmed that it is the wreck of the *Modern Greece.*

The wreck lies just beyond the surf zone in 25–30 feet of water off the beach at Fort Fisher opposite the radar domes. The visibility is generally in the range of 5–10 feet, but it may be much lower during a rising or falling tide. As in the case of any near-shore wreck, the best time to dive the *Modern Greece* is at slack tide.

Condor

The *Condor* was a 300-ton, three-funnel, side-wheel steamer that served as a blockade runner assigned to carry goods from London to the Confederate port of Wilmington. The steamer left London in August 1864 and arrived at the mouth of the Cape Fear River on September 30. On October 1, Captain Hewett, the commander of the *Condor*, sighted what he thought was a Union ship and gave orders to change course in order to swerve out of the way of the object; but the pilot panicked and altered course so abruptly that the vessel ran aground on New Inlet bar near Fort Fisher. The object that Captain Hewett had seen was the *Night Hawk*, a blockade runner which had become stranded the night before. The *Condor* broke in two in the rough seas, but the crew and most of the passengers got to land safely.

One of the passengers was Mrs. Rose O'Neal Greenhow, a Southerner who was very prominent in Washington society during the Buchanan administration. Though she was a personal friend of President Buchanan and of other Washington notables of the time, Mrs. Greenhow always had a strong feeling for and identification with the South, and at the urging of fellow Southerners in Washington she became a spy for the Confederacy. Mrs. Greenhow provided the information to General Beauregard as to where the Union army would cross the Potomac into Virginia which led to the rout of the Union forces at Manassas. She was caught shortly thereafter. However, following a brief period of imprisonment, Mrs. Greenhow was allowed to return to Richmond, and from there she left the South for England aboard a blockade runner. In 1864, she boarded the *Condor* in London to return to the South with information and support from British sympathizers. When the ill-fated vessel ran aground, Mrs. Greenhow begged Captain Hewett to let her escape to shore in a boat so that she could avoid being captured as a spy for a second time. Put aboard a small boat with a sizable amount of gold sovereigns, she got within a few yards of land when the craft capsized and she drowned. The body of Mrs. Greenhow washed ashore the next day and was then buried, wrapped in a Confederate flag, with full Confederate military honors in Oakdale Cemetery in Wilmington.

The location of the *Condor* has been passed down through time and is confirmed by an 1865 Coast and Geodetic Survey Chart. The *Condor* lies in 20 feet of water approximately 800 yards offshore of Fort Fisher headed into the mouth of New Inlet. Although the wreck has been examined by professionals from the early 1960s to the present, the most thorough description comes from a local sport diver's report written in 1974. The bow and stern sections are separated by about 50 yards. Visibility is five feet or less. Much of the wreckage is above the sand, and the major portions of the Condor's remains are the hull, the boiler, two oscillating engines, paddle wheel shaft, and port paddle wheel. The propulsion system on this site is one of the best preserved of the Civil War wrecks.

Douro

The early history of the *Duoro* is not well known. It was apparently outfitted for blockade running in Liverpool during late 1862 and registered at 185 tons. In the spring of 1863, the *Duoro* was captured by Union blockaders and taken to the North to be sold at auction. Ironically, she was purchased through an agent in Halifax, Canada, for the Confederate government. Within a month, she was re-outfitted for sea and docked at Nassau.

On October 11, 1863, the *Douro* tried to run the blockade at New Inlet loaded with 550 bales of cotton, 279 boxes of tobacco, turpentine, and rosin. By 8:30 P.M. she had made it past Federal blockaders and was headed up the shore toward Masonboro Inlet in water 15 feet deep when she was spotted by the USS *Nansemond*. The blockader tried to get between the *Douro* and the beach. Failing to do this because of the shoal water, the *Nansemond* returned to deeper water. Then, instead of continuing toward Masonboro and the freedom she could have achieved because of her speed, the *Douro* turned about and headed back to New Inlet where she was run aground by the *Nansemond*. The captain and all but five crew members escaped in lifeboats and made shore safely. The five crew members who remained on board were captured by the Federals on the *Nansemond*. Attempts to remove the stranded vessel by the *Nansemond* were thwarted by Confederate fire from shore.

The Confederates completely destroyed the vessel, and the remains of the *Douro* now lie in 20 feet of water near Carolina Beach Inlet. The wreck site is heavily sanded and only a twenty-foot iron bow section is exposed. The presence of a steam-powered anchor windlass lying in place

8.4 *Ella.* Courtesy of the Peabody Museum of Salem, Salem, Massachusetts.

indicate that much of the wreckage at site is scattered about under the sand and is probably in good condition. Visibility on the site is three to five feet at slack high tide. Much of the *Duoro* is completely buried in the Inlet shoals. Occasionally, the top of her engine and boiler, and a portion of her hull are visible.

Ella

The *Ella* is an example of a late-model blockade runner. Built in Dumbarton, Scotland, in the summer of 1864 the 404-ton iron sidewheel steamer measured 22 feet by 28 feet by 13 feet. It was owned by the Bee Company of Charleston, South Carolina. It had made four successful trips through the blockade before running aground in Old Inlet loaded with a large supply of both military goods, arms and ammunition, luxury items, food, and whiskey. Loaded with these goods the *Ella* was intercepted and chased by several Union blockaders as she attempted to run to the mouth of the Cape Fear River on December 3, 1864. Seeing no escape, the captain ordered his men to run the ship ashore near the southeast corner of Bald Head (Smith's) Island, where he and the crew abandoned the ship and got to land safely. The hapless vessel sank on the south end of Marshall Shoal near the light on Bald Head Island. For several days following the grounding furious attempts to salvage the vessel and its valuable cargo were made from both sides. A company of Confederate troops from Edenton Battery led by Captain Bedham boarded the stricken vessel and removed her cargo while enduring heavy Union bombardment. The end result was the partial recovery of cargo by the Confederates. The steamer was then set afire and completely destroyed.

The wreck lies on a northwest heading parallel to the south shore of Bald Head Island in about 30 feet of water. The site has been identified as the *Ella* from its location, vessel features, and recovered artifacts. The visibility on this wreck is better than on most beach wrecks but it is still less than 15 feet on the best days. The most prominent features on the site are the remains of two large boilers, steam machinery, and paddle wheel shaft. In addition, significant portions of the hull and structural framing, as well as a small amount of cargo, remain intact. The few artifacts that have been found at the site include wine bottles, spice and mustard jars, and brass handles. Shifting bottom sands cover the site to varying degrees in response to tidal currents and ocean swells.

The *Ella* was the last of 30 blockade runners lost near the Cape Fear River during the Civil War.

Bendigo

The *Bendigo* was a 500-ton Clyde River steamer, fast but of weak construction, that was called into service as a transatlantic blockade runner when the demand for more conventional blockade runners exceeded the supply. The Clyde River steamers that were used as blockade runners were often lost on the runs between London or Bermuda and Wilmington because they were not constructed to endure the hardships of oceanic travel.

The small iron sidewheel steamer was built in a British shipyard in the mid-1863s for Fraser, Trenholm, and Company who also owned the ill-fated *Elizabeth*. The *Bendigo* departed from Liverpool, England, loaded with rifles and carpentry tools bound for Wilmington, and made the transatlantic crossing successfully. When the *Bendigo* arrived off Lockwood's Folly Inlet on January 4, 1864, the men on board mistook the wreck of the blockade runner *Elizabeth* for a Federal cruiser, and trying to run between the wreck and the beach they stranded their vessel. The captain and crew abandoned ship and made shore safely in small boats. After the USS *Fahkee* discovered the *Bendigo* at 11:00 A.M., five Federal vessels made repeated, but fruitless, attempts to dislodge the newly stranded blockade runner. Confederate batteries on shore bombarded the Union ships and drove them off, sinking one of them, the USS *Iron Age*. The Confederates successfully unloaded the *Bendigo's* cargo onto shore. Then they set the vessel on fire and destroyed it to prevent it from falling in Union hands. The *Bendigo* grounded on its third attempt at running the blockade.

Lying on the western margin of the inlet channel in less than 15 feet of water at high tide, the wreck appears to have remained entombed in sand since the stranding. The visibility on the site is about three to five feet. It is accessible today at low tide by venturing out on the western bar shoal as its hull is clearly visible. Local tradition has maintained that the hull is that of the *Bendigo*. The bow of the wreck points in a southeast direction which puts the vessel heading toward the mouth of the Cape Fear River but angled away from shore. The bow protrudes near or in the inlet channel and therefore had been subjected to tidal currents, creating a break in the hull near the forward boiler. Although deteriorated, the framing on the two boilers survive so that it is possible to see their construction details.

The steam machinery is in a good state of preservation. In addition, from midship to the stern, the main deck beams are still in place indicating that the majority of the hull remains intact. While the port paddle wheel shaft has broken from the wreck and is sanded over, the starboard shaft is in place and displays features such as the paddle-wheel hub, lower spurs, and bracket mounts. The stern of the wreck extends under the sand for about 60 feet from the after boiler. The *Bendigo* was formerly known as the *Milly*.

USS *Iron Age*

The *Iron Age* was a 424-ton, 144-foot-long, wood screw steamer built by Captain Nathaniel Lord Thompson at Kennebunk, Maine, in 1862. She had a beam of 25 feet and a depth of 12 feet 6 inches. Purchased in April 1863, by the U.S. Navy, she was outfitted with three 30-pounder Dahlgren rifles and six VIII-inch Dahlgren S.B. and commissioned at Boston on June 25, 1863. The *Iron Age* arrived on station off Wilmington in September 1863, and participated in the destruction of the blockade runner *Venus* and the raiding of salt works near Bear Inlet. The USS *Iron Age* grounded at Lockwood's Folly Inlet on January 10, 1864, while attempting to tow the recently wrecked *Bendigo* off the western shoal. After futile attempts to get free, the *Iron Age* was bombarded by Confederate gunfire causing her magazine to explode and destroying the ship. The *Iron Age* was the only Union blockader lost to gunfire during the Civil War while engaging in blockading activities. It was, however, the third vessel to meet its fate at Lockwood's Folly Inlet.

The remains of the *Iron Age* are located on the eastern side of the present channel lying in ten feet of water about 100 yards from shore and lies in the same orientation as the *Bendigo* wreck. The forward section of the vessel is obscured due to heavy sanding. Her steam machinery is heavily damaged and collapsed, but the remains of a rectangular boiler and a single cylinder vertical operating steam engine may be seen. The midship portion of the hull is broken out near the turn of the bilge. Hard oak frames, oak exterior planking, and bilge ceiling, possibly pine, are present. The hull deterioration is marked until twenty feet from the stern where the sides gradually rise to a height of seven feet. Her frame members are preserved as well as remnants of copper sheathing. The four-bladed iron propeller and a wood rudder remain in place. Three feet of sediment covers the hull from the machinery area to the stern including an eight-inch-diameter propeller shaft which lies in this area. A number of small artifacts have been recovered including several round cannon shot and a navigational lantern. Fused coal, metal, and miscellaneous debris indicate a very hot fire at the time of wrecking. The wreck field is estimated to be 200 feet by 50 feet.

Ranger

The *Ranger,* 400 tons and 200 feet long, was a side wheel steamer which was operated as a blockade runner. The steamer sailed from New Castle, England, November 11, 1863, to Bermuda. On January 6, 1864, loaded with Austrian rifles and carpentry tools, the *Ranger* sailed from Bermuda under the command of Captain George Gift. They reached the North Carolina coast on January 10 about five miles north of Murrell's Inlet, South Carolina, near Lockwood's Folly Inlet off Oak Island. Union forces had put out the lightship off Frying Pan Shoals, and Captain Gift, concerned about his ship's drift in the Gulf Stream, headed inshore to get an exact position. On the morning of January 11, Captain Gift unloaded his passengers and cargo at Murrell's Inlet. Then, having determined his position, he ran the *Ranger* along the coast toward the western bar near Fort Caswell.

Eight miles from the fort, Captain Gift sighted the USS *Minnesota* about a mile away. The pilot on the *Ranger* panicked and turned inshore, and in an instant the ship was aground one mile west of Lockwood's Folly Inlet. Aided by covering fire from Confederate sharpshooters, the captain and crew were able to set the *Ranger* on fire before abandoning her. While the men from the *Ranger* made shore safely, the USS *Minnesota,* assisted by the USS *Buckingham,* the USS *Daylight,* and the USS *Aries,* attempted to haul the stranded ship off and put the fire out. Confederate fire from shore drove the Union ships away, and the *Ranger* was burned and bombarded until she was destroyed.

The *Ranger* lies in 15 feet of water (high tide) one mile west of Lockwood's Folly Inlet, 50 yards offshore of the pavilion at Holden Beach. The wreck has yielded interesting artifacts including several well-preserved

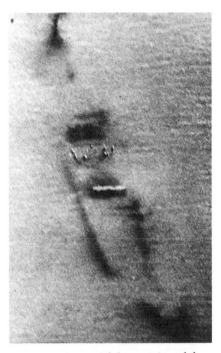

8.5   Aerial view of the remains of the
blockade runner, *Ranger.*

cases of rifles from its hold which were a portion of its remaining ill-fated war supplies. The wreckage is well-preserved, particularly from midship forward. The machinery area, engine, and aft boiler remain intact as well as large sections of the bow and stern structure. Although the sides of the vessel are collapsed out in the hold areas, they remain as they fell with minimal shifting. Visibility on the wreck is three to five feet. However, at low tide, her rusting hulk may be seen above water.

Vesta

The *Vesta* was a 500-ton, double-propeller blockade runner. Early in 1864, she was transporting supplies for the Confederate army from Bermuda to Wilmington. However, on January 10, three Union ships spotted the *Vesta* near Tubb's Inlet and gave chase, and the blockade runner went aground between Tubb's Inlet and Little River Inlet. Setting their ship on fire before they departed, the captain and crew made shore safely in lifeboats. One of the three Union ships reported seeing smoke in the distance near Little River, and the USS *Aries* was sent to investigate. When the *Aries* found the *Vesta* burning close to shore, Confederate sharpshooters prevented the Union vessel from getting near until the blockade runner had burned to the water line. Once the *Aries* did reach the wreckage, there was nothing to retrieve except two anchors.

The *Vesta* lies in 10 feet of water south of Tubb's Inlet off Vesta Pier. Parts of the remains of the vessel are exposed at low tide. Her iron boiler and engine are partially buried in the sand. Visibility is three to five feet.

CSS *Raleigh*

The CSS Raleigh was a Richmond Class steam ironclad built in Wilmington, North Carolina, to serve as a key component in the defense of the harbor. Completed in the spring of 1864, it was a typical Confederate ironclad with thick iron plating over a heavily constructed wooden hull and a subsurface ram fitted at the bow. The *Raleigh,* measuring 150 feet by 32 feet by 12 feet, was powered by totally inefficient steam engines, a problem common to most Confederate warships. Outfitted with four-inch rifles, the CSS *Raleigh* was to help break the blockade by confronting and driving off Union warships from the Cape Fear River inlet. However, her very brief career was ended when, after a few hours of indecisive naval maneuvers off Fort Fisher, the Confederate warship ran aground inside New Inlet and was severely damaged. Unable to refloat the ironclad, the Confederates ordered it destroyed. The *Raleigh* wreck site has been well-known from the time of its sinking because it posed a dangerous hazard to ship traffic until New Inlet was closed. The location has been well-marked on navigational charts and can still be seen on charts today. The *Raleigh* was partially salvaged in 1881 when a portion of its turret was removed after the wreck was dynamited. Lying perpendicular to the river channel shoulder, only a small portion of the remains protrude into the river.

Unknown Vessel

The remains of this vessel are the least understood within the Shipwreck District wreck group because of its lack of features and poor visibility at the site. Although divers have confirmed it as a wreck by the presence of sections of iron hull and two large iron anchors, features such as boilers, machinery, or means of propulsion have not been found. There are a series of open metal cylinders on the site that may be barrels. From inside one of these barrels an intact unidentifiable stoneware jug has been recovered. Not only do the conditions at the site present a problem for divers and for the identification of the wreck, historical records provide few likely candidates. In the mouth of New Inlet channel a wreck, labeled "2nd wreck", was charted on the 1865 Coast and Geodetic Chart in the exact location of this site. Therefore, it is probable that the wreck occurred during the Civil War. The Federal transport, USS *Union*, is the only wreck in the vicinity which remains unaccounted. This 149-ton stern wheel steamer was abandoned on April 3, 1864, while in tow near New Inlet. Leaking badly, it was set afire, cut loose, and then drifted to within a half mile of the beach at Fort Fisher and sank. Perhaps this wreck is the USS *Union*.

USS *Louisiana*

USS *Louisiana* was built in Wilmington, Delaware, in 1860 and a year later was purchased by the U.S. Navy. Measuring 145 feet by 27 feet and screw-driven, the iron hull vessel drew only eight-and-a-half feet of water making it an excellent blockader of southern ports. After actively serving in the shallow sounds and rivers of northern North Carolina, the USS *Louisiana* was selected to carry out an ill-fated plan to blow up Confederate earthworks at Fort Fisher. In December 1864, she was stripped of her mast, coal, guns, and extra equipment and loaded with 300 tons of explosive powder. After being towed to within 250 yards of the fort, the anchors were set and fuses ignited. Soon afterward, after a tremendous explosion, the USS *Louisiana* sank. However, the ship was sacrificed for nothing as it failed to inflict any damage to the fort. The site has been identified as that of the USS *Louisiana* by its general position to Fort Fisher and from measurements. Although thought to have been obliterated at the time of its sinking, it retains relatively good structural integrity. The propeller and drive shaft, machinery, and boiler remain in place. Iron hull plating remains intact up to the turn of the bilge at midship, while two to four feet of sand cover the hull bottom.

Arabian

The *Arabian* is an example of a prewar steamer pressed into blockade running. A wooden vessel with side paddle wheels propelled by a vertical beam engine, she was constructed in Ontario, Canada, in 1851. The *Arabian* operated on Lake Ontario and the St. Lawrence River until it was converted for blockade running by Canadians in 1863. Following conversion, the *Arabian* measured 174 feet by 24 feet by 18 feet. On its third attempt to run the blockade from Wilmington to Nassau, the *Arabian* was discovered leaving New Inlet. Reversing its course in an effort to run back under the guns from Fort Fisher, it ran aground short of the inlet. Within a few days, a storm had pounded its hull to pieces, but not before a majority of the *Arabian's* cargo of cotton was salvaged and later sold. Positive identification of the wreck is based on the presence of the supporting structure for a vertical beam engine. The *Arabian* was the only vessel with this type of steam machinery lost in this area. The wreck is pointing toward shore as determined by the relationship of the boiler to the machinery. Although scattered wreckage is at least ninety feet forward of the machinery, the extent of remains at either extreme is not known. A second screw-propelled vessel may lie wrecked in the same position although it is unclear what this wreck may be.

USS *Aster*

The USS *Aster* had been on blockade duty off New Inlet less than 24 hours before it was lost on October 7, 1864. While chasing a blockade runner, it grounded on the eastern extremity of Carolina Shoals. After attempts to free the USS *Aster* failed, a fire was set over the magazine to destroy the stranded vessel.

The USS *Aster* was purchased late in the war on July 25, 1864, at Philadelphia and converted for blockade duty as an bar tender. The wood screw steamer was built as an ocean going tug and measured 122 feet by 23 feet. The USS *Aster's* draft was registered at 10 feet, however, it was apparently drawing 12 feet, which was considered to be too deep to operate effectively on the Cape Fear inlet bars. The officers of the *Aster* in their hasty attempt to capture a quick prize, proved this to be the case. A wreck location labeled *Aster* on the 1865 Coast and Geodetic Chart confirms the wreck. A four-blade iron propeller connected to a drive shaft may be seen about thirty-five feet forward of the stern. Although poor visibility and heavy marine growth makes recognition of specific features difficult, the machinery area is basically intact. All that remains of the hull is the very bottom portion in the stern. The size of the propeller indicates the vessel had a draft of 10 feet or more. The heavy deterioration of the hull suggests the wreck was constructed of wood. Both of these findings add support to the USS *Aster's* identification.

Stormy Petrel

The *Stormy Petrel* represents the last generation of blockade runners constructed specifically for the American Civil War. It was built in Scotland in the fall of 1864. The steamer was attempting to make New Inlet on its maiden voyage when driven aground by Federal gunboats well out on the south breakers on December 15, 1864. After two days of unsuccessful Union attempts to destroy it a northeast gale succeeded in completing the task. The *Stormy Petrel* was reputedly carrying a cargo of arms and munitions; the only wartime salvage reported was a full load of clothing by the Confederates. The remains of a sidewheel steamer constructed of iron may be seen at the site. The recovery of the ship's bell, inscribed with the vessel's name, *Stormy Petrel*, has provided positive identification. The wreckage has deteriorated considerably. The machinery and boilers remain intact as well as a 30-foot section of the bow. The hull in the fore and aft cargo holds has collapsed out at the turn of the bilge. The hull frames and bottom are partially covered with one-to-three feet of sand. The wreck field indicates that the vessel was 240 feet long with a beam of 32 feet. The extreme stern cannot be detected due to sanding. The ship's bell and other artifacts were recovered in 1984.

Elizabeth

The *Elizabeth* was a 216-foot-long wooden hull sidewheel steamer. Powered by a vertical beam or a walking beam, low pressure steam engine, the vessel had a beam of 26 feet and drew ten feet of water. It was built in New York and owned and operated by Charles Morgan's Southern Steamship Company. The *Elizabeth* was seized by Confederate General Mansfield Lovel, in New Orleans in January 1862, but later released because it was considered too inadequate for military service. Private investors converted the *Elizabeth* for blockade running and successfully made seven runs before it was lost on September 4, 1863. The *Elizabeth* was attempting to run in at Old Inlet, twelve miles east of Lockwood's Folly Inlet, with a load of steel and saltpeter. While creeping along the shore it grounded on an inlet bar shoal. After unsuccessfully attempting to free the vessel she was burned by her crew to avoid capture. The wreck site lies on the outside of the western bar shoal and the remains of a walking beam may be seen. Only portions of the steam machinery are exposed above the bottom. The support structure or walking beam, piston rods, cylinder, and steam pipes are reasonably intact, but an adequate determination of the condition of the wreckage is difficult due to the sanded condition of the wreck. No vessel measurements nor orientation have been determined for the vessel. There are artifacts roughly estimated to lie within a 250-foot-diameter area centering on the steam machinery. The *Elizabeth* was formerly known as the *Atlantic*.

Wild Dayrell

Built in Liverpool, England, in the summer of 1863, the *Wild Dayrell* was an iron, side-wheel steamer measuring 215 feet by 20 feet by 11 feet. It was built along the same lines as the *Banshee I* making it an example of the first class of steamers built exclusively for blockade running. On its fifth run through the blockade, the *Wild Dayrell* was run aground at New Topsail Inlet on February 2, 1864. Most of its cargo of shoes, blankets, and provisions had been taken off by Confederates. Pillaging of the cargo remains and final destruction of the vessel was completed by a Union boarding party. The wreck does not lie in the historical wreck location reported for the *Wild Dayrell*, although it is strongly suspected to be that vessel.

The wreckage measures 220 feet by 21 feet, all of which corresponds to the *Wild Dayrell*. No other vessel of the *Wild Dayrell's* description has been found at New Topsail Inlet nor were any wrecks reported lost in nearby Rich Inlet. Lying in the inlet the wreck has been sanded over and is well-preserved. In addition to its steam machinery, much of its hull is intact to the deck level. Part of the superstructure lies just outside of the hull. Sport divers removed some portholes from the wreck in the early 1960s.

[Historical information for some vessels in this chapter is from James Sprunt, 1920; Frances B. C. Bradlee, 1925; and James Delgado, 1989. Information for wrecks that are part of the Cape Fear Civil War Shipwreck District is an edited version of material from the National Register of Historic Places Nomination Form for the Cape Fear Civil War Shipwreck District written by Mark Wilde-Ramsing, Archaeologist, Underwater Archaeology Unit, North Carolina Division of Archives and History and is used with permission.]

9. *New Artificial Reefs*

THE North Carolina Division of Marine Fisheries of the Department of Environmental Health and Natural Resources is in charge of the Artificial Reef program of the state of North Carolina. With the assistance of different sportsfishing associations, the state has sunk several ships off North Carolina's coast for the purpose of attracting marine life. The ships also serve as new dive sites. A brief list of the shipwreck sites is given below. Local dive stores can give detailed information about the sites and provide dive trips to them. In the future several more large ships are to be sunk as the artificial reef program expands over the next few years.

Cape Lookout Area

Hardee's Reef—The *YO-FS26*, a 174-foot-long yard oiler was obtained from the James River Reserve fleet and sunk in 92 feet of water south of Cape Lookout and east of the *Aeolus*. It sits upright and contains three decks and a stern pilot house that rises up to 55 fsw.

Novelty—The *Novelty* is a 140-foot-long, steel-hulled menhaden fishing trawler that was sunk in 52 feet of water three miles offshore of the Ramada Inn. Relief on the *Novelty* reaches up to 35 fsw.

Nancy Lee, ex *Verbena*—The *Verbena* was a 170-foot-long U.S. Coast Guard buoy tender. Later the ship was decommissioned and sold to become the *Nancy Lee*, a menhaden fishing vessel. The *Nancy Lee* was sunk in 70 feet of water on the east side of Cape Lookout and inshore of the *Caribsea*.

Cape Fear Area

Hyde—The *Hyde* was a 215-foot-long U.S. Army Corp of Engineer dredge that was sunk in 25 feet of water off of Masonboro Inlet. It was the only dredge to circumnavigate the globe and spent a tour of duty in Vietnam.

Underwater Photography

THERE ARE MANY CHOICES of cameras available for the underwater photographer. The most widely used formats are 35mm and 110, and models include just about all on-land cameras safely placed in a protective underwater housing as well as cameras ready-made for underwater submersion. Two examples of the latter type of camera are the Sea-and-Sea 110 camera made for direct use underwater and Nikon's Nikonos in the 35mm format.

I recommend a 35mm camera for several reasons. Many divers already have a favorite on-land 35mm camera, and it is a relatively simple matter to obtain the appropriate underwater housing for it. Such housings are made by several companies and are designed for easy placement and removal of the camera, making it easy to alternate between on-land and underwater use. Housings are easy to use and the controls are conveniently placed on most models. They are, however, large and bulky, and transporting them underwater, although easy under normal conditions, becomes more difficult in a current or rough seas.

The Nikonos is a compact 35mm camera designed to be used directly underwater without additional housing. Early models (I, II, and III) are rangefinder types which have been around for a number of years. They are easy to use and compact, and with certain lenses they can be used on land as well. These older Nikonos models have evolved into and been replaced by the much newer and more advanced Nikonos IVA and V 35mm rangefinder cameras which offer auto-exposure and through-the-lens metering, coupled with auto-flash exposure. They are designed like land cameras, so film loading, the camera back, and placement of control knobs and dials are very familiar to anyone who has used an on-land camera. These cameras are also quite compact; you can stuff one into your BC pocket during a dive if you don't wish to carry it in your hands. There are several interchangeable lenses available for the Nikonos IV and V cameras, some of which allow the camera to be used on land as well. I prefer the housed SLR because it allows me to use my on-land camera system underwater. Before investing in one system or the other, go to a camera dealer or dive shop and check out all of the options that are available.

The lens to use underwater requires more deliberation. The choice depends in part on an understanding of the behavior of light in water, which is different in several respects from its behavior in air. Rays of light are refracted, or bent, as they pass from one medium to another of differing density. This will result in the image being either larger or smaller depending upon the difference in densities of the media. Light from an underwater subject travels through water and passes into the less dense air of the camera housing and lens where it is refracted in such a fashion as to produce an image which appears about one-third larger and one-third closer than it actually is. Focusing of the lens must be done on the basis of the apparent image distance rather than the actual distance and is easily accomplished by eyeball judgment since light from the subject will be refracted in the same way as it passes from water through the air in your mask. Set the focus on the distance scale of your lens at the distance you see, or if you actually measure the distance, subtract one-third the distance to determine the distance setting on the lens. Refraction also affects the focal length and angle-of-view of the lens, increasing the former and thereby decreasing the latter. For example, a lens of with a focal length of 35mm and an angle-of-view of 63 degrees *on land* will behave *underwater* as though the focal length were 47mm with an angle-of-view of only 50 degrees. This means that a 35mm wide-angle lens behaves underwater as though it were a "normal" lens.

To get a wide-angle view underwater requires the use of a lens with an above-water focal length of 28mm or less. The 28mm lens will produce an underwater image with an angle-of-view equivalent to that of a 35mm lens used above water. Wide-angle lenses are used most extensively underwater because they increase depth of field, thereby minimizing focusing errors. If you wish to produce a telephoto effect, choose a normal (50mm) or moderate telephoto lens to use underwater.

Another effect of water on light passing through it is the selective removal of color. Red is filtered out at about 10 feet, orange at around 20 feet, and yellow at about 45 feet. If you take available-light photographs at depths greater than 10 feet, the images will have altered color balance, and at depths greater than 45 feet the images will appear blue. A red filter on the camera lens may help reduce the bluish image, and other filters (81A and 81B) will help warm the image.

However, if you want normal color in your underwater images you must use an electronic strobe (flash) at depths greater than 10–15 feet. These strobes are balanced for sunlight, and images produced under their influence will be as colorful as they would be if they were taken in direct sunlight. There are many strobes for underwater use on the market, and like cameras some are ready-made for direct submersion without additional housing. Any on-land flash can be housed for underwater use. However, on-land flashes housed for underwater use are recommended only for special circumstances such as when only a spot of light is required on a subject. The same refraction effect that reduces the angle-of-view of lenses underwater will reduce the angle-of-coverage of underwater flash units. The strobe that adequately covers the image on land will behave like a spotlight underwater and leave the edges of the subject dark and underexposed.

For added lighting, the best results are generally obtained with strobe units designed for underwater use. The flash reflector in such strobes has been designed so that adequate coverage of the underwater subject is obtained with all but the fisheye type of wide-angle lens. There are many types of underwater strobes available for use with housed and Nikonos-type cameras. They come in many varieties for manual use or equipped with sensors for automatic use. Some strobes are coupled through the camera's metering system so that the camera turns off the strobe when the film has received enough light. In spite of this electronic wizardry, I recommend a manual-use strobe for those who are already familiar with on-land flash use and for those who wish to have the additional versatility allowed by these manual strobes.

The principles that govern the manual use of a strobe underwater are the same as those on land, although there are several important considerations that must be understood for successful underwater photography. The amount of light generated by a strobe to produce a properly exposed image at a given distance on land will not be sufficient for the same apparent distance underwater. There are several reasons for this. Part of the light is absorbed by water, part is blocked or scattered by particles in the water; and since apparent distances are used underwater to estimate camera-to-subject distances, the light is actually travelling one-third further to reach the subject and to reflect back to the camera. All three factors work together to decrease the amount of light a strobe puts out to the subject. To understand how these factors may be compensated for, it is necessary to understand how the power of a strobe is determined.

Of the common ways of measuring and comparing the light output of a strobe, the two most often used are *watt-second* and *guide number*. Guide number is directly related to exposure whereas watt-second is not. Watt-second is a measure of how much electricity a strobe's capacitor can store. The capacitor stores and concentrates electricity from the strobe's battery so that when the strobe is fired by triggering the shutter release on the camera, the electrical energy stored in the capacitor is quickly released into the flash tube which then produces the flash of light. Capacitors vary in size—i.e., they vary in the amount of electrical energy they can store. The more energy a capacitor stores, the brighter the flash of light when the charge of electricity is released to the flash tube. Thus, a strobe incorporating a capacitor with twice the storage capacity of another will produce twice the brightness of flash and consequently requires one f-stop less exposure to produce a properly exposed image. For example, consider a strobe rated at 150 watt-seconds which requires the use of, say, f/11 at a given distance from a subject for proper exposure. Another strobe rated at 75 watt-seconds would have to be used at f/8 to achieve the same exposure. Many underwater strobes are designed with a power switch that regulates the number of equivalent capacitors which fire the strobe's flash tube. At full power, for example, four capacitors equivalent to 150 watt-seconds will be fired in the Ikelite 150; at only half-power only two capacitors equivalent to 75 watt-seconds will be fired; and at one-quarter power a single capacitor equivalent to 37.5 watt-seconds will be fired. Suppose that at full power the camera's lens has to be set at f/11 for proper exposure. For equivalent exposures at a given distance, a setting of f/8 would have to be used at one-half power, and a setting of f/5.6 would have to be used at one-quarter power.

By contrast, guide number (GN) relates flash directly to exposure through the f-stop system. A guide number, when divided by subject-to-flash distance, gives the f-stop to use in making a correct exposure. The GN is determined by the manufacturer for each flash model and varies depending upon the model and brand. For a given flash, the GN is different for each ASA film used, so there are several GN's for a given strobe depending upon the film in use. A table of GN's should appear in the instruction manual provided with the strobe or may be obtained from a camera store or dive shop carrying the particular unit. If the GN is unavailable, it can be easily determined for a particular film by a series of exposures made as follows: On land (even though you are using an underwater strobe) set up a colorful subject 10 feet from the strobe and make a series of exposures one-half to one f-stop apart, beginning with the smallest aperture of the lens. Process the film and determine which f-stop produced the correct exposure. The correct f-stop multiplied by the distance, 10 feet, equals the GN for the flash using that particular film. For example, say you determined that f/8 is the correct f-stop for proper exposure for ASA 64 film, then the on-land guide number for the flash would be 80. Now it is necessary to convert the on-land guide number to an underwater guide number. I have already mentioned the three factors that act together to reduce the amount of light from the strobe reaching the subject underwater. These are compensated for by dividing the on-land guide number by three for clear water, by four for average clarity, and by five for less than average. In water off the North Carolina coast it is necessary to divide the GN by four. You will seldom be using a strobe in conditions that require the GN to be divided by five. This correction of the on-land GN by dividing by three, four, or five depending upon the water clarity results in requiring an opening of the lens aperture one f-stop as water clarity changes from clear to average and from average to below average.

Watt-second power designations and guide numbers should be provided by the manufacturer for each strobe unit. Guide numbers for underwater strobes will be underwater GN's, and GN's for on-land strobes will be on-land GN's. They may be interchanged quite easily as I have described. For underwater strobes, the GN's are given for use in *clear* water and a table of these GN's and corresponding f-stop/distances can be taped to the outside of the strobe for easy reference. When going from *clear* water to water of *average clarity*, open the lens one f-stop from those indicated in the table. For North Carolina wreck photography it is necessary to open the lens one f-stop as the water is of average clarity. Once the underwater GN has been determined for your strobe in the type of water you will be using it in, it is a relatively simple matter to make properly exposed images. The general procedure is as follows: Using your camera's light meter or an underwater light meter, determine the correct f-stop to use under existing natural light conditions. Divide this f-stop into the GN to get the proper subject-to-flash distance. By placing your strobe at that distance from the subject and setting the lens at the f-stop for existing light, the subject will be properly illuminated by the strobe and the background behind the subject will be properly exposed by the natural light.

One problem in using a strobe underwater is backscatter of unwanted light bouncing off particulate matter between the camera and the subject. To reduce backscatter, which appears as snow in the image, hold the strobe at arm's length above and away from the camera at about 45 degrees. Practice this technique since aiming the strobe properly is important for complete and correct illumination and exposure of the subject.

How far away you can shoot effectively underwater depends upon the visibility. Film limits the maximum shooting distance to about 25 percent of the visibility, but you should always try to shoot as close to your subject as possible. This is one reason why wide-angle lenses are used a lot in underwater photography; with the proper wide-angle lens, the subject can be approached closely and still be entirely included in the frame. For shooting over long distances, you will find that, underwater, "infinity" is about six to eight feet. The best time to dive and do photography is between 10 A.M. and 2 P.M. when the sun is high in the sky and more sunlight penetrates the water.

Selection of film depends on water quality and what the film is to be used for. In clear water like that found in the Florida Keys, the Caribbean, or the South Pacific, use Kodachrome 25 (K25), Kodachrome 64 (K64), or Ektachrome 100 (E100) slide film for flash photography. These slide films will produce wonderful results. However, each type differs in the quality of color rendition and graininess. The least grain will be obtained with K25 film, but the use of this film will be limited to extremely clear water because of its slow speed. The best all-round film for clear water is K64 which produces the best quality color image. That is not say images produced with E100 film will be poor. Quite the contrary, E100 film produces good color rendition but lacks the rich, saturated colors of K64. K64 film must be sent to a processing laboratory for development whereas E100 film can be processed in your own home. Also, dive resorts generally have facilities for quickly processing E100 film.

The exposure latitude of slide films is maximally around plus or minus three-quarters of an f-stop. You must, therefore, be very careful not to make a mistake in exposing slide films. On exotic dive trips carry several rolls of K64 film and a few rolls of E100 if you are going someplace where there are facilities for rapid processing of E100 film. Shoot your initial underwater exposures with E100 film based upon the rated GN information for your strobe at the appropriate f-stops. Have this film processed locally and then shoot the rest of your dives with K64 film using the proper exposure determined with E100. K64 is two-thirds of a stop slower than E100 film, and thus requires opening the lens two-thirds of an f-stop, or decreasing strobe-to-subject distance by about 20% from those parameters determined with E100. There is nothing worse than discovering after you have returned from a beautiful dive trip with a batch of unprocessed film that your slides were improperly exposed. Another sure-fire method of avoiding that kind of disappointment is to bracket your exposures. Make one exposure at the f stop you think is correct and then make an exposure at an f-stop on either side of the first one. Film is cheap. Getting back to the dive site is not.

For flash photography in water off the North Carolina coast, I primarily use Ektachrome 200 (E200) slide film. I do not like Ektachrome 400 (E400) film because of its graininess and less-than-good color rendition under dim light conditions. E200 is a far superior "fast" film and it is only one stop slower than E400. E400 or even faster ASA 1000 film (made by 3M) is useful for non-flash photography, and E400 can be "push-processed" one to two f-stops if used under really dim light conditions. The exposure latitude of E200 and E400 films is the same as for the other slide films, plus or minus three-quarters of an f-stop.

Color or black-and-white negative films, such as Kodacolor VR (ASA 100, 200, 400, and 1000) or Plus-X (ASA 125), Tri-X (ASA 400), and HP-5 (ASA 400), respectively, may be used for underwater photography but really should be avoided if at all possible. These films will produce very flat and dull images because of the inherent lack of contrast underwater. However, these films might be useful to a beginner since the exposure latitude of negative films is plus one-and-a-half to minus one-and-a-half f-stops. There is a larger margin for error when shooting with these films than with slide film. However, even the most inept beginner can, with proper instruction, learn to use a camera and strobe well enough to keep exposure errors to within the tolerance required for slide films and should not have to resort to negative films for underwater photography. There are some cases where black-and-white negative film is useful for underwater photography, but these are more specialized applications.

My recommendation for shipwreck photography off the North Carolina coast is Ektachrome 200 film. Under sunlight conditions normally found on offshore shipwrecks off the North Carolina coast from May to November, my parameters for flash photography, using E200 film and a 75-watt-second strobe set at half-power, are f/5.6 at four feet for depths of 30 to 160 feet. In normal circumstances, ambient light conditions at depths of 40–140 feet with E200 film require a setting of f/2.8 to f/5.6 for a proper exposure at 1/90 of a second. Under good ambient light conditions, found several times during the summer off the North Carolina coast, E200 film will be properly exposed at f/8-f/11 at depths from 60 to 100 feet.

Although necessarily brief for the purposes of this book, the foregoing information should give you a start with underwater photography. Several very good books on the subject are available at dive shops and camera stores, and I recommend the purchase of one or more of these for more complete information to begin your adventure in underwater photography.

Federal Laws
Abandoned Shipwreck Act of 1987

AN ACT

To establish the title of States in certain abandoned shipwrecks, and for other purposes.

Be it enacted by the Senate and House of Representatives of the United States of America in Congress assembled.

Section 1. Short title.
This Act may be cited as the "Abandoned Shipwreck Act of 1987."

Sec. 2. Findings.
The Congress finds that—
(a) States have the responsibility for management of a broad range of living and nonliving resources in State waters and submerged lands; and
(b) included in the range of resources are certain abandoned shipwrecks, which have been deserted and to which the owner has relinquished ownership rights with no retention.

Sec. 3. Definitions.
For purposes of this Act—
(a) the term "embedded" means firmly affixed in the submerged lands or in coralline formations such that the use of tools of excavation is required in order to move the bottom sediments to gain access to the shipwreck, its cargo, and any part thereof;
(b) the term "National Register" means the National Register of Historic Places maintained by the Secretary of the Interior under section 101 of the National Historic Preservation Act (16 U.S.C. 470a);
(c) the terms "public lands," "Indian lands," and "Indian tribe" have the same meaning given the terms in the Archaeological Resource Protection Act of 1979 (16 U.S.C. 470aa-470ll);
(d) the term "shipwreck" means a vessel or wreck, its cargo, and other contents;
(e) the term "State" means a State of the United States, the District of Columbia, Puerto Rico, Guam, the Virgin Islands, American Samoa, and the Northern Mariana Islands; and
(f) the term "submerged lands" means the lands—
(1) that are "lands beneath navigable waters," as defined in section 2 of the Submerged Lands Act (43 U.S.C. 1301);
(2) of Puerto Rico, as described in section 8 of the Act of March 2, 1917, as amended (48 U.S.C. 749);

(3) of Guam, the Virgin Islands and American Samoa, as described in section 1 of Public Law 93-435 (48 U.S.C. 1705); and

(4) of the Commonwealth of the Northern Mariana Islands, as described in section 801 of Public Law 94-241 (48 U.S.C. 1681).

Sec. 4. Rights of access.

(a) *Access rights.*—In order to—

(1) clarify that State waters and shipwrecks offer recreational and educational opportunities to sport divers and other interested groups, as well as irreplaceable State resources for tourism, biological sanctuaries, and historical research; and

(2) provide that reasonable access by the public to such abandoned shipwrecks be permitted by the State holding title to such Shipwrecks pursuant to section 6 of this Act, it is the declared policy of the Congress that States carry out their responsibilities under this Act to develop appropriate and consistent policies so as to—

(A) protect natural resources and habitat areas;

(B) guarantee recreational exploration of shipwreck sites; and

(C) allow for appropriate public and private sector recovery of shipwrecks consistent with the protection of historical values and environmental integrity of the shipwrecks and the sites.

(b) PARKS AND PROTECTED AREAS.—In managing the resources subject to the provisions of this Act, States are encouraged to create underwater parks or areas to provide additional protection for such resources. Funds available to States from grants from the Historical Preservation Fund shall be available, in accordance with the provisions of title I of the National Historic Preservation Act, for the study, interpretation, protection, and preservation of historic shipwrecks and properties.

Sec. 5. Preparation of Guidelines.

(a) In order to encourage the development of underwater parks and the administrative cooperation necessary for the comprehensive management of underwater resources related to historic shipwrecks, the Secretary of the Interior, acting through the Director of the National Park Service, shall within nine months after the date of enactment of this Act prepare and publish guidelines in the Federal Register which shall seek to:

(1) maximize the enhancement of cultural resources;

(2) foster a partnership among sport divers, fishermen, archaeologists, salvors, and other interests to manage shipwreck resources of the States and the United States;

(3) facilitate access and utilization by recreational interests;

(4) recognize the interests of individuals and groups engaged in shipwreck discovery and salvage.

(b) Such guidelines shall be developed after consultation with appropriate public and private sector interests (including the Secretary of Commerce, the Advisory Council on Historic Preservation, sport divers, State Historic Preservation Officers, professional dive operators, salvors, archaeologists, historic preservationists, and fishermen).

(c) Such guidelines shall be available to assist States and the appropriate Federal agencies in developing legislation and regulations to carry out their responsibilities under this Act.

Sec. 6. Rights of Ownership.

(a) *United States Title.*—The United States asserts title to any abandoned shipwreck that is—

(1) embedded in submerged lands of a State;

(2) embedded in coralline formations protected by a State on submerged lands of a State; or

(3) on submerged lands of a State and is included in or determined eligible for inclusion in the National Register.

(b) The public shall be given adequate notice of the location of any shipwreck to which title is asserted under this section. The Secretary of the Interior, after consultation with the appropriate State Historic Preservation Officer, shall make a written determination that an abandoned shipwreck meets the criteria for eligibility for inclusion in the National Register of Historic Places under clause (a) (3).

(c) *Transfer of title to states.*—The title of the United States to any abandoned shipwreck asserted under subsection (a) of this section is transferred to the States in or on whose submerged lands the shipwreck is located.

(d) *Exception.*—Any abandoned shipwreck in or on the public lands of the United States is the property of the United States Government. Any abandoned shipwreck in or on any Indian lands is the property of the Indian tribe owning such lands.

(e) *Reservation of rights.*—This section does not affect any right reserved by the United States or by any State (including any right reserved with respect to Indian lands) under—

(1) section 3, 5, or 6 of the Submerged Lands Act (43 U.S.C. 1311, 1313, and 1314); or

(2) section 19 or 20 of the Act of March 3, 1899 (33 U.S.C. 414 and 415).

Sec. 7. Relationship to other laws

(a) *Law of salvage and the law of finds.*—The law of salvage and the law of finds shall not apply to abandoned shipwrecks to which section 6 of this Act applies.

(b) *Laws of the United States.*—This Act shall not change the laws of the United States relating to shipwrecks, other than those to which this Act applies.

(c) *Effective date.*—This Act shall not affect any legal proceeding brought prior to the date of enactment of this Act.

APPENDIX C

NC *Statute on Underwater Salvage*

STATE OF NORTH CAROLINA SUBMERGED CULTURAL RESOURCES LEGISLATION: *Salvage of Abandoned Shipwrecks and other Underwater Archaeological Sites (Excerpts of Article 3)*

Sect. 121–22. Title to bottoms of certain waters and shipwrecks, etc., thereon declared to be in State. Subject to chapter 82 of the General Statutes, entitled "Wrecks" and to the provisions of chapter 210. Session Laws of 1963 [sections 121–7, 121–8.1 to 121–8.3 and 143–31.2], and to any statute of the United States, the title to all bottoms of navigable waters within one marine league seaward from the Atlantic seashore measured from the extreme low watermark; and the title to all shipwrecks, vessels, cargoes, tackle, and underwater archaeological artifacts which have remained unclaimed for more than 10 years lying on the said bottoms, or on the bottoms of any other navigable waters of the State, is hereby declared to be in the State of North Carolina and such bottoms, shipwrecks, vessels, cargoes, tackle, and underwater archaeological artifacts shall be subject to the exclusive dominion and control of the State. (1967, c.533, s.1.)

[Section 10 of of Session Laws 1967, c.533, makes the act effective July 1, 1967.]

Sect. 121–23. Department to be custodian of shipwrecks, etc., and underwater archaeological artifacts; rules and regulation.—The custodian of shipwrecks, vessels, cargoes, tackle and underwater archaeological artifacts as defined in sect. 121–22 hereof shall be the State Department of Archives and History, which is empowered to promulgate such rules and regulations as may be necessary to preserve, protect, recover, and salvage any or all underwater properties as defined in sect. 121–22 hereof; such rules and regulations, when approved by the Governor and Council of State, shall have the force and effect of law. (1967, c.533, s.2.)

Sect. 121–24. Department authorized to establish professional staff.—The Department of Archives and History is also authorized to establish a professional staff for the purpose of conducting and/or supervising the surveillance, protection, preservation, survey and systematic underwater archaeological recovery of underwater material as defined in sect. 121–22 hereof. (1967, c.533, s.3.)

Sect. 121–25. License to conduct exploration, recovery or salvage operations.—Any qualified person, firm or corporation desiring to conduct any type of exploration, recovery or salvage operations, in the course of which any part of a derelict or its contents or other archaeological site may be removed, displaced or destroyed, shall first make application to the Department of Archives and History for a permit or license to conduct such operations. If the Department of Archives and History shall find that the granting of such permit or license is in the best interest of the State, it may grant such applicant a permit or license for such a period of time and under such conditions as the Department may deem to be in

338

the best interest of the State. Such permit or license may include but need not be limited to the following:

1. Payment of monetary fee to be set by the Department
2. That a portion or all of the historic material or artifacts be delivered to custody and possession of the Department
3. That a portion of all of such relics or artifacts may be sold or retained by the licensee
4. That a portion or all of such relics or artifacts may be sold or traded by the Department.

Permits or licenses may be renewed upon or prior to expiration upon such terms as the applicant and the Department may mutually agree. Holders of permits or licenses shall be responsible for obtaining permission of any federal agencies having jurisdiction, including the United States Coast Guard, the United States Department of the Navy and the United States Army Corps of Engineers prior to conducting any salvaging operations. (1967, c.533, 2.4.)

Sect. 121–27. Law-enforcement agencies empowered to assist Department. —All law-enforcement agencies and officers, State and local, are hereby empowered to assist the Department of Archives and History in carrying out its duties under this article. (1967, c.533, s.6.)

Sect. 121–28. Violation of article a misdemeanor.—Any person violating the provisions of this article or any rules or regulations established thereunder shall be guilty of a misdemeanor and upon conviction thereof shall be punished as in cases of misdemeanor. (1967, c.533, 2.8.)

For further information relative to North Carolina's submerged cultural resources legislation, please contact:

Underwater Archaeology Branch
Division of Archives and History
P.O. Box 58
Kure Beach, North Carolina 28449

APPENDIX D

Divers Alert Network (DAN)

THE DIVERS ALERT NETWORK (DAN) is a membership association of individuals and organizations sharing a common interest in diving safety. DAN operates a 24-hour national hotline, (919) 684-8111, to provide advice on the early treatment, evacuation, and hyperbaric treatment of persons suffering from diving-related injuries. In addition, DAN provides diving safety information to members of DAN to *prevent* accidents. For $15 a year every member receives: the DAN *Underwater Diving Accident Manual*, which describes symptoms and first aid for the major diving-related injuries, plus emergency-room physician guidelines for drugs and i.v. fluids; a membership card listing diving-related injury symptoms on one side and DAN's emergency and non-emergency phone numbers on the other; one tank decal and three small equipment decals with DAN's logo and emergency number; and a newsletter, *Alert Diver*, which provides diving medicine and safety information in layman's language and includes articles for professionals on case histories and medical questions related to diving. Special memberships for dive stores, dive clubs, and corporations are also available. Posters and brochures for dive stores, dive clubs, dive boats, and emergency rooms are free. The DAN manual is available separately for $4.

In an emergency a diver or his physician dials (919) 684-8111 to reach DAN. (Collect calls are accepted in the case of an emergency.) The caller is answered by an operator at Duke University Medical Center in Durham, North Carolina, the site of DAN headquarters. When diving accidents or emergencies are reported, contact is made with a physician trained in diving medicine (on call 24 hours a day). The physician may advise the caller directly or refer him or her to one of DAN's six other Regional Coordinators. DAN divides the U.S. into seven regions, each coordinated by a specialist in diving medicine who has access to the hyperbaric chambers in his region. Non-emergency or information calls are connected to the information number of the DAN office, (919) 684-2948. Non-emergency, information callers should dial this number direct, between 9 A.M. and 5 P.M. (eastern time zone) Monday through Friday. Divers should *not* call DAN to inquire about chamber location information for general knowledge. Chamber status changes frequently make this kind of information dangerous because it may be obsolete at the time of an emergency. Instead, divers should contact DAN as soon as a diving emergency is suspected. DAN does not *directly* provide medical care. All divers should have comprehensive medical insurance and check to make *sure* that hyperbaric treatment and air ambulance services are covered internationally. Medical insurance for divers is available from DAN.

Diving is a safe sport, and there are very few accidents compared to the number of divers and number of dives made each year. But when the infrequent injury does occur, DAN is ready to help. DAN, originally 100 percent federally funded, is now largely supported by the diving public. Membership in DAN or purchase of DAN manuals or decals provides divers with useful safety information and provides DAN with necessary operating funds. Donations to DAN are tax-deductible as DAN is a legal non-profit public service organization.

For more information about DAN, and to become a member of the network, write to:

Divers Alert Network
Box 3823
Duke University Medical Center
Durham, North Carolina 27710

North Carolina Dive Stores and Charterboats

THE FOLLOWING LIST of North Carolina dive stores is based upon up-to-date information as of the date of publication. It is intended solely to indicate sources of current information about the shipwrecks, their location, prevailing diving conditions and other pertinent information that would be useful to divers.

Coast Dive Stores

1. Aquatic Safaris
   5751-4 Oleander Drive
   Wilmington, NC 28403
   (919) 392-4386

2. Discovery Diving Company
   414 Orange Street
   Beaufort, NC 28516
   (919) 728-2265

3. EJW Bicycle and Sports Shop
   2204 Arendell Street
   Morehead City, NC 28557
   (919) 726-6959

4. Hatteras Divers
   P.O. Box 213
   Hatteras, NC 27943
   (919) 986-2557

5. Nag's Head Pro Dive Center
   P.O. Box 665
   Nag's Head, NC 27959
   (919) 441-7594

6. Olympus Dive Shop
   P.O. Box 486
   Morehead City, NC 28557
   (919) 726-9432

7. Scuba South Diving Company
   222 South River Drive
   Southport, NC 28461
   (919) 457-5201

8. Wilmington Scuba
   5028-A Wrightsville Avenue
   Wilmington, NC 28403
   (919) 799-0868

Inland Dive Stores

1. Adventure Scuba
   8700 Pineville-Matthews Road #530
   Charlotte, NC 28226
   (704) 541-8541

2. Aqua-Nut Dive Service, Inc.
   3703-1 Bragg Blvd.
   Fayetteville, NC 28303
   (919) 864-3577

3. Aquatics Unlimited
   212 Adams Street
   Eden, NC 27288
   (919) NC-DIVER

4. Aqua Sport
   1422 N. Bragg Blvd.
   Spring Lake, NC 28390
   (919) 436-3483

5. Blue Dolphin Dive Center
3010 S. Stratford Road
Winston-Salem, NC 27103
(919) 760-9226

6. Blue Water Dive Company
2257 New Hope Church Road
Raleigh, NC 27604
(919) 878-6131

7. Bottom Time
2651 N. Marine Blvd.
Jacksonville, NC 28546
(919) 347-2826

8. Cape Fear Scuba
5441 Yadkin Road
Fayetteville, NC 28303
(919) 867-2844

9. Carolina Divers
4724 Old Pineville Road
Charlotte, NC 28217
(704) 523-4029

10. Charlotte Dive Center, Inc.
1741 E. Independence Blvd.
Charlotte, NC 28205
(704) 334-3483

11. Country Scuba
Rt. 5 Box 9
Leland, NC 28451
(919) 371-3220

12. Crystal Coast Diving Adventures
713 New Bridge Street
Jacksonville, NC 28540
(919) 347-DIVE

13. Dane Lane Enterprises
Rt. 9 Box 329
Hendersonville, NC 28739
(704) 685-8574

14. The Dive Shop
P.O. Box 877
Claremont, NC 28610
(704) 459-7440

15. Gypsy Divers
1019 E. Whitaker Mill Road
Raleigh, NC 27608
(919) 833-9810

16. Island Hoppers Dive Center
2827 C Spring Garden Street
Greensboro, NC 27403
(919) 854-DIVE

17. Paradise Island Divers
2600 South Blvd.
Charlotte, NC 28209

18. Piedmont Divers
P.O. Box 976
Burlington, NC 27215
(919) 226-5206

19. Pro Scuba Center
1167 N. Wesleyan Blvd.
Rocky Mount, NC 27804
(919) 985-3951

20. Reef and Ridge Sports
532 E. Chatham Street
Cary, NC 27511
(919) 467-3831

21. Rum Runner Dive Shop
2905 East 5th Street
Greenville, NC 27858
(919) 758-1444

22. Sea Wolf of Clinton
P.O. Box 707
Clinton, NC 28328
(919) 592-5708

23. Smokey Mountain Water Sports, Inc
38 Westgate Parkway
Asheville, NC 28806
(704) 253-8125

24. Tar Heel Divers
2601 Highway 70 East
New Bern, NC 28560
(919) 633-4544

25. Water World Marine Services, Inc.
135 S. Miami Blvd.
Durham, NC 27703
(919) 596-8185

North Carolina Dive Charterboats

Carolina Cape Divers
P.O. Box 208
Long Beach, NC 28461
(919) 278-5611

Easy Step Charters
203 Neuse Avenue
Morehead City, NC 28557
(919) 726-2311

Fanta-Sea Charters
6819 Myrtle Grove Road
Wilmington, NC 28403
(919) 395-5841

Gale Anne Charters
P.O. Box 1754
Atlantic Beach, NC 28512
(919) 726-3550

Jaws Charters
515 Neptune Drive
Swansboro, NC 28584
1-800-345-5774 (NC)
(919) 393-2754

Little Clam Charters
P.O. Box 322
Hatteras, NC 27943
(919) 986-2365

Lou-Ton Charters
221 Lullwater Drive
Wilmington, NC 28403
(919) 799-5329

Olympus
P.O. Box 486
Morehead City, NC 28557
(919) 726-9432

Outrageous
414 Orange Street
Beaufort, NC 28516
(919) 728-2265

Quiet Waters Charters
P.O. Box 572
Hatteras, NC 27943
(919) 986-2477

Rod's Charters, Inc.
Rt. 1 Box 48AB
Cedar Grove, NC 27231
(919) 732-3934

Saltshaker Dive Service
P.O. Box 275
Morehead City, NC 28557
(919) 726-8852

SeaDiver Charters
112 Stillbrook Center
Jacksonville, NC 28540
(919) 455-2955

Sea Wife Charters
Rt. 2 Box 614
Beaufort, NC 28516
(919) 726-5670

Tarheel Aqua Ventures
102 Deerpark Lane
Cary, NC 27511
(919) 859-5200

Wet and Wild Diving Excursions
4625 Lord Elkins Road
Wilmington, NC 28405
(919) 799-4659

Whipsaw Charters
409 Windemcrc Road
Wilmington, NC 28405
(919) 791-7682

APPENDIX F
Charter Dive Services

THE CHARTER DIVE BOATS LISTED in this section regularly carry divers to the shipwreck sites described in this book. I have chartered most of these boats at one time or another and have found them to be sturdy ocean-going vessels run by competent and helpful boat captains who are knowledgeable about divers and North Carolina wreckdiving; I heartily recommend them all. I have also included possible advantages and limitations of each charter boat. All boats included in this section are licensed for charter by the Coast Guard and are fully equipped with navigation electronics including loran C, recording fathometer and marine radio.

There are charter dive boats as well as charter fishing boats willing to take divers to offshore shipwrecks from nearly every marina found along the North Carolina coast. The charter boat services listed in this section carry the vast majority of divers who come to visit these shipwrecks. Each charter captain generally carries divers to wrecks within a maximum of four to five hours running time from the inlet nearest the marina. Most charter dive boats are chartered by a single group of divers to go to a specific wreck site. On these regular charter dive boats the group decides the wreck site destination and the boat is hired to take the divers to that site, weather permitting. Another kind of charter dive service operates on a "head" basis whereby an individual diver pays for a single space on a dive charter and has little or no control over the choice of wreck sites. All head boats accept group and walk-on divers on all charters and a few regular charter dive boats will occasionally accept walk-on divers. The price for chartering the entire boat or for a single "walk-on" varies depending on the boat. Some boats are licensed to carry six divers plus a divemaster while some are licensed to carry up to 25–30 divers. Some charter captains allow divers to sleep on the boat the night prior to a dive trip and some provide other diver-related services such as air fills, gear rentals, repairs and box lunches. Most are willing to recommend good, reliable, nearby accommodations for your dive party. Non-diving boat riders are generally allowed, if prior arrangements have been made, but numbers of riders allowed and costs vary depending on the boat. A few charter services utilize nearby motels and restaurants to offer complete dive charter packages including motel and restaurant accommodations. Public and private campgrounds are also located near charter boat marinas and offer inexpensive accommodations for tent and vehicle camping.

The following list of charter dive boats is not complete; however, as a group these boats probably account for most of the charter dive boat businesses which carry dive trips off the coast of North Carolina. For those charter boats I may have missed, I apologize for the oversight. Additionally, charter fishing boats may sometimes be hired to carry divers to wrecks and often operators of marinas can provide names of fishing boat captains willing to provide this service. Don't expect a lot of trips along these lines because fishing boat captains are frequently

345

reluctant to take divers to their fishing spots for fear of driving the fish away, a groundless fear. Local dive shops in the area have up-to-date information about all the boats willing to take divers to wreck sites and should be contacted for specific charter dive information. There is a list of coast and inland dive shops in Appendix E.

RUM RUNNER DIVE SHOP, INC.
Ray Scharf
2905 East 5th Street
Greenville, NC 27836   (919) 758-1444 (919) 758-2072

Boat name	Captain	Length	Beam	Engine	Cruising Speed
Pelican	[1]Ken Ball [2]Ray Scharf	45 ft.	14 ft.	twin diesel	16 knots

Boat is docked at: Morehead City Yacht Basin

Trip data		Dive shop services	
Maximum no. of divers	10	Scuba lessons	yes
Sleep on board the night before the dive?	no	Equipment	yes
		Air fills	yes
Walk-on divers accepted?	yes	Gear rentals	yes
Riders accepted?	yes	Repairs	yes
Is the captain a diver?	[1]y/[2]y	Divemaster for charters?	yes
Scuba instructor?	[1]n/[2]y		

Facilities near boat dock: Motels and restaurants within a short walk; campgrounds within five miles.

Wrecks visited:
Cape Lookout area shipwrecks

Comments:
Nice boat with competent boat captain. Safety first is the rule on this boat. No deep diving.

JAWS CHARTERS
George Harper
515 Neptune Drive
Swansboro, NC 28584   (919) 393-2754

Boat name	Captain	Length	Beam	Engine	Cruising speed
Jaws	George Harper	45 ft.	16½ ft.	twin diesel	10 knots

Boat is docked at: Island Harbor Marina, Emerald Isle, NC; it is not affiliated with a dive store.

Trip data		Dive shop services	
Maximum no. of divers	six plus divemaster	Scuba lessons	NA
		Equipment	NA
Sleep on board the night before the dive?	yes	Air fills	yes
		Gear rentals	NA
		Repairs	NA
Walk-on divers accepted?	no	Divemaster for charters?	if necessary
Riders accepted?	no		
Is the captain a diver?	yes		
Scuba instructor?	no		

Facilities near boat dock: Motels and restaurants within a short walk; campgrounds within five miles.

Wrecks visited:

Via Bogue Inlet: *Theodore Parker, Suloide, W. E. Hutton, Atlas, Caribsea, Senateur Duhamel, Fenwick Island, Ea, Portland, Ashkhabad, Thistleroy, U-352, Schurz, Papoose, Naeco, Normannia, Lobster Wreck, Cassimir, Proteus, Tarpon, British Splendour, Empire Gem, Dixie Arrow, Manuela, Tamaulipas, F. W. Abrams*

Comments

Jaws is one of the finest charter dive boats operating off the North Carolina coast, is equipped with full electronics, and features on-board air compressor, zodiac chase boat, refrigerator, stereo, color TV, video, couches, double beds and hot shower. Captain Harper is a competent boat captain and one of the most experienced operating in the area. He is quite knowledgeable about divers and diving and will move the boat to Ocracoke for long weekends of diving the wrecks in the Hatteras-Ocracoke area. He and his mate provide friendly, enthusiastic service and *Jaws* provides some of the most comfortable diving off the North Carolina coast.

LITTLE CLAM CHARTERS
Spurgeon Stone
P.O. Box 322
Hatteras, NC 27943   (919) 986-2365

Boat name	Captain	Length	Beam	Engine	Cruising Speed
Little Clam	Tom Bibbey	42 ft.	13 ft.	single diesel	20 knots

Boat is docked at: Oden's Dock, Hatteras

Trip data		Dive shop services	
Maximum no. of divers	16	Scuba lessons	no
Sleep on board the night before the dive?	no	Equipment	no
		Air fills	no
Walk-on divers accepted?	no	Gear rentals	no
Riders accepted?	yes	Repairs	no
Is the captain a diver?	no	Divemaster for charters?	yes
Scuba instructor?	no		

Facilities near boat dock: Dive shop, motels and restaurans located within walking distance; campground within five miles.

Wrecks visited:

Ocracoke-Hatteras area wrecks.

Comments:

The austere accommodations are offset by the speed of the boat.

NAGS HEAD DIVERS
Fil Nutter
P. O. Box 665
Mile Post 13
Nags Head, NC 27959   (919) 441-7594

Boat name	Captain	Length	Beam	Engine	Cruising speed
Sea Fox	Doogie Pledger	50 ft.	16 ft.	twin diesel	25 knots

Boat is docked at: Pirates Cove Marina, Nags Head-Manteo Causeway; it is affiliated with a dive shop.

Trip data		Dive shop services	
Maximum no. of divers	20	Scuba lessons	yes
Sleep on board the night before the dive?	no	Equipment	yes
		Air fills	yes
		Gear rentals	yes
		Repairs	yes
Walk-on divers accepted?	yes	Divemaster for charters?	if necessary
Riders accepted?	yes		
Is the captain a diver?	no		
Scuba instructor?	no		

Facilities near boat dock: Motels and restaurants within one mile; campgrounds within five miles.

Wrecks visited:

Nags Head area via Oregon Inlet: *U-85, Byron D. Benson, Norvana, Buarque, Zane Grey, Dionysus, Ciltvaira, City of Atlanta, Proteus, Tarpon, F. W. Abrams, Dixie Arrow.*

Comments

The *Sea Fox* is equipped with full electronics and is one of the nicest and fastest dive boats operating off the coast of North Carolina. Captain Pledger is not a diver but Nags Head Divers sends an experienced divemaster to assist each dive group.

BOTTOM TIME DIVE CHARTERS
Gordon Smith
P.O. Box 933
Beaufort, NC 28516   (919) 728-6002

Boat name	Captain	Length	Beam	Engine	Cruising Speed
Bottom Time	[1]Gordon Smith [2]Howard Scott	36 ft.	14½ ft.	single diesel	15 knots

Boat is docked at: Morehead City Yacht Basin

Trip data		Dive shop services	
Maximum no. of divers	6	Scuba lessons	no
Sleep on board the night before the dive?	yes	Equipment	no
		Air fills	no
Walk-on divers accepted?	yes	Gear rentals	no
Riders accepted?	no	Repairs	no
Is the captain a diver?	[1]y/[2]y	Divemaster for charters?	yes
Scuba instructor?	no		

Facilities near boat dock: Motels and restaurants within walking distance; campground within five miles.

Wrecks visited:

Cape Lookout and Ocracoke-Hatteras area wrecks.

Comments:

Comfortable, fast boat. Very competent boat captains and knowledgeable wreck divers.

DISCOVERY DIVING COMPANY
Debbie Boyce
414 Orange Street
Beaufort, NC 28516   (919) 728-2265

Boat names	Captain	Length	Beam	Engine	Cruising speed
Outrageous V	Terry Leonard	47 ft.	15 ft.	twin diesel	16 knots
Seaquest	Jerry Smith	42 ft.	14 ft.	single diesel	13 knots
Atlantis I	Bobby Edwards	33 ft.	12 ft.	single diesel	12 knots
Outrageous VI	Jonathan Pharr	33 ft.	12 ft.	single gas	22 knots
My Mistress	David Haskovec	30 ft.	12 ft.	single diesel	18 knots
Captain's Lady	Leroy Crayton	30 ft.	12 ft.	single diesel	18 knots

Boats are docked at: Discovery Diving Company, 414 Orange Street, Beaufort, NC; they are affiliated with a dive store.

Trip data		Dive shop services	
Maximum no. of divers	*Out. V:* 16 plus divemaster all others: six plus divemaster	Scuba lessons	yes
		Equipment	yes
		Air fills	yes
		Gear rentals	yes
		Repairs	yes
Sleep on board the night before the dive?	no	Divemaster for charters?	if necessary
Walk-on divers accepted?	yes		
Riders accepted?	yes		
Is the captain a diver?	yes		
Scuba instructor?	no		

Facilities near boat dock: Motels and restaurants within a short walk; campgrounds within five miles.

Wrecks visited:

Via Beaufort Inlet: *Theodore Parker, Suloide, W. E. Hutton, Atlas, Caribsea, Senateur Duhamel, Fenwick Island, Ea, Portland, Ashkhabad, U-352, Schurz, Papoose, Naeco, Proteus, Tarpon, Dixie Arrow, British Splendour, Cassimir.*

Comments

All six boats are equipped with full electronics. Terry Leonard is an experienced and competent boat captain and diver. The *Outrageous V* is a comfortable, fast dive boat equipped with a large dive platform. Jerry Smith and Bobby Edwards are also experienced captains and divers and are quite knowledgeable about divers and wreck diving. Discovery Diving Company has a diver's lodge nearby, which will accommodate 22 divers.

SEA WIFE CHARTERS
Buck Wilde
Rt. 2 Box 614
Beaufort, NC 28516   (919) 728-5670

Boat name	Captain	Length	Beam	Engine	Cruising speed
Sea Wife IV	Buck Wilde	51 ft.	16½'	single diesel	14 knots

Boat is docked at: Foot of 8th. Street, Morehead City, NC. Although not affiliated with a dive shop, air fills are available at the dock.*

Trip data		Dive shop services	
Maximum no. of divers	20	Scuba lessons	NA
Sleep on board the night before the dive?	yes	Equipment	NA
		Air fills	yes *
		Gear rentals	NA
Walk-on divers accepted?	yes	Repairs	NA
Riders accepted?	yes	Divemaster for charters?	if necessary
Is the captain a diver?	yes		
Scuba instructor?	no		

Facilities near boat dock: Motels and restaurants within a short walk; campgrounds within five miles.

Wrecks visited:

Via Beaufort Inlet: *Theodore Parker, Suloide, W. E. Hutton, Atlas, Caribsea, Senateur Duhamel, Fenwick Island, Ea, Portland, Ashkhabad, U-352, Amagansett, Schurz, Naeco, Papoose, Cassimir, Proteus, Tarpon, Dixie Arrow, British Splendour, Tamaulipás.*

Comments

The *Sea Wife IV* is one of the nicest charter dive boats operating on the North Carolina coast. The boat is fully equipped with electronics and Captain Wilde is an experienced and competent captain; he is a diver, and is enthusiastic about wreck divers and diving. Licensed to carry 20 divers, the *Sea Wife IV* can accommodate most dive group needs. Most groups charter the whole boat and I have taken as many as 19 people on a charter without too much inconvenience. However, unless you don't mind riding among tanks, dive bags, ice chests, wet suits, weight belts, cameras, strobes and the like, charters should be limited to 12–15 divers. Buck Wilde was the first captain from Morehead City to find the USS *Tarpon* and is one of only two charter boats running to the *Naeco* and *Cassimir*, two of the top five wrecks off the North Carolina coast. Captain Wilde will also move the *Sea Wife IV* to Ocracoke Island for long weekends exploring the wrecks in the Ocracoke-Hatteras area.

SALTSHAKER DIVE SERVICE
Mike McKay
Post Office Box 275
Morehead City, NC 28557   (919) 726-8852

Boat name	Captain	Length	Beam	Engine	Cruising speed
Saltshaker IV	No longer in service; replaced by Saltshaker V				
Saltshaker V	Mike McKay	36 ft.	15 ft.	single diesel	12 knots

Boat is docked at: Olympus Dive Shop, foot of 8th Street, Morehead City, NC; it is affiliated with a dive shop.

Trip data		Dive shop services	
Maximum no. of divers	six plus divemaster	Scuba lessons	no
		Equipment	yes
Sleep on board the night before the dive?	yes	Air fills	yes
		Gear rentals	no
		Repairs	yes
Walk-on divers accepted?	yes	Divemaster for charters?	if necessary
Riders accepted?	yes		
Is the captain a diver?	yes		
Scuba instructor?	no		

Facilities near boat dock: Motels and restaurants within one mile; campgrounds within five miles.

Wrecks visited:
Via Beaufort Inlet: *Theodore Parker, Suloide, W. E. Hutton, Atlas, Caribsea, Senateur Duhamel, Fenwick Island, Ea, Portland, Ashkhabad, U-352, Schurz, Naeco, Papoose, Amagansett, Cassimir, Proteus, Tarpon, Dixie Arrow, British Splendour, Tamaulipas.*

Comments
The *Saltshaker V* is a brand new dive boat replacing the older but larger and more plush *Saltshaker IV*. Captain McKay is a certified divemaster and has had several years experience diving on wrecks off the North Carolina coast. He is a

very competent boat captain and he and his crew are very helpful, courteous and a delight to dive with. Captain McKay will move the *Saltshaker V* to Ocracoke Island for long weekend trips to visit wrecks in the Hatteras-Ocracoke area. I highly recommend Captain McKay and the *Saltshaker V* for safe, reliable and friendly dive charter service.

OLYMPUS DIVE CHARTERS
George Purifoy
Post Office Box 486
Morehead City, NC 28557   (919) 726-9432

Boat name	Captains	Length	Beam	Engine	Cruising speed
Olympus	George Purifoy Robert Purifoy Ben Day	65 ft.	17 ft.	twin diesel	16 knots

Boat is docked at: Pier 8, foot of 8th Street, Morehead City, NC; it is affiliated with Olympus Dive Store.

Trip data		Dive shop services	
Maximum no. of divers	25	Scuba lessons	yes
		Equipment	yes
Sleep on board the night before the dive?	no	Air fills	yes
		Gear rentals	yes
Walk-on divers accepted?	yes	Repairs	yes
Riders accepted?	yes	Divemaster for charters?	if necessary
Is the captain a diver?	yes		
Scuba instructor?	no		

Facilities near boat dock: Motels and restaurants within a short walk; campgrounds within five miles.

Wrecks visited:

Via Beaufort Inlet: *Theodore Parker, Suloide, W. E. Hutton, Atlas, Caribsea, Senateur Duhamel, Fenwick Island, Ea, Portland, Ashkhabad, Bedfordshire, U-352, Schurz, Papoose, Proteus, Tarpon, Dixie Arrow, British Splendour.*

Comments

The *Olympus* is great for walk-on divers since the boat is rarely chartered in its entirety by a single group; instead there is usually a mix of several different groups and individual walk-on divers sharing the boat on any given dive trip. The boat is fully equipped with electronics and is air conditioned. It has an on-board air compressor, microwave oven, hot deli sandwiches and drinks, dive platform, zodiac chase boat and lifting davit for recovering artifacts. Olympus Dive Charters also has an air conditioned and heated diver's lodge with room for 18, conveniently located a few blocks from the boat dock. George Purifoy, his son, Robert, and Ben Day are competent boat captains and good divers. Captain Day has many years' experience diving North Carolina shipwrecks and Captain Robert Purifoy has worked and dived with his father, George, for a number of years. Captain George Purifoy has been a diver for 24 years; with the assistance of others he has discovered the locations of several of the wrecks offshore of Morehead City such as the *U-352*, *Schurz*, *HMS Bedfordshire* and others. George Purifoy probably has more experience diving on wrecks in the Cape Lookout area than most, and he is willing to share his interesting experiences with divers on the way out to a wreck site.

The *Olympus* will move up to Ocracoke Island for long weekend dive trips to visit wrecks in the Ocracoke-Hatteras area.

GALE ANNE CHARTERS
Scot Whitfield
Post Office Box 1754
Atlantic Beach, NC 28512   (919) 726-3550 (day)
                            (919) 247-3694 (night)

Boat name	Captain	Length	Beam	Engine	Cruising speed
Gale Anne	Scot Whitfield	42 ft.	14 ft.	single diesel	15 knots

Boat is docked at: Behind Fisherman's Inn, Atlantic Beach Causeway, Atlantic Beach, NC; it is affiliated with a dive shop.

Trip data		Dive shop services	
Maximum no. of divers	6 plus divemaster	Scuba lessons	no
		Equipment	yes
Sleep on board the night before the dive?	no	Air fills	yes
		Gear rentals	yes
		Repairs	yes
Walk-on divers accepted?	no	Divemaster for charters?	if necessary
Riders accepted?	yes		
Is the captain a diver?	yes		
Scuba instructor?	no		

Facilities near boat dock: Motels and restaurants within a short walk; campgrounds within five miles.

Wrecks visited:

Via Beaufort Inlet: *Theodore Parker, Suloide, W. E. Hutton, Atlas, Caribsea, Senateur Duhamel, Fenwick Island, Ea, Portland, Ashkhabad, U-352, Schurz, Papoose.*

Comments

The *Gale Anne* may be chartered directly through Captain Whitfield or through EJW Bicycle and Sports Shop in Morehead City (919)726-6959. Scot Whitfield is a competent captain and a diver who has spent a number of years diving shipwrecks off the North Carolina coast. The *Gale Anne* is fully equipped with electronics.

EASY STEP DIVE CHARTERS
Bob Eastep
203 Neuse Avenue
Morehead City, NC 28557   (919) 726-2311

Boat name	Captain	Length	Beam	Engine	Cruising speed
Easystep I	Bob Eastep	39 ft.	13 ½ ft.	single diesel	10 knots
Easystep II	Bob Eastep	32 ft.	12 ft.	single diesel	10 knots

Boats are docked at: Morehead City Yacht Basin, Arendell St. (Hwy. 70), Morehead City, NC; they are affiliated with EJW Bicycle and Sports Shop.

Trip data		Dive shop services	
Maximum no. of divers	six plus divemaster	Scuba lessons	yes
		Equipment	yes
Sleep on board the night before the dive?	yes	Air fills	yes
		Gear rentals	yes
Walk-on divers accepted?	yes	Repairs	yes
		Divemaster for charters?	if necessary
Riders accepted?	yes		
Is the captain a diver?	yes		
Scuba instructor?	yes		

Facilities near boat dock: Motels and restaurants within a short walk; campgrounds within five miles.

Wrecks visited:

Easystep I and II via Beaufort Inlet: *Theodore Parker, Suloide, W. E. Hutton, Atlas, Caribsea, Senateur Duhamel, Fenwick Island, Ea, Portland, Ashkhabad, Thistleroy, U-352, Schurz, Papoose.*

Comments

Both boats are equipped with full electronics. Captain Eastep is an experienced charter captain and a 24-year veteran scuba instructor; he has several years' experience carrying divers to North Carolina shipwrecks. Bob Eastep also knows of a few "private" wreck sites available for special trips, and he always has interesting stories to tell on the way out to the wreck site.

COUNTRY SCUBA
Dale and Gwen Davis
Rt. 5 Box 19
Leland, NC 28451   (919) 371-3220 (919) 392-3195

Boat name	Captain	Length	Beam	Engine	Cruising Speed
Country Scuba #1	[1]Dale A. Davis	22 ft.	8 ft.	single gas	30 knots
Lou-Ton	[2]Robert Prevatte	32 ft.	12 ft.	twin gas	12 knots

Boat is docked at: Bridgetender Marina

Trip data		Dive shop services	
Maximum no. of divers	7	Scuba lessons	yes
Sleep on board the night before the dive?	no	Equipment	yes
		Air fills	yes
Walk-on divers accepted?	yes	Gear rentals	yes
Riders accepted?	yes	Repairs	yes
Is the captain a diver?	yes	Divemaster for charters?	yes
Scuba instructor?	[1]y/[2]n		

Facilities near boat dock: Motels and restaurants within one mile; campground within five miles.

Wrecks visited:
Cape Fear area wrecks.

WHIPSAW CHARTERS
Ed Wolfe
409 Windemere Road
Wilmington, NC 28405   (919) 791-7682

Boat name	Captain	Length	Beam	Engine	Cruising speed
Whipsaw	Ed Wolfe	42½ ft.	15 ft.	twin diesels	10 knots

Boat is docked at: Seapath Boatominium, Seapath Tower, Causeway Drive, Wrightsville Beach, NC; it is not affiliated with a dive shop.

Trip data		Dive shop services	
Maximum no. of divers	6 plus divemaster	Scuba lessons	NA
		Equipment	NA
Sleep on board the night before the dive?	yes	Air fills	NA
		Gear rentals	NA
Walk-on divers accepted?	no	Repairs	NA
		Divemaster for charters?	no
Riders accepted?	yes		
Is the captain a diver?	no		
Scuba instructor?	no		

Facilities near boat dock: Motels and restaurants within one mile; campgrounds within five miles.

Wrecks visited:

Via Masonboro Inlet: *Alexander Ramsey, John D. Gill, Normannia, Esso Nashville, Peterhoff, Condor, Raritan.*

Comments

The *Whipsaw* is a very nice boat which is fully equipped with electronics. Although not a diver himself, Captain Ed Wolfe knows wreckdiving and divers and is one of the most experienced boat captains in the area. Charter dive bookings with Ed Wolfe are usually filled for the season by April and are generally made up of long-standing customers. About the only way to get on a *Whipsaw* charter is to join the Triangle Dive Club of Durham (919) 732-3934 or the North Carolina Diver's Cooperative of Raleigh (919) 467-3831. Both organizations have long-time charter arrangements with Ed Wolfe for regular visits to the *Normannia, Esso Nashville,* and the *John D. Gill.* Occasionally, Captain Wolfe is able to squeeze in one or two more dive charters during the season. He is the only charter dive captain carrying divers to the *Normannia* and *Esso Nashville,* two of North Carolina's top wrecks. He also has several "private" wrecks he will take divers to visit. Ed Wolfe always has an interesting story or two to tell to pass the time on the way out to the dive site. Seapath Boatominium has hot shower and dressing room accommodations which are refreshing after a long day on the ocean and are convenient for those who spend the night on the boat.

There is a full service dive shop, Undersea Sales and Engineering (919) 256-3057, located five minutes from the boat dock.

SCUBA SOUTH DIVE CHARTERS
Wayne Strickland
222 S. River Drive
Southport, NC 28461   (919) 457-5210 (919) 392-3195

Boat name	Captain	Length	Beam	Engine	Cruising Speed
Scuba South I	Wayne Strickland	42 ft.	12 ft.	single diesel	12 knots

Boat is docked at: American Fish Company dock, foot of Bay Street, Southport, NC; it is affiliated with a dive shop

Trip data		Dive shop services	
Maximum no. of divers	10 plus divemaster	Scuba lessons	yes
		Equipment	yes
Sleep on board the night before the dive?	no	Air fills	yes
		Gear rentals	yes
		Repairs	yes
Walk-on divers accepted?	yes	Divemaster for charters?	if necessary
Riders accepted?	yes		
Is the captain a diver?	yes		
Scuba instructor?	yes		

Facilities near boat dock: Motels and restaurants within a short walk; campgrounds within five miles.

Wrecks visited:
Via Cape Fear River: *Raritan, Mount Dirfys, George Weems, City of Houston*

Comments

The Scuba South I is a relatively new dive boat which is fully equipped with electronics. The boat cruises at 12 knots, has a walk-through transom for easy dive access, and is equipped with a compressor for air-fills. The captain and crew are helpful and courteous; they make diving with the *Scuba South I* a pleasant experience.

Captain Strickland is a very competent boat captain, a scuba instructor, a commercial salvage diver, and an ardent sport diver. His knowledge of the wreck sites he visits is exceptional. The wrecks he will carry divers to are limited to those located south of Frying Pan Shoals; Captain Strickland has several "private" wrecks he will occasionally take divers to visit. He has been in the charter business for a number of years and is the only captain carrying divers to the wreck of the *George Weems,* one of the prettiest, in terms of marine life, off the North Carolina coast. Strickland was the first boat captain to take divers to the *City of Houston.*

Captain Strickland also owns and operates a full service dive shop, Scuba South Diving Company (919) 457-5201 to provide a complete package for the wreck diving enthusiast.

APPENDIX G

Type, Tonnage, and Depth of Offshore Wrecks

Table 1. Offshore Wrecks by Type

Tanker	Freighter	Ocean fishing
Byron D. Benson	City of New York	Amagansett
Australia	Marore	Fenwick Island
Empire Gem	City of Atlanta	**Submarine**
F. W. Abrams	Ciltvaira	
Dixie Arrow	Ella Pierce Thurlow	U-701
British Splendour	Thistleroy	U-85
Tamaulipas	Ea	USS Tarpon
Atlas	Suloide	U-352
W. E. Hutton	Aphrodite	**Armed trawlers**
Papoose	Normannia	
Naeco	Raritan	Senateur Duhamel
Cassimir	Mount Dirfys	HMS Bedfordshire
John D. Gill	George Weems	**Ocean Tug**
Esso Nashville	Malchace	
E. M. Clark	Portland	Keshena
Ario	Ashkhabad	**Passenger/Cargo**
Liberty ship	Caribsea	
	Norvana	City of Houston
Zane Grey	Manuela	Proteus
Dionysus	**Navy cruiser**	Buarque
Theodore Parker		Central America
Alexander Ramsey	USS Schurz	**Civil War blockader**
		USS Peterhoff

Table 2. Wrecks by Tonnage and Length

Name	Gross tons	Length in feet	Name	Gross tons	Length in feet	Name	Gross tons	Length in feet
John D. Gill	11,641	523	Proteus	4,836	406	U-85	500	220
Australia	11,628	510	Manuela	4,772	393	Keshena	427	142
E. M. Clark	9,647	516	Aeolus	4,087	426	George Weems	416	141
F. W. Abrams	9,310	485	Thistleroy	4,027	345	Fenwick Island	230	125
Marore	8,215	550	Ciltvaira	3,779	347	Amagansett	226	135
Empire Gem	8,139	463	Malchace	3,516	334			
Dixie Arrow	8,046	468	Suloide	3,235	334			
Byron D. Benson	7,953	465	Caribsea	2,609	251			
Esso Nashville	7,943	445	Normannia	2,681	312			
Zane Grey	7,176	441	Raritan	2,649	251			
Dionysus	7,176	441	Norvana	2,677	253			
Theodore Parker	7,176	441	Portland	2,648	289			
Alexander Ramsey	7,176	441	Central America	2,141	272			
British Splendour	7,138	441	USS Schurz	1,630	295			
Atlas	7,139	430	City of Houston	1,515	290			
W. E. Hutton	7,076	435	Ella Pierce Thurlow	1,509	221			
Ario	6,952	435	USS Tarpon	1,316	298			
Tamaulipas	6,943	435	Ea	1,269	235			
Papoose	5,939	412	Aphrodite	1,098	206			
City of Atlanta	5,433	378	USS Monitor	981	173			
Naeco	5,372	412	HMS Bedfordshire	900	170			
Mount Dirfys	5,242	400	U-701	871	220			
Ashkhabad	5,284	400	USS Peterhoff	800	210			
Buarque	5,152	390	U-352	786	218			
Cassimir	5,030	390	Senateur Duhamel	739	165			

Table 3. Offshore Wrecks by Depth

30–70 feet	80–90 feet	100–115 feet	120–140 feet	150–210 feet
Theodore Parker*	Caribsea	U-352	Cassimir*	Tamaulipas*
Alexander Ramsey*	Dixie Arrow	USS Schurz	Papoose*	E. M. Clark
Fenwick Island	John D. Gill	Normanna	Proteus	Manuela
W.E. Hutton	Byron D. Benson	U-85	USS Tarpon	
Suloide	Empire Gem	Ciltvaira	Naeco	
Portland	Raritan*	HMS Bedfordshire	Buarque	
Senateur Duhamel	Australia	Norvana	Amagansett	
Ashkhabad	Zane Grey*	City of Atlanta	Atlas*	
Ea	Dionysus	Esso Nashville	Marore	
USS Peterhoff	City of Houston	British Splendour	Ella Pierce Thurlow	
F.W. Abrams			Lobster Wreck	
Keshena				
City of New York				
Mount Dirfys				
Thistleroy				
George Weems				
Aeolus				
Aphrodite				

*John D. Gill, 60–90 feet; Cassimir, 85–120 feet; Papoose, 80–130 feet; Atlas, 90–130 feet; Zane Grey, 40–80 feet; Dionysus, 50–80 feet; Theodore Parker, 20–50 feet; Raritan, 55–80 feet; Alexander Ramsey, 20–50 feet; Tamaulipas, 130–150 feet.

Fate of U-Boats Involved in Sinking off the NC Coast

Boat*	Type	Name of Commander	Ship sunk or damaged	Fate of U-Boat
U-66	IX-C	Fregattenkapitän Richard Zapp	Norvana Empire Gem	Sunk off Cape Verde Islands, May 6, 1944 by USS *Buckley*.
U-71	VII-C	Korvettenkapitän Walter Flachsenberg	Dixie Arrow	Scuttled at Wilhelmshaven, Germany, May 2, 1945.
U-85	VII-B	Kapitänleutnant Eberhard Greger	—	Sunk off Nags Head on April 14, 1942 by USS *Roper*.
U-123	IX-B	Kapitänleutnant Reinhard Hardegen	City of Atlanta Ciltvaira	Paid off, Lorient, France, August 19, 1944. Turned over to French as *Blaison* in 1945. Scrapped in 1957.
U-124	IX-B	Korvettenkapitän Johann Mohr	E. M. Clark Papoose W. E. Hutton Esso Nashville (D) Naeco	Sunk west of Orporto, Portugal, April 3, 1943 by HMS *Blackswan* and HMS *Stonecrop*.
U-158	IX-C	Kapitänleutnant Erich Rostin	Caribsea John D. Gill Ario	Bombed and sunk west of Bermuda, June 30, 1942.
U-160	IX-C	Kapitänleutnant Georg Lassen	Malcbace	Sunk south of the Azores, July 14, 1943 by aircraft from USS *Santee*.
U-332	VII-C	Kapitänleutnant Johannen Liebe	Australia	Bombed and sunk north of Cape Finisterre, Spain, May 2, 1943.

APPENDIX H, *continued*

Boat*	Type	Name of Commander	Ship sunk or damaged	Fate of U-Boat
U-352	VII-C	Kapitänleutnant Helmut Rathke	—	Sunk May 9, 1942 off Cape Lookout by the Coast Guard cutter *Icarus*.
U-402	VII-C	Korvettenkapitän Siegfried v. Forstner	*Ashkhabad*	Bombed and sunk mid-Atlantic, October 13, 1943 by aircraft from the USS *Card*.
U-404	VII-C	Korvettenkapitän Otto v. Bulow	*Manuela*	Bombed and sunk in the Bay of Biscay, July 28, 1943.
U-432	VII-C	Kapitänleutnant Heinz-Otto Schultze	*Marore*	Sunk in mid-Atlantic by the French corvette, *Aconit*, March 11, 1943.
U-552	VII-C	Korvettenkapitän Erich Topp	*British Splendour* *Atlas* *Tamaulipas* *Byron D. Benson*	Scuttled at Wilhelmshaven, May 2, 1945.
U-558	VII-C	Kapitänleutnant Gunther Kretch	HMS *Beafordshire*	Bombed and sunk northwest of Cape Ortegal, Spain on July 20, 1943 by a U.S. B-24 Liberator.
U-576	VII-C	Kapitänleutnant Hans-Dieter Heinicke	—	Sunk July 15, 1942 20 miles east of Ocracoke Inlet by USS *Unicoi* and two planes from Squadron VS-9 at Cherry Point.
U-701	VII-C	Kapitänleutnant Horst Degen	—	Bombed and sunk off Cape Hatteras, July 7, 1942.

*These and other U-Boats sank or damaged additional ships off the coast of North Carolina, but the wrecks in question lie in water too deep for scuba diving or their locations are unknown.

SELECTED BIBLIOGRAPHY

Albion, Robert G. *Five Centuries of Famous Ships*, New York: McGraw-Hill, 1978.

Alden, John D. *The Fleet Submarine in the U.S. Navy*. Annapolis: Naval Institute Press, 1979.

Bagnasco, E. *Submarines of World War II*. Annapolis: Naval Institute Press, 1977.

Berman, Bruce D. *Encyclopedia of Marine Shipwrecks*. Boston: Mariners Press, 1972.

Bernath, Stuart L. "Squall Across the Atlantic: The Peterhoff Episode." *Journal of Southern History* 34 (1968): 382–401.

Bradlee, Francis B. C. *Blockade Running During the Civil War and the Effect of Land and Water Transportation on the Confederacy*. Salem, Massachusetts: The Essex Institute, 1925.

Bright, Leslie S. *The Blockade Runner Modern Greece and Her Cargo*. Raleigh, North Carolina: Fort Fisher Preservation Laboratory, Division of Archives and History, North Carolina Department of Cultural Resources, 1977.

Burgess, R. H. "The Metropolis on Currituck Bank: Wreck on the Beach Recalls Disaster of 75 Years Ago." *Norfolk-Virginia Pilot*, 31 January 1954.

Colledge, J.J. *Ships of the Royal Navy: An Historical Index*. New York: Augustus M. Kelley, 1970.

Delgado, James P. *Assessment of Shipwreck Remains on the Beach: Cape Hatteras National Seashore, North Carolina*. National Park Service, National Maritime Initiative, 1989.

Dickerson, Michael T. "Saga of the *U-352*." *Skin Diver*, November 1981, 28–30.

Foard, Charles H. Chart of Vessels Sunk or Captured near Wilmington, North Carolina circa 1861–1865. Carolina Beach, North Carolina: privately published, 1968.

Govert, Gary. "Dive On In, the Water's Fine." *Carolina Lifestyle*, August 1982, 50–55.

Harker, J. and B. Lovin. *The North Carolina Divers Handbook*. Chapel Hill, North Carolina: Marine Grafics, 1976.

Heyl, Erik. Early American Steamers. 2 vols. Buffalo, New York: privately published, 1952.

Hickam, Homer. "Day of Anger, Day of Pride." *American History Illustrated*, January 1983, 30–39.

———. "The Night of the Roper." *American History Illustrated*, October 1984, 10–17.

Hocking, Charles. *Dictionary of Disasters at Sea During the Age of Steam, 1824–1962*. 2 vols. London: Lloyd's Register of Shipping, 1969.

Holdcamper, Forrest M. *Merchant Steam Vessels of the United States, 1807–1868*. New York: Steamship Historical Society of America, 1952.

Horner, Dave. *The Blockade Runner: True Tales of Running the Yankee Blockade of the Confederate Coast*. New York: Dodd, Mead and Co., 1968.

Jane, Frederick T. *Jane's Fighting Ships*. London: S. Low, Marston and Company, Ltd., 1916.

La Dage, John H. *Merchant Ships: A Pictorial Study*. Cambridge, Maryland: Cornell Maritime Press, 1955.

Lloyd's of London. *Wreck Returns*. 61 vols. London: Lloyd's Register of Shipping, 1885–1946.

Lonsdale, A. L. and H. R. Kaplan. *A Guide to Sunken Ships in American Waters*. Arlington, Virginia: Arlington Compass Publications, 1964.

Lytle, William M. *Merchant Steam Vessels of the United States, 1807–1868*. Mystic, Connecticut: Steamship Historical Society of America, 1952.

Mitchell, C. Bradford. *Merchant Steam Vessels of the United States, 1790–1860*. Staten Island, New York: privately published, 1975.

Moore, Arthur R. *A Careless Word . . . A Needless Sinking*. King's Point, New York: American Merchant Marine Museum, 1983.

Naisawald, L. VanLoan. *In Some Foreign Field*. Winston-Salem, North Carolina: John F. Blair, 1972.

Naval History Division, Department of the Navy. *Dictionary of American Naval Fighting Ships*. Washington, DC: Government Printing Office, 1976.

Newton, John G., A. H. Pilkey and J. O. Blanton. *An Oceanographic Atlas of the Carolina Continental Margin*. Raleigh, North Carolina: North Carolina Department of Conservation and Development, 1971.

New York Times, "Normannia," 17 January 1924.

———, "Normannia," 19 January 1924.

Philadelphia Press, "U.S.S. Schurz," 26 June 1918.

Office of the Chief of Naval Operations. 1942. Summary of Statements by Survivors of Ship Sinkings. Washington, DC. photocopy.

Office of Naval Intelligence. Post-Mortems on Enemy Submarines. Washington, DC: Commander-in-Chief U.S. Fleet, 1942. microfilm.

Ridgely-Nevitt, Cedric. *American Steamships on the Atlantic*. East Brunswick, New Jersey: Associated University Presses, 1981.

Rössler, Eberhard. *The U-Boat*. Annapolis, Maryland: Naval Institute Press, 1981.

Sawyer, L. A. and W. H. Mitchell. *The Liberty Ships*. Devon, England: David and Charles, Ltd., 1970.

Shomette, Donald G. *Shipwrecks of the Civil War: The Encyclopedia of Union and Confederate Naval Losses*. Washington, D.C.: Donic Ltd., 1973.

Showell, J. P. M. *Under the Swastika*. New York: Arco, 1974.

Sprunt, James. Derelicts: An Account of Ships Lost at Sea in General Commercial Traffic and a Brief History of Blockade Runners Stranded Along the North Carolina Coast, 1861–1865. Wilmington, North Carolina: privately published, 1920.

Stern, Robert C. *U.S. Subs in Action*. Carrollton, Texas: Squadron/Signal, 1979.

Stick, David. *Graveyard of the Atlantic*. Chapel Hill, North Carolina: University of North Carolina Press, 1952.

————. 1952. "A List of Vessels Probably Lost on the North Carolina Coast." Kill Devil Hills, North Carolina. Typescript.

Strobridge, Truman R., 1956. Tanker Losses of WWII. The Mariners' Museum, Newport News, Virginia. Typescript.

Underwater Archeology Branch, North Carolina Department of Cultural Resources. *Underwater Archeology in North Carolina*. Kure Beach, North Carolina: Underwater Archeology Branch, Division of Archives and History, North Carolina Department of Cultural Resources, 1981.

United States Office of Naval Records and Library. *Official Records of the Union and Confederate Navies in the War of the Rebellion*. 31 vols. Washington, DC: Government Printing Office, 1894–1927.

Wilde-Ramsing, Mark. Nomination form for the Cape Fear Civil War Shipwreck District. Underwater Archaeology Unit, Division of Archives and History, North Carolina Department of Cultural Resources, 1985.

GLOSSARY

Blockader. Union warships that patrolled offshore of major Confederate ports during the U.S. Civil War to prevent essential war supplies from Europe reaching the South and southern goods from reaching Europe.

BC. Bouyancy compensator. An inflatable flotation device worn by divers to provide "face-up" flotation when on the surface and to provide additional buoyancy at depth. May be a vest type or "horse collar" type similar to the old "Mae West" life jacket.

Bottom Time. Time spent by a diver at depth during a dive.

Blockade Runner. Ships that ran the Union naval blockade of Confederate ports during the U.S. Civil War bringing supplies to the South from Europe and returning loaded with cotton and other Southern goods which were in demand.

Clyde River Steamer. Fast but delicate steamers built for commerce on the Clyde River in Scotland. These swift river steamers were pressed into service as blockade runners when the demand for sturdy ocean-going steamers exceeded the supply.

Cross-wreck Line. A light line of great length used by divers to aid underwater navigation under conditions of low visibility. Carried on a spool, one end of the line is attached to the wreck near the dive boat's anchor and the rest of the line is played out across the wreck site. This serves to guide divers back to the anchor line for the ascent after completing the dive.

Dive Light. Bright underwater flashlight.

Eighty-cubic-foot Scuba Cylinder. Scuba cylinder slightly over two feet tall by seven or so inches in diameter, which, when filled to the maximum of 3000 psi, contains 80 cubic feet of air or an amount of air slightly greater than that contained in a telephone booth.

fsw. Feet of sea water. Depth in water from the surface measured in feet.

League. Unit of distance equal to approximately three miles.

Liberty Ship. An emergency type of cargo steamer which was mass-produced by assembly-line methods during WWII by the United States and Great Britain to keep the Allied lifeline open from America to Europe as German U-boats were sinking conventional ships faster than they could be built.

List (nautical). Incline to one side.

loran C. System of ocean navigation which involves land-based transmitters which send radio signals that are picked up by special receivers on shipboard. The time delay between the transmission of the signal from land until its reception at sea is measured by the receiver and is a function of the distance from the ship to the transmitting station. Equivalent distances from the transmitter can be represented on a map by lines of arc, and points along the arc will have the same time delay in receiving the signal from the transmitter. Special navigation maps are overprinted with loran C time-delay lines. When two widely spaced land transmitters are monitored at sea, the intersection of their time-delay lines is the location of the ship on the ocean.

Port. Left-hand side of a vessel facing forward.

psi. Pounds per square inch. Unit of pressure. Normal atmospheric pressure is 14.7 psi. Pressure in a full scuba cylinder can be as high as 3000 psi.

Recording Fathometer. Electronic device used on shipboard to measure and record the depth and topography of the ocean bottom directly beneath the ship. It is used to "see" a wreck on the ocean floor as the ship passes over it.

Relief. Projection of a wreck above the ocean bottom.

Starboard. Right-hand side of a vessel facing forward.

Twin-50's. Two identical scuba cylinders, each with a maximum air-fill capacity of 50 cubic feet, worn in tandem to provide a diver with a supply of 100 cubic feet of air.

U-boat. German *Unterseeboot* or submarine.

Wire-dragging. Process by which large cables are pulled beneath the water between two surface vessels to clear portions of sunken ships which protrude near the surface and present a hazard to navigation.

INDEX

Aeolus, 174–76

Aldersgate. See *Ashkhabad*

Alexander Ramsey, 11, 250

Amagansett, 142

Amassia. See *Suloide*

Ambrotype, 269

Aphrodite, 132–35

Arabian, 301, 323–24

Ario, 147–48

Ashkhabad, 8, 149–51

Atlantic sand tiger shark, 25–27

Atlas, 8, 139–41, 216

Australia, 19, 66–67

Bendigo, 300, 302, 318–19

Bernini. See *Mount Dirfys*

Bird City. See *Buarque*

British Splendour, 7, 124–27

Buarque, 7, 32–33

Byron D. Benson, 7, 19, 34–36

Caribsea, 8, 143–46

Carl Gerhard, 10, 283–84, 286–87

Cassimir, 10, 230–35

Central America, 157–59

Charles M. Everest. See *Naeco*

Charter dive services, 345–60

Chickamauga. See *Malchace*

Ciltvaira, 7, 52–53

City of Atlanta, 7, 64–65

City of Houston, 261–69

City of New York, 7–8, 19, 84–86

Compass, 15, 18

Condor, 10, 301, 315–16

CSS *Raleigh,* 301, 322

CSS *Virginia,* 68–71

Cross-wreck line, 15, 18

Current line, 15

Detroit Wayne. See *Raritan*

Dionysus, 11, 48

Dive boats. See Charter dive services

Dive flag, 14

Dive light, 15, 18

Dive shops, 342–43

Divers Alert Network, 340–41

Diving conditions
  surge, 4, 304–305
  visibility, 3–4, 304–305
  water temperature, 4, 304–305

Dixie Arrow, 7, 19, 96–102

Dnesprostroi. See *Ashkhabad*

Douro, 302, 316–17

Ea, 9, 168–69

Ella, 303, 317–18

Ella Pierce Thurlow, 204–07

Elizabeth, 302, 325

E. M. Clark, 90–91, 212

Empire Gem, 7, 19, 82–83

Endsleigh. See *Ciltvaira*

Esso Nashville, 212, 241–43

Eugomphodus taurus, see Atlantic sand tiger shark

Fanny and Jenny, 10, 299, 309, 311

Farb Monitor Expedition, 73–77

Fenwick Island, 9, 169

F. W. Abrams, 7, 19, 94–95

Freedom, 60

Geier. See USS *Schurz*

General Beauregard, 10, 300, 303, 313–14

George Law. See *Central America*

George S. Blake. See *George Weems*

George Weems, 10, 270–72

Gulf Stream, 3, 4

Harbor Branch Oceanographic Institution, 26

Hardee's Reef, 327
Hebe, 302, 312–13
HMS *Bedfordshire*, 162–67
Hugoton. See *Tamaulipas*
Hyde, 327
Irma, 284
Iron Age, 10, 319–20
Jacox. See *Portland*
John D. Gill, 10, 50, 255–60
Keshena, 7, 8, 92–93
Kutais. See *Ashkhabad*
Kyzickes, 10, 283–84, 285–87
Labrador Current, 4
Lake Fairton. See *Raritan*
Lake Flattery. See *Caribsea*
Lake Gatun. See *Norvana*
Lobster Wreck, 236–40
Lynx, 302, 311–12
Maceio. See *Suloide*
Malchace, 19, 21, 87–89
Manuela, 8, 128–30
Marore, 49–50
Mary Ellen O'Neill. See *Australia*
Metropolis, 11, 280–282
Milazzo. See *Ashkhabad*
Mistley Hall. See *Ashkhabad*
Modern Greece, 10, 299, 301,
    314–15
Mount Dirfys, 10, 273–74
Naeco, 9, 212–15
Nancy Lee, 327
National Oceanic and Atmospheric
    Administration (NOAA), 6,
    72–73
Nora, See *F. W. Abrams*
Normannia, 10, 244–48
Norvana, 7, 37–38
Novelty, 327
Nutfield, 308–9
Odontaspis tauris, see Atlantic sand
    tiger shark
Oriental, 305–7
Panulirus argus, see Spiny lobsters
Papoose, 9, 208–11, 212, 216
Paraguay. See *Kyzickes*

Permits
    artifact collection, 6, 254, 304
Phantom, 303, 307–08
Portland, 8, 152–54
Portola Plumas. See *W. E. Hutton*
President Bunge. See *Ciltvaira*
Proteus, 7–8, 20–24, 103–12, 240
R. B. Drisko, see *Ella Pierce
    Thurlow*
Ranger, 10, 300, 303, 320–21
Raritan, 10, 274–75
Salvage laws
    Federal, 335–37
    North Carolina, 338–39
Sand tiger shark, see Atlantic Sand
    Tiger Shark
Scaupenn. See *Buarque*
Sea sickness
    medication, 12
    prevention, 11–13
Senateur Duhamel, 9, 163, 170–73
Shipwrecks
    depth, 363
    length, 362
    physical condition, 5
    tonnage, 362
    type, 361
Silvanus. See *Papoose*
Sophia, 303, 310
Spiny lobsters, 236
Stars and Stripes. See *Metropolis*
Stormy Petrel, 301, 324–25
Suloide, 9, 93, 95, 221–24, 226
Surge, 4, 17, 18
Tag line, 14
Tamaulipas, 8, 136–38
Theodore Parker, 11, 217–20
Thistleroy, 155–56
Triangle Wrecks, 11, 284, 287
Turandot, see *Aeolus*
Twyford, 52
U-boats
    crews lost, 62
    fate of, 62, 364–65
U-85, 7, 19, 24, 39–45, 59, 163

Underwater photography
  cameras, 329
  color, 330
  film, 331–34
  lenses, 329–30
    angle-of-view, 330
    focusing, 329–30
  strobes, 330–32
    guide number, 331–32
    watt-second, 331
USS *Aster*, 301, 324
USS *Columbia*, 310–11
USS *Huron*, 11, 288–93
USS *Iron Age*, 302, 319–20
USS *Louisiana*, 301, 323
USS *Merrimack*, see CSS *Virginia*
USS *Monitor*, 6, 68–81
USS *Peterhoff*, 6, 10, 251–254, 303
USS *Roper*, 41–44
USS *Schurz*, 9, 197–203
USS *Tarpon*, 7–8, 20, 22–27,
  113–23

U-701, 54–63
U-352, 9, 24, 59, 163, 177–96
Venus, 299, 302, 311–12
Verbena, see *Nancy Lee*
Vesta, 299, 321–22
Vironia. See *Ciltvaira*
War Hostage. See *Ashkhabad*
War Penguin. See *Mount Dirfys*
W. E. Hutton, 9, 93, 95, 208, 212,
  221, 225–28
W. E. Johnson. See *Thistleroy*
Wild Dayrell, 303, 326
William Rockefeller, 60
Wire dragging, 5
Wreck diving techniques
  from a boat, 11–17
  from shore, 17–18
York. See *Norvana*
Zane Grey, 11, 46–47